A New Working Class

POLITICS AND CULTURE IN MODERN AMERICA

Series Editors: Keisha N. Blain, Margot Canaday,
Matthew Lassiter, Stephen Pitti, Thomas J. Sugrue

Volumes in the series narrate and analyze political and social change in the broadest dimensions from 1865 to the present, including ideas about the ways people have sought and wielded power in the public sphere and the language and institutions of politics at all levels—local, national, and transnational. The series is motivated by a desire to reverse the fragmentation of modern U.S. history and to encourage synthetic perspectives on social movements and the state, on gender, race, and labor, and on intellectual history and popular culture.

A NEW WORKING CLASS

The Legacies of Public-Sector Employment in the Civil Rights Movement

Jane Berger

UNIVERSITY OF PENNSYLVANIA PRESS

PHILADELPHIA

Copyright © 2021 University of Pennsylvania Press

All rights reserved. Except for brief quotations used
for purposes of review or scholarly citation, none of this
book may be reproduced in any form by any means without written
permission from the publisher.

Published by
University of Pennsylvania Press
Philadelphia, Pennsylvania 19104-4112
www.upenn.edu/pennpress

Printed in the United States of America
on acid-free paper
10 9 8 7 6 5 4 3 2 1

Library of Congress Cataloging-in-Publication Data
Names: Berger, Jane, (Jane Alexandra), author.
Title: A new working class : the legacies of public-sector employment in
the civil rights movement / Jane Berger.
Other titles: Politics and culture in modern America.
Description: 1st edition. | Philadelphia : University of Pennsylvania
Press, [2021] | Series: Politics and culture in modern America |
Includes bibliographical references and index.
Identifiers: LCCN 2021003510 | ISBN 9780812253450 (hardcover)
Subjects: LCSH: Government employee unions—Maryland—Baltimore—
History—20th century. | African Americans—Employment—Maryland—
Baltimore—History—20th century. | African Americans—Civil
rights—Maryland—Baltimore—History—20th century. | African Americans—
Maryland—Baltimore—Economic conditions—History—20th century. |
African Americans—Maryland—Baltimore—Social conditions—History—
20th century. | Urban policy—Maryland—Baltimore—History—20th century. |
Baltimore (Md.)—Economic conditions—20th century. | Baltimore (Md.)—
Social conditions—20th century.
Classification: LCC HD8005.2.U53 B47 2021 | DDC 330.9752/6008996073—dc23
LC record available at https://lccn.loc.gov/2021003510

CONTENTS

List of Abbreviations	vii
Introduction. Public-Sector Workers and the Battle over Cities	1
1. "Boom Times" in Baltimore?	12
2. "A New Mood" Is Spreading: The Great Society as Job Creation	33
3. "We Had to Fight to Get This": Antipoverty Workers Take on City Hall	55
4. "Better Wages and Job Conditions with Dignity": Unionizing the Public Sector	76
5. "A Posture of Advocacy for the Poor": Fighting Poverty in an Era of Austerity	98
6. "The Hell-Raising Period Is Over": New Federalism in Baltimore	116
7. "Polishing the Apple While the Core Rots": Carter and the Cities	140
8. "A Tourist Town at the Expense of the Poor": The Making of Two Baltimores	160
9. "A Revolving Door for Impoverished People": Reaganomics and American Cities	184

10. "There's Tragedy on Both Sides of the Layoffs": Privatization and the Urban Crisis	205
Conclusion	228
Notes	247
Index	289
Acknowledgments	301

ABBREVIATIONS

AFDC   Aid to Families with Dependent Children
AFGE   American Federation of Government Employees
AFSCME   American Federation of State, County and Municipal Employees
AFT   American Federation of Teachers
ALEC   American Legislative Exchange Council
BDC   Baltimore Development Corporation
BPD   Baltimore Police Department
BTU   Baltimore Teachers Union
BUILD   Baltimoreans United in Leadership Development
BUL   Baltimore Urban League
CAA   Community Action Agency
CAC   Community Action Commission
CDBGs   Community Development Block Grants
CETA   Comprehensive Employment and Training Act of 1973
CIG   Civil Interest Group
CMEA   Classified Municipal Employees Association
CORE   Congress of Racial Equality
CRC   Baltimore Community Relations Commission
CSC   Civil Service Commission
DPW   Department of Public Welfare
DSS   Baltimore Department of Social Services
EEOC   Equal Employment Opportunities Commission
EOA   Economic Opportunity Act
FEPC   Fair Employment Practices Commission
GOP   (allow without definition)
GRS   general revenue sharing
HUD   Department of Housing and Urban Development
HWC   Health and Welfare Council of the Baltimore Area, Inc.

MCEA	Maryland Classified Employees Association
NAACP	National Association for the Advancement of Colored People
NEA	National Education Association
NUL	National Urban League
PSTA	Public School Teachers Association
SDS	Students for a Democratic Society
SNCC	Student Non-Violent Coordinating Committee
SSA	Social Security Administration
TANF	Temporary Aid to Needy Families
TIF	tax increment financing
U-JOIN	Union for Jobs or Income Now
UDAGs	Urban Development Action Grants
USA	Urban Services Agency

INTRODUCTION

Public-Sector Workers and the Battle over Cities

Following the death of Freddie Gray while in police custody in Baltimore in 2015, city residents took to the streets in large numbers to protest police brutality and press the claim that Black Lives Matter. "We're in a state of emergency," Tawanda Jones passionately declared at one demonstration. Two years earlier, Jones herself had lost a brother, who died following a struggle with police officers who were never prosecuted.[1] She had been holding weekly rallies ever since to call attention to her brother's case and the larger issue of police brutality, and she joined the Gray protests as well.[2] Jones was not the only person in Baltimore to mourn Gray's loss without having known him personally. "Most of us are not here because we knew Freddie Gray; most of us are here because we knew a lot of Freddie Grays. Too many," grieved William "Billy" Murphy, a prominent local attorney who was representing the Gray family and who was speaking at Freddie's funeral.[3] Elijah Cummings, who represented Baltimore in the U.S. Congress, spoke at the funeral as well. And he also called attention to the issue of who knew—and did not know— Gray and other Black Baltimoreans like him. "When I look at all the cameras, I wonder: did you recognize Freddie when he was alive? Did you see him? Did you see him? Did you see him?"[4] Jones made a similar point, but even more trenchantly: "We are not the enemy."

Jones's comment that Black Baltimore was not the enemy was most immediately a rebuke of the Baltimore Police Department, which had been the subject of an investigation by the U.S. Justice Department because of brutality cases even before Gray's death. Her remark also, however, communicated a powerful critique of a reality in Baltimore that was not caused solely by the behavior of the police. The city certainly served as an example of the devastating consequences of the nation's racially biased carceral state. But more generative of Baltimore's pressing problems was the tremendous race- and class-based economic gap that sharply divided the city. The journalists who descended on Baltimore following Gray's death could hardly fail to notice the glaring disparities between the city's commercially redeveloped downtown area and the hypersegregated, overpoliced, low-income African American neighborhoods such as Sandtown-Winchester, where Gray had lived. Hugging Baltimore's harbor were glistening skyscrapers and office buildings that were home to such investment and wealth management firms as Legg Mason and T. Rowe Price and such transnational professional services corporations as PricewaterhouseCoopers, companies that were thriving in the nation's postindustrial economy. Luxury condominium complexes and upscale hotels also bordered the harbor and provided many of the patrons for nearby boutiques, high-end restaurants, Major League stadiums, and waterfront tourist attractions.

But not too far away from downtown in the city's poorest neighborhoods there existed another Baltimore, one that looked familiar to the fans of HBO's drama series *The Wire*. There, the boards that sealed the door and window openings of two- and three-story row houses identified the many properties that were vacant or abandoned and reflected the reality that the neighborhood had seen better days. Corner convenience and liquor stores were fairly easy to come by, as were pawn shops, but a trip to the grocery store required of many a bus ticket, taxi ride, or very long walk.[5] And while residents certainly took pride in their neighborhoods, achievements, and potential, grim statistics painted a portrait of the consequences of decades of neglect. In Sandtown-Winchester, children were more likely to go to jail than to college, and half lived in poverty. The infant mortality rate surpassed that in some developing countries, and life expectancy was more than a decade less than the American average—despite the presence of two internationally renowned hospitals in the city. In addition, the unemployment rate spoke volumes about two pressing problems that were the source of much economic hardship in the city. At 21.5 percent, almost four times the national average, this rate signaled the urgent need for new employment opportunities in the city. Simultaneously, it reflected the alarming fact that most residents already had at least one job but were still struggling to get by.[6] And while waterfront condominiums and the city's poorest neighborhoods represented the two extremes between which most Baltimore residents lived, it was hard to imagine how such discrepancies existed without concluding that many local and national policy makers did in fact consider Black Baltimoreans the enemy.

There was a time some sixty years earlier when a different future for Baltimore had seemed possible, when the city's Black and low-income residents were not seen as ubiquitously as the enemy. During the 1960s, the federal government passed sweeping civil rights legislation and launched a War on Poverty. For decades, civil rights activists in Baltimore had been fighting white supremacy in the Jim Crow city, and among their top priorities were better employment opportunities for Black workers, increased political influence in the local government, and access to the quality of government services and public provisions available to whites. The activists saw in the War on Poverty, and the jobs it created in the municipal government, a means to achieve some of their goals. They leveraged the power of the Black electorate, which was increasing in importance as the city experienced white flight and pressured predominantly white and reluctant elected officials to open new antipoverty jobs and other positions in existing municipal departments to Black workers. The efforts met with considerable success. By 1970, half of the city government's workers were African American, a figure that had risen dramatically in just six years.[7] In turn, a vocal contingent of the city's new Black employees—such as Parren Mitchell, the director of the city's Community Action Agency, and Pearl Cole Brackett, who led Baltimore's community schools program—used their positions within the government to pursue the goals of civil rights activists. And though the federal government's commitment to fighting poverty quickly proved lackluster, the dedication of those who had become municipal antipoverty warriors did not. They attacked the racial and economic status quo in the city, fought to have low-income residents represented on the oversight bodies of municipal agencies, and used their new influence to attempt to shape urban planning. The efforts put them at odds with local business interests who had long called the shots in municipal governance and who favored trickle-down commercial revitalization projects to solve the city's problems rather than the redistributive approach preferred by antipoverty workers.

As they sought a voice for low-wage city residents in municipal decision-making, African American municipal employees also advocated on their own behalf as workers. Government jobs by no means guaranteed a living wage, so municipal employees—from sanitation workers to teachers—joined unions and demanded that the city consider their views when determining the terms of their employment. As historian Lane Windham argues about the nation's "new working class" of the era, which included large numbers of public- and private-sector service providers and many people of color and women, commitments to civil rights campaigns hardly precluded workers from embracing collective forms of activism.[8] African Americans played leading roles in public-sector unionization efforts in Baltimore. Raymond Clarke, the president of the city's largest local of the American Federation of State, County and Municipal Employees (AFSCME), helped lead the fight for recognition for his union and fought to improve the wages and working conditions of many of the municipal government's lowest-paid employees. Dennis Crosby pursued similar goals for his members as the president of the Baltimore Teachers Union. Unionization campaigns in Baltimore, which mirrored efforts under way in other cities, helped to turn public-sector unions into some of the fastest-growing and most dynamic participants in the American labor movement. And public-sector unions became influential advocates for both government workers and the many important public services they provided. Although industrial unions were in decline at the time, and historian Jefferson Cowie's focus on their predominantly white and male members has led him to dub the 1970s "the last days of the working class," those in the new working class, which included Baltimore's public-sector workers, were just getting started.[9]

This book traces efforts by Black women and men in Baltimore to fight racial and economic injustice in their city and to play a role in charting their city's future. I focus in particular on African American public-sector workers and their unions. During the 1960s and 1970s, the unionized public sector became a critical source of employment for African Americans that gave rise to the city's Black middle class and also to the relative economic security enjoyed by many with pink- and blue-collar government jobs.[10] During a period in urban history remembered primarily for deindustrialization and joblessness, civil rights and Black labor leaders had built an influential and union-protected job niche for African Americans that provided a refuge in the storm.[11] Black women outpaced Black men in entering the public sector, and my focus on government employment enables me to emphasize the important role played by gender in African American urban history.[12] At the same time that manufacturing job losses were creating the debilitating problem of structural unemployment among Black men, the job prospects of African American women were improving—as was service delivery to Black communities; as a result, the era was not only one of crisis. Black women's overrepresentation in the government workforce was a source of the vital economic contributions they made to their families and communities. It also positioned them, as well as the sizable number of Black men who worked for the government, in the middle of some of the most divisive public-policy debates of the late twentieth century. African Americans entered the public sector in large numbers just as Republicans undertook a major effort to delegitimize American liberalism and the expansive role the government had come to play in the national economy. Black public-sector workers and their unions assumed especially important roles in the debates, and their efforts were not simply self-serving. They defended their jobs and their right to collective bargaining but also the nation's welfare state and the principle that the government has a responsibility to provide for the well-being of its citizens. The battles in Baltimore were iterations of struggles under way around the globe during the 1980s and 1990s over the appropriate distribution of wealth and power.

As Baltimore's public-sector workers and their unions attempted to make their voices heard within public-policy debates, they simultaneously found themselves the subjects of the debates. Critical to conservative efforts to delegitimize American liberalism was the criminalization of Black urban residents, and despite their status as workers and taxpayers, government employees quickly found themselves thrown into the mix. During the late 1960s, presidential candidate Richard Nixon and his running mate, Spiro Agnew, the governor of Maryland, began employing coded appeals to racial hostility in an effort to win disaffected white Democratic voters to the Republican Party. The tactic worked, and the use of what became known as dog-whistle politics became a staple GOP strategy.[13] During the 1970s and 1980s, Republican rhetoric described cities like Baltimore as overpopulated with African American street criminals, so-called welfare cheats, and inefficient and overpaid unionized public-sector workers. Hostile conservative rhetoric cast government workers as a group apart from productive, contributing American citizens and instead as part of the supposed excesses of liberalism.[14] Further, conservatives racialized as lazy and undeserving not only public-service recipients but also public-service providers, an effort abetted by the fact that African Americans were overrepresented in government employment not only in Baltimore but across the nation. Meanwhile, conservatives implicated public-sector unions in the supposed web of criminality by conflating strikes with the urban uprisings, or "riots," of the era. "Public-employee unions encourage violence and sabotage, boast when they break the law," proclaimed the back cover of a popular screed against public-sector collective bargaining endorsed by Senator Jesse Helms and former governor of California and future United States president Ronald Reagan.[15] The use of dog-whistle politics enabled national lawmakers to build and defend an expansive criminal justice infrastructure that extended deeply into Black neighborhoods in cities such as Baltimore, and it also supposedly legitimized their decision to largely call off the War on Poverty.[16] Collectively, rhetoric that criminalized urban African Americans, including government workers, helped to justify the rolling back of the welfare state and the federal neglect of cities that characterized the 1970s and 1980s.

As hostility to cities and their African American residents grew, American political leaders simultaneously faced serious challenges to U.S. global hegemony. Confronted by a crisis of profitability in the face of mounting global competition, corporate interests pressed elected officials for relief. Meanwhile, the international agreements that had governed the global economy since the end of World War II verged on the brink of collapse. In response, American presidents, Democrat and Republican alike, presided over the financialization of the American economy. They lent the weight of the federal government not to job creation or the protection of the nation's labor-intensive manufacturing sector but instead to the creation of a healthy business climate in which the banking and finance industries could flourish.[17] Toward that end, the presidents pursued macroeconomic policies that contributed to reorienting the national and global economies away from liberalism and toward a revived free-market orthodoxy, which became known as neoliberalism. The changes occurred as both factory decline and white flight were already draining cities like Baltimore of the tax revenue needed to pay for municipal services and those who provided them. The new policies made things worse. They accelerated deindustrialization, eroded the city's competitiveness in increasingly global contests for credit and investment, worsened the city's vulnerability to capital flight, and spurred job creation predominantly in low-wage employment categories. The policies also compelled municipal austerity and budget cuts that cost city residents both critical government services and public-sector jobs. Elected officials justified the disinvestment with dog-whistle claims. They argued that redistributed federal aid had been squandered on such cities as Baltimore and its residents, who they claimed had self-inflicted problems.

In Baltimore, African American municipal workers responded with protests to efforts to derail the War on Poverty, weaken the welfare state, and disrupt local campaigns to redistribute power and wealth in the city. Black leaders protested as well. And public-sector unions staged strikes to ensure that their members did not pay the price for the new macroeconomic priorities and the austerity pressures they imposed. The influence that African

Americans could wield over the municipal agenda in their capacity as government workers and increasingly also as elected officials was under assault, however. Over the course of the 1970s and 1980s, American presidents pursued domestic and urban policies that shifted the authority over the declining funds the federal government redistributed to other levels of government away from African Americans and women and toward white men. During the 1960s, the considerable influence African Americans exerted over the city's antipoverty strategies resulted largely because their municipal agencies and departments were the direct recipients of federal grants. The grants gave Baltimore's municipal workers the access to resources and independence from locally elected officials that they needed to pursue their ambitious agenda. But beginning during the 1970s and in response to the rebellion that had erupted in cities such as Baltimore in the 1960s, presidents began consolidating federal grants into what Nixon called block grants. And they sent the block grants first to elected officials on the municipal level, who in Baltimore were predominantly white men, and then during the 1980s to elected officials on the state level, where the new recipients were also predominantly white and male and where Baltimoreans' elected representation was in decline due to the city's population losses. The pursuit of federalism and reassertion of states' rights by American presidents threatened the gains civil rights leaders had made in recent decades. Meanwhile, the presidents also made available to cities aid that subsidized trickle-down remedies to poverty and increasingly abandoned the redistributive approach pursued by activist workers.[18] As a result—although over the course of the 1970s and 1980s, African Americans continued to increase their representation in the city workforce, met with growing success at winning seats on the city council, and in 1987 elected a Black mayor—meaningful sources of power over local affairs remained elusive. For each move down the field that African Americans made to increase their control over local decision-making and public policy, American presidents moved the goal post farther away. The policy shifts made it difficult for African Americans to effectively combat the conservative changes under way.

Local- and state-level officials, including Democrats, were hardly mere bystanders to the conservative assault on the welfare state and its workforce, and Democrats played a role in creating the divisions that fractured their party. As occurred in Maryland and throughout the nation, Democrats sometimes attempted to score political points with voters by challenging the integrity of public-sector unions.[19] The practice pitted constituents of Democratic voters against one another. And, as also occurred in Maryland, Democrats were known to accuse social-services providers of acting in cahoots with their supposedly conniving clients to lengthen welfare rolls and defraud taxpayers, which eroded faith in liberalism and further sowed division in the party.[20] Meanwhile, flagging commitment to rust-belt cities and the increasing embrace of neoliberal policy-making in Washington deeply constrained municipal agenda setting, forcing Democrats on the local level to make difficult choices. The policy context compelled many mayors to assume the role of entrepreneur rather than municipal manager.[21] Some elected officials resisted the constraints, but Baltimore's William Donald Schaefer, a white Democrat who served as mayor from 1971 to 1987, enthusiastically embraced the role. Painfully aware of the challenges involved in luring businesses to and keeping them in his city, Schaefer closely monitored Baltimore's credit rating and practiced austerity to create a healthy business climate—regardless of the toll the priority took on the actual health of city residents. He also negotiated multiple tax-relief packages for businesses to secure investment, even as some feared that the practice would create a race to the bottom among rival distressed cities that would further erode sources of tax revenue.[22] Schaefer's concessions came at a significant cost to city services and the workers who provided them. They also set the low bar that investors' responsibility to local residents was limited to job creation. The cost of helping to sustain schools, parks, public-health initiatives, and other municipal services became negotiable.

Nevertheless, Schaefer attracted the enthusiastic attention of the nation's mayors for the innovative methods he used to dole out trickle-down redevelopment funds—even as the methods led many city residents to protest their exclusion from local decision-making. As the mayor plotted the city's postindustrial future, which involved creating a tourism industry centered on Baltimore's inner harbor, he was unwilling to see his plans fall victim to missed business opportunities occasioned by the slow pace of city council debate or contract riders requiring potential investors to make direct contributions to the economic well-being of constituents of city residents. As a result, the mayor and his advisers created a web of public-private corporations that traded largely in federal and state urban aid and were charged with handling the wheeling and dealing required to achieve Schaefer's revitalization ambitions.[23] By so doing, however, the mayor robbed both residents and the members of the city council of the chance to participate in critical decisions regarding their city's future. Moreover, by excluding African Americans from the process, Schaefer foreclosed opportunities for them to negotiate Black wealth–creating possibilities as part of the commercial redevelopment process such as minority business set-asides.[24] The facelift Schaefer gave the inner harbor exceeded all expectations, and the mayor had many supporters, both Black and white. But the postindustrial jobs he helped create to replace the manufacturing jobs the city was bleeding were largely in the low-wage service sector and ultimately expanded the ranks of the city's working poor.[25]

Nationally and in Baltimore, civil rights and feminist organizations, groups known primarily for their assertions of identity-based politics, played leading roles in campaigns against the erosion of American liberalism and the embrace of neoliberalism. Even as they remained mindful of ways that the nation's welfare state had disadvantaged their constituents, they became some of its staunchest defenders. Civil rights leaders urged nationally elected officials to use the power of the federal government to promote job creation and pointed out the perils for African Americans of the revival of federalism.[26] Feminist leaders made similar points and also protested the demonization of welfare recipients and the feminization of poverty, which resulted in part from the low-wage service jobs the new economy was engendering.[27]

Organized labor also played a major role in campaigns opposing the macroeconomic and domestic policy changes and advocated for the federal government to remain focused on job creation. And public-sector unions often took the lead in efforts to safeguard the activist state. By the late 1970s, AFSCME leaders understood themselves as the protectors of both the welfare state and the workers who staffed it.[28] The union fiercely resisted privatization and warned of the dangers posed to both the public good and the welfare of government employees by the commodification of such public services as education and health care and the outsourcing of such provisions to the lowest or best-connected bidder. And public-sector union officials described their opposition to privatization as a defense of American democracy. They believed that voters via their elected officials rather than those concerned with profit making should be the arbiters of public policy and service provision. Moreover, as the strength of private-sector unions declined during the last decades of the twentieth century, public-sector union officials also rose to become leading champions of collective bargaining and the right of workers to play a role in determining the terms of their employment.

The resistance mounted by civil rights, feminist, and labor organizations to the macroeconomic and domestic policy changes of the 1970s and 1980s met with limited success. Conservatives had landed on a winning formula for justifying their embrace of neoliberalism and federalism. By linking American liberalism with supposed urban and African American dysfunction—crime, welfare fraud, governmental inefficiency, and high taxes—conservatives sowed division among Democratic voters that yielded Republicans the margins they needed to win elections. And by shifting important policy-making to the state level, they made their opponents' resistance efforts more difficult. Meanwhile, in cities like Baltimore, the policy changes under way contributed to increasing hardship and insecurity. Urban African Americans were being scapegoated for the nation's economic woes at the same time that they paid some of the steepest tolls for the new neoliberal macroeconomic regime.

The ramifications of the policy changes of the 1970s and 1980s and the racist rhetoric that justified them were often gendered. The crisis of mass incarceration that emerged at the end of the twentieth century grossly disproportionately entrapped Black men in the criminal justice system and limited the opportunities of those with criminal records.[29] Meanwhile, the contraction of the public sector compelled by budget cuts and austerity shrank a segment of the labor force in which African Americans and Black women in particular had made critically important gains over the previous two decades. And because job losses were often concentrated in human-services departments—health and welfare agencies, for example—the employment prospects of African American women were the most gravely imperiled. Simultaneously, the financialization of the American economy forestalled an already unlikely industrial recovery in Baltimore, which kept Black male unemployment rates high. And the proliferation of nonunionized, low-wage, private-sector service jobs in Baltimore's postindustrial economy meant that new employment opportunities were typically inferior in terms of wages and conditions to the unionized manufacturing and public-sector jobs that had been more available in the past.

And Black women paid an additional cost for the ascendancy of neoliberalism. During the 1960s, the municipal government had begun providing federally funded antipoverty services in such realms as health care, nutrition, and recreation. African Americans had also gained access to new entitlements, such as Food Stamps, Medicare, and Medicaid, and improved access to preexisting programs, such as Aid to Families with Dependent Children. The governmental support, though inadequate, did reduce poverty. It also contributed to easing the gendered responsibilities that women often bore for providing for their families: tending to the ill, food preparation, the supervision of children, the care of elders. As a result, not only were entitlement programs a form of wealth redistribution but social services were as well—because they had replaced at least in part labor that women performed in the domestic sphere. The government began paying workers to do tasks that women earlier had done themselves for free. The loss of public services and tightening of entitlement eligibility requirements during the 1970s and 1980s compelled women to reassume the responsibilities.[30] They could pay for needed services in the private sector, provide them themselves, or watch their families do without. As financialization and tax cuts for the wealthy concentrated wealth at the top of the economic ladder, low-income women, among whom African Americans were overrepresented, were left to attempt to fix on their own the holes nationally elected officials rent in the nation's social safety net. During the 1970s and 1980s, African American populations in Baltimore were increasingly tasked with responding independently to worsening urban problems at the same time that the champions of neoliberalism continued to tout supposed Black criminality to justify attempts to further erode the welfare state. And the dynamic continued into the early twenty-first century as neoliberalism grew more entrenched. No wonder Tawanda Jones felt like the enemy.

CHAPTER 1

"Boom Times" in Baltimore?

In early 1951, the *New York Times* predicted "boom times" for the Baltimore region. The business community had already identified 1950 as its best year since World War II, and executives in several industries planned to expand production to meet demand for defense orders, making the new year even better. Unemployment in Maryland was at its lowest level since the war's end, and industrial employers expected to have to search out of state to fill a projected ten thousand positions for skilled workers. Many residents of Baltimore shared in the prosperity the city's boom times created. Studies of local economic activity revealed that they were celebrating the flush times with shopping sprees and splurging on big-ticket items. Retail sales were on the rise, as was demand for electricity to power the many consumer products that had flooded the market after the war, items such as televisions, washing machines, and refrigerators. Area residents were also taking to the roads with increasing frequency. Car registrations were up, and gasoline consumption was rising quickly. For growing numbers, cars sustained suburban lifestyles as city natives abandoned Baltimore entirely for a new start.[1]

But not everyone in Baltimore benefited equally from the city's boom times. Persistent employment discrimination kept Black city residents on the margins or at the bottom of the city's industrial economy. Anna "Nan" Butler's family was representative. In 1950, she was thirty-seven years old and the mother of four. Although as a child she had sometimes imagined for herself a career in nursing, the aspiration had proven difficult to achieve in Jim Crow Baltimore. Instead, like most Black women of her generation, Butler turned to domestic work. She might have preferred the life of a housewife, attending to her own children and home instead of juggling family responsibilities with the demands of cleaning and caring for others. But her husband's income as a laborer, the occupational category that included the largest number of Black men in Baltimore during the first half of the twentieth century, could not sustain their family. So Butler cleaned for white families to help make ends meet. Her wages were low—minimum-wage laws excluded domestic workers—but she did what she could to boost them. When she took on new clients, she exaggerated prevailing wage rates and sometimes won herself a raise. The small victories were important but not enough to lift her family out of poverty. "We were poor," one of her daughters recalled, but then added pensively, "but we didn't know we were poor. Everyone was poor."[2] Her recollection was not far off. During Baltimore's boom times, when employers anticipated recruiting relatively highly paid skilled workers from out of state, well over half of the city's Black residents lived in poverty.[3]

To combat widespread insecurity, during the postwar era, civil rights leaders worked relentlessly to incorporate African Americans into their city's boom times. The task was daunting. Known as the nation's northernmost southern city and southernmost northern city, Baltimore had an industrialized, Jim Crow economy, and there were few forms of discrimination Black residents did not confront. Nevertheless, building on campaigns with roots in the 1930s, African American leaders endeavored to improve conditions. They took on Jim Crow segregation and sometimes met with success.[4] Simultaneously, they remained unwavering in their determination to fight employment discrimination. The ticket to the city's boom times lay in integrating the mainstream economy and thereby winning for African Americans both better jobs and greater protection from the nation's welfare state—access to Social Security and unemployment insurance, the right to join a union and earn the minimum wage. Such protections were buoying the economic fortunes of many white workers but did not consistently extend to laborers, domestic workers, and others in the precarious jobs often filled by African Americans. The health of the local—and national—economy had long depended on a racially segmented labor market in which whites confined African Americans to low-wage jobs. Change did not come easily. Despite some very hard-won and important civil rights victories, the system largely remained in place through the 1950s. As a result, gains accrued by many in the white working class during Baltimore's boom times remained out of reach for many Black families.

The marginalization of African Americans in Baltimore's vibrant postwar economy had far-reaching and also gendered implications. For men, their concentration in laboring positions made them particularly vulnerable to efforts by manufacturers to mechanize production. Technological changes meant that new machines rather than men increasingly did the grunt work on the city's job sites, which saved on labor costs but increased the Black male unemployment rate. What is more, by the postwar years, Baltimore was no longer the magnet for industrial employers that it once was. New firms often located in the city's suburbs, and manufacturers with aging plants in the city increasingly found it cost-effective to move elsewhere. Mechanization and early deindustrialization threatened to erode the city's manufacturing base before Black men had won full inclusion. Meanwhile, for many Black women like Butler, economic hardship meant juggling the demands of paid employment with family obligations—obligations that the nation's welfare state was easing for white women but that substandard housing, inadequate sanitation services, separate and unequal access to health care, and other vestiges of Jim Crow made all the more challenging. To be sure, the momentum achieved by Baltimore's civil rights leaders during the 1950s paved the way for important changes to come. Nevertheless, during an exceptional era in the history of American capitalism during which many workers shared to an unprecedented level in the profits of their employers, Baltimore's boom times did not extend far into Black communities.

"A Ready Supply of Common Labor": Civil Rights Leaders and Black Employment

As postwar civil rights leaders attempted to dismantle the Jim Crow–dominated system in Baltimore, they encountered considerable resistance. Local white power brokers, as well as much of the white population more generally, shared a deep commitment to maintaining the city's rigid racial hierarchy. During the 1940s, Baltimore became the nation's sixth largest city, and by the war's end, the Black population had reached about two hundred thousand. Although African Americans accounted for approximately 20 percent of the city's residents, which was a larger fraction than found in most other industrial cities, they wielded little political or economic power. The trappings of white supremacy were everywhere. African Americans held no elected offices; Jim Crow segregation dictated where people could and could not go; residential segregation prevailed; and most Black workers had menial jobs.[5] Civil rights activists had a lot to tackle.

The key to improving the economic fortunes of African Americans lay in moving Black men into and upward in the city's industrial sector, many activists believed. Despite its location below the Mason-Dixon line, Baltimore resembled economically cities in the Northeast and the Midwest rather than cities in the South. Although Baltimore's economic roots were in commerce, by the start of the twentieth century an extensive rail system had attracted manufacturers to the city. The Baltimore port, which became one of the largest and most important on the U.S. Atlantic coast, fueled the industrial development. A wave of mergers early in the twentieth century consumed many locally owned firms and added nationally recognizable names to the city's business directories, and so Baltimore became known as a city of branch plants. Western Electric and Glenn Martin Aircrafts opened facilities in the area during the 1920s, as did Procter and Gamble, Coca-Cola, Montgomery Ward, McCormick Spice, and American Sugar. By the 1930s, Bethlehem Steel, which had purchased mills in Sparrows Point just outside the city in 1916, was Baltimore's largest employer, and it remained so after the war. Bethlehem Steel also ran shipyards at "the Point" and in South Baltimore. General Motors began operations during the 1930s just outside the city, and by the start of World War II, General Electric and Westinghouse also had Baltimore branches. As in most northeastern cities, Baltimore's economy was diversified. Commerce remained important, and the city had a small but significant banking and financial sector; the contemporary firms Legg Mason and T. Rowe Price were products of the city. In 1940, 40 percent of Baltimore's workforce labored in trade and service jobs. The city's economic diversity persisted through the postwar years, making Baltimore representative of similarly sized cities in the industrial belt. Nevertheless, the industrial sector powered the city's economy.[6]

The exploitation of Black labor long had been critical to the city's economic growth. At the start of the Civil War, Baltimore had been home to the largest population of free African Americans in the nation, and the city had been known as the Black capital of the United States. But Baltimore's tradition of free Black labor had hardly prevented whites from excluding most African American men from skilled jobs and the lucrative trades after the Civil War. And white employers used racism to justify low wages for Black workers. In fact, during the Great Depression, business boosters made the availability of inexpensive African American labor a selling point in a campaign to attract investors to the city. "The percentage of Negroes is 17.7 affording a ready supply of common labor," the Baltimore Industrial Bureau touted in an advertisement.[7] White employers confined Black men to low-wage positions to reduce labor costs and also to prevent unionization. In some cases, employers intentionally denied Black workers regular jobs so as to hire them as scabs during strikes. Employers' manipulation of race limited most Black men to poverty-level wages. It also impeded labor organizing. By World War II, Baltimore's labor movement was notoriously weak.[8]

Wartime labor demands had opened opportunities for Black workers, and civil rights leaders pursued them assertively. The percentage of Black men employed in the industrial sector rose from 7 percent to 17 percent. Black women made gains as well. Although still largely confined to low-wage service positions, the percentage engaged in domestic service dropped from 70 to less than 45.[9] While important, the changes did not go far enough. Discrimination continued to confine most African American workers to the least secure and most unprotected jobs in the city. As the white director of Baltimore's Department of Public Welfare, T. J. S. Waxter, explained in 1944, "Perhaps the greatest handicap under which Negroes live in Baltimore is in the restriction of job opportunities in many areas. Numerous concerns in the city will not employ Negroes for semi-skilled, skilled and professional work." Despite wartime improvements, he noted, "It is still true . . . that the overwhelming number of Negroes find employment in unskilled work and domestic service."[10] In the midst of the city's modern industrial economy, most African Americans struggled to get by in low-wage jobs.

"The Constitution Meant Just What It Said"

Postwar civil rights activists knew well the challenges they faced. Many who engaged in postwar campaigns for jobs began their activist careers during the 1930s. The people and organizations behind Baltimore's Depression-era and wartime civil rights efforts were numerous. Black neighborhoods housed an extensive network of institutions, some of which had roots in antebellum America. Black churches had an especially long and important history in the city. In Sunday-morning sermons, clergy across the city—some lecturing in the stern tone of patriarchs, others fired by the passion of revelation—blended spiritual guidance and political advocacy. Although church members differed in their assessments of the responses required to pernicious racism in the city, from their ranks emerged many of the leaders and foot soldiers of the city's civil rights movement. Meanwhile, clergy members played important roles in interracial relations.[11]

Baltimore also boasted a critically important Black-owned press. The *Afro-American*, a newspaper purchased by John Murphy in 1890 and edited from the 1920s through 1967 by his son, Carl, was the most important Black business in the city. The paper covered events of interest to its national African American readership in editions published in cities across the country. Its Baltimore edition included stories on local politics. The paper's editorial page provided readers with perspectives on both international and domestic events. It also included trenchant insights into Baltimore's ongoing civil rights struggles, battles in which Murphy and his paper were often intimately involved. The editor, who held degrees from Howard and Harvard Universities as well as Friedrich Schiller University Jena in Germany, was a member of the national board of the National Association for the Advancement of Colored People (NAACP). During the 1930s, he helped to revive the city's branch of the organization, which had become dormant during the 1920s. No resident in Baltimore had the ear of as many of the city's Black citizens as Carl Murphy.[12]

Murphy's paper was hardly limited to political content. Articles in the *Afro-American* kept readers updated on the goings-on within the city's many civic and social organizations, including numerous fraternal groups, sororities, lodges, and other private clubs. Readers could also look to the paper for news of the latest events at Morgan State and Coppin State, two historically Black colleges that had graduated many of the city's African American professionals. In addition, the *Afro-American* covered the cotillion dances, elaborate weddings, overseas escapades, and other exploits of the small but notoriously class-conscious who's who of Black Baltimore. The paper included articles on the city's vibrant cultural scene as well, reporting on the hottest acts appearing in clubs on Pennsylvania Avenue in West Baltimore, the heart of the city's African American arts scene. And the paper kept readers current on all forms of sporting events, providing scores and analyses of high school, college, amateur, and professional matchups. In other words, the sources of the energy and perseverance that sustained the city's civil rights activists through difficult battles was described in the paper's articles that were not related to civil rights.

From the mid-1930s onward, many issues of the paper did include news of local civil rights activism. The Baltimore chapter of the NAACP led many of the battles. The organization, the second NAACP branch in the nation, received its charter in 1913. During its early years, members spearheaded fights against lynching in Maryland and campaigned against housing segregation laws that the Baltimore City Council repeatedly but unsuccessfully attempted to enact. Concerned about African Americans' access to jobs and public services, local NAACP leaders also protested rampant employment discrimination in the municipal government.[13]

Lillie May Jackson was a primary force behind the resurgence of the Baltimore NAACP during the mid-1930s, and she remained at the organization's helm until 1970. Born in Baltimore in 1889, Jackson graduated from Coppin Teachers College. She worked in the city's public schools, and then married Kieffer A. Jackson, an exhibitor of religious films. Together the couple had four children. Lillie May Jackson was devoutly religious and not a little righteous. She understood her efforts in the NAACP to be God's work, and she grew the Baltimore branch of the organization into one of the nation's biggest primarily by working within the city's Black religious communities. In keeping with the ideology that motivated many African American activists of her generation and class, Jackson asserted that it was her "job to help [her] people and lift them up." Yet she also believed strongly that it was her responsibility to "prove that the Constitution meant just what it said."[14] She valued action, and upon assuming the leadership of the Baltimore NAACP, she replaced some on the organization's "polite preacher-teacher" board with representatives from organized labor.[15] Her reputation as a leader who produced results—and also the membership dues needed to finance the local and national organizations—eventually extended beyond Maryland, and during the late 1940s, she won a spot on the board of directors of the national NAACP. Many knew Jackson not only for her activism but also for her sharp tongue and domineering leadership style. Baltimore NAACP board members who disagreed with her dictates sometimes opted to skip meetings rather than battle with, in the words of one member, their "sort of autocratic" leader.[16] Yet as her son-in-law later noted, "She made [Maryland] a lot closer to what it ought to be than anybody ever imagined it would be, and I think she did it by the sheer force of her determination with very little resources to work with."[17]

Working side by side with Jackson at the helm of the NAACP was her daughter, Juanita Jackson Mitchell. Mitchell was born in 1913 and attended Baltimore City schools. She received both a bachelor's and a master's degree from the University of Pennsylvania. Returning home during the Depression, she cofounded and became president of the Citywide Young People's Forum, a progressive, Popular Front–type organization with a membership that included Thurgood Marshall, who later argued the *Brown v. Board of Education* case that outlawed segregation in public schools and who in 1967 became the nation's first African American Supreme Court justice. With the NAACP's blessing, the Young People's Forum launched a "Don't Buy Where

You Can't Work" campaign. The willingness of activists in Baltimore to use the picket line in addition to the legal strategies typically associated with the NAACP won them a reputation for militancy, and Mitchell's influence was critical. After beginning her activist career in Baltimore, Mitchell served as a special assistant to national NAACP leader Walter White and as the national youth director of the NAACP.[18]

In 1938, then Juanita Jackson married Clarence Mitchell, who was also an early leader of the Young People's Forum. The union joined two of the city's most powerful African American families and soon further strengthened the link between the Baltimore branch and the national NAACP. Following World War II, Clarence Mitchell became the labor secretary of the national NAACP and then the director of its Washington, DC, bureau and its chief lobbyist in the nation's capital. In the latter position, he played a major role in shaping all of the federal civil rights legislation passed during the 1950s, 1960s, and 1970s, work that earned him a Presidential Medal of Freedom in 1980. Juanita Mitchell's reputation as a civil rights activist and leader was well established before her marriage, however, and remained distinct from her husband's. During the late 1940s, she embraced a challenge put to her by NAACP legal giant Charles Houston. In 1950, she became the first African American woman to graduate from the University of Maryland Law School, which the NAACP had earlier compelled to integrate, and to practice law in the state. She used her legal training to combat Jim Crow segregation and discrimination in Baltimore. Her reputation as an advocate extended beyond Baltimore. Three presidents, Franklin Roosevelt, John Kennedy, and Lyndon Johnson, appointed her to federal commissions or conferences.[19]

Under the powerful mother-daughter team of Jackson and Mitchell, the Baltimore NAACP became one of the most active branches in the country. Although few women held top positions nationally in civil rights organizations, Jackson's and Mitchell's decades at the helm of the organization indicate that African Americans in Baltimore adjusted to female leadership. "God opened my mouth and no man can shut it," Jackson once declared.[20] For that, many Black residents were grateful. The fight for jobs and employment equity consistently appeared on the NAACP's agenda. In addition to its endorsement of the pickets of the Young People's Forum, during the 1930s Jackson worked with Marshall on a county-by-county effort in Maryland to equalize the salaries of Black and white teachers. The NAACP also fought for government posts for African Americans in segregated public institutions, on the police force, and in the fire department. Then during the war years, the NAACP played a critical role in the campaign to win industrial jobs for Black workers. By the postwar era, the organization already had amassed an impressive record of civil rights activism.[21]

Critical in NAACP efforts to improve the job prospects of Black workers was F. Troy Brailey, who served as labor secretary. Born in South Carolina in 1916, Brailey hitchhiked his way to Baltimore as a teenager during the Depression and then eked out an existence shining shoes. He later became a railroad porter and an associate of African American labor leader and civil rights legend A. Philip Randolph. Brailey served as the president of the Baltimore division of the Brotherhood of Sleeping Car Porters, a union founded by Randolph. He also worked with Randolph on the proposed March on Washington in 1941 to protest discrimination in the war industries. After the war, Brailey became the president of the Baltimore chapter of the Negro American Labor Council, an organization founded by Randolph to fight discrimination in labor unions. In 1966, Brailey won a seat in the Maryland House of Delegates, where he was a founder of the Maryland Legislative Black Caucus. He later served in the state's Senate. Somewhat exceptional among Baltimore's postwar civil rights luminaries because of his deep and personal connection to organized labor, Brailey was fiercely committed to keeping the civil rights movement focused on labor issues.[22]

Joining the NAACP at the forefront of Baltimore's civil rights movement was the Baltimore Urban League (BUL). Members of an interracial coalition founded the organization in 1924. In keeping with the mission of its parent organization, the BUL focused on advocating for employment opportunities and access to public services for the city's African Americans. Initially committed to the almost exclusive use of moral suasion to achieve its goals, BUL leaders generally eschewed the picket lines and lawsuits that were the hallmarks of the NAACP. The BUL favored instead the research study that documented the ill effects of discrimination. During the 1930s, the organization conducted a survey of New Deal relief recipients and exposed bias in the distribution of services. They used the results to push for improved services for Black residents and to win African Americans positions as caseworkers with the Baltimore Emergency Relief Commission. The BUL also worked to open low-cost housing options to African Americans and to win better health and recreation services for Black city residents. During the war, the BUL probably outpaced the NAACP in efforts to convince white employers to hire Black workers. As a result, by the conclusion of the war, the BUL like the NAACP had quite a significant civil rights track record.[23]

By the postwar period, the BUL had a reputation for moderation and was dominated by a largely white leadership. The organization's board was entirely male, and many members had affiliations with important businesses or labor organizations. The BUL's leadership also included some prominent African Americans, including those often found on the Baltimore NAACP's masthead. Juanita Mitchell served for a time as a member of the BUL's Ladies Auxiliary, and her husband was an early board member, where he served alongside the *Afro-American*'s Murphy. The BUL's most influential Black leader during the war years and again during the 1950s and 1960s was Furman Templeton. An alumnus of Lincoln University, Templeton joined the BUL as the United States was preparing to enter World War II. In 1941, as the BUL's industrial secretary, Templeton's advocacy on behalf of prospective Black war workers won him a place on the *Afro-American*'s "Honor Roll." He left the league for a federal job during the war and then worked for Murphy's paper. In 1950, he returned to the BUL as the organization's executive secretary, and from that position he played a leading role in the fight to improve access for African Americans to jobs and social services.[24]

In addition to African American activists, a small but important number of white liberals also fought for civil rights. Although relations between African Americans and Jews were sometimes tense in Baltimore, Jewish leaders frequently participated in fights against segregation and discrimination. Leon Sachs, of the Baltimore Jewish Council, played a tremendously important role in postwar activism, especially on behalf of equal employment. Some white Protestant and Catholic leaders were also active in civil rights battles, as were the leaders of several labor unions. And Baltimore was home to a chapter of the Congress of Racial Equality (CORE), which had a predominantly white membership. In addition, the Citizen's Housing and Planning Association and several other groups attracted an interracial membership that worked to improve race relations in the city.[25]

"Sweep and Scrub, Push and Haul, Tote and Carry": The Fight for Postwar Jobs

Although battles against Jim Crow segregation in Baltimore often attracted headlines during the postwar era, civil rights leaders also remained focused on fighting employment discrimination. The campaign was critical. Postwar prosperity in Baltimore stemmed largely from the city's privileged position within the global capitalist economy. The United States emerged from World War II an undisputed superpower and with its physical infrastructure worn but unscathed. Meanwhile, much of Europe and Japan lay in ruins. U.S. manufacturers and other business leaders were more than happy to supply the industrial needs of their war-torn competitors, and U.S. policy makers brokered the international agreements that provided them with advantageous means to do so. Meanwhile, although some lamented the reliance of much U.S. prosperity on militarism, defense spending on a global war against communism precluded a return to economic depression and powered economic growth.[26]

But the midcentury was not only a bonanza for elites. Workers had spent more than the last half-century battling the labor conditions that had prevailed under the system of laissez-faire capitalism. They won incomplete but important concessions. The New Deal produced legislation that protected many workers' right to join labor unions. Union membership surged, and collectively bargained contracts won wage increases and better working conditions for many. Meanwhile, federal welfare measures eased some of the economic hardship often associated with old age and unemployment; enforced baseline labor standards; maintained tax incentives to induce employers to provide fringe benefits, such as health insurance and pension plans; and provided mortgage assistance that enabled families to realize the dream of homeownership. To be sure, the labor legislation and welfare measures that protected workers were the product of compromises that conservative politicians and business interests tried to renegotiate throughout the postwar years. Nevertheless, for many, the system worked admirably well. The problem for African Americans, however, is that much New Deal legislation did not extend to many of the jobs in which they were concentrated. The racial discrepancies meant that while many white families could start to get ahead, many African Americans continued to struggle just to get by.[27]

Civil rights advocates in Baltimore had launched battles for postwar jobs even before the war came to an end. Some efforts involved securing federal legislation. Thousands in Baltimore actively participated in national campaigns to make the Fair Employment Practices Commission (FEPC) permanent. Created during the war, the FEPC combated employment discrimination in the war industries. African Americans wanted to see federal prohibitions against discrimination extended. Clarence Mitchell commuted from his home in Baltimore to champion the issue in D.C. on behalf of the national NAACP. Meanwhile, the Baltimore NAACP helped to coordinate efforts by more than a hundred local organizations that were engaged in lobbying and letter- and telegram-writing campaigns intended to sway Maryland's congressional officials to the cause.[28] Baltimore activists also supported efforts to secure full-employment legislation, which would require the federal government to guarantee a job to all Americans in search of work. In Baltimore, the issue did not garner the level of activism fair employment received, but it had staunch advocates. The editors of the *Afro-American* called on readers to "stand solidly behind the Full Employment Bill by urging our representatives in Congress to back it to the hilt. We clamored for war jobs. Let us clamor with equal vigor for jobs in peacetime."[29] Ultimately, however, neither fair nor meaningful full employment legislation made it through the Congresses of the late 1940s.

Civil rights leaders led by Mitchell did meet with success in efforts to ban employment discrimination in the federal workforce. In Baltimore, the issue garnered considerable support. The Social Security Administration (SSA) was headquartered in the city and served as a critical local employer. Moreover, the U.S. Post Office, known in Black communities as the Negro graveyard because it often employed Black men in positions well below their skill level, had long been an important source of stable African American male jobs.[30] In response to a pressure campaign, in 1948, President Harry Truman signed Executive Order 9980, which banned discrimination, although not segregation, in the federal workforce.

Under the watchful eyes of such leaders as Jackson and Juanita Mitchell, Executive Order 9980 had immediate ramifications in Baltimore. Following an internal investigation into discrimination at the agency, SSA officials agreed to fully desegregate its facilities, hire African American personnel officials, make employment decisions without consideration of race, and make promotion decisions based on merit regardless of the racial composition of the employees a prospective supervisor would oversee. Completely out of step with the Jim Crow culture of Baltimore, Social Security became an imperfect but pathbreaking employer. The change was particularly consequential for Black women as the SSA's workforce was predominantly female. Overall, as a result of the executive order and its actual if incomplete implementation, in 1949 the BUL noted with enthusiasm "a marked increase in the colored employment in Federal agencies."[31] African Americans, by that time constituting nearly a fourth of the city's population, made up 16 percent of local Social Security employees and more than a quarter of Baltimore's U.S. postal workers. In the one realm in which civil rights activists had won a nondiscrimination provision, the measure seemed to be helping.[32]

Unfortunately, changes in federal agencies were among the very few positive developments for Black workers in Baltimore. The situation at Bethlehem Steel, the most important employer in the city, was a disappointing best-case scenario for African Americans in the private sector. Historically, about a third of the company's workforce had been Black. But as McCall White, who started working for the company during the 1940s, recalled, "Wages [for African Americans] were much lower, much lower than for white workers. Job classes ran from 1 to 32. Black workers usually stayed around job class 1 and no higher than job class 4."[33] During a successful unionization drive during the war years, an effort in which Black workers played an important role, union officials promised they would combat discrimination. Postwar contracts, however, failed to effectively challenge the segregation of Black workers into the lowest grades. Company officials divided the workforce into departments, and African Americans generally worked in departments with limited opportunities for advancement regardless of accrued seniority. Black workers fought the discrimination and, with eventual union support, won modest changes. Token numbers of Black workers started to make inroads into skilled and supervisory positions during the 1950s. Greater numbers moved into semiskilled or operative jobs. Nevertheless, the concentration of African Americans in unskilled positions persisted. The problems at Bethlehem Steel were far from unique. Despite slow but important changes in the city's industrial sector, discrimination remained rampant.[34]

Civil rights leaders were ever vigilant. During the 1950s, BUL officials worked directly with Maryland Department of Employment Security officials as well as with private employment agencies in an effort to open new jobs to Black workers. In addition, they held vocational fairs, monitored African American access to and participation in vocational education, worked with government officials to open public-sector employment, mediated strikes, helped job candidates prepare for trade-specific examinations, and negotiated with business leaders and union officials.[35] Meanwhile, the NAACP, often led by Brailey, monitored the distribution of federal contracts in Baltimore and worked to ensure the enforcement of the equal-opportunity provisions such contracts mandated. The organization also pressed the city council unsuccessfully for legislation prohibiting employment discrimination in publicly funded construction projects and worked with employers and unions to win positions for Black workers. By the mid-1950s, the NAACP had helped to secure limited numbers of African Americans jobs as plumbers, electricians, and telephone workers, as well as bus, streetcar, and taxi drivers. The organization also opened paths for African Americans to some professional jobs by winning the integration of some graduate schools. Victories by both the NAACP and BUL, however, were largely piecemeal. Without the muscle of a permanent FEPC, the pace of change was painfully slow.[36]

Aware that efforts to persuade employers and unions to abandon discriminatory practices met with only minimal results, during the mid-1950s Black leaders began to pressure elected officials for a local fair-employment practices ordinance. And they had a powerful weapon to mobilize on behalf of the cause: Black voters. During the early twentieth century, efforts by whites in Maryland's State House to disenfranchise African Americans had failed repeatedly (largely because Baltimore's sizable population of immigrants suspected the proposed legislation would eventually be used against them). Since the 1930s, however, white officials had gerrymandered Black residents out of political representation. During World War II, as African American migration swelled the city's Black population and local Black leaders yearned for increased political influence, civil rights activists successfully mobilized voting power to affect the outcome of a citywide election. In 1943, Black voters helped moderate Republican Theodore McKeldin beat the city's aging Democratic machine and win the mayor's office. In exchange for their support, African Americans expected and received appointments and municipal jobs. The gains were far from substantial, but the achievement was important.[37] During the war, the city's Black population was finally able to flex its political muscle. And aided by white flight from the city and continuing Black in-migration, those proposing a local fair employment measure decided it was time to try to flex that muscle again.

By the mid-1950s, twelve states and twenty-nine cities had passed what activists called "Baby FEPCs." Baltimore's civil rights leaders hoped to make their city the first below the Mason-Dixon line with such a provision. In 1954, a large coalition of labor, civic, religious, and welfare organizations came together to support the local fair employment law. The BUL played a leading role in the campaign, as did Sachs of the Baltimore Jewish Council. The NAACP also sponsored the measure, which the *Afro-American* strongly endorsed.[38] Supporters faced a daunting task as they tried to convince a majority of the all-white city council to support the FEPC, however. Unlike the city's mayors and city council presidents, who had to prevail in citywide elections, council members typically owed allegiance only to those in their districts.[39] In March 1954, four members introduced the bill, which would ban discrimination in employment based on race, color, creed, or religion. Hundreds of African

Americans wrote to the city council to urge passage of the measure, and at a hearing on behalf of the bill, more than two hundred supporters crowded into the council chambers as thirty speakers presented their case. Jackson spoke in favor of the measure, as did William Passano, then president of the BUL.[40] But despite the tremendous effort on behalf of the FEPC, the measure did not pass.[41]

A year later, Black Baltimore finally had succeeded in electing an African American city council member. Demographic changes and voter registration drives overwhelmed white efforts to exclude Black politicians from municipal office. "Our goal was not just political representation, but the power to make changes in a society that excluded and victimized us," recalls city resident Verda Welcome, who later became the first Black woman to serve in a state Senate.[42] In late 1955, Walter Dixon won a seat on the council, and the following spring, he reintroduced the FEPC ordinance. This time the bill did pass— or at least a watered-down version of it did. A new ordinance created an Equal Employment Opportunities Commission (EEOC). The law, however, denied the EEOC the power to pursue legal action against employers it found guilty of discrimination. The EEOC, in other words, had no enforcement power. In an effort to be upbeat, the *Afro-American*'s editorial board described the new FEPC as "another step forward." The paper's editors could not fully contain their skepticism, however. "If discrimination in employment can be cured by persuading employers and unions then it should be done that way. This is an effort to see if this method can be successful," the editors, mindful of the past failures of just such an approach, reflected doubtfully.[43]

And it quickly became apparent that most city officials, including Mayor Thomas D'Alesandro Jr., who succeeded McKeldin, had no intention of even letting the EEOC put the persuasion method to the test. D'Alesandro's appointments to the EEOC evinced inconsistent interest in battling employment discrimination. A year later, aware of multiple instances in which Black workers had been unfairly denied jobs, the editors of the *Afro-American* noted with obvious disappointment, "IT WAS hoped" that the EEOC would do something to improve employment opportunities for Black workers (emphasis in the original).[44] But it had not.

Despite obstacles and an impotent EEOC, African Americans did make some important employment gains during the 1950s. Black men's representation in the industrial sector rose from its wartime peak of 17 percent to 20 percent. And Black men in semiskilled work reached wage parity with their white counterparts. Black women made some significant gains as well. A fortunate few won clerical jobs or spots in federal agencies. And the percentage who worked in domestic service continued to decline. Yet the movement of Black women out of domestic and into other types of low-wage service work largely accounted for the postwar changes. Certainly some Black families did win a share of the city's boom times. As Pete Wallace, an employee of Bethlehem Steel, recalled, "If the man worked [in the steel mills] . . . and his wife worked for Social Security, we thought we had it made."[45] Such families were the aristocracy of the Black working class, and it showed. "The purses matched the shoes and the gloves matched the coats, and you could easily pick those people out," recalled Juanita Cole about the wives of some Black employees of Bethlehem Steel.[46]

But most Black men did not work in unionized factories, and only a small minority of Black women held government posts. The 20 percent of African American men in industrial positions compared to well over 30 percent for white men. And the whites generally had better-paying jobs. By 1960, African Americans made up nearly 70 percent of the city's unskilled workers while whites accounted for 92 percent of skilled workers.[47] Domestic service remained the occupational category that included the largest number of Black women. In fact, the concentration of African American women in menial positions led researchers studying Baltimore's labor scene to identify "the Negro woman" as "the least utilized pool of potential urban industrial labor power" in the city.[48]

Ongoing employment discrimination created a tremendous income gap between Black and white families. During the mid-1950s, the median African American income in the city was a mere 56 percent of the white median income. Worse, the gap between Black and white earnings had actually increased since 1949. By the end of the 1950s, nearly a third of Black families earned incomes less than the $3,000 the federal government soon identified as the poverty line, and almost two-thirds of families earned less than the $5,180 the Bureau of Labor Statistics calculated was needed to sustain a family at a "moderate but adequate" level. Despite important changes, "when all the advances are ticked off, the employment picture remains a gloomy one," concluded researchers studying Baltimore's "progress towards equity." "There are a few secretaries, a few foremen, a few engineers and telephone operators, but the great majority of colored Baltimoreans continue to sweep and scrub, push and haul, tote and carry in menial, unskilled occupations."[49] Many Black workers remained trapped in low-wage, insecure jobs, where they typically lacked access to many of the supposedly universal welfare programs of the

New Deal as well as fringe benefits the federal government subsidized. The city's boom times were passing by Black Baltimore, and despite their best efforts, civil rights activists had not been able to do enough about it.[50]

Making matters worse, the bottom literally began falling out of the city's industrial economy. The number of jobs for unskilled laborers, the positions on which so many Black families depended, was in decline. During the postwar years, manufacturers throughout the United States built on wartime innovations in an effort to automate production. They aimed both to lower labor costs and to increase productivity. The trend toward automation became increasingly evident in Baltimore during the 1950s. Machines replaced laborers on many of the city's construction sites as well as in Baltimore's factories. The changes reduced the need for unskilled labor and also stalled growth citywide in the number of semiskilled positions. Automation took a particularly hard toll on African Americans. As the *Baltimore Sun* reported, "Negro unemployment, locally as nationally, is being magnified by automation and other technological advances which are steadily reducing the need for unskilled and blue-collar workers."[51] During Baltimore's boom times, Black men were even losing their niche at the bottom of the industrial sector.

Moreover, deindustrialization promised to make Black men's employment prospects even bleaker. As a consulting firm studying Baltimore's regional economy explained, continuous wartime use had "worn out" industrial machinery in many older urban factories. Then, after the war, "lack of space, increasing congestion, unfavorable cost-price movements, and inflation accompanying the increased wage demands acted as tremendous disruptive forces for older areas of the Northeast and Middle Atlantic states."[52] In some instances, firms responded by relocating outside of aging cities. In the Baltimore region, the military contracts that helped to produce the city's boom times often went to suburban-based firms. The shift had serious consequences for the city. During the Depression, manufacturing employment in Baltimore had dropped by 10 percent, but it had mushroomed by more than 250 percent in nearby suburbs. During the 1950s, the city lost 338 manufacturing firms. Manufacturing remained the city's largest employment category into the 1960s. Nevertheless, as mechanization eroded the lowest tiers of the industrial economy, deindustrialization made uncertain the future of the entire manufacturing sector. The change imperiled a critical job base for men in Baltimore—both Black and white. White men had the option of relocation, but fiercely policed residential segregation largely precluded African Americans from moving to the city's suburbs where job prospects were better.

Baltimore's economy was in the midst of fundamental structural change that was devastating the job prospects of Black men, and there was very little Jackson, the Mitchells, Brailey, Templeton, and the city's other civil rights leaders could do about that.[53]

"We Are the Mothers Whose Children Suffer This Damage": Gender and the Security Gap

While Black men bore the brunt of the employment costs associated with technological and structural economic changes, Black women paid a gendered price for economic insecurity. Not only did they participate in the paid labor force in larger numbers than white women—and usually in lower-paid positions—but they also often attempted to compensate for poverty and low incomes by working extra hard at home. As one city native recalls, "Throughout most of my childhood, my mother seemed to be working constantly. If she wasn't putting in hours at the factory, or cleaning the houses of the white people on the weekends, she was busy at home cooking, tidying up, and keeping an eye on us."[54] Feminist economists have long argued that women often respond to tough times not only by working for wages but also by doing extra tasks around the house to stretch family budgets. They repair rather than replace broken items; provide rather than purchase health, child, and elder care; and make from scratch or by hand items available ready-made on the market. Such practices were stock-in-trade for many Black and also white women in Baltimore prior to World War II. Boom times, however, alleviated some of the pressures on the white women while Black women saw fewer changes. Ongoing employment discrimination and the lack of access African Americans had to many of the nation's most generous welfare provisions had gendered consequences that Black women bore. And segregation made Black women's gendered caretaking roles all the more challenging.

As the social safety net began to ease the conditions of working-class life during the postwar era, a security gap emerged between Black and white families that had implications for women. During the 1930s, as New Dealers were building the nation's social security system, NAACP lawyer Charles Houston commented that "from the Negro's point of view," the new system looked like "a sieve with the holes just big enough for the majority of Negroes to fall through."[55] Large numbers of Black workers were excluded from such programs as old age and unemployment insurance because of their concentration in agricultural labor and domestic work. And they secured only inconsistent protection from subsequent welfare-state provisions as well. The consequences of the exclusion became increasingly stark after the war. Elderly parents, even if they qualified for means-tested old age assistance, could still need financial support, which created added strain on already tight family budgets and pressure on women to adopt labor-intensive, cost-cutting strategies. Visits to doctors were expensive, compelling adult daughters to provide needed care and other support themselves. Moreover, the family of a brother who did not receive unemployment insurance during a bout of joblessness because he worked outside of the system might need an extra few meals that took time and resources to prepare. Meanwhile, the lack of employer-provided health insurance might mean trying to substitute a mother's touch for a costly hospital visit. In countless ways, Black women provided for their families' security with labor that white women could increasingly abandon as their families received welfare protections from the government.

And as in the past, Jim Crow practices exacerbated the caretaking demands borne by Black women. As one city resident recalls, "The city government didn't really care how we lived, and their neglect could be seen in our communities."[56] Substandard housing, separate and unequal public and private facilities, and the inferior quality of services the city provided to African American residents meant that Black women had to "sweep and scrub, push and haul, tote and carry" far more than white women in their homes and neighborhoods.[57] During the 1950s, the number of neighborhoods into which Black families could safely move without fear of retaliatory violence by whites increased. Often aided by federal mortgage assistance to which Black families had less access, many whites left the city to realize the dream of suburban homeownership. The whites thus acquired an asset they could later use to help put a child through college or pass down an inheritance, wealth-generating practices that could lead to upward mobility and that were less available to African Americans.[58] Although housing options increased for Black Baltimoreans, by the mid-1950s, the city classified over 40 percent of the housing occupied by African Americans as substandard, meaning either the units were dilapidated or lacked a private toilet, bath, or hot running water. In addition, almost 40 percent of dwellings occupied by African Americans lacked central heating.[59] In their homes, Black women scrubbed and cleaned and tried to combat the symptoms of housing decay. As one low-income African American woman explained, mothers who "lived in the slums" knew only too well the fear and sadness of "stay[ing] up nights chasing rats . . . [and] listen[ing] to the wind whistling through the walls."⁶⁰ Thus they devised strategies for keeping out vermin and the cold. Black women also worked collectively as they paid a gendered price for white supremacy. For generations, African American women in Baltimore had relied on kin and other social networks as well as religious communities to meet the needs of their families and communities. Grassroots and voluntary organizations also helped women navigate the segregated landscape. African American women were consistently prominent among those participating in the *Afro-American*'s Clean Block campaigns, community projects intended to improve neighborhood sanitation. Like the progressive reformers of the late nineteenth century, Black women in 1950s Baltimore often used their own muscle and resources to combat neglect by the city as they also pressed elected officials for change.⁶¹

Unmet sanitation needs in many Black neighborhoods and the concentration of African American families in the city's most dilapidated housing made it a challenge to find places where children could safely play. In addition, the segregation of the city's libraries, parks, and recreation services denied Black children access to Baltimore's best-resourced public facilities. "We are the mothers whose children suffer this damage," Juanita Mitchell of the NAACP later argued in response to the slow pace the city took toward integration.⁶² More immediately, she used her legal talents and attempted to build on the momentum achieved by the *Brown* decision that declared school segregation unconstitutional. She prevailed upon the courts to ban segregation in public parks and places of recreation, a case that was ultimately won.⁶³

Overcrowding in substandard housing also contributed to alarming health statistics for the city's African American communities that women tried to combat. Baltimore's Department of Health reported that between 1940 and 1950, tuberculosis struck five times as many Black residents as white. In 1950, African Americans also had higher rates of typhoid fever, measles, whooping cough, influenza, and several other major diseases. African Americans suffered 90 percent of the city's cases of accidental lead poisoning. In addition, the Jim Crow system caused Black women to pay with the lives of their children and their own lives as well. In 1950, when African Americans made up almost a quarter of Baltimore's population, Black mothers bore more than 40 percent of the stillbirths in the city, and Black babies made up almost half of the infants who died at an age younger than one. The same year, Black women accounted for more than 55 percent of maternal deaths.⁶⁴ As the tragic health statistics indicate, Black women could not fully compensate for the health implications of poverty, segregation, the lack of health insurance, and the inferior quality of public and private services African Americans could access in Baltimore.[65] The reality fueled unsuccessful but ongoing campaigns by civil rights activists and Black politicians on the local and state levels on behalf of desegregation.[66]

During the fifteen years following World War II, the concentration of Black workers—both women and men—at the bottom or on the periphery of the industrial sector and Black men's growing vulnerability to automation kept economic insecurity high in many African American neighborhoods. As they had for generations, Black women responded to hardship and segregation in a myriad of ways, both paid and unpaid, to support and sustain their families and communities.[67] Welfare-state protections eased conditions for some—even a growing number—but the holes of the sieve that was the nation's safety net remained sized in a manner that continued to allow many African Americans to fall through. And segregation and the city's provision of Jim Crow services continued to compel compensatory efforts by Black women to keep their families safe. For far too many African Americans in Baltimore, the city's boom times had not amounted to very much.

Yet civil rights leaders had scored some critical victories in their pursuit of improved job prospects during the postwar era that merited dividends that had yet to be paid and that activists were determined to collect. Significantly, they had persuaded Truman to ban discrimination in the federal workforce, and they had wrangled from the overwhelmingly white and socially conservative Baltimore City Council a fair employment-practices law. Meanwhile, the number of African American residents was continuing to grow in the city as the number of whites remained in decline. Black leaders began the 1960s determined to use the power of the ballot box to influence the outcome of the upcoming national election, win more locally elected offices for African Americans, and pressure white elected officials to make good on their promise of equal employment opportunities.

CHAPTER 2

"A New Mood" Is Spreading

The Great Society as Job Creation

In 1960, the editors of the *Afro-American* sent a reporter to the offices of the Baltimore City Municipal Building and City Hall to do some investigative journalism. Four years earlier, civil rights leaders had wrangled from the city council Baltimore's fair employment practices ordinance. Thereafter, municipal officials had repeatedly promised that the new law would be used to root out discrimination in municipal agencies. Most recently, the newly elected president of the city council had told a group of African Americans rather patronizingly, "I am convinced that there is discrimination practiced in the city government.... I believe [the Equal Employment Opportunity Commission] should start with the city government. Clean house there before going out crusading."[1] Having endorsed the same "good starting point" three years earlier, editors at the *Afro-American* had become increasingly impatient with the lack of results.[2] So this time they decided to take matters into their own hands by conducting an informal head count of African American city-government workers. Peering into offices in the municipal building and city hall, the *Afro* journalist sought Black faces in the sea of white. The municipal building investigation yielded only fourteen African Americans as compared to five hundred whites while the search to find Black workers in City Hall proved almost fruitless. Only the presence of a lone "colored messenger boy" prevented the paper from having to report it could find no African Americans at all in the seat of the city government.[3] The paper's editors expressed outrage. While their methods were hardly scientific and underestimated the actual number of Black municipal employees, their point was dead on. "When you have 32 percent of the population and no [or next to no] personnel employed in City Hall, you are in a bad way—and this is the situation facing the colored citizens of Baltimore," an *Afro-American* editorial argued. "Not even the rosiest of rose-colored glasses can hide the fact that City Hall is shot through with racial discrimination and when it comes to jobs it is as if the colored citizens of Baltimore do not even exist."[4] The editors demanded immediate redress.

African American leaders in Baltimore had good reason to push hard for jobs in the municipal government. The public-sector workforce expanded steadily during the postwar era while the city's manufacturing sector, although still a critical source of employment, was in decline. Moreover, public-sector employment, which the city's civil rights activists had been monitoring and attempting to secure for Black workers for decades, served as potential partial solutions to three of the most pressing and ongoing problems that African Americans faced: rampant racial discrimination in the private-sector job market, the near total lack of Black influence over municipal policy-making, and the gross inadequacy of the historically separate and unequal public services to which African American residents had access. Black government workers would have stable jobs, could potentially influence policy, and could help improve service quality.

During the 1960s, President Lyndon Johnson's Great Society reforms, which included the nation's War on Poverty, were the engines behind continuing public-sector growth. In 1960, Black leaders had worked tirelessly to help John F. Kennedy win the presidency, and they supported Johnson's subsequent bid as well. In turn, they closely monitored the implementation of the liberal Democrats' reforms in their city, identifying new federal programming as sources of the jobs, political power, and services that they sought. They demanded African American influence over the city's War on Poverty and pressured elected officials to comply with the federal mandate that residents with low incomes play key roles in antipoverty efforts. They also pressed hard for government jobs for Black workers. The efforts met with remarkable success. During the 1960s, Black representation on the oversight bodies of municipal agencies, while still low, grew to levels that would have been inconceivable during the 1950s. Meanwhile, the number of African Americans who worked for the city government mushroomed as that sector expanded due to the infusion of federal funds. Critics at the time and since have faulted Johnson for failing to include a full-employment guaranteed among his Great Society reforms.[5] Such a measure might have served as an antidote to the worsening structural unemployment among Black men. Nevertheless, the Great Society itself was an engine of job creation that quickly became critical to the economic health of the city's working- and middle-class Black families.

African Americans' public-sector employment gains proved gendered, however. Black men certainly increased their representation in government workforces—and won more leadership posts than did Black women. Yet far more Black women than men entered the public sector; much of the job growth was in fields and employment categories typically dominated by women. New government positions—as well as the many new service jobs in the private sector in fields such as health care that the Great Society also helped to create—buoyed the economic fortunes of Black women, albeit unintentionally. Ironically, an administration that dubbed Black women matriarchs and blamed their supposed dominance in their families for high African American poverty rates, structurally transformed Baltimore's economy in a way that favored women workers.[6] To be sure, Black women became overrepresented at the bottom of public-sector hierarchies. And to the extent that they secured white-collar and leadership positions, both African American men and women gained the most authority in government agencies in which they dealt largely with other African Americans. White officials hardly ceded much ground in critical realms such as planning and finance. Nevertheless, African Americans' increasing political influence and improved job prospects in the public sector were critical changes. The gains Black women made in the public sector were a primary source of their tremendous importance to the economic health of African American families and communities during the 1960s and the decades that followed. Despite important limitations, the successful campaign by Black leaders to win increasing influence for African Americans within the municipal government and to open public-sector jobs to Black workers stand as two of the most important victories of Baltimore's civil rights movement.

"We Are Not Children": The Fight for Maximum Feasible Participation

As Black leaders anticipated continuing their campaigns against employment discrimination into the 1960s, they fully appreciated the difference that federal civil rights legislation could make. Convinced that John F. Kennedy would be their best bet for meaningful change in the 1960 presidential election, they began mobilizing Black voters on his behalf. And they were quite mindful of the fact that despite their location below the Mason-Dixon line, they had the ability and thus the responsibility to do just that. "In Baltimore we don't have to die for the right to vote," NAACP activist Juanita Mitchell was known to remind Black city residents.[7] The franchise was a powerful weapon in the battle against racism and economic injustice. As the election loomed, the leaders of multiple African American organizations coordinated a major voter-registration drive. The NAACP joined forces with volunteers from church groups and members of the Civic Interest Group (CIG), who the *Afro-American* described as "the sit-downers" because of their involvement in ongoing direct-action campaigns to integrate Baltimore's lunch counters.

Together Baltimore's older and younger activists convinced the city's board of elections to keep their office open late one night a week to allow residents who worked during the day an opportunity to register. They also provided babysitting services and bus transportation to the voter-registration office. Recent migrants were among the targets of the campaign. "I never had the chance to register before.... We couldn't vote down home," reported George W. Collins, a newcomer to the city.[8] Although the *Afro-American* did not tally the total number of new voters activists added to the rolls, by Election Day more than 106,000 African Americans were registered, and Black residents made up 20 percent of the city's voters. "Hip, Hip Hurrah!" cheered the editors.[9] The paper predicted that the Baltimore city returns would decide the election in Maryland. And they did. Despite residual support for the Party of Lincoln among some Black voters, Kennedy's "landslide in [the] city's colored areas" was pivotal in helping the Democrat win the state. African Americans in Maryland gave Kennedy more than 58,000 votes in a state election that he won by 55,000. Although Black turnout was not as high as civil rights leaders would have liked, as in several other states, the *Afro-American* reported "the Colored vote" created "the margin of victory."[10]

Despite early enthusiasm for the young president, Kennedy quickly proved a disappointment to Baltimore activists, who sought immediate redress for civil rights abuses and attention to urban issues. Johnson, who became president following Kennedy's assassination in November 1963, more successfully responded to African Americans' concerns. When introducing his vision of the Great Society he pledged to create, Johnson married the goals of eradicating racial injustice and poverty. "Unfortunately, many Americans live on the outskirts of hope—some because of their poverty, and some because of their color, and all too many because of both. Our task is to help replace their despair with opportunity," Johnson argued in his 1964 State of the Union address.[11] Then, as the nation grieved its recently slain leader, Johnson brokered the passage of the Civil Rights Act of 1964, a remarkable achievement given the tremendous institutional power of southern defenders of white supremacy in the Congress. The voting-rights provision of the law proved woefully inadequate, however. In response to ongoing activism, Johnson also helped secure the Voting Rights Act of 1965.

Activists in Baltimore hailed Johnson's civil rights achievements and also his decision to declare a war on poverty as part of his Great Society programming. The fact that one in five Americans lived in poverty was a source of profound national disgrace, Johnson believed. Between 1964 and 1967, he and the Congress passed more progressive legislation than at any time since the New Deal years. Unlike many New Dealers, however, Johnson was convinced that poverty could be best defeated by national economic growth that was supposed to "lift all boats" rather than through wealth redistribution. Determined to combat poverty by offering Americans with low incomes "a hand up, not a handout," the centerpieces of his antipoverty efforts were education and vocational training.[12] Congress did, however, also enact the Economic Opportunity Act (EOA) that funded the War on Poverty and created Medicare and Medicaid. In addition, the federal government made permanent the Food Stamps program and established the Model Cities program. To coordinate the implementation of urban policies, in 1966 Congress created the Department of Housing and Urban Development, which established a cabinet-level position for a representative of cities. Ultimately, Johnson's Great Society initiatives, although not all specifically urban policies, dramatically increased the amount of federal resources cities and their residents received.

Johnson's Great Society programs sparked criticism from those to his political left who believed that poverty could not be alleviated without intentional federal job-creation efforts. As could already be seen in Baltimore, mechanization and deindustrialization were transforming urban economies in the industrial belt in ways that had dire implications, particularly for Black male workers. And the problems seemed likely to worsen. By the 1960s, American manufacturers faced far stiffer international competition than they had in the immediate postwar era, when much of Europe and Japan had been in shambles. Yet American markets remained open to imports due to Cold War commitments. U.S. officials had failed to plan for this inevitability, and U.S. manufacturers and their workers were paying the price.[13] In search of lower labor and production costs to boost competitiveness and profitability, growing numbers of U.S. companies relocated to the outskirts of industrial cities or moved south within the United States or even overseas.[14] Accelerating deindustrialization during the 1960s presaged the loss of entire categories of manufacturing jobs, and nothing appeared on the horizon likely to produce equivalent employment opportunities for men in rusting cities that were increasingly populated by African Americans. Training programs were fine, but cities such as Baltimore, which lost more than thirteen thousand factory jobs between 1963 and 1972, also needed new sources of employment. To those living in the shadows of shuttered factories, the prospect of vocational programs was a partial solution at best.[15]

Despite the warnings, Johnson remained committed to growth liberalism. He was also receptive to the idea that urban Black male unemployment resulted largely from African American cultural dysfunction rather than structural economic problems. That notion gained currency during the mid-1960s, fueled by the publication of a controversial report by Assistant Secretary of Labor for Policy, Planning and Research Daniel Patrick Moynihan. Although himself a proponent of federal job creation, in "The Negro Family: The Case for National Action," Moynihan attributed high levels of African American poverty to a lack of education and job skills—and also to a "tangle of pathology" within Black families. Slavery and racism produced the pathology, Moynihan argued, and one of its most overt symptoms was matriarchal culture. Because Black men faced ongoing employment discrimination, Black women entered the labor market in larger numbers than white women. "This dependence on the mother's income undermines the position of the father and deprives the children of the kind of attention, particularly in school matters, which is now a standard feature of middle-class upbringing," Moynihan contended.[16] He conceded that the patriarchal model prevalent among middle-class whites was itself a social construct. Nevertheless, because it was the norm, African Americans deviated from it at their peril. And the fact that many families already had, he argued, contributed significantly to their economic marginalization. The claim, which attracted widespread attention and outraged many African Americans, shifted the national conversation about Black poverty further away from economic changes, such as mechanization and deindustrialization, and toward supposed Black cultural dysfunction.[17]

Despite the disputes among liberal policy makers over the causes of Black male economic insecurity, most shared a blind spot for the employment concerns of Black women. Advocates of growth liberalism and proponents of such interventionist strategies as job creation believed that the best antidote to poverty, particularly in African American communities, was to provide men with the means to become breadwinners. Such an outcome, they anticipated, would restore men to their supposedly proper position of authority within their families, slow the pace of family dissolution, and reduce demand for welfare services. Historians Marissa Chappell and Robert Self describe this outlook as "breadwinner liberalism."[18] For the most part, policy makers and activists, both Black and white, failed to take women seriously as economic actors, and the War on Poverty reflected the bias. As initially conceived, for example, the first Job Corps training programs were intended only for men. Only intervention by women secured a federal commitment to including women in Job Corps programs from the start.[19]

Despite their serious inadequacies, Great Society programs nevertheless did create opportunities for African Americans such as those in Baltimore to seize a greater role in policy-making than they had ever had in the past. As had been the case since the 1930s when Franklin Roosevelt created the nation's first urban policies, the infusion of federal funds on the local level had the potential to alter the balance of power in municipal affairs. New revenue led to contests over power as various interest groups vied to control the agendas of new or growing bureaucracies or the implementation of federal mandates. Most recently during the 1950s, the urban-renewal emphasis of Republican president Dwight Eisenhower's policies had provided cities with resources that enhanced the ability of business leaders to push municipal planning in the direction of commercial redevelopment. In many cities, such efforts resulted in projects that often displaced large numbers of African Americans; efforts to remove "blight" led to the destruction of African Americans' homes for which alternatives were frequently not provided. In fact, African Americans often referred to urban renewal as Negro removal.[20]

In Baltimore, federal funding for urban redevelopment and highway construction wreaked havoc in some of the city's Black neighborhoods and also helped business elites to exert increased influence over municipal affairs. To be sure, business leaders had long been powerbrokers in the city. During the 1950s, however, they had increased their influence. James Rouse, a local real estate developer later known for his urban commercial showplaces, such as Faneuil Hall in Boston and Harborplace in Baltimore, helped found the Greater Baltimore Committee (GBC). Rouse and other members of GBC identified downtown commercial redevelopment as the most significant ingredient for revitalizing Baltimore. During the mid-1950s, the group hired urban planners to draft a long-term plan for the city, and in 1958, the members of the city council adopted GBC's proposal. In so doing, they rejected a plan they themselves had commissioned, which prioritized neighborhood over center-city revitalization. With the vote, members of GBC secured significant influence over municipal policy-making, influence they were not inclined to relinquish in the face of the new federal priorities of the 1960s.[21]

African American leaders, however, hoped to use the new federal priorities to move the city in a new direction. Unconvinced that urban renewal and trickle-down commercial revitalization strategies would adequately redress African American poverty, many Black leaders favored more redistributive approaches and championed "human renewal," a phrase used to emphasize a focus on people rather than infrastructure. And Black leaders were determined to make their voices heard in municipal public-policy debates. In fact, they had already been demanding attention for their concerns and ambitions before the War on Poverty even started.

In 1962, the Health and Welfare Council of the Baltimore Area, Inc. (HWC) published an indictment of the city that they titled "A Letter to Ourselves." In it, the white, liberal leadership of the private organization argued that Baltimore's response to urban poverty was inadequate and proposed that the city formulate a new approach. They created a Steering Committee on Human Renewal to develop a long-term strategy. Only one member of the committee, Reverend Robert T. Newbold Jr. of the Interdenominational Ministerial Alliance, was African American. While the HWC committee was formulating its plan, Congress passed the Economic Opportunity Act of 1964. Anticipating that new federal funds could make their "Plan for Action" a reality, committee members drafted their proposal to correspond to the federal law's provisions.[22]

Not long after the steering committee began its work, African Americans in Baltimore began protesting their near exclusion from the antipoverty planning effort. In February 1964, Reverend Herbert O. Edwards of Trinity Baptist Church complained to HWC about the committee's composition. "The fact that the Negro represents more than 1/3 of the population of Baltimore City seems to have escaped the attention of those planning this far-reaching project," he wrote. He accused HWC of doing what whites in Baltimore always did to marginalize Black views. "The 'traditional approach,'..." Edwards explained, "is to make plans for the City of Baltimore in order to cope with its problems, ignoring the Negro Community until such time as you have decided what *should be done*" (emphasis in the original). Then, he predicted, the city would select a few African American representatives "and send them back to the Negro Community to tell them what to do. Surely you cannot be unaware of the past ineffectiveness of such a paternalistic approach!"[23] Melvin G. Roy, the president of the Eastside Community Committee, Inc., echoed Edward's concern in a telegram to Mayor Theodore McKeldin. "Better results will accrue when we plan together with ethnic groups rather than plan for them," Roy protested.[24] The pressure yielded some results. McKeldin, a racially liberal Republican who had served as the city's mayor during the mid-1940s and as Maryland's governor during most of the 1950s, had recently won reelection as mayor. He owed all of his political offices at least in part to Black support, and he quickly appointed six African Americans to an advisory committee on the antipoverty effort.[25] The issue, however, was hardly resolved.

By late 1964 the steering committee had completed its Plan for Action, and officials applied for federal antipoverty funds. Whites in Baltimore had planned the city's war on poverty with very limited African American participation and with no involvement of residents with low incomes. Angered by the exclusion, Juanita Mitchell of the NAACP sent a telegram to Sargent Shriver, who was directing the nation's War on Poverty. She requested that funds be withheld from Baltimore because those who would be affected by new antipoverty programs had had insufficient participation in the planning process. "We are tired of people planning about us and not with us," she explained to a *Baltimore Sun* reporter. "We are mature and want to be partners with the city in all of its activities. We are not children."[26]

Revealing increasing ideological tensions within the city's Black communities, Mitchell's telegram angered conservative Black leaders and won the scorn of younger activists. The Interdenominational Ministerial Alliance immediately telegrammed Shriver to refute the NAACP's claim. The ministers described the plan as "a bold and imaginative attempt by city officials, public and private agencies to make a coordinated and cooperative effort toward taking the slum attitude and outlook out of our culturally deprived citizen."[27] Meanwhile, younger activists also took the NAACP to task. Robert E. Hinton Jr., a Morgan State student affiliated with the Student Non-Violent Coordinating Committee (SNCC) and Students for a Democratic Society (SDS), wrote to the *Baltimore Sun* incensed that the "Black Bourgeoisie" who ran the NAACP had the gall to represent itself as the voice of poor African Americans.[28] Poor people themselves, Hinton intimated, rather than middle-class leaders, deserved the right to plan for their own communities. Ultimately, and no doubt chastened, the NAACP rescinded its request that funds be withheld. But despite the controversy, the point had been made: African Americans refused to be sidelined while whites conducted a war on poverty.

Federal legislation bolstered efforts in Baltimore to secure for African Americans and residents with low incomes influence over the local War on Poverty. The Economic Opportunity Act of 1964 created the Community Action Program and mandated the "maximum feasible participation" of low-income residents in antipoverty efforts. The legislation thus compelled elected officials to listen to poor people, and that is exactly what some of the architects of the War on Poverty intended. They recognized that many New Deal programs had not served African Americans well, and they wanted a different outcome for their reforms. In addition, some of the union leaders Johnson included in the planning hoped to politically mobilize low-income citizens and encourage democratic decision-making in policy planning and implementation. Their intention represented a stunning departure from past welfare-policy practices, which tended to figure recipients of government assistance as objects of pity, suspicion, or both. Whereas Eisenhower's urban policies had enhanced the authority of business leaders in municipal planning, Johnson's domestic agenda created opportunities for African Americans to win a greater role in shaping their cities' futures.[29]

"I Am a Citizen Who Has a Job to Do": Democratizing Decision-Making

In Baltimore, the influx of federal funds to fight poverty raised the stakes considerably in ongoing struggles over political power and control over municipal planning that had long pitted civil rights activists against white municipal officials. By the mid-1960s, African Americans made up more than 40 percent of the city's population. The number of African Americans on the city council had only grown by one since the 1950s, bringing the total of Black council members to a mere two. Together they constituted 9 percent of the body. Reapportionment compelled by the 1960 Census ended with the decision by elected officials to shrink the size of the council and redraw district lines. Keenly aware of the import of redistricting, African Americans pressed for opportunities to win more representation and met with some success. In the 1967 local election for seats on the newly constituted body, Black candidates, including the first woman to be elected to the council, won four seats. The African Americans served alongside fourteen whites and under a white council president, however. In addition, at least ten of the white victors had reputations as racial conservatives.[30] Even though African Americans had doubled their number on the council, they remained grossly underrepresented and outnumbered.

As an additional route to achieving some influence over policy-making and service delivery, Black leaders had long sought positions for African Americans on the oversight bodies of government departments. The efforts had not yielded much. In 1965, African Americans composed only 5 percent of the members of municipal boards and commissions. With minimal official representation, Black Baltimore had almost no formal means of influencing policy-making and agenda setting in the city. Not surprisingly, African American leaders set their sights on making sure the city complied with maximum feasible participation.[31]

Although the city would have to abide by federal mandates if it accepted federal funds for antipoverty efforts, ultimately decisions concerning the organization and leadership of Baltimore's War on Poverty fell to elected officials. The members of the city council, most of whom were staunch defenders of the racial status quo, were hardly inclined to hand authority over to Black residents. Although in February 1965 council members did create a Community Action Agency (CAA) to carry out the local War on Poverty, to maximize the council's control, they subsumed the agency within the municipal government. As a result, all of the CAA's programming and all appointees to the Community Action Commission (CAC) that would oversee the CAA would require council approval.[32]

The council's decision served as a rebuke to the members of a new organization in the city. Members of Baltimore's chapter of SDS had recently founded the Union for Jobs or Income Now (U-JOIN). The organization included students from Johns Hopkins University, Goucher College, and Morgan State College. Several labor unions also lent their support to U-JOIN, and community activist Walter Lively headed the organization. An African American from Philadelphia, Lively earlier had helped to create chapters of the NAACP and CORE in his hometown. He had also been an organizer of the 1961 Freedom Rides.[33] Baltimore native and Morgan State student Robert "Bob" Moore, who later became a prominent activist and labor leader in the city, was also an early member of U-JOIN. He, Lively, and other members of the organization described the HWC's antipoverty program as "welfare colonialism" and drafted an alternative proposal that called for the creation of a nonprofit, nongovernmental antipoverty agency.[34] They also suggested that almost all members of the organization's governing body be community residents with low incomes or representatives from organized labor. In addition,

U-JOIN argued, "To guarantee that decision-making will originate with the poor and not with the professionals," the administrative staff of the agency should be "*subordinate*" to the decision-making body (emphasis in the original).[35] Not surprisingly, the city council had rejected the proposal.

Ultimately, the task of nominating the CAC's members fell to McKeldin, and the mayor did not relish handing power over a municipal agency to people likely to be hostile to the city government any more than the members of the city council did. Many of the nation's mayors shared his view. In fact, McKeldin had already written a letter to President Johnson on behalf of the Board of Advisors of the U.S. Conference of Mayors expressing concern about the War on Poverty. He urged the president to rein in the enthusiasts of community participation.[36] And in his own city, the mayor took steps to circumvent community involvement. Although he nominated five African Americans to the CAC, he gave whites the majority with six seats and the chairmanship. In addition, none of the nominees were residents of the action area where antipoverty efforts would be targeted.[37]

Reflecting the divisions within Baltimore's African American communities, some Black leaders applauded as a win the mayor's appointments, while others deemed them entirely unacceptable. Among those declaring victory was the leadership of the BUL, whose officials had been working for decades to increase Black representation on public boards and commissions—with very limited success.[38] The leadership of U-JOIN, alternatively, did not view the composition of the CAC as a victory at all and instead urged city residents with low incomes to protest at city council meetings to fight their exclusion. They did. And ultimately Baltimore's CAC grew to include more low-income members than required by federal law.[39] Activists had made community participation a reality in Baltimore.

In the wake of their success securing influence over the CAC, African Americans and residents with low incomes began demanding seats on additional municipal boards and commissions. The efforts reflected a growing confidence among marginalized groups and a belief that they deserved to be listened to and treated with dignity. It also likely reflected an unprecedented conviction that officials in the city of Baltimore, and perhaps even the state of Maryland, might actually prove responsive to their concerns. And change was indeed under way. In 1963, the leaders of Baltimore's mainstream civil rights organizations had faced an uphill battle when they pressed Maryland officials simply to appoint a second African American to the state's welfare board. Three years later, thirty-five members of a new welfare rights organization crashed a meeting of Maryland's legislative council to demand representation on the welfare board. The request was granted.[40] Residents of public housing also met with success in battles with the city for inclusion in housing-related decision-making. Baltimore was one of the first cities in the nation to establish a Resident Advisory Board, and as activist Shirley Wise recalled, the victory "gave [residents] their true rights to sit at the table with the decision-makers and effect some changes in their community."[41] Poor residents also fought for representation on the policy-making body that oversaw the city's Model Cities program, an initiative launched in Baltimore during the late 1960s. By the early 1970s, nearly two-thirds of the membership board had been elected by residents.[42]

The leadership of some municipal departments also proved receptive to demands for community participation. Officials in the Department of Health agreed to create a Parents' Advisory Council at a community health clinic. More remarkably, in 1967 the white superintendent of the Baltimore City Public Schools and the mostly white members of the school board explained their support for demands by African Americans for community involvement by echoing rhetoric more typically heard from civil rights advocates. The superintendent and board explained they did not want the school system to become "another form of paternalism."[43] During the second half of the 1960s, African Americans and residents with low incomes secured limited but unprecedented influence over policy-making in the fields of health, education, and welfare, a democratization of decision-making few could have imagined possible at the dawn of the decade.

The adoption of community participation opened opportunities for women, and particularly Black women, to exercise leadership in a city run almost entirely by white men. By the end of the 1960s, Black and white women together accounted for only 16 percent of the members of municipal oversight bodies. Over half of the city's fifty-one boards and commissions had no female representation whatsoever, and twelve had only a single woman. But in 1968, almost half of the community representatives on the CAC were women, and in 1969, eight of the ten women on the Model Cities' thirty-member Policy Steering Committee had been elected by community groups. Residents of low-income neighborhoods put women into policy-making positions at a far higher rate than the city's mayors did. Although outnumbered by men on all boards and commissions—including those overseeing agencies that served predominantly female clienteles—women had seized opportunities to shape public policy. Those involved felt the changes keenly. As Margaret McCarty, the head of Baltimore's welfare rights organization Mother Rescuers from Poverty, explained, "I'm a citizen who has a job to do, instead of a poor forgotten colored woman, like some of our people feel."[44]

Despite the remarkable changes under way, white leaders in Baltimore maintained a tight grip on power. In January 1968, for example, a coalition of groups that included CORE, U-JOIN, SNCC, Mother Rescuers from Poverty, and the Interdenominational Ministerial Alliance sent a letter to the mayor. "We demand that half of the members of all boards and commissions be Black to reflect the racial make up of the city; that no white individuals be appointed until the composition of these boards is at least half Black and at least half of the chairmen of these boards and/or commissions are Black," group members wrote.[45] Meanwhile, aware that their perspectives were universally relevant, welfare recipients pressed for representation not just on poverty-related bodies but on "all policy-making and advisory boards, state and city."[46] Such efforts made little headway. Under duress, white officials had granted African Americans and low-income residents an increased level of influence over agencies responsible for poor people or over departments that provided such services as health and education, for which whites could seek private or suburban alternatives. But the officials were not willing to go much further than that.

Though limited in scope, the influence African Americans and low-income residents won represented an important threat to the status quo. In 1966, the *Afro-American* reported that there was a "new mood creeping slowly through the Black ghetto of Baltimore like sunlight at early dawn—a mood that demands rights and respect and a chance for a decent life as the natural birthright of all."[47] Many African Americans, women, and low-income residents took the promise of the Civil Rights Act of 1964 and the maximum feasible participation mandates of the Equal Opportunity Act to heart. They demanded and won a voice in the decision-making bodies that were waging the city's war on poverty. In so doing, they challenged the near monopoly white men had historically maintained over policy-making in the city. And it seemed pretty clear that armed with federal funds, they intended to use their new influence to shift the focus of municipal policies away from the trickle-down commercial revitalization projects long touted by the business community and toward efforts to redistribute power and wealth in the city.

"Some Progress Has Been Made": The Great Society as Job Creation

Even as they waged battles in the city over community participation, civil rights leaders hardly relented on their campaign to open job opportunities to African Americans. And as became evident during the mid-1960s, although Johnson's Great Society measures did not include full-employment legislation, new federal programs created a considerable number of new public-sector jobs, and federal funds also helped to swell the staff of existing municipal agencies. In addition, federal funding also triggered job creation in the private sector. The introduction of Medicare and Medicaid, for example, increased local demand for health care and also for health care providers.[48] The government expansion boded particularly well for Black workers. The use of moral suasion on private employers to combat discrimination had led only to modest results through the early 1960s. Exerting the heft of Black voting power yielded better results in the public sector, where hiring practices were open to public scrutiny. And the size of the African American population in Baltimore was still on the rise. During the 1960s, Black leaders used the growing importance of the Black electorate to win municipal jobs for African American workers and applied pressure on federal and state officials and agency heads for equal employment opportunities as well.

Although the size of the public sector had been increasing for much of the twentieth century, the 1960s was a period of particularly rapid growth. During the 1950s, Baltimore's municipal government had increased by approximately 7,000 positions. It nearly doubled that growth during the 1960s. During the decade, the city workforce grew by about 13,000 positions to reach a total of about 35,000 jobs. Meanwhile, state and federal agencies with offices in or near the city expanded their workforces as well. By 1970, the state and federal governments employed 16,900 and 16,200 Baltimore workers, respectively.[49] The growth of the public sector during this period of industrial decline dramatically reconfigured Baltimore's labor market. In 1960, 27.8 percent of Baltimore's workers labored in manufacturing jobs. By 1970, the percentage was 25.6, and by 1980 it had plummeted to 15. Meanwhile, government employees made up 15.1 percent of city workers in 1960, 18.7 percent in 1970, and 20.8 percent in 1980.[50] Although manufacturing job losses outpaced the expansion of the public sector, the growth in government jobs helped to compensate for industrial decline.

Breaking into the municipal workforce—and especially its upper echelons—was not going to be easy. The city was a notorious discriminator.[51] Yet the jobs were worth the fight. They were often full time and stable, lacking the insecurity of domestic, low-wage service and day-laboring work and the periodic layoffs associated with factory jobs. The public sector also provided employees with better workplace protections than were available to African Americans generally. And some public-sector jobs came with fringe benefits, such as pension plans and health insurance. Civil rights advocates certainly never abandoned the fight for private-sector jobs. But mindful of the perks associated with government employment and because the public sector was expanding, activists intensified the pressure on officials to win government jobs for Black workers.

Although born toothless because the city council had stripped it of enforcement power, the municipal EEOC became a critical tool for increasing Black public-sector employment. During the early 1960s, African Americans gained increased authority within the EEOC, which Black city council member Walter Dixon helped win some enforcement powers and was renamed the Community Relations Commission (CRC).[52] The CRC remained responsible for combating discrimination in both the public and private sectors, but ultimately the commissioners more effectively redressed the employment practices of the city government. In order to improve African Americans' representation in the municipal workforce, both CRC officials and activists needed reliable statistics. In 1964, CRC staffers conducted a comprehensive survey of African American municipal employment. They found that at a time when African Americans accounted for more than 40 percent of the city's population, Black workers made up only a little over a quarter of the workforce. (Had they included employees of the Department of Education, the figure would have been somewhat higher.) They also discovered that African Americans were concentrated in only a handful of agencies. Ninety percent of the city's Black classified employees—those in civil service rather than at-will laboring positions—worked in only five city departments: Education, City Hospitals, Health, Parks and Recreation, and Fire. In addition, Black workers made up 41 percent of the employees of the Department of Public Welfare and the majority of the staff of CAA. In contrast, sixty-two city departments, most significantly those that controlled the city's finances and planning, had no or minimal numbers of African Americans on their payrolls. Thus, the CRC staff concluded, "While some progress had been made in some city agencies in the employment of Negroes, there was a dismal lack of progress and concern by other agencies, and/or those who run them."[53]

In light of their findings, CRC staffers demanded greater oversight of hiring practices and the right to investigate all instances in which African Americans were passed over for promotions in the municipal government. City officials rejected the request. Nevertheless, thereafter, the CRC closely monitored employment practices and pressured agency directors with poor minority hiring records to make improvements. The CRC soon began receiving support for its efforts from the Employment Subcommittee of the Mayor's Task Force on Equal Rights. McKeldin created the task force in 1966 as a proactive measure following the announcement by CORE that it had chosen Baltimore as a "target city" because of the city's poor civil rights record.[54] By 1967, the employment subcommittee included some of the most outspoken critics of the city's minority-hiring practices. Reverend Marion Bascom, the chair of the Interdenominational Ministerial Alliance, was one such prominent critic. Bascom was the pastor of the influential Douglas Memorial Church, and he played an important role in desegregation battles in the city during the 1950s and 1960s. He and others on the committee declared their intention to make the city government a "model" employer.[55]

To achieve their ends, activists picketed city agencies with poor minority-hiring records, and in 1967, an election year, they made minority hiring a campaign issue. A coalition of groups accused the personnel director and members of Baltimore's Civil Service Commission (CSC) of racism. Bascom threatened a mass protest by the members of "two or three hundred groups" if immediate action was not taken.[56] The challenge produced immediate results. Democratic mayoral candidate Thomas D'Alesandro III, the son of the D'Alesandro who had sabotaged the EEOC during the 1950s (and the brother of future speaker of the U.S. House of Representatives Nancy Pelosi), promised "a top-to-bottom review and revision" of the city's civil service system if he was elected.[57] His Republican opponent also pledged to make significant changes. Leon Sachs, a leader of Baltimore's Jewish community who had been critical in the city's fair-employment campaign years earlier, summed up the situation well. Access to city jobs had become "a festering sore in race relations in our community and call[ed] for immediate therapy."[58] Elected officials needed to make serious changes, or they would face the wrath of the Black electorate.

The political pressure worked. Following the 1967 municipal election, Black city council member Robert L. Douglass introduced a resolution that called for the city to revamp the CSC's procedures. Newly elected Mayor D'Alesandro, whose earlier work on behalf of open housing had won him considerable African American support, followed through on his campaign promise to address civil service issues. Determined to make application procedures accessible to "low-income, low-skilled persons," the mayor proposed revisions to the City Charter to change civil service procedures.[59] He also attempted to secure administratively those reforms he could not get through the city council. In addition, he appointed several African American men to high-level positions. For its part, the CRC entered into agreements with departments or agencies to compel improvements in minority hiring and adopted affirmative action–type strategies to increase minority hiring. Meanwhile, angry that white suburbanites held many of the municipal government's highest-paying jobs, city activists also pressed officials to limit eligibility for municipal employment to Baltimore residents. In 1969, the city council passed a hiring-preference ordinance. The measure was challenged and repealed, however, and the issue remained a source of contention throughout the 1970s.[60]

Although they did not neglect women entirely, the staff of the CRC and many local activists concerned with using public-sector employment to combat unemployment frequently concentrated their efforts on agencies with predominantly male staff members. Concerns about police brutality were perennial, and activists continued to target the Baltimore Police Department to win better African American representation. They were also especially attentive to the hiring and promotion practices of the Departments of Highways, Public Works, and Sanitation, agencies with few female employees.[61] The attention paid to Black male employment concerns made sense given the devastating impact mechanization and deindustrialization were having in the private sector. Yet African American women had valid employment concerns that also warranted redress, but they received little attention.

Efforts to improve Baltimore's record of minority hiring were remarkably successful. By 1970, almost 40 percent of municipal employees—as compared to about 25 percent six years earlier—were African American. Including the Department of Education in the calculation raised the percentage to 50. African Americans' representation in the municipal workforce had surpassed their percentage in the city's population. In just five years African Americans had made tremendous gains in one of the few sectors of Baltimore's economy that was experiencing growth.[62] And despite widespread concerns about Black male unemployment, Black women ultimately won a greater share of municipal jobs than did Black men. In fact, by the end of the 1960s,

African American women made up the largest demographic group in the city workforce, outnumbering not only Black men but also white women and white men. Nearly a third of all municipal employees were African American women.[63] Many of the jobs Black women filled resulted from federal-level spending on antipoverty services. Ironically, an administration that had produced the problematic "Moynihan Report" had fundamentally transformed labor markets in deindustrializing cities such as Baltimore in ways that advantaged women and did little to combat structural Black male unemployment.

Although Black women made unprecedented job gains in the municipal government, race- and sex-based discrimination persisted. White men and in a few cases Black men served in most leadership roles; white women filled many professional positions; and African American women and men predominated in the lowest-paid jobs.[64] Training programs reinforced gendered and racialized employment patterns. "When you're offered job training, it's always something with 'aide' behind it," African American welfare rights activist McCarty complained in 1969. "I suppose some kind of job beats nothing, but it tells you what people think of you when they only think of your being a nurse's aide when you could be a nurse or teacher's aide when you could be a teacher."[65] In the mid-1960s, the concentration of Black workers in low-level positions contributed to a Black-white earnings gap in the municipal workforce of $2,000 per year.[66] Yet low-wage positions in human-services agencies could serve multiple productive roles. As historian Rhonda Williams notes, African American women with low incomes became increasingly assertive in the demands they made of the state. "[Antipoverty] jobs," Williams contends, "further validated poor black women's concerns and empowered them to speak; after all, they believed they had the federal government behind them."[67]

And not all African American municipal employees labored in menial posts. Over the course of the 1960s, white-collar public-sector employment served as an anchor of Baltimore's Black middle class. Activists had more success winning leadership positions for Black men than women. And most of the positions were managerial jobs within rather than at the helm of municipal departments. Nevertheless, Black men won high-level jobs in human-services and antipoverty agencies, including the Departments of Health and Education, the Baltimore City Hospitals, the CRC, the CAA, and the Model Cities program.[68] In addition, in 1968, D'Alesandro hired George Russell to fill the post of city solicitor, the most senior position an African American had ever held in the Baltimore city government. The mayor also hired F. Pierce Linaweaver to head the Department of Public Works.[69]

While African American men made slow but steady progress in the upper echelons of the civil service, Black women secured fewer high-level positions. By 1969 Black and white women together made up less than 9 percent of Baltimore's 202 officials. Thirty-five of the city's forty-seven agencies had no women in top positions at all, and of the remaining twelve, ten had only one female administrator. White women were much more likely than African Americans to hold senior posts. Still, Black women secured important positions in the Departments of Education, Welfare, and Housing and Community Development as well as in the mayor's office.[70]

"No More Tokenism": The Battles for State and Federal Jobs

Fights for jobs for African Americans played out in the state and federal governments as well with similarly gendered outcomes. During the 1960s, federal aid contributed to the expansion of the state's public workforce. Between 1962 and 1967, Maryland's payroll grew by nearly 11,500 jobs, and state officials opened close to 18,000 positions over the next five years.[71] While only a fraction of the new jobs were in Baltimore, the state of Maryland nonetheless became an important local employer. Ultimately, Black workers did not make as much headway into state employment as they did into the municipal workforce. African American political pressure did not produce the same results at the state level as it did in Baltimore. The Maryland Commission on Interracial Problems and Relations monitored minority hiring, however, and activists maintained pressure on state officials. By 1970, African Americans made up close to 20 percent of Maryland state employees.[72] As in the municipal government, most of the job gains at the state level were in a handful of agencies, largely in the human services, and Black women outnumbered Black men. African Americans were concentrated in the lowest levels of employment, and the relatively small number of professional and leadership positions they achieved were largely in human-services departments or agencies. As a result, Black workers as a group earned less than white workers did. Those holding leadership positions in human-services agencies generally earned lower salaries than those paid to other government administrators, which contributed to the discrepancy and reflects the price Black men paid for the devaluation of "women's" labor.[73]

Baltimore's federal workforce also grew during the 1960s. Much of the expansion occurred at the Social Security Administration. Both local and national civil rights activists closely monitored the federal government's employment practices, pressed for the enforcement of antidiscrimination and affirmative-action measures, and demanded that the U.S. Civil Rights Commission monitor compliance. Activists had been tracking Black employment at the SSA for decades and had important achievements to show for it. Nevertheless, in the summer of 1963, frustration about ongoing discrimination prompted the president of the Baltimore NAACP, Lillie May Jackson, to send a letter of protest to President Johnson. The move produced results. NAACP and SSA officials met, and the agency agreed to conduct an internal investigation into its employment practices. Nevertheless, problems persisted. In May 1964, frustrations peaked, and activists and SSA employees took what they believed to be an unprecedented step: they picketed a federal agency. Harts Brown, who worked at the agency at the time and also volunteered as a coach for African Americans prepping for the federal civil service exam, was among the approximately one hundred who demonstrated. The professionally clad protesters, many of them women, carried placards reading "No More Tokenism" and "Stand Up for Freedom" and marched on the sidewalk in front of the agency.[74] The ongoing pressure appears to have had some effect. In 1969, the *Afro-American* reported that African American representation in the SSA workforce had reached 30 percent.[75]

By the end of the 1960s, a decade-long campaign by civil rights leaders to push open the door to public-sector employment for large numbers of African Americans had yielded impressive results. In 1970, African Americans made up more than 50 percent of the city's residents employed by the state and federal governments. State and federal workers accounted for almost 15 percent of employed African Americans in the city. When combined with job gains in the municipal government's labor force, over a quarter of all employed African Americans in Baltimore worked in the public sector. The numbers for Black women alone were even more impressive. In 1950, about 12 percent of African American women held government jobs in Baltimore. By 1970, the number had nearly tripled; almost one out of three Black women worked for the city, state, or federal government. Meanwhile, a smaller but still important 20 percent of Black men worked for the government.[76] The shifts in Baltimore corresponded to national trends. Nationwide, the percentage of Black women employed in the public sector rose from 10 percent to

24 percent between 1950 and 1970. During the same two decades, Black men increased their representation in government employment from 10 percent to 19 percent.[77] Discrimination certainly persisted. Nevertheless, during a decade often associated with deindustrialization, the hard-won public-sector job gains that Black women and men achieved during the 1960s helped to account for the rising economic security of African American families in Baltimore. Meanwhile, not only the African Americans and residents with low incomes serving on the boards and commissions of municipal agencies but also many new government workers were determined to use their new influence within the state to fight poverty and inequality in Baltimore.

CHAPTER 3

"We Had to Fight to Get This"

Antipoverty Workers Take on City Hall

On a chilly November night in 1967, a crowd of more than 1,500 gathered at Baltimore's downtown Federal Office Building plaza for a rally. The staff of the city's Community Action Agency, led by their director Parren Mitchell, were launching a multistage demonstration to protest what they considered to be the woeful inadequacy of the federal government's funding of the War on Poverty. Waving placards with such slogans as "No More Broken Promises," "To C.A.A. with Love," and "Don't Mess with Poor People," they cheered speakers who demanded the government significantly increase the resources it had committed to fighting poverty.[1] Several days later, Mitchell announced the group's next move. The hardiest among them would march from Baltimore to Washington, DC, and take their concerns directly to the nation's lawmakers. On November 12, between 200 and 300 of "the city's highest and lowest ranking veterans of the war on poverty," according to a local journalist, set off on the forty-five-mile trek.[2] Most wore sturdy boots and carried knapsacks, and Mitchell donned a thick green sweater and raincoat. Before they left, Mitchell reminded members of the CAA staff that they would have to forfeit two days' pay to participate in the march; as employees of the city of Baltimore, they needed to be off the clock when they made their political statement. With all in agreement, they set off. They spent the night in a church along the way and reached Washington the next day.

Not everyone greeted their arrival with enthusiasm. A conservative congressional representative from Michigan sniped that if the protesters could march from Baltimore to D.C., they could certainly "walk to the employment office."[3] The comment reflected disdain for Black women with low incomes and mounting hostility to federal antipoverty efforts. But those who participated in the pilgrimage, predominantly African American women by all accounts, took great pride in the statement they were making. As city residents who had witnessed firsthand the benefits of the War on Poverty as service providers or recipients—and in some cases as both—they wanted their voices heard. Congress needed to understand how vital federal antipoverty efforts were. As Nellie Brewer, a CAA neighborhood aide, explained about her participation in the march, "I feel I should be here. . . . The program has helped me in many ways and I feel some responsibility for its continuation."[4]

As African Americans secured jobs in the municipal government in rising numbers during the 1960s, many were determined to use their new positions within the state in pursuit of racial and economic justice. Those in antipoverty agencies and human-services departments in particular worked to engage and politicize African Americans and low-income residents, who had long been excluded from the political process. The workers also pressured locally elected officials to prioritize redistributive antipoverty campaigns as opposed to the trickle-down commercial redevelopment projects championed by the city's business elites. Policies of the federal government informed and abetted the workers' cause. Grants earmarked by Congress for the War on Poverty and other Great Society initiatives transferred federal revenue into the coffers of public agencies charged with fighting economic insecurity, the very agencies in which African Americans had growing influence. Perpetually insufficient in the opinion of many antipoverty activists, the grants nevertheless accorded service providers with a measure of autonomy from the predominantly white and male elected city officials. Federal legislation and grants also fueled efforts by service providers, sometimes working in collaboration with residents with low incomes, to both democratize decision-making and redistribute power and resources in the city. In other words, rather than employees simply putting in their hours, many workers in antipoverty and human-services agencies—the majority of whom were African American women—were deeply engaged in the political struggles of their era. And they made their mark on Baltimore's municipal agenda by forcing reluctant elected officials to adopt redistributive responses to poverty and tend to the concerns of African Americans and low-income city residents.

Efforts by workers in antipoverty agencies and human-services departments contributed significantly to alleviating economic hardship. By seeking out and then enrolling needy residents in entitlement programs, staffing new programs, and improving old ones, they helped to reduce the poverty rate in the city. Their efforts also had gendered implications. Entitlement benefits and antipoverty services eased some of the responsibilities poor women bore for caring for their families. Access to health, sanitation, recreation, and other public services relieved women at least in part of the obligation of trying to provide such services on their own. And although economists and elected officials at the time hardly recognized the unpaid labor that women did for their families as economic activity, the expansion of the welfare state revealed it as such. The government began to pay employees—admittedly often very low wages—to do work that women previously did for their families and communities for free. The provision of new social services, as a result, was an important form of wealth redistribution that replaced some of the invisible caretaking labor that low-income women earlier performed and that was needed to keep Baltimore's economy functioning.

"The Passion of the Time": The Great Society and the Redistribution of Power

As African Americans, and especially Black women, increased their representation in the municipal workforce during the 1960s, many secured posts in antipoverty and human-services agencies. The workers entered government service during an intensely politicized era. Young African American activists from CORE and from newer organizations, such as U-JOIN, SNCC, and the Black Panthers competed with those in older and more mainstream organizations to set the Black agenda. Meanwhile, as women's liberation movements gained momentum, many women across the city attempted to make sense of the implications of feminism for their lives and called attention to the legacies and persistence of sexism.[5] Race-, gender-, and other identity-based struggles for justice were concurrent with spirited student protests in the city and impassioned demonstrations against the Vietnam War. And the antiwar protests and other battles led some of the city's more progressive white Democrats to split from older Democratic clubs, establish new organizations, and fight for influence within their party.[6] In such a context, it is hardly surprising that Clarence Blount, who headed the oversight board of Baltimore's CAA and who also later served in the Maryland State Senate, recalled many municipal workers of the 1960s as being inspired by "the passion of the time."[7] For many, a city job in an antipoverty or human-services agency meant not just a paycheck but an opportunity to create meaningful change in the city on behalf of racial and economic justice.

By accepting government jobs, municipal employees became part of the very system activists and other critics held largely responsible for some of the city's persistent problems. For that reason, some African Americans eschewed government employment and appointments, asserting that they could achieve bolder change by working outside of the system. But people needed jobs, and even some of Baltimore's most outspoken activists accepted municipal posts. Thus, despite their insider status, many antipoverty workers and municipal service providers were fiercely committed to making the state more responsive to residents who historically had been underserved by the government. Ultimately, city employees could not control the level of funding the federal, state, and city governments allotted to fighting poverty. They could, however, endeavor to alter power relations; ensure the city made full use of available federal antipoverty grants; identify needy residents to enroll in entitlement programs; and improve the quality and delivery of city services, many of which until very recently had been provided on a separate and unequal basis. When government workers failed to push hard enough, organized and assertive low-income residents pressed them to move faster and fight harder. Tensions between service providers and recipients persisted during the 1960s, but as the many protests Mitchell initiated indicate, solidarity emerged as well.

The method the federal government used to distribute revenue to the local and state levels enhanced the authority and clout of those waging Baltimore's War on Poverty. Since the 1930s, Congress had transferred funds to lower levels of government in the form of categorical grants or grants-in-aid. Federal-level policy makers determined the specific purposes for which the money could be used and then transferred the funds. They used this method of distributing revenue to prevent elected officials on the local or state level from diverting federal funds for alternative uses and also to compel compliance with federal mandates such as nondiscrimination.[8] The Johnson administration's commitment to building a Great Society meant that municipal agencies in Baltimore gained access to many new categorical grants earmarked for antipoverty efforts. The availability of the grants gave administrators in antipoverty and social services agencies a degree of independence from locally elected officials who controlled the local budgeting process and on whose largesse municipal departments had earlier largely been dependent.

Accessing categorical grants and then coordinating service delivery were not necessarily easy. City workers had to complete detailed and time-consuming applications, and in some cases the federal government made available grants to varying agencies for the same types of programs. Service providers complained of excessive red tape and redundancy, and some taxpayers complained of wasted federal dollars.[9] Meanwhile, locally elected officials were not left out of the grant application process entirely. Before seeking federal funds, applicants generally had to secure the approval of elected officials as well as a level of local financial commitment for the program the grant would fund. Despite the requirements, the availability of antipoverty grants gave agencies staffed by growing numbers of African Americans—and in a few cases also headed by Black administrators—significant influence over setting the municipal agenda and controlling the use of millions of dollars of federal funds. Given the continuing influence of conservatives on the Baltimore City Council, it is certain that antipoverty efforts would not have received the level of funding they did had Congress simply channeled resources into city coffers with limited or no oversight.

The enhanced autonomy exercised by workers in antipoverty and human-services agencies greatly alarmed Baltimore's lawmakers, who accurately identified the challenge to their authority the change represented. It also excited a bit of paranoia. As the War on Poverty got under way, Mayor Theodore McKeldin and members of the city council began suspecting that workers in municipal agencies were subverting mandated procedures and securing federal grants without the lawmakers' knowledge. The specter of rogue grant writing by activist African Americans and do-gooder whites in antipoverty agencies and human-services departments jolted the white officials into action. In 1965, McKeldin sent a memo to all city department heads pointedly reminding them that his approval was required for all new municipal programs. The members of the city council did McKeldin one better. So concerned were they that workers were seeking unauthorized funds that they commissioned a private welfare agency to investigate the extent of the practice. Ultimately, the agency determined that while covert grant writing had indeed occurred, it was not as prevalent as the lawmakers feared. The findings must have come as a relief to the officials. Nonetheless, their suspicions reveal the extent to which the lawmakers worried that federally subsidized autonomy in antipoverty and human-services agencies and the increasing influence of African Americans in those agencies threatened the status quo. Not surprisingly, elected officials subjected antipoverty agencies to close scrutiny and frequent audits. They also, however, were cowed enough by the new political context to take the War on Poverty seriously.[10]

Aware that they were the cause of suspicion, activist employees nevertheless boldly championed community participation and also worked to make resident engagement meaningful rather than simply symbolic. Adding the voices of poor people with legitimate gripes against the city to already contested debates over public policy hardly had a calming effect on municipal affairs, and city workers sometimes found themselves caught in the middle of fierce battles. Residents pushed for fast and meaningful change, while city council members, outraged to have people on the city's payroll fomenting discontent and by what historian Jon C. Teaford describes as "the unusual spectacle of government-sponsored rebellion," tried to slow things down.[11]

Probably the most ardent proponents of community organization and participation within the municipal government were many of the administrators and staff members of the CAA. Although theoretically hired to coordinate and deliver poverty-alleviating services, many were dissatisfied with that narrow role. Political scientist Peter Bachrach, who studied Baltimore's War on Poverty firsthand, argues that federal antipoverty legislation provided inner-city residents with what the Wagner Act had given workers during the 1930s; the laws gave federal sanction to and implied presidential endorsement of organizing efforts among those with limited power and influence. Not all staffs of CAAs across the nation pursued grassroots organizing in addition to service delivery, but under the leadership of Mitchell, the employees of the Baltimore agency seized the opportunity. As Mitchell asserted, although not necessarily designed for purposes beyond service delivery, "It's possible to use an anti-poverty program for community organization and subvert [the intended goal]."[12]

Born in 1922, Mitchell had grown up in Baltimore. His commitment to combating racial injustice had hardened when he was a young boy. At the time, his older brother, Clarence, was working as a journalist for the *Afro-American*. In 1931, Clarence traveled to Cambridge, on Maryland's Eastern Shore, to cover the case of a Black man accused of murdering his white employer. Clarence arrived in town just as white residents were setting aflame the lynched body of the accused. They then dragged him through the African American section of the town. On learning of the brutal crime, Parren committed himself to fighting racism. He participated in local demonstrations against segregation during the 1930s and early 1940s. After high school, he served in World War II and subsequently attended Morgan State College in Baltimore. He next combined his desire to continue his education with his determination to fight discrimination and successfully sued the segregated University of Maryland to gain admittance into a graduate program. After receiving a master's degree in sociology, he returned to Morgan to teach and remained involved in civil rights efforts. He also served as executive secretary for the Maryland Human Relations Commission. Then in 1965 he assumed the leadership of Baltimore's Community Action Agency. After later leaving that post, he became the first African American from Maryland to be elected to the U.S. Congress, and while there, he helped to found the Congressional Black Caucus. Over the course of his career, Mitchell used multiple strategies to fight racial and economic injustice, and while heading the CAA, he committed himself and his staff to community organizing.[13] "My theory is this," he explained. "If you organize the poor people and show them where they can get some services which were previously denied them, they'll begin thinking politically."[14]

Among the responsibilities borne by Mitchell and his staff was the coordination and oversight of the use of federal War on Poverty grants in the city by municipal departments and nongovernmental entities alike. Mitchell, his staff, and the members of the Community Action Commission, the governing body of the CAA, used their authority to compel maximum community participation. In 1965, the CAA issued guidelines for those seeking federal antipoverty funding. All proposals had to demonstrate that there had been and would be "in-depth involvement of poor residents" at every stage of the planning and program implementation process.[15] The guideline's authors, including Madeline Murphy, an outspoken advocate for racial and economic justice and a columnist for the *Afro-American*, also described what they considered inadequate community participation. Clearly mindful of the strategies whites in the city often used to give the pretense of having included African Americans in decision-making, the authors explained, "Gathering of information from residents, incorporating this into the proposal and subsequent proposal review by poor residents do not constitute involvement of the poor per se."[16] Poor people had to play meaningful roles in programming conception and design. The mandate validated the conviction that low-income residents had important insights into the causes of and best ways to alleviate poverty. As community activist and municipal employee Elizabeth Ward later explained, "Maybe I don't have a degree, but I knew I could do it better than the planners could. White people would always come in and say, what you need is this or that, and I'd just tell them, 'Don't tell me what I need; ask me what I need.'"[17]

Just as CAA staffers raised the bar on community participation for recipients of Office of Economic Opportunity (OEO) grants, they held themselves to high standards. The staff of the CAA was largely African American and, although the city did not monitor employment by sex during the 1960s, undoubtedly predominantly female. Many on the staff, such as Martina Madden, Joan Foster, and Charlotte Clark, had grown up or lived in low-income communities.[18] They ran forty neighborhood centers in designated action areas and offered a variety of educational, medical, vocational, recreational, and family services. They also used neighborhood centers to mobilize residents into political action, with elected representatives governing each center. Community organizing was hardly new in Baltimore, and some low-income residents were already politically engaged. Others needed encouragement. As Goldie Baker, a public-housing and community activist and resident, recalls, the staff members of the CAA neighborhood centers were important in bringing "people together . . . [and] telling them how to stand up, be strong and organize."[19]

CAA staffers employed multiple community-organizing strategies. They used their influence and resources to help low-income residents establish independent organizations, demand input in municipal decision-making, and pressure the city for more and better public services. CAA staffers assisted welfare recipients and their advocates establish Mother Rescuers from Poverty, a welfare rights organization. They also accompanied public-housing residents to a meeting with the head of the Department of Housing and Community Development and endorsed the residents' demand for greater influence. The meeting led to the creation of a Resident Advisory Board. Residents also used CAA letterhead to pen complaint letters to multiple city officials. Improving living conditions in low-income neighborhoods was a top priority. Members of newly formed neighborhood councils demanded cleaner streets, intensified rat eradication efforts, better parks and playgrounds, and more youth programs and recreation centers.[20] Although city officials sometimes accommodated them, the pace of change was far too slow for CAA staffers and residents alike. "Why must the requests and desires of inner city residents always be denied?" Mitchell complained to the traffic commissioner, whose staff had ignored requests that traffic signals be installed at several busy intersections that children had to cross to get to school.[21] Despite serious obstacles, rarely if ever in the city's history had so many low-income residents—particularly African Americans—believed change was possible.

Given their different views on the importance of community mobilization in low-income neighborhoods, the staff of the CAA and the conservative members of the city council locked horns repeatedly. Remarkably, the CAA won some important battles. In 1967, Mitchell sought the council's approval of Self-Help Housing, a program conceived of and planned entirely by low-income residents. The residents sought funds that could be used for property repairs and neighborhood upkeep. They also wanted to control hiring for the program. As Leander Douglas, the head of the Neighborhood Housing Action Committee, explained, the residents desired "a chance to work in our own communities."[22] The council balked. Revealing a level of condescension about low-income city residents that some of his fellow council members doubtlessly shared, Reuben Caplan complained, "There's $330,000 involved in this program. It would be turned over to a group of people who have been unable to earn a living."[23] Eventually, however, only two council members voted against funding the program. The increasing importance of Black voting power—combined with the availability of federal funding for the initiative—tipped the balance of power in favor of the residents and their CAA supporters. The victory, while modest, was nonetheless monumental. Only four years earlier in Jim Crow Baltimore it would have been inconceivable that the city council would award low-income African Americans hundreds of thousands of dollars to hire themselves to combat neglect in their neighborhoods.[24]

The staff of the Model Cities project also exhibited a strong commitment to community mobilization. Elva Edwards, an African American social worker and native of Baltimore who joined the Model Cities project after a stint in the CAA, recalled, "Model Cities started from the streets. It was born there."[25] The Model Cities project in Baltimore did not become fully functioning until the 1970s. During the late 1960s, an informal staff worked out of the mayor's office. Walter Carter, known by some as the Martin Luther King of Baltimore, served as the project's community-relations specialist. Carter, a native of North Carolina and a social worker, was the chair of the city's branch of CORE from 1961 to 1963. He led Freedom Rides to Maryland's Eastern Shore and also spearheaded efforts to desegregate eating establishments along the state's highways. In 1963, he was Maryland's coordinator for the March on Washington. During the second half of the 1960s, much of his activism targeted housing discrimination. Like many civil rights activists of the time, he was painfully aware that residential segregation by race, and increasingly by class, was isolating low-income African Americans in neighborhoods and in a city with limited employment opportunities and paths to upward mobility. But he was also committed to improving conditions in the city. On assuming his post in Model Cities, like Edwards, Carter traveled through low-income neighborhoods and worked with residents to plan the next front of the city's War on Poverty.[26]

African Americans, and Black women in particular, played important roles in fostering community participation in older municipal departments and in new federally funded antipoverty agencies. It also often fell to them to ensure that community participation meant more than mere tokenism. In the Department of Education, Pearl Cole Brackett, an African American former public school teacher, took the lead. Brackett was born in Washington, DC, in 1917 and moved to Baltimore as a young girl. She attended Morgan State College where she was president of the school's chapter of Delta Sigma Theta. Because the University of Maryland was segregated, Brackett pursued graduate study at New York University and the University of Massachusetts at the expense of the state of Maryland. When in 1968, the school board hired Brackett as the assistant superintendent of community schools, she assumed the most senior position a Black woman had ever held in a school system in Maryland.[27]

Reflecting on her early years in the job, Brackett described sexism as a serious obstacle that she faced; some on her staff were reluctant to serve under a woman. Financial constraints quickly became a second, pressing concern. Brackett found it far easier to secure resident volunteers than funds for their proposals. By 1969, she had organized community councils composed of residents and professionals for each school in the program, which was itself directed by a citywide advisory board. Yet she lacked adequate resources. A grant from the state eventually enabled her staff and community residents to institute a multitude of programs. Community schools offered adult education courses, high school equivalency classes, job training programs, and child-care services for parents attending the schools. Some schools also housed social-service clinics and had staff able to conduct health screenings. Community councils installed lights on playgrounds so that recreational facilities could be used after dark. In addition, Brackett intentionally included law enforcement officials in the program. Police brutality was an ongoing problem in Baltimore, and Brackett hoped to ease tensions. Mincing no words, she argued, "The Police Department belongs in this project, so kids at an early age can see the police as someone to help them, not someone who is going to beat their brains in."[28] Despite the success of many community school activities, funding remained scarce, and some residents complained that their ideas did not result in programming. Other parents, however, remained enthusiastic. "I see great things coming out of community schools. I see links between fathers, mothers, sons, daughters, teachers, school staff and community and understanding like a hard clenched fist, communities working together to build great things," explained one mother involved in the program.[29]

Brackett was not unique as a Black female administrator in a municipal department intent on realizing the potential of community participation. F. Eulalian Ferguson and Gordine Blount pursued the goal for the Department of Housing and Community Development, and they had counterparts elsewhere in the city government, such as the Departments of Welfare and Health.[30] Meanwhile, pressure from activists and residents to make the government more responsive led Mayor Thomas D'Alesandro III, who replaced McKeldin in 1967, to hire Marguerite Campbell to serve as his community relations specialist. "Aggressive . . . in a very diplomatic way," D'Alesandro later recalled, Campbell quickly earned a reputation for helping residents with low incomes cut through "bureaucratic red tape" and solve problems they had with the city government.[31] Like other municipal employees, Campbell appreciated the limitations of what the War on Poverty could achieve. And like Carter of Model Cities, she was particularly worried that residential segregation precluded poor city residents from accessing economic opportunities available outside of the city. Nevertheless, she did her part to hold the city accountable to all of its residents and advocated on behalf of community participation.[32]

The presence of activist agency administrators and staffers promoting community involvement hardly quelled tensions between municipal workers and low-income residents. When they felt city employees were failing to deliver on the promise of the War on Poverty, residents pressed for greater representation and bolder action. And when they believed service providers disrespected them or treated them unfairly, they protested.[33] Some of the most dramatic showdowns occurred between Mother Rescuers from Poverty and the staff of the Department of Public Welfare (DPW). Created in 1966 by Margaret McCarty, Daisy Snipes, and Zelma Storey, three African American women who were recipients of Aid to Families with Dependent Children (AFDC), and Joan Berezin, a young white activist, Mother Rescuers quickly became the city's most active welfare rights organization. Members raised numerous concerns about the DPW staff and the injustices inherent in federal and state welfare policies. As McCarty argued, "Welfare robs a person of his dignity and his rights. When you apply, automatically everything you say is assumed to be a lie. By the time you get on welfare, you just don't think much of yourself. And once you get on the rolls there are 'policies' to keep you feeling that way."[34] Insensitivity on the part of DPW workers was part of the problem. "Investigators are trained to be nasty," McCarty explained. "They just come to your home whenever they feel like it, one at the back door while another rings the front bell. They look everywhere. 'Do you have a boyfriend?

What's in the icebox?' is what they ask."[35] Throughout the late 1960s, Mother Rescuers engaged in many forms of protest—including a sleep-in in the DPW lobby—to pressure the agency's leadership and staff to respond to their critiques. In some cases, they met with success. The sleep-in won Mother Rescuers permission from the Maryland DPW to set up shop in the agency's Baltimore offices, where they provided support for those seeking assistance and monitored workers to ensure they were courteously following the law.[36]

While racial solidarity and sisterhood only inconsistently characterized the relationship between city workers and residents with low incomes, members of the two groups did join forces to press for change. Clarence Blount recalled that Mitchell and the staff of the CAA were especially adept at rallying residents to participate in demonstrations. The 1967 protest at the city's Federal Office Building and subsequent march to Washington were but two examples of many.[37] Employees of municipal departments also took to the streets to demand improvements in services and the nation's welfare state. And despite confrontations and mistrust between the staff of DPW and AFDC recipients, members of the two groups also sometimes found common cause. In 1969, for example, an interracial group of eighty AFDC recipients and DPW staffers traveled to Maryland's State House in Annapolis. In a series of meetings arranged by Geraldine Aronin, a white woman who was the Baltimore DPW's community relations chief, the contingent made demands of two legislative committees and spoke with the governor to request increased welfare benefits and greater representation for low-income residents on the city's and state's welfare boards.[38] Although their demands were inconsistently met, the cross-class, interracial organizing was sometimes successful and contributed to the momentum for democratizing decision-making in Baltimore.

African American men, such as Mitchell and Carter, also played critically important leadership roles in community organizing efforts and engaged in considerable activism in defense of the War on Poverty and on behalf of a more generous welfare state. Some whites were deeply committed as well. Most antipoverty warriors in Baltimore, however, were Black women. Some were service providers, some were service recipients, and others were both. Moreover, women in the city's lowest-wage positions often had much in common with recipients of welfare-related services; they were sometimes nothing more than a training program, paycheck, or pink slip removed from the clients they served, if their low wages had not already qualified them for government benefits. As a result, they were intimately familiar with the hardship of those struggling to get by on limited means and clearly believed low-income residents deserved a voice in municipal affairs. Certainly, tensions continued to emerge. Nevertheless, the joint efforts by Black women with varying connections to antipoverty agencies on behalf of democratic decision-making and a more generous welfare state were an important dimension of 1960s activism in Baltimore. It also reflected staunch determination on the part of African American women to play a role in charting the course the city took to respond to urban problems.

"The Agony of This Kind of Existence": Campaigns to Strengthen the Welfare State

As battles to increase democratic decision-making raged in the city, service providers also attended to the important task of improving service availability and delivery. Activist providers were outspoken in their critiques of both the War on Poverty and the welfare state. They were also innovative when it came to attempting to fix the system's flaws. They worked hard to make sure the city made use of all available federal grants, tried to fill gaps in the safety net with new programs, and protested encroachments on funding. They also attempted to make service delivery more convenient and accessible.

Even as they operated from within public agencies, many service providers harbored deep suspicions regarding the government's commitment to fighting poverty. As their engagement in protest evinces, few appeared to believe that Johnson's inadequately resourced War on Poverty could accomplish enough. Carter and Campbell were among those who called attention to the dire and long-term implications of ongoing residential segregation. Meanwhile, Mitchell and many on the staff of the CAA also protested the toll the president's commitment to fighting the Vietnam War took on levels of antipoverty funding.[39] Moreover, the lack of a job-creation component in federal poverty-fighting efforts led CAA staff and residents to propose grant-funded programs intentionally designed to employ community residents. In 1966, for example, the CAA partnered with U-JOIN and the Baltimore Neighborhood Commons, Inc., on a playground-building initiative that would have a staff of a hundred. The following year, the CAA embraced a jobs drive as one of its key initiatives. Because the federal government was not creating enough jobs, CAA staffers and community residents attempted to at least use their small-scale initiatives to fight unemployment.[40]

Some administrators and employees of DPW were also openly critical of the welfare programs they themselves staffed. And although it may have come as a surprise to some welfare rights advocates, among the critics was Esther Lazarus, DPW's Baltimore director. A white native of the city who had joined the department's staff during the Great Depression, Lazarus, the only woman to head a municipal department, was intimately familiar with critiques of the welfare system—and she agreed with many of them. Concerned that benefit levels were too low and welfare workers too intrusive, in 1967, she asserted, "I believe strongly that, if welfare gave a really adequate family grant, people would be able to arrange their lives better than we could arrange it for them."[41] Like welfare rights advocates, Lazarus also expressed concern that the welfare system—from the courts to service agencies—compromised the dignity of low-income recipients. As a solution, Lazarus advanced the controversial position that Congress should get rid of the AFDC entirely and instead simply guarantee all Americans a minimum income. "Instead of all this effort we expend trying to make people prove their need, we should have a declaration of income and then set a standard below which no one should live," she declared.[42]

Others on the staff of DPW shared Lazarus's frustration with the miserly nature of the American welfare state and the treatment received by welfare recipients and tried to raise public awareness. Barbara Mikulski, a white social worker employed in the community relations division of DPW, was among them, and she was also the advocate who became the most famous. Mikulski went on to serve on the Baltimore City Council, in the U.S. House of Representatives, and in the U.S. Senate. Although Mikulski helped to create and then rode into office on a wave of white ethnic pride, her political ascent was not a product of race-baiting. Instead, she consistently attempted to build racially diverse coalitions around economic issues, an effort she pursued at DPW. During the late 1960s, she was a critic of the welfare system, which she fully appreciated inadequately met the needs of low-income African Americans and whites alike. In 1969, for example, she made a joint presentation with a welfare recipient and did not sugarcoat her message. "Public welfare keeps families in poverty," she stated. Welfare payments did not raise recipients' incomes even to the poverty line, and intrusive surveillance policies, such as unannounced home visits, led to family breakups, she argued.[43]

Others at DPW also agreed. Roger Brown, an African American social worker, described the unfortunate tensions that often divided service providers and recipients. "We represent the system. We're the guy that's saying 'No,

No, No, No.'"[44] And Edmond Jones, an African American DPW social service director, shared Mikulski's and Brown's critique. "Even if a recipient somehow kept every expense within the allotted grant," he explained, "[the recipient] would have a maximum of $5 a month left over. If one child became ill and had to be rushed by cab to a doctor that would be it. . . . Anyone ought to be able to see the agony of this kind of existence." Jones also called into question the sincerity of the federal government's commitment to reducing hunger. The nation's Food Stamp program "was never intended really to aid welfare clients," he argued. "It is administered by the U.S. Department of Agriculture and it is designed actually to aid farmers and the national economy, not to relieve the burdens of the poor."[45]

Even as they were critical of the systems that they staffed, activist antipoverty and human-services workers attempted to use the limited influence they had to make improvements. Although they never engaged in the level of activism for which the staff of the CAA and DPW became notorious, employees of the Department of Health were particularly successful at finding and securing federal grants to ease hardship. They also tried to devise methods the city could use to coordinate service delivery so as to avoid having multiple agencies offering duplicated or piecemeal programming. In 1968, Dr. Matthew Tayback, a white man who was the city's deputy health commissioner, urged elected officials to create a single agency "to work with appropriate Federal and State offices so Baltimore may better receive an appropriate share of funds allocated for the nutrition of children."[46] Tayback estimated that an alarming 55,000 infants and children in the city could benefit from programs intended to combat malnutrition. Yet the city was failing to make full use of available aid. Baltimore also lacked a free milk program, and underserved children who qualified for free school lunches were not receiving them, Tayback protested. "To get the best for the city," he argued, Baltimore could leave no funding source untapped.[47] His alert prompted action; the city sought new nutrition grants and attempted to coordinate delivery. Tayback also helped the city secure funds from the federal government for health care services, including a program for low-income expectant mothers.[48] Efforts by the staff of the Baltimore Health Department won their agency a reputation among city officials for "aggressively pursuing the federal dollar."[49]

While some city employees helped to bring new welfare services to Baltimore, others worked to ensure that all who qualified for such entitlement programs as AFDC and Food Stamps found their way onto the rolls. Although the city's rapidly expanding pool of welfare recipients angered some taxpayers and elected officials in both the city and the state, many DPW workers took considerable pride in securing critical benefits for residents who needed them. Meanwhile, DPW employees also fought welfare-funding reductions—independently as well as with recipients. In 1968, more than a hundred welfare workers signed a petition protesting state-level cuts. Beatrice Langford, the supervisor of the DPW training department, initiated the petition drive. "The ways of the State can be inscrutable, if not bungling and inhumane," she complained.[50] In addition, in 1968, DPW staffers and welfare-service recipients joined forces and inundated the mayor and state officials with letters in an unsuccessful bid to win resources for a demonstration project in which they were involved.[51]

Other municipal employees also attempted to improve the ways their agencies delivered services. In the mid-1960s, many began to argue that the city should replace large, impersonal, centralized office buildings with smaller outposts modeled on CAA neighborhood centers. Supporters believed decentralization would make government agencies more accessible and convenient. They also hoped community residents would be able to win increased authority over decision-making in decentralized locations and that agency staff members would become more empathetic if they worked in the neighborhoods where their clients lived. By the end of the decade, many city agencies, including the Departments of Health, Education, and Welfare had adopted decentralization at least in part. Even the Baltimore Police Department created community-relations centers, and D'Alesandro began organizing mayor's stations around the city. Decentralization was hardly compensation for the inadequacy of antipoverty funding and welfare benefits. Nonetheless, it represented an attempt by agency administrators to alter the power relationship between service providers and recipients. Instead of compelling residents to travel to distant, impersonal central offices, city workers moved to be closer to those they were hired to serve.[52]

Efforts by workers in antipoverty agencies and municipal departments to bring new programs to Baltimore and strengthen the welfare state sometimes led to showdowns with elected city officials. Conflict between the staff of the CAA and members of the Baltimore City Council were most frequent. In some cases, the council simply rejected CAA proposals. Such was the fate of plans to create food cooperatives and credit unions.[53] In other cases, the council engaged Mitchell and his staff in protracted wrangling over proposals. It took two years to open Legal Aid offices in the city, for example. Not surprisingly, conservative council members were hardly inclined to approve a request likely to ensnare the city in legal battles brought by low-income residents.[54] Ultimately, Mitchell and other advocates of Legal Aid prevailed—at least in part. They had hoped for ten neighborhood Legal Aid offices, but the city council approved only two. It was still a victory. "We had to fight to get this," declared Tilghman G. Pitts Jr., chair of the Legal Aid board, at the ribbon-cutting ceremony for the first office in 1967.[55] And the importance of the victory grew over the next years. In 1968, the board of Legal Aid granted their attorneys permission to represent at no cost "neighborhood groups, tenant groups, welfare protest organizations, and civil rights groups in slum neighborhoods."[56] Organized low-income city residents gained a new and important tool in their efforts to fight poverty and injustice in Baltimore, and Mitchell and the staff of the CAA deserved much of the credit.

"The Wind Whistling Through the Walls": Welfare Services and Gendered Caretaking

The new antipoverty and social welfare programs that municipal workers and residents with low incomes helped to secure in Baltimore, in addition to improved access to entitlement programs, alleviated hardship for many in the city. The changes also produced gendered outcomes that proved particularly important for women. In fact, ultimately, the Great Society benefited women in two very significant albeit unintended ways. First, federal spending created many jobs that women were more likely than men to fill. And second, new programs made available from the state services that women had earlier attempted to provide for their families on their own. The increased availability of public provisions—in health care, nutrition, and recreation, for example—replaced or mitigated some of women's gendered caretaking obligations. At the same time, civil rights legislation that outlawed segregation opened access to new or better services than had previously been available to African Americans, also alleviating caretaking labor. The ramifications for women with low incomes were particularly significant because they were the least able to purchase labor-reducing services in the private sector.

In the mid-1960s, while conducting a home visit, a social worker from DPW witnessed firsthand the level of the usually invisible labor that poverty extracted from poor women. While chatting with an AFDC recipient in her well-maintained but rundown home, the social worker learned that the client had made all of her children's clothing by hand. She also had sewn the curtains that hung in her windows. Gifts of food from family and friends supplemented her welfare check and helped her to scrimp by. But her dependence on gifts reflected the inadequacy of her means to stave off hunger. A washboard in her tub indicated that she did her family's laundry by hand, sparing the expense of a laundromat. And her children's sleeping quarters revealed the extent of her ingenuity—and also the lengths women went to on behalf of their families. Her two children had their own beds because she had sawed a single mattress in half.[57] Great Society programs were hardly an adequate antidote to the hardship the welfare recipient and others like her faced. They could and did, however, prove a source of some relief that alleviated some of the caretaking obligations low-income women bore.

Dramatic improvements in the availability and accessibility of health insurance and health care services during the 1960s were a tremendously important source of relief for not just the ill but also the mothers, daughters, and other women who cared for them. When introducing Americans to the Medicare program that his administration created, President Lyndon Johnson noted, "Every American family will benefit by the extension of social security to cover the hospital costs of their aged parents."[58] Medicare also had specific implications for the adult daughters of aging parents, as they were often the health care providers who filled in when professional care was too expensive. The introduction of Medicaid produced similar outcomes for mothers and wives. In 1966, welfare officials in Baltimore estimated that Medicaid was going to extend health coverage to two hundred thousand city residents, doubling the number who had access to some medical services under the state's indigent-care program.[59] Both the ill and those who previously cared for them at home were the beneficiaries.

Meanwhile, legal desegregation made more medical facilities in the city available to African Americans, and federally funded public health programs that were part of the War on Poverty also increased access to medical care. The decision by city officials to adopt some community-based health services provisions and to include residents in decision-making bodies also made medical services more accessible and accountable. As one mother explained about a neighborhood pediatric center, "We can walk here. . . . They have good doctors here, and everything you need is right here."[60] By 1968, three hundred thousand city residents, about a third of the population, were assisted by public health programs. But serious problems with health care availability persisted. The city relied on sixteen sources of federal, state, and local funding to provide for public health. Each funding source had its own set of standards for implementation, and as a result, Tayback of the health department complained, service delivery was "confusing" and in some cases "inefficient."[61] Nevertheless, the greater access to health insurance and medical services relieved not only physical suffering but also the tremendous pressure earlier borne by women to compensate for inadequate state support, segregation, and low incomes.

Federal nutrition programs were also among the Great Society initiatives that helped to ease caretaking responsibilities. During the 1960s, low-income women in Baltimore repeatedly protested the quality of food they could provide their families on limited budgets. In 1966, for example, members of Mother Rescuers from Poverty prepared a meal for Baltimore's Mayor McKeldin that represented the types of food AFDC recipients were constrained to offering their families. The featured entrée was Spam, a low-cost canned-meat product consisting of pork mixed with ham. The mayor politely refused the offer.[62] Meanwhile, concern about food quality and affordability led some women to work with CAA employees to plan the creation of food cooperatives. Although the city council rejected the proposal, antipoverty warriors did manage to carry out a buy-in-bulk program in an effort to make food more affordable. Meanwhile, the Baltimore chapter of the Black Panthers did execute the food cooperative idea. The Food Stamp program, which the Johnson administration made permanent, and other nutrition programs created as part of the War on Poverty provided some relief to women concerned about and responsible for their family's nutritional needs. Although federal programs failed to fully respond to the problems women with low incomes faced, even structurally flawed programs such as Food Stamps alleviated to some extent women's fears that they would not be able to provide for their families. So too did school lunch and milk programs and nutritional programs aimed at older Americans.[63]

Increases in federal funding for programs that served elderly Americans and youth further eased gendered caretaking responsibilities. During the 1960s, older African Americans, and Black women in particular, were overrepresented among the city's poor residents. Those who earlier had worked as domestic workers or in other precarious jobs had been excluded from participation in the nation's top-tier Social Security program, and so they typically qualified only for a less generous benefit. Black family members no doubt tried to compensate financially for the income gap that left many older African American in far tougher straits than most white seniors, and many women surely also provided caretaking support. War on Poverty funding that enabled antipoverty agencies and municipal departments to increase not only medical and nutrition programs but also recreation and housing services for older Americans eased hardship and likely also relieved women of some of the stresses involved in caring for older relatives.[64]

Meanwhile, federal grants enabled city employees to provide new programs for children and youth. To be sure, some officials' enthusiasm for recreational programming and other War on Poverty initiatives stemmed from an interest in preventing "riots." Nevertheless, as was the case with nutritional services, youth programming was a top priority among women with low incomes; mothers frequently voiced the concern that youth deprived of recreational services and structured activities would end up in trouble. War on Poverty funds subsidized considerable programming for children. Head Start and other early-childhood educational programs granted women some child-care relief while enabling them to give their children access to educational resources many families could otherwise not afford. Grant-funded programs carried out by the city's public library system, museums, zoo, and symphony orchestra created enriching activities that families independently might not have been able to provide. CAA neighborhood centers, community schools, and other entities used federal funds to provide children with opportunities to take African dance classes and music lessons, participate in fashion shows, and engage in a wide range of extracurricular activities. Meanwhile, federally and locally sponsored recreation programs and summer camps relieved mothers of not just supervisory responsibilities but also of the worry of finding safe places for their children to play.[65]

The introduction or improvement of other municipal services during the 1960s also helped alleviate women's caretaking responsibilities. As city resident Aloha Burrell complained, she had "worn out a dozen brooms" doing work that should have been performed and paid for by the city.[66] Not surprisingly, the quality of sanitation and housing services available in their neighborhoods was of considerable concern to mothers worried about health and safety. Self-help initiatives such as the *Afro-American*'s annual Clean Block campaigns continued through the decade—in some cases subsidized by federal rather than private funds. And the CAA's community-run Self-Help Housing program responded to residents' determination "to expedite and supplement existing City services to improve housing and environmental conditions."[67] New programs and improved services were hardly an adequate response to decades of neglect and the ongoing problem of residential segregation. Even modest improvements, however, helped to make neighborhoods and housing complexes cleaner and at least partially alleviated the responsibilities women assumed to keep their family members safe.[68]

The relationship between the provision of public services and women's caretaking roles casts welfare-state expansion and the Great Society in a new light. Because care work is economic activity, to the extent that new services replaced unpaid labor, it was a form of wealth redistribution. The state rather than women wearing out brooms assumed a measure of responsibility for the well-being of its citizens. To be sure, in cities like Baltimore, the municipal government often paid African Americans who carried out the new public services wages that kept the workers themselves in or near poverty. Meanwhile, policy makers hardly acknowledged the economic transactions under way, and the gendered caretaking responsibilities that women continued to perform remained invisible in national accountings of economic activity. Nevertheless, even if inadequately, the state did assume as public responsibility the provision of some of the caretaking labor earlier performed by women.

* * *

In her eloquent account of the War on Poverty in Las Vegas, Annelise Orleck describes the battles low-income African American women waged against elected officials to secure federal funding for antipoverty efforts.[69] In Baltimore, some among the largely African American and female staffs of the CAA, the Model City program, and municipal human-services providers waged similar fights, sometimes in solidarity with activists and low-income residents. The government workers used their positions within the state to increase democratic participation in decision-making and improve the welfare state, while activists and residents pushed from outside of the system. Grants from Congress earmarked for antipoverty efforts provided the antipoverty workers and service providers with a degree of independence from elected city officials, which allowed them to pursue a revitalization plan for the city that did not center on downtown commercial revitalization. The War on Poverty, despite its many limitations, enabled Black Baltimoreans and women to exercise unprecedented influence over the municipal agenda, an outcome of grave concern to conservative members of the city council. But government jobs hardly guaranteed workers a living wage, a problem public-sector unions stood ready to address.

CHAPTER 4

"Better Wages and Job Conditions with Dignity"

Unionizing the Public Sector

In September 1968, inspired by a strike by African American sanitation workers in Memphis, Tennessee, six months earlier, garbage collectors in Baltimore launched a work stoppage of their own. And like their fellow workers to the south, Baltimore's strikers demanded union recognition and better pay. A tragic event separated the two events, however. The protest in Memphis had attracted the participation of Martin Luther King Jr., who had commended the sanitation workers for demanding that their city "respect the dignity of labor" and had fully endorsed their cause. "It is criminal," King told a Memphis audience, "to have people working on a full-time basis and a full-time job getting part-time income."[1] The civil rights giant pledged to remain involved in the workers' cause—and he had, until an assassin in Memphis took his life. King's murder, as well as his words of support, surely reverberated in the minds of Baltimore's sanitation workers a few months later as they marched the picket line. To honor the slain leader and the workers he championed and to compel sympathy for their own circumstances, Baltimore's strikers carried placards identical to those used in Memphis. Their signs declared "I Am a Man" and demanded "Decency and Justice" as they marched for "better wages and job conditions with dignity."[2] They protested not just for themselves but for all of the municipal government's low-wage workers whose labor enabled the city to function but whose incomes left some living in poverty.[3]

Just as the politicized "spirit of the times" of the 1960s inspired municipal employees in Baltimore to advocate with and on behalf of city residents with low incomes, so it empowered them to take action to better their own situations as workers. As the size of the public sector swelled during the 1960s throughout the nation, growing numbers of government workers turned to unionization as a means of improving the terms and conditions of their employment. In Baltimore, as elsewhere, some full-time public-sector workers earned so little that they qualified for welfare benefits. And even those with better pay knew their wages or salaries generally trailed those earned by workers in equivalent positions in the private sector or in wealthier jurisdictions. Meanwhile, much of the nation's protective labor legislation, including the right to join a union, did not extend to government workers. As employees of the people rather than "the man," government workers historically had been seen as relatively invulnerable to exploitation. During the 1960s, however, many government workers came to feel that their interests were not taken seriously enough by elected officials. Government workers demanded the right to collectively bargain over issues including wages; fringe benefits, such as health insurance and sick leave; workplace safety; and bias and favoritism in hiring, promotion, and firing. At the same time that many public service providers were championing community participation in municipal affairs, government workers also fought for a role in decision-making that affected their futures.

In Baltimore, African Americans such as Raymond Clarke and Dennis Crosby played leading roles in the efforts to win union rights for municipal workers. And the receptivity of Black workers to their organizing overtures evinces the considerable faith many put in the power of collective bargaining. As historian Lane Windham argues, many African Americans of the era saw no contradiction between advocating for both individual civil rights and collective union rights.[4] In Baltimore, those in the public sector were particularly assertive in seeking unionization, but they were hardly the only workers in the city with that goal. Low-wage service providers in the private sector, most notably many African American women employed in health care, also actively sought union representation during the late 1960s. Having gained increased access to jobs in the mainstream economy during the 1960s, many Black workers lost no time before fighting for the protections and benefits they believed their new employers should provide, and they looked to unions to achieve that end. Successful union drives, particularly those in the public sector, had considerable significance for local Black communities given the increased presence of African Americans in the government workforce and the otherwise bleak labor market in the deindustrializing city. And the Baltimore workers' victories had national implications as well. As the fortunes of the predominantly white and male unionized industrial workforce waned, government employees in Baltimore, as elsewhere, breathed new life into the American labor movement. And they served as a vanguard for many other low-wage public- and private-sector service workers, predominantly women and people of color, who sought union representation in the decades that followed.

But not everyone in Baltimore understood growth, activism, and unionization in the public sector as positive developments. Some, including many conservatives, believed the changes—in combination with the victories of activists pursuing other progressive causes such as civil rights—came at their expense. And some were clearly threatened and angered by Black advancement. The riots and rebellions that followed the assassination of Martin Luther King as well as concerns that urban crime rates appeared to be on the rise heightened many whites' long-held suspicions of African Americans. Defenders of white supremacy had long attempted to delegitimize Black protest by equating it with criminality, and it did not take long for whites, not only in Baltimore but throughout Maryland, to conflate activism in the public sector and strikes by government workers with "riots" and crime. The sentiments reinforced conservative claims that criminality and lawlessness increasingly characterized rusting cities and their African American residents. Those harboring or receptive to such views in Maryland found a spokesperson in their state's governor, Spiro Agnew, who rose to national prominence in 1968 as a voice of the "silent majority." As African Americans in Baltimore attempted to capitalize on their new influence over the municipal agenda to win public policies to fight poverty and simultaneously worked to build public-sector unions that would protect the economic interests of a significant portion of the city's Black working and middle classes, the governor of their state championed a backlash gravely detrimental to the efforts.

"The People Who Need It Most": Public-Sector Unionization in Baltimore

During the 1960s, labor activism among public-sector workers nationwide reached unprecedented heights. Unions representing government employees were not new, however. Instead, some public-sector unions shared early twentieth-century origins with many of their private-sector counterparts. Government officials were not obligated to recognize public-sector unions, however, and in some cases, they were specifically prohibited from doing so. In addition, government workers were largely excluded from New Deal legislation, which created Social Security and unemployment insurance and established the minimum wage and overtime procedures. The nation's history of antiradicalism helps to explain why the United States trailed most industrialized countries in granting recognition to government unions; opponents argued that unionization would lead to communist subversion of the government. In Baltimore, for example, business leaders responded to an organizing drive among municipal workers during the Great Depression by charging that "100% communistic" and "foreign elements" were bent on taking over the city.[5] Historian Joseph Slater notes that such claims were common in the United States but also often disingenuous; outspoken critics of government unions frequently expressed equally as hostile sentiments about private-sector unions. Nevertheless, the red-baiting met with success in Baltimore as elsewhere.[6] As a result, although public-sector unions sometimes wielded unofficial negotiating power, as was the case in Baltimore, most did not win recognition until the 1960s.[7]

Early unionization campaigns occurred among state and federal workers in the Baltimore area as well. Efforts to win union recognition from Maryland officials made almost no headway. In fact, in 1941, concern about public-sector union activism led the Maryland General Assembly to consider legislation that would punish participants in public-sector strikes as harshly as the state censured those convicted of treason. Resistance to public-sector unionism remained fierce in Annapolis well beyond the postwar years, and state workers did not win union rights until the 1990s. Federal unions had greater success. Postal unions had a long and proud history in the United States and counted many Baltimore workers among their members. And a federal union had acted on behalf of Social Security employees since at least the early 1940s. The extent to which federal unions could achieve their goals, however, depended entirely on the largesse of individual agency administrators.[8]

Employee associations and professional organizations existed in Baltimore and Maryland alongside public-sector unions and also wielded a measure of influence in labor relations. The Classified Municipal Employees Association (CMEA) courted members from among the city's white, nonlaboring, and non–per diem employees. The Maryland Classified Employees Association (MCEA) sought members in similar positions on the state level and was likely also an exclusively white organization. Both CMEA and MCEA began as social groups, and neither adopted the adversarial stance toward elected officials more typical of the unions.[9] The racist membership requirement of the CMEA was doubtlessly one reason why African American classified workers in Baltimore created the Association of Classified Municipal Employees, which by 1942 boasted a membership of almost one thousand. Teachers and nurses also formed organizations in the city prior to 1960.[10]

Racist membership requirements in government workers' organizations served as an obstacle to Black advancement and the increased strength of the public-sector labor movement. By the early 1960s, all public-sector unions and employee associations appear to have been integrated, but the change had not come without a fight. Under pressure from the city's Equal Employment Opportunities Commission (EEOC), CMEA had disavowed its whites-only membership requirement in 1960 but also refused to admit that it had ever discriminated.[11] The same year, and also under pressure from the EEOC, the Baltimore Firefighters Association (part of the American Federation of Labor and Congress of Industrial Organizations) agreed to admit African American members. But the union demanded twenty-five dollars in back dues from veteran Black firefighters. "Why should firefighters be penalized for not joining a union when they were prevented from doing so by that union?" demanded an outraged Troy Brailey, the chair of the labor committee of the Baltimore branch of the NAACP and the president of the Maryland chapter of the Negro-American Labor Council.[12] The Black firefighters took their complaint to the national leadership of the AFL-CIO and won support for their case. In the end, they paid only the ten-dollar fee the union charged to other new members.[13]

The showdowns that pitted the EEOC against the employee organization and firefighters' union reveal African Americans' interest in collective organizing but also the tense state of race relations within the municipal workforce and its labor movement. Public-sector union organizers would have to tread carefully if they hoped to grow their organizations during the 1960s. The local leadership of AFSCME was intimately familiar with the city's racial minefields. Raymond Clarke became the president of Baltimore's AFSCME Local 44 in 1962, two years after he and other union representatives launched a major organizing drive in the city. Clarke, who was African American, had been a chauffeur-foreman in the Bureau of Sanitation when he joined the union, and he was certainly no stranger to the city's racial politics; he had grown up in Baltimore. He was a fierce advocate of the labor movement, he later explained, because his father had been a union man. Clarke knew firsthand the benefits unionization could accrue to working families. As a result, when the International Brotherhood of Teamsters had begun organizing a union among sanitation workers in Baltimore, Clarke quickly joined the effort. He then helped spearhead AFSCME's organizing drive. Other African

Americans, including Earlyne Moir, a nurse at the Baltimore City Hospital—who was a rare woman among the union's predominantly male leaders—also served terms as officers during the early 1960s.[14]

The white leadership of AFSCME on the state level also had familiarity with race relations in Baltimore as well as backgrounds in the private-sector labor movement. During World War II, P. J. Ciampa and Ernest Crofoot had been affiliated with the United Automobile Workers when members of that union and local civil rights leaders successfully won jobs for African Americans at Glenn L. Martin Company, an aircraft-producing firm in the city. Crofoot described the experience as formative in terms of his own awareness of race relations. Later, once they moved to AFSCME, Ciampa became the director of field services and then an area director, and Crofoot became the president of AFSCME's Council 62, which included Clarke's Baltimore local. Crofoot also later served as an international vice president of AFSCME. During much of the 1960s, Clarke, Ciampa, and Crofoot used their familiarity with the city's racial politics, knowledge of the municipal workforce, and organizing skills to grow AFSCME's membership rolls and increase the union's influence in local and state politics.[15]

Despite lacking official recognition from the city, AFSCME leaders aggressively fought on behalf of municipal workers during the early and mid-1960s. They organized among hourly rather than salaried workers and took considerable pride in working on behalf of the city's lowest-paid employees. The leaders consistently demanded raises and full payment of workers' medical and life insurance policies. They also called for a city-financed unemployment insurance system, pension benefit, and disability policy. Further, they pressed the city to consider seniority in promotion decisions, fought to increase fringe benefits and overtime allowances, and tried to get the city to extend some benefits to per diem employees. In addition, AFSCME officials joined the city's civil rights leaders and the staff of the Community Relations Commission (formerly the EEOC) in protesting racial discrimination in civil-service testing procedures.[16]

AFSCME also challenged as discriminatory the city government's failure to train and then promote low-level workers. The city's tendency to keep unskilled workers in dead-end jobs and to hire new workers for vacant skilled positions reinforced racial- and gender-based segmentation in the municipal workforce. To counter the problem, AFSCME International secured federal funding for programs to prepare low-wage employees for higher-paid positions. In Baltimore, AFSCME trained custodial workers to become operation engineers, and union leaders convinced the Civil Service Commission to honor the license the union awarded those who successfully completed the program. (The program's graduation ceremonies could reduce burly union members to tears, Crofoot recalled, as licensure created access to promotions never before possible.[17]) Thus, even before they secured official recognition from the city, AFSCME leaders had made considerable gains on behalf of low-wage workers. The efforts won the union new members from a range of municipal agencies. AFSCME attracted school cafeteria workers in addition to custodians, patient aides in addition to orderlies, and employees of the Department of Welfare in addition to prison guards. As a result, the union won many female as well as male members and large numbers of African Americans. It also grew to include many who were fighting the war on poverty as well as those staffing the city's criminal justice system—even as those groups increasingly represented opposing sides in debates over appropriate responses to urban poverty.[18]

Meanwhile, on the national level, AFSCME officials, such as the union's president Jerry Wurf and secretary-treasurer William "Bill" Lucy, often aligned personally and also affiliated their union with politically progressive causes. Wurf, a white native of Brooklyn, became the president of AFSCME International in 1964. He had become a union organizer as a young man and had helped to establish the first state chapter of CORE in New York. In 1958, after becoming the president of AFSCME's District Council 37 in New York City, Wurf helped win collective-bargaining rights for municipal workers in that city. As the president of AFSCME International, Wurf worked with and then served alongside Lucy, who *Ebony* magazine often described as one of the nation's top one hundred most influential African Americans. Lucy was born in Memphis in 1933 and grew up in California. After attending the University of California, Berkeley, he became an engineer with a county government and then joined the public-sector labor movement in the mid-1950s. He served as the president of his local union before moving into leadership roles in AFSCME International. In 1972, he cofounded the Coalition of Black Trade Unionists, and in 1994, he served as the president of Public Services International, a coalition of unions representing government service providers around the world.[19] Together, Wurf and Lucy transformed AFSCME International into a nationally prominent union. With its membership base in large cities, AFSCME officials closely tracked and lobbied on behalf of urban policies. AFSCME International also partnered with the National Welfare Rights Organization in policy fights and to improve relationships between service providers and recipients. Under Wurf's admittedly sometimes caustic leadership and guided by Lucy's incisive analyses of complex political issues, AFSCME became one of the most important unions in the United States during the 1960s and 1970s.[20]

Although on the national level their union sometimes engaged in coalitional politics, on the ground in Baltimore, local AFSCME leaders largely confined themselves to addressing the bread-and-butter concerns of their members and potential members. The union's influence in city hall was increasing during the mid-1960s, but it was hardly secure, with growth and eventually union recognition top priorities. Local AFSCME leaders did not consistently seek common cause with public-service recipients or connect claims for higher wages with demands for improved government services. Instead, they considered their efforts on behalf of low-wage workers a critical component of the larger struggle for racial and economic justice. In 1965, for example, Crofoot denounced the city for paying male custodial workers in the public schools between $2,628 and $3,336 and female custodial workers between $2,052 to $2,628 per year. The Johnson administration had recently declared $3,000 the national poverty level. Full-time municipal employment should at the very least raise workers out of poverty.[21]

Unlike those affiliated with AFSCME, the leadership and members of organizations representing Baltimore's public-school teachers overtly linked their demands for better working conditions with efforts to improve the quality of the services they provided. Despite their lack of official recognition from the city, like other organizations representing municipal employees, the Baltimore Teachers Union (BTU) and the Public School Teachers Association (PSTA) had long advocated on behalf of their members. During the 1960s, they also engaged in activism to improve urban education, and they called for increased local and state spending on public schools. To be sure, teachers had a vested interest in working for a well-resourced school district. Nonetheless, their concerns about the impacts of the city's shrinking tax base and mounting urban problems on the quality of the public education in the city were more than self-serving. Members of the two groups, who were relentlessly at odds with one another over their divergent approaches to labor relations, fought to ensure that young people in Baltimore had access to educational opportunities of the same quality as children elsewhere.[22]

Members of the BTU which was affiliated with the American Federation of Teachers (AFT), and PSTA, which was affiliated with the National Education Association (NEA), pursued different strategies in their efforts to improve local schools. Their divergent tactics—and the rivalry between them—mirrored the tense relationship between their national-level parent organizations. BTU attracted a disproportionately male membership and a large number of high school teachers. The union tended to adopt the confrontational stance of the AFT and advocated for policy changes intended to combat urban poverty and empower and engage African American students. To compensate for funding mechanisms detrimental to children from Baltimore and other relatively poor districts in Maryland, BTU officials demanded that the state legislature use subsidies to equalize spending across jurisdictions. BTU also championed the community schools model that the city ultimately did in part adopt.[23]

The union's concern with African American students and history reflected not only the concerns of both the local membership and AFT, which had a long history of fighting racism and segregation, but also the expertise of Dennis Crosby, who became the president of BTU in the mid-1960s. Crosby, an African American high school teacher, was a member of CORE and had served as the chair of that organization's education committee. Under his leadership, BTU partnered with CORE and ran a Freedom School during the summer of 1966. The staff of the school sponsored discussions on racial justice and taught Black history. AFT previously had sent volunteer teachers to Freedom Schools in Virginia, Mississippi, and elsewhere in the South. In Baltimore, until 1964 a Jim Crow city, BTU members could simply commute from home to address the deficiencies of an education system inadequately concerned with the interests of Black children.[24]

Members of PSTA, a fiercely proud professional organization, also fought to improve the quality of the city's public schools. In 1966, the six-thousand-member-strong organization issued sanctions against the Baltimore school system, promising to lift them "only when it can be assured that adequate financial support for the schools will be forthcoming."[25] The teachers imposed the sanctions through work-to-contract measures; they did nothing beyond the tasks specifically assigned to them in their employment contracts to call attention to the extent to which they had been personally compensating for their underfunded schools. Then, shortly after they announced their sanctions, three thousand members, many of them women and elementary school teachers, rallied at city hall. Their efforts to improve the schools won the endorsement of the Maryland School Teachers Association and the NEA, which added its own sanctions on the city. The organization declared, "The public school system of Baltimore is so extremely deficient that many of the children of the city are being denied the minimum level of educational opportunity to which every child is entitled."[26] Although city officials disputed the claims, they did increase funding for the city schools to have the sanctions withdrawn.[27]

While teachers met with some success in their efforts to improve the quality of the services they delivered and the terms of their employment, the fact that their organizations participated in discussions with the city only at the discretion of elected officials became a point of deepening contention. During the second half of the 1960s, members of municipal unions—and some in associations as well—began to prioritize the fight for union recognition and collective-bargaining rights. Municipal workers took inspiration from the achievement of their counterparts in the federal workforce. Following a decades-long campaign by federal workers' unions for recognition, President John F. Kennedy issued Executive Order 10988 in 1962. The order extended limited collective-bargaining rights to nearly two million federal employees. Workers seized the opportunity, and the membership rolls of previously unrecognized federal unions grew quickly. By 1965, the nation's postal unions had a combined membership of 180,000, and the American Federation of Government Employees (AFGE), among the largest of the federal unions, included 150,000 members.[28]

Kennedy's executive order had immediate ramifications in Baltimore beyond the inspiration it provided to municipal workers. Local 1923 of AFGE became the bargaining agent for workers at Social Security's headquarters. By 1965, more than 8,500 Baltimore-area workers were represented by the local, which Social Security employees believed to be the biggest in the nation representing white-collar workers. Kennedy's executive order also galvanized Baltimore's postal workers, and in 1963, the Post Office Department began negotiating with several postal unions that had prevailed in local contests. Although unions had been unofficially representing federal workers for decades, recognition conferred legitimacy, and the promise of union-negotiated contracts enhanced the security of federal employment. The development was important for all federal workers and particularly for African Americans. In Baltimore, jobs at Social Security had long been a source of coveted employment, particularly among women, and civil rights activists had monitored and fought discrimination at the agency since its founding. Meanwhile the post office was the nation's largest employer of African Americans during much of the 1960s. The increased wages and fringe benefits federal unions won grew and strengthened the Black middle and working classes and were critical to the economic health of Baltimore's African American communities during the era of deindustrialization.[29]

Following the lead of federal workers' unions, in Baltimore, locals of AFSCME and AFT championed collective-bargaining rights for municipal employees. Ultimately, the BTU was the first to crack the city council's resistance to unionization. In December 1966, the BTU formally and forcefully requested that the city schedule an election between itself and the PSTA and agree to negotiate with the winner. The following May, Crosby and his members staged a one-day strike. One hundred thirty people were arrested, a third of them women, and 1,200 out of 7,200 teachers did not report for work. In response to the mounting pressure, the city council agreed to schedule an election, which BTU won. As was the case at Social Security, unionization enhanced the well-being of all workers represented by unions. It also helped make the Department of Education, which employed significant numbers of African Americans, particularly women, an even more important source of economic security than it already had been.[30]

Following the city's decision to grant collective bargaining to teachers, public-sector labor leaders in Maryland took their case to Annapolis and demanded that state legislators grant all government workers union rights. They did not meet with success. The legislators did pass a law requiring all jurisdictions in Maryland to recognize and negotiate with teachers' organizations. They did not, however, extend the protection to other public-sector employees. Despite persistent efforts, union leaders in Maryland were unable to win a place for public-sector collective-bargaining rights in the state's new constitution, which was completed in 1968. Moreover, a "Little Wagner Act" for public employees that would have guaranteed union recognition sat stalled in committee, held hostage by the Baltimore Chamber of Commerce and the Associated Builders and Contractors of Maryland.[31] The failures angered AFSCME officials in particular, who were frustrated that middle-class teachers had won a right that low-wage employees lacked. As Harold Shaw, an AFSCME official, later recalled, "It just [didn't] make sense that the people who needed it most [didn't] have it."[32]

Without state-level protection, AFSCME officials turned their attention to campaigns on the local level. In Baltimore, AFSCME's Clarke and Crofoot championed the fight for collective-bargaining rights. Although the city's new mayor, Thomas D'Alesandro III, endorsed collective bargaining during his 1967 campaign, union leaders faced opposition from the majority of the members of the city council.[33] As AFSCME and other union leaders pressed their case, events to their south soon diverted their attention.

In February 1968, 1,300 sanitation workers in Memphis walked off the job following the deaths of two of their coworkers, who were crushed in the back of a malfunctioning garbage truck. The striking workers, all African American, demanded union recognition, improved workplace safety measures, and an increase in their wages, which were so low for many that they qualified for public assistance. The workers, who had been organized by Thomas Oliver "T. O." Jones, were affiliated with AFSCME. Initially, AFSCME International officials expressed alarm at the sanitation workers' walkout and hoped to convince those striking to return to work; no plans or resources were in place to sustain a strike. Visits by Ciampa and Wurf to Memphis and their encounters with the city's white mayor Henry Loeb, his segregationist supporters, and the workers themselves changed their minds. Loeb and his supporters were arrogantly indifferent to the hardships borne by sanitation workers and evinced what the workers derided as a "plantation mentality"; white elected officials and city residents seemed to assume it natural that African Americans would occupy a submissive and inferior position in society.[34] Outraged by the mayor's insensitivity and hubris, Wurf endorsed the strike and promised the workers the full support of AFSCME International. The strike also had won the support of members of the local African American community, including Reverend James Lawson, who invited his friend Martin Luther King to visit Memphis and meet with the striking workers.[35]

Witnessing the sanitation workers' fierce defense of their dignity and right to a decent standard of living, King found a cause he readily embraced. He had recently begun work organizing a Poor People's Campaign because he wanted to call attention to the persistence of economic injustice in the United States. As he explained to the striking sanitation workers at a rally on their behalf, "Now our struggle is for genuine equality, which means economic equality.... It isn't enough to integrate lunch counters. What does it profit a man to be able to eat at an integrated lunch counter if he doesn't have enough money to buy a hamburger?"[36] King worried that economic injustice—full-time wages that did not lift workers out of poverty, miserly welfare allowances that trapped people in poverty, and the inadequate availability of jobs, for example—imperiled the promise of the United States and squandered the talents of its citizens. In Memphis's striking sanitation workers and their supporters, he identified a community taking a bold and noble stand against the problems that most threatened the nation.

King's support for the strike brought the workers, AFSCME, and the cause of public-sector unionization national attention. It also validated for workers the righteousness of their cause. Tragically, it was during a trip to Memphis on behalf of the sanitation workers in April 1968 that an assassin took King's life. His death sent shock waves across the nation. It also hastened the resolution of the Memphis strike—although not immediately. Even on the evening of King's death, the mayor remained firm in his refusal to grant union recognition. Only pressure from the federal government and a silent march of more than forty thousand people in his city led by Coretta Scott King and other leaders compelled the mayor to reluctantly capitulate. The victory was bittersweet, but the sanitation workers had won.[37]

King's assassination prompted rioting and rebellion in many cities across the nation, and Baltimore was no exception. In that city, two days after King's death, protest, looting, and arson broke out in an African American neighborhood in East Baltimore. Maryland governor Spiro Agnew responded by declaring a state of emergency, establishing a curfew, and calling up the Maryland National Guard. The disorder, which many called riots but which those sympathetic to the latent and articulated political ambitions of the participants called uprisings or rebellions, soon spread to other sections of the city with predominantly Black populations. In response, D'Alesandro requested that President Lyndon Johnson send army troops to the city. Meanwhile, as the former mayor later recalled, many of the city's African American ministers and leaders walked the streets in an effort to quell the violence. The bulk of the disorder persisted for only a few days. Nevertheless, over the course of two weeks, six people died; more than 5,500 were arrested, most for curfew violations; and the city accrued over $12 million in damages.[38]

King's murder prompted organized as well as unorganized protest. Particularly noteworthy was a surge in activism among low-wage private- and public-sector workers, many of whom owed their jobs to the nation's expanding welfare state and the jobs it created. Some of the workers had been seeking union recognition since before King's death. A little over a year following her husband's murder, Coretta Scott King visited Baltimore to help low-wage health care workers win union rights from the Johns Hopkins Hospital. Although one of the top-rated hospitals in the nation, Johns Hopkins was, in the words of Annie Henry, an African American employee at the time, "not a nice place to work." She recalled, "They assumed that because you were doing a menial job that you were an ignorant person, but that was not the case."[39] Buoyed by Coretta King's endorsement, the workers won their campaign in December 1969. They were represented by the Hospital and Nursing Homes Employee Union, Local 1199E, which later merged with the Service Employees International Union, and the union continued to organize low-wage workers during the decades that followed.[40]

Meanwhile, AFSCME leaders had redoubled their efforts on behalf of unionization for municipal employees in Baltimore. King's endorsement of their goal, and his death while in pursuit of it, lent their cause both moral legitimacy and a sense of urgency. Mounting political pressure and the mayor's support for collective bargaining made the city council's endorsement of public-sector union recognition a near inevitability in 1968. What remained to be determined, however, was with which organization or organizations the city would eventually negotiate. D'Alesandro indicated that he would prefer to bargain with a single entity, which intensified already fierce rivalries among the unions and organizations representing municipal workers.[41] Local AFSCME officials had returned from Memphis primed for battle, and many of the city's African American sanitation workers hardly needed encouragement to take a bold and principled stance on their own behalf. What followed in September was a four-day strike for a cause that had largely already been won.[42]

The Baltimore strike, which sanitation workers initiated, quickly attracted the participation of municipal employees in the departments of highways, parks, and sewers. On the first day of the strike about 1,750 city employees joined the sanitation workers, with a larger number participating the following day.[43] Even some CMEA members walked the AFSCME-led picket line.[44] To be sure, Baltimore was not Memphis. The Department of Public Works had long been a source of patronage jobs in the city, and more than 40 percent of Baltimore's sanitation workers were white. An "I AM a Man" placard in the hands of a white man did not have quite the same resonance that it had had when carried by a Memphis sanitation worker. Moreover, the recently appointed director of the Department of Public Works, F. Pierce Linaweaver, was himself African American. Nevertheless, like their counterparts in Memphis, many of Baltimore's low-wage Black male workers who launched the strike did so to protest their exploitation and defend their dignity.

As the strike was under way, about thirty-five Black leaders met to debate the role they should play. Among the groups represented were the NAACP, BUL, CORE, Civic Interest Group, Interdenominational Ministerial Alliance, and U-JOIN. Some in the meeting, including several agency heads and program administrators as well as Roger Brown, the president of the AFSCME-affiliated social workers local that unofficially bargained with state legislators, were public-sector employees themselves. Their dual status as government workers and prominent activists put the leaders in a bind as they risked jeopardizing their jobs by endorsing an illegal strike. As a result, a reporter from the *Afro-American* was the only member of the press allowed to cover the meeting. Ultimately, the group voted unanimously to support the strike, and Walter Lively of U-JOIN became the head of a newly formed Concerned Citizens' Committee.

The striking workers' concerns, Lively explained, were "an issue of survival."[45] In the end, the Concerned Citizen Committee played an instrumental role in bringing the strike to an end. The city agreed to a wage increase that benefited about 1,500 workers, and the strike hastened the city council's decision to grant municipal employees collective-bargaining privileges. Ten days after the strike's resolution, the council approved union elections, and D'Alesandro signed legislation granting union recognition on September 30, 1968. And given the rivalries among groups claiming to represent municipal workers, the city agreed to bargain with multiple organizations instead of a single union.[46]

Although they had participated in BTU's earlier strike, had been active in AFSCME's local organizing drives, and had a history of protesting the terms of their municipal employment, women did not participate in the 1968 work stoppage. Perhaps in light of Memphis, they viewed it the sanitation workers' hour. Like men, however, women certainly benefited from the strike's resolution. In the union elections that followed, workers from multiple departments, including public works and education, chose to be represented by AFSCME, as did employees in the city's jail and hospitals. After the votes were counted, AFSCME's membership total reached ten thousand. CMEA, which abandoned its no-strike clause and officially became a union during the strike, won uncontested elections among classified workers. Teachers' aides voted to join the BTU. Two firefighters' unions and a professional nursing organization also became official bargaining agents for city workers, and an AFSCME-affiliated union represented police officers.[47]

Collective-bargaining rights did not result in dramatic changes in city workers' wages, benefits, and working conditions. After all, public-sector unions and organizations informally had been winning improvements for decades. Union recognition did, however, gain city workers the right to be represented in future deliberations critical to their economic well-being. The workers "who needed it most" had secured protections recently won by federal employees and teachers. The change bolstered the status of all union members but was particularly important for African Americans. As the industrial sector of their city continued to decline, a significant contingent of Black workers had gained for themselves a relatively safe haven in the local labor market. Discrimination certainly persisted, yet unionized government jobs enabled a growing number of Black families to experience upward mobility, buy houses, and send children to college. And at the same time, Baltimore's municipal workers helped make AFSCME one of the fastest-growing and most vibrant unions in the nation.

Together the private- and public-sector labor activism in Baltimore during the late 1960s represented a turning point in the history of the American labor movement. Although accelerating deindustrialization did not bode well for the fate of the predominantly white and male members of industrial unions, upon whose fortunes the labor movement had long rested, new energy and enthusiasm for collective action on the part of workers of color and white women in the low-wage private and public service sectors served as a force for potential rejuvenation.[48] And from their relatively advantaged position in the public sector, government workers were taking the lead. Although historian Jefferson Cowie describes the 1970s as "the last days of the working class," during that decade in Baltimore, working-class private- and public-sector service employees, many of them African American and women, were just getting started.[49]

"Civic Chaos" and "Permissiveness": The Backlash Against Changes in the Public Sector

The expansion and unionization of the municipal workforce did not uniformly strike Baltimore city residents and the citizens of Maryland as improvements. Alternatively, some associated government growth and collective bargaining with rising taxes that were used to cover the cost of bloated bureaucracies rather than with needed services and jobs. Simultaneously, some viewed the riots and rebellion that occurred in Baltimore and other cities during the 1960s as evidence that the War on Poverty was not only failing but also engendering a culture of entitlement and lawlessness among poor African Americans. Fear of rising urban crime rates exacerbated the notion that cities and their Black residents were becoming ungovernable and falling sway to the influence of radical Black nationalists. Meanwhile, public-sector unionization also raised the specter for some observers of outsider influence over local affairs. To those harboring such suspicions, the sanitation workers' strike appeared little more than a sequel to the disorder that had followed King's assassination. Certainly taxpayers had legitimate grounds for monitoring public spending and objecting to waste or abuse. Yet like conservative city council members, many critics of the recent changes seemed to automatically assume that government unions and social programs that served and were staffed by large numbers of African Americans were inefficient and corrupt. The suspicions exacerbated an ongoing backlash among whites to civil rights victories. Fearful that the government was rescinding its commitment to them while giving African Americans special privileges, angry whites aimed their ire at an expanding pool of targets during the late 1960s.[50] Not just rioters but also strikers, Black antipoverty workers, and low-income service recipients became suspect. Agnew became a spokesperson for conservative white anger. In fact, Agnew rose to national prominence due to his willingness to aggressively condemn African American protest in Baltimore.

The uprising that followed King's assassination and then the sanitation workers' strike occurred at a time when many in Baltimore and Maryland at large already were harboring deep concerns about growing urban crime rates. The fear had at least three sources. Some was the result of manipulation. During the 1950s, southern whites alarmed by civil rights advances deliberately stoked the racist notion that African Americans were somehow innately prone to criminality. They sought anticrime legislation in an effort to undermine the civil rights movement.[51] Racist rhetoric about crime was reinforced in Baltimore by a procedural change carried out by the police department. In keeping with national trends, the department instituted protocols that required officers to report all crimes they encountered and rescinded their authority to exercise reporting discretion. As a result, the policy change artificially increased crime rates. At the same time, however, evidence does suggest that the rates of some crimes were indeed rising in U.S. cities.[52] Racist hype, the procedural change, and actual increases in criminal activity all contributed to mounting anxieties that the nation's cities were crime-ridden.

In Baltimore, African Americans and whites as well as liberals and conservatives shared alarm over the crime problem, yet the solutions they proposed often differed. Many of the city's liberal leaders largely concurred with the authors of the Kerner Report, which Lyndon Johnson commissioned to determine the causes of the urban "riots" of the mid-1960s. The authors associated crime with unmet expectations and a lack of economic opportunity. Convinced of the same logic, African Americans who were engaged in Baltimore's War on Poverty tended to propose community involvement in policing and social programs to combat crime. Alternatively, conservatives, including members of the Baltimore City Council, tended to advocate harsher criminal justice policies, such as stiffer sentencing to fight crime. They also blamed individuals rather than context for criminal behavior.[53]

The policy debates in Baltimore mirrored those under way on the federal level. Johnson, under pressure from his advisers that he "start acting less like a social worker and more like a cop" in the wake of the growing concerns, began making increasingly bolder calls for anticrime legislation during the second half of the 1960s.[54] In 1967, he proposed anticrime legislation. The measure called for federal grants for training programs for local officers, gun control, prisoner rehabilitation, and other initiatives. As the bill made its way through Congress, however, Republicans and southern Democrats led by Representatives Everett Dirksen and Gerald Ford, dramatically transformed it. In the end, the law that Johnson signed was far more punitive than the original bill had been. The new legislation extended the reach of the federal government over crime control far into local and state law enforcement agencies. And as historian Elizabeth Hinton argues, even before Johnson left office, his War on Poverty was giving way to a War on Crime.[55]

Fear of rising crime rates led some in Baltimore not only to demand tougher crime policies but also to complain that their hard-earned tax dollars were being squandered on antipoverty programs that did not seem to work. Despite the city's success at winning federal aid, during the 1960s, the city's tax rates were well above those in surrounding suburbs. Baltimore was its own jurisdiction rather than part of a larger county. It was also home to a considerable number of residents with low income. The city's population of taxpayers had to help cover the cost of the maintenance of the city's infrastructure, regular budget items, and the municipal government's contribution to antipoverty efforts. Rising tax rates accelerated white flight, and many of those who left were homeowners. To those homeowners who remained fell the increasingly weighty burden of paying for costly public services and the growing municipal payroll.[56] Critics voiced their frustration by complaining of freeloaders. As Harry How Jr. wrote to Mayor McKeldin in 1967, "I am against any of my tax money being used for someone who doesn't want to work. How long do you think the people of Baltimore City are going to put up with your give away programs of Anti-Poverty, welfare and unemployment."[57]

The increasing size of the municipal workforce also attracted conservative ire. In 1966, the Commission on Governmental Efficiency and Economy, a conservative business organization with a long history in the city, complained that Baltimore had the largest number of municipal employees among cities of its size in the nation. The following year, the *News-American*, a major Baltimore newspaper with a large white, working-class readership, reported sarcastically that the city was losing three thousand residents but adding a thousand municipal workers annually. The paper estimated that one out of eleven city residents worked for the city. "But once the employee is hired, no checks are made to see if that employee is writing love letters all day or performing his job efficiently," the reporter complained.[58] Many city residents had long harbored suspicion of welfare recipients, and the hostility only grew as Black and white DPW workers added previously neglected low-income African Americans to the rolls. In addition, as the ranks of the public sector swelled, and as African Americans filled many of the new positions—particularly in human-services agencies—the suspicions of conservative whites began to grow to include public-service providers.

The man who rose to represent the mounting white backlash in Maryland was Governor Spiro Agnew. Ironically, Agnew, a Baltimore native, had won the governorship in 1966 in large measure because his Democratic opponent was a segregationist. George Mahoney, a Baltimore contractor and frequent political candidate, ran on the slogan "Your home is your castle—protect it," a declaration intended to communicate his opposition to open housing and other civil rights measures.[59] His primary victory in a three-way contest led some Democrats, including African Americans, to cross party lines on Election Day. At the time, many considered Agnew a fairly moderate Republican. Moderation was not evident, however, in his reactions two years later to the uprising in Baltimore that followed King's assassination. He blamed the disorder on "riot-inciting, burn-down-America" Black militants and a culture of entitlement and permissiveness.[60] Contributing to the discourse that linked African Americans with cultural deviance and criminality, Agnew asserted that riots were "caused in too many cases by evil men and not evil conditions."[61]

Days later, as the nation was still reeling from the shock of King's death, Agnew pushed the envelope further. At a public meeting to which many of the city's self-described "moderate" Black leaders had been invited, and at which they expected to be updated on plans for the aftermath of the disorder, Agnew lashed out again—directly at the African American attendees, a group that included stalwarts of the Baltimore civil rights movement, such as Lillie May Jackson and her daughter Juanita Mitchell.[62] Their fear of being "stung by insinuations that [they] were Mr. Charlie's boy, by epitaphs like 'Uncle Tom'" had prevented them from preventing the riots, Agnew angrily charged.[63] Stunned by a diatribe that then turned to lampooning "militant" activists, most of the African Americans walked out. "He's got to be out of his mind," commented Brailey to a reporter as he exited.[64] "Agnew Insults Leaders" read the front-page headline of the *Afro-American* following the exchange.[65] The paper's editorial board expressed outrage and accused the governor of acting "out of blind anger or sheer stupidity. . . . We reject out of hand any talking down to us, paternalism, condescension, or scolding whether it flows from the lips of kings or beggars," the editors pronounced.[66]

Having been trounced by Maryland's Black leaders as well as some liberal whites, Agnew kept a low profile on matters pertaining to Baltimore following the meeting. The sanitation workers' strike, however, reignited his ire. Although he kept his distance from Baltimore, he nonetheless seized the moment of the strike to reiterate the law-and-order rhetoric for which he was gaining notoriety. AFSCME's illegal strike was "another indication of the breakdown of duly constituted authority in our society," the governor declared.[67] Whereas King had identified in the Memphis sanitation workers' strike a community taking a bold stance on behalf of the dignity of labor, Agnew saw in Baltimore's predominantly Black strikers criminality and an instinct to incite to mayhem. And he was hardly alone. The *News-American* responded to the strike by proclaiming, "Baltimore today is experiencing the civic chaos which goes hand in hand with one form of the permissiveness which engulfs our modern society."[68] The interchangeable rhetoric Agnew and others used to describe the disorder and the strike reflects the extent to which Black protest was being simultaneously criminalized and trivialized.

Emboldened by the changing political tides to which Agnew gave voice, the conservative members of the city council began to push back against federal antipoverty agencies in the city and the influential activists within them. In June 1968, Parren Mitchell announced his resignation from the top post of the CAA. Although he cited "strangling bureaucracy" as a major source of his decision, it also soon became clear that he intended to pursue elected office as the means to securing the progressive changes he sought.[69] On the recommendation of the members of the CAC, D'Alesandro nominated Walter Carter, the former CORE president who was directing the Model City's community-organizing efforts, to replace Mitchell. The nomination had tremendous support in low-income neighborhoods and among African Americans, and many liberal whites endorsed it as well. Conservative council members did not share the enthusiasm.[70] Some were concerned that the mayor was conceding too much power to African Americans. As Councilmember William J. Meyers asserted, "[The mayor] has to look at two different sides, our side and the other, and it's about time he started appointing some of our people to some of these jobs. I mean white people."[71] The council rejected the Carter nomination by a vote of ten to eight.[72]

Outraged by the decision, Carter's supporters inundated the mayor and council members with protest letters. Twelve members of the CAC, most of them community residents, resigned in anger.[73] Mitchell described the rejection as "part of the sequence of what I see happening in Baltimore, throughout the State and across the country. The backlash conservative group is determined there will be no further advances for the Black community.... The gauntlet has really been thrown now."[74] Brailey concurred. They "want a yes-man," he protested.[75] Mary Sollars, a prominent African American antipoverty activist and member of the CAC, agreed as well. She described the vote as a deliberate effort to undermine the city's War on Poverty.[76] For his part, and not one to mince words, Carter compared the council members to those who joined white citizens' councils in the South to defend Jim Crow after the Supreme Court declared school segregation unconstitutional.[77]

D'Alesandro, whose family had considerable power in the city's Democratic Party, made repeated efforts to convince the council to reverse its decision—to no avail.[78] The conservative members of the body had had enough of community organizing and demands from "militants," and they retained the power to put on the brakes. Certainly the rejection of Carter for the top post at the CAA did not bring the War on Poverty in Baltimore to an end. Carter and the staff of the Model Cities program redoubled their community-organizing efforts, and that agency replaced the CAA as the heart of the city's activist antipoverty efforts. Meanwhile, support for community participation remained firm in many municipal departments, and residents with low incomes were hardly willing to relinquish the influence they only recently had won. In addition, Baltimore was home to a growing population of white liberals who made their mark on city politics by supporting like-minded city council candidates and helping to elect D'Alesandro in 1967.[79] Nevertheless, Mitchell was right; the gauntlet had indeed been thrown.

The goings-on in Baltimore—and particularly the actions of Agnew—did not escape the notice of Richard Nixon, who was running for president on the Republican ticket in 1968. Convinced that Agnew's law-and-order rhetoric and willingness to talk tough to civil rights leaders would be attractive to many of the voters the candidate was already courting, Nixon invited the Maryland governor to join his campaign and run for vice president. Agnew's ascension to national politics was a sign of trouble to come for Baltimore's Black population. Civil rights leaders' decades-long effort to open the municipal workforce to African Americans had paid dividends during the 1960s. President Johnson's Great Society programs expanded the public sector, and African Americans, particularly Black women, secured many of the new jobs. Grants from the federal government earmarked for antipoverty efforts afforded Black municipal employees a degree of independence from the city's predominantly white elected leaders and enabled them to pursue an antipoverty agenda that differed considerably from the trickle-down commercial revitalization efforts usually championed by business leaders and city officials. Black leaders, activists, and city workers, meanwhile, seized the opportunities maximum-feasible community participation mandates opened and attempted to politicize city residents with low incomes. Their goal was to redistribute power and resources in the city. Although confined largely to antipoverty and human services agencies, African Americans nevertheless gained more influence over municipal affairs than they had ever had. They also worked hard to increase and improve service delivery, efforts that often eased the gendered caretaking responsibility of women, especially those with low incomes. Simultaneously, successful unionization campaigns enhanced the security of government employment, raised wages, and increased benefits. In a city hemorrhaging manufacturing jobs, unionized public-sector positions were a shelter in the storm. But many of the changes that African Americans recently had achieved were contingent on a stream of federal grants to cities to fight poverty. As a result, the stakes in the 1968 election were quite serious. Odds were not high that a Nixon-Agnew administration would continue the flow of federal aid to African American–controlled government agencies in Baltimore.

CHAPTER 5

"A Posture of Advocacy for the Poor"

Fighting Poverty in an Era of Austerity

Even in the face of waning local and national support for the War on Poverty, activist employees in Baltimore's antipoverty agencies and human-services departments attempted to sustain the passion for change that had exploded in the city in the 1960s. Employees of the Department of Public Welfare played leading roles. Some welfare workers, aware that their clients often saw them as representatives of an antagonistic state and that many elected officials both expected and wanted them to play that role, defiantly dubbed themselves "client advocates."[1] And they took the role very seriously. Client advocates complained publicly of welfare regulations that impeded them from effectively serving low-income residents and expressed outrage that the state provided inadequate resources to combat need. As a result, it sometimes became necessary to "bend the rules," in the words of one advocate. Maryland lacked funding to help residents pay for utility bills, she offered as an example. But the state did have an emergency furniture allotment. "We'll just say to the client: 'Don't you need a chest of drawers?'" she commented to explain how she and her coworkers got families the cash they needed to keep their lights on.[2] And when rule-bending proved inadequate, DPW workers were known to propose more dramatic interventions. As one welfare recipient recalled, "Sometimes caseworkers will tell us about harsh or unfair state regulations they can't do much about and suggest that we try to do something, like organize a protest to the state."[3] Client advocates participated in protests as well. "Often they join militant Welfare Rights Organization demonstrators on a picket line," a local journalist reported about DPW workers.[4] And their union, a local of AFSCME that included more than five hundred caseworkers, paraprofessionals, and clerical workers, also sometimes joined welfare rights protests. In 1972, for example, led by their African American union president Carolyn Murray, DPW workers rallied in solidarity with their clients on behalf of welfare reform.[5] Although the tide of public opinion was turning on an aggressive war against poverty, activist municipal employees were not ready to give up.

Many conservative Maryland voters and elected officials did not appreciate client advocates' rule-bending and activism. Instead, they considered DPW workers troublemakers—and conservatives were not the only critics. As the *Baltimore Sun* reported, welfare workers were frequently "criticized for irresponsibility with tax-payers money, for being overly-solicitous of their clients, for either helping clients to 'cheat,' in [Lieutenant Governor Blair] Lee's words, or more mildly in [Governor Marvin] Mandel's words, for being 'uncooperative.'" They performed their jobs with "a missionary zeal— just adding people to the rolls," the lieutenant governor complained.[6] And he and the governor were Democrats. Activist city workers remained impassioned, but they were running short on allies. Meanwhile, Democrats were creating dangerous divisions within their party by selling out government workers and their clients.

DPW workers were not unique among municipal employees during the late 1960s and early 1970s in being determined to maintain the activist spirit that had motivated many public service providers during the height of the War on Poverty. Their efforts to promote democratic decision-making and accessible and accountable neighborhood-level service delivery reflected the conviction that the opinions of low-income city residents merited respect and that the hardships service recipients endured were legitimate and required significant government intervention. The sentiments were not as widely shared as they once were. Alternatively, growing numbers of Americans, particularly white Americans, both in Maryland and nationally increasingly regarded low-income urban residents, particularly African Americans, with mistrust. And candidate and then president Richard Nixon and his running mate Spiro Agnew stoked the hostility in an effort to win new Republican voters. Mounting racial resentment and Nixon's legitimation of it on the campaign trail and again while in office contributed to imperiling federally funded antipoverty programs and the well-being of those who depended on them.

Meanwhile, significant policy changes that President Nixon made in the realm of global macroeconomics undermined activist workers' efforts to win resources to combat poverty. In an effort to preserve American global hegemony, Nixon abandoned the multilateral agreements that had governed the global economy since the end of World War II and that had reflected mid-century liberal economic orthodoxy. He adopted instead policies that paved the way for the neoliberal global world order that characterized the late twentieth century. But the policies the president pursued did not bode well for rust-belt cities and their residents. The policies contributed to eroding the cities' competitiveness in global contests for credit and investment, all but foreclosing the already unlikely possibility of industrial recoveries that would restore needed jobs and tax revenue. Moreover, the policies increased already intense pressure on locally elected officials to practice cost-cutting in order to make ends meet and to attract new investment. In Baltimore, such austerity pressures were among the factors that led elected officials to closely monitor and attempt to improve the city's credit ratings and to offer tax incentives to lure new businesses to the city, regardless of the tolls the practices took on municipal jobs and services. By offering the tax relief, however, Baltimore made rivals of other struggling cities, whose elected officials would have to attempt to best the incentives offered elsewhere, setting off a race to the bottom that would come at the cost of needed tax revenue. The combination of fiscal strains facing elected officials had dire implications for the agendas of client advocates, other activist municipal employees, and their unions.

"I See What They're up Against": Defending the War on Poverty

During the late 1960s and early 1970s, activist municipal employees in antipoverty and human-services agencies endeavored to keep city officials committed to fighting the War on Poverty. Efforts to revitalize the city via trickle-down commercial redevelopment strategies had certainly persisted through the 1960s, but the availability of federal antipoverty grants had enabled the workers, abetted and pushed by activist groups, to compel the city to also invest in bottom-up solutions to the city's problem. Decreasing federal interest made the task more difficult. During the early 1970s, the number of Black city residents surpassed the number of whites. African Americans remained grossly underrepresented in elected office throughout the decade, however, so municipal jobs, particularly high-ranking positions, and positions on oversight boards and commissions remained a critical source of Black influence in local decision-making. To be sure, disillusionment with the federal government's lackluster dedication to antipoverty and urban programs was widespread, bitter, and growing. And frustration mounted as the Vietnam

War slogged on and continued to steal lives and sap resources that city workers believed they could put to much better use. "It's like paying for the [war] out of the hide of a 16-year old neighborhood kid," complained Marion Pines, who ran Baltimore's Office of Manpower Resources.[7] Meanwhile, Parren Mitchell's departure from the Community Action Agency and Walter Carter's decision to leave the Model Cities program a year later cost the city's federally supported antipoverty efforts dynamic leadership. Nevertheless, many workers, such as the client advocates at DPW, and elected representatives on municipal oversight bodies did what they could from within the state to make sure low-income residents were included in policy-making and to safeguard and even improve the social safety net.

Following the 1968 decision by conservative members of the Baltimore City Council to prevent Carter from assuming the directorship of the CAA, many of that agency's employees along with others committed to aggressively combating poverty sought positions in the Model Cities program, which became the new heart of the city's War on Poverty.[8] In 1969, William Sykes became the director of Model Cities. Born in Virginia in 1926, Sykes was an African American social worker with experience garnered in multiple public agencies, including the Baltimore Departments of Education and of Health. A principled yet pragmatic leader, he skillfully shepherded the staff, steering board members and city officials through the posturing and power-seeking phase of program planning into actual policy implementation. Model Cities adopted the neighborhood-based service-delivery model of the CAA and developed a network of community-run neighborhood councils that served as centers of both advocacy and policy innovation. Model Cities staff also helped low-income city residents win representation on the boards of government agencies and local institutions. Meanwhile, the Model Cities Policy Steering Board and the Community Action Commission remained the only two oversight bodies in the city that included a significant number of African Americans, women, and residents with low incomes.[9]

Many workers in municipal human-services departments also remained committed to an aggressive War on Poverty. During the mid-1960s, the Department of Health had not garnered a reputation for activism. In fact, as a mayoral adviser noted, the department's leadership was often criticized in comparison to leadership in other city departments for "not being radically innovative." Its administration and staff were good, however, at "aggressively pursuing the federal dollar," the observer noted.[10] Thus, despite the lack of fire at the top of the department, during the late 1960s and early 1970s, health officials oversaw considerable new programming. And the city's interracial team of community health nurses and aides joined the staffs of antipoverty agencies as an additional army of largely female workers committed to improving and expanding the government's provision of welfare services.

Health care providers introduced new services and programming, some of which were aimed at women and children. Health department staff helped create well-baby services and family-planning programming. In addition, they staffed tuberculosis and venereal disease clinics, made home visits to the elderly and disabled, advocated for lead-poisoning prevention remedies, and worked in the schools. Many public-health employees staunchly defended community-based service provision. As African American nurse Leola Washington noted about working in neighborhoods, "That's why I like what I do. As a nurse, I deal with the complete person. . . . Besides their medical problems, I see what they're up against as people too."[11]

Meanwhile, activist leadership at Baltimore's DPW reinforced the assertiveness of the staff. In 1969, Maurice Harmon replaced Esther Lazarus as the department's director. A white social worker, Harmon was a staunch proponent of a generous welfare state. He also expressed frustration with conservatives' critiques of welfare programs and concerns with cheating, which he believed distracted attention from the magnitude and gravity of need in the nation. "The issue," he argued, "should be how to redistribute the wealth of this country."[12] From that perspective, Baltimore's growing pool of Aid to Families with Dependent Children recipients served as evidence of his department's success; DPW workers were getting the job done, and low-income residents were receiving at least some of the support they needed. At the same time, Harmon embraced the community-based service model, and he championed the decentralization of his agency, which was renamed the Department of Social Services. Instead of requiring welfare recipients to report to a large, impersonal, and inconveniently located government building, Harmon wanted to shift the power dynamics between service providers and recipients and base his workers in neighborhoods. Among other benefits, such a method of organization "place[d] staff people in a posture of advocacy for the poor," Harmon explained.[13] Once the plan was realized, at least some on his staff felt it worked. "When you consistently walk through the same neighborhoods, when you buy at the same stores they do and see the same children on the street, you begin to experience some of their frustrations," explained social services employee Mary Stevenson.[14]

Efforts to include poor people in decision-making and policy implementation and to move government offices and service delivery into low-income neighborhoods evinced a faith on the part of employees in antipoverty and human-services agencies that poor people's opinions and time were important and that the state should be responsive and accommodating. Certainly, residents with low incomes continued to receive and to complain of poor and disrespectful treatment by city workers. Not all municipal employees shared the passion and commitment to social and economic justice of Harmon and his department's client advocates. And certainly activists with low incomes, civil rights activists, and other progressive leaders continued to battle city hall independently and with the conviction that city workers were part of the problem.[15] Nevertheless, within the municipal government, activist workers had become the city's conscience. Administrators in antipoverty and human-services agencies often proved willing to speak up for some of the concerns of African Americans and residents with low incomes when city officials deliberated over the municipal agenda and policy-making. The need for their voices only grew stronger after Nixon and Agnew won the White House and began rescinding the federal government's commitment to the War on Poverty. The reliance of their agencies on federal funding made the services the workers delivered—and the jobs they depended on—vulnerable to the shifting mood of the national electorate.

"Why, Oh, Why Are the Loud and Violent Given All the Privileges?" American Political Realignment

During the late 1960s, the United States entered a period of significant political realignment. In the wake of the Great Depression, many Americans had accepted as necessary and beneficial a more expansive regulatory role for the federal government than had previously existed. Diverse groups of voters that included blue-collar workers, white southerners, African Americans, and members of other minority ethnic and religious groups served as the electoral power behind the changes. Historians dub the group the New Deal coalition. During the decades that followed, those seeking to expand the regulatory powers of the state wrangled repeatedly with those hoping to shrink them. Both sides scored noteworthy victories. Nevertheless, the size of the federal government and the scope of its involvement in American life continued to grow under both Democratic and Republican administrations.

Republican Richard Nixon's elections in 1968 and 1972 signaled the beginning of the splintering of the New Deal coalition. Staunch advocates of laissez-faire capitalism had been working for decades to discredit New Deal liberalism and promote their own agenda. They were joined during the 1950s and 1960s by constituencies who shared their hatred of communism and concern with government growth, some of whom hailed from the small but growing religious right. Nixon, however, owed the bulk of his electoral support less to the stridently conservative groups than to those in what he called the "silent majority," predominantly white Americans still largely content with the federal government's regulatory role but increasingly hostile to liberal antipoverty efforts and civil rights and other protest movements.[16] They were voters such as those in Maryland who cheered Governor Agnew's decision to berate civil rights activists and deride the Baltimore sanitation workers' strike in 1968. They were those who wondered along with one frustrated Baltimore resident, "Why, oh, why are the loud and violent given all of the privileges and the law-abiding citizens deprived of what is rightfully his?"[17]

On the campaign trail, Nixon and Agnew had assiduously courted Democratic voters who they correctly perceived to be alienated from their party and its leaders. The candidates targeted white working- and middle-class Americans, southerners and nonsoutherners alike. A broad range of issues angered these voters. They were frustrated by the Democrats' inability to effectively execute the war in Vietnam and by antiwar protesters whom they viewed as unpatriotic—even as they harbored their own doubts about the war's wisdom and viability. Rising inflation and a slowing in the growth of real wages during the mid-1960s also contributed to voters' dissatisfaction with Democratic leadership as did resentment against taxes. Additionally, many who pulled the lever for Nixon in 1968 and 1972 were concerned with the state of race relations in the United States.[18] In 1969, according to a national opinion poll, 81 percent of respondents agreed that the United States was suffering from a breakdown in law and order, and the majority of them blamed "Negroes who start riots."[19]

Nixon and his surrogates conveyed sympathy with the concerns of disaffected white Democrats, including their racial resentment. They typically did so, however, not in the overtly racist style of segregationists nor by adopting the crass approach Agnew took with Baltimore's Black leaders following the death of Martin Luther King. Instead they communicated between the lines. Nixon described himself as a supporter of civil rights. He also made clear that as president he would be the arbiter of the pace of race-related changes and that he intended to slow things down. As he stated in 1968 when accepting his party's nomination for the presidency, at an event usually known for bold campaign pledges, "Tonight I do not promise the millennium. I don't promise that we can eradicate poverty and end discrimination in the space of four or even eight years." Instead, distinguishing himself from Democratic president Lyndon Johnson, the candidate vaguely promised "action."[20]

Nixon also knew how to intimate to more reactionary potential voters that he might share their bigotry. During an interview on the national news program *Face the Nation* shortly before the election, Nixon sanitized the exchange that had occurred between Agnew and Baltimore's Black leaders. The Maryland governor had "stood up at the time that his city, Baltimore, was being burned and said, 'Look, we're going to rebuild our cities but we don't have to burn them down in order to rebuild them,'" Nixon disingenuously reported about an infamous diatribe that had actually involved yelling and name-calling. Agnew's supposedly measured response had been "criticized by some of the all-out civil rights people," Nixon continued, suggesting that it was Black leaders rather than the governor who were intemperate. But, the candidate continued, "I agree with him on that statement. I think we need that kind of strength and that kind of firmness."[21] Although he did not literally wink and nod, Nixon, who surely knew what had really happened in Baltimore, endorsed Agnew's aggressive, get-tough stance with civil rights leaders.

On the campaign trail, Nixon and Agnew also used language that invoked but did not specifically mention race and that was intended to reinforce white racial resentment and foment division within the Democratic Party. To woo working-class whites in particular, Nixon described them in language borrowed from Franklin Roosevelt. As they had been during the early years of the Great Depression, they were once again the "forgotten Americans." This time, however, Nixon suggested, it was the Democratic Party that had left them behind—because they were "the non-shouters, the non-demonstrators."[22] Concerned more with special interest groups such as African Americans, the Democrats had abandoned their base, Nixon suggested.

But Nixon and Agnew did not identify members of the silent majority only as nonprotesters; they also described them economically. The voters who they courted were "taxpayers," "hard-working," and "homeowners," an assertion that perniciously implied that protesters, including African Americans with jobs such as government workers, were not. In their effort to chip away at the New Deal coalition, Nixon and Agnew erased from the political conversation Black working people, some of whom were protesting simply to secure the protections the New Deal had extended to many white forgotten Americans a few decades earlier. Meanwhile, Nixon and Agnew's frequent calls for "law and order" were references to anti–Vietnam War demonstrators and often intended to invoke the specter of urban crime and African American protest. The use of coded appeals to racial prejudices became known as "dog-whistle politics," and Nixon employed such rhetoric to great effect.[23] To be sure, many backlash voters, as the media and political scientists dubbed those who cast ballots motivated at least in part by white identity politics, had harbored racial hostilities well before the 1960s.[24] But Nixon perfected a formula for stealthily invoking and stoking prejudices recently made impolitic by the successes of the civil rights movement. And Agnew certainly pulled his own weight, at times less delicately. Both helped to convince many white American voters that despite the tremendous political and economic power they commanded both domestically and internationally, they were the victims of the reforms enacted during the 1960s to redress centuries of exploitation and oppression. At the same time, they communicated that Black protest, be it in the service of civil, welfare, or unions rights, was illegitimate.

Ultimately, Nixon's electoral success in 1968 and 1972 reflected his ability—and the failure of successive Democratic candidates—to demonstrate convincing concern for the multiple problems facing many working- and middle-class white American voters. It also, however, represented his effectiveness at conveying his agreement with reactionary hostilities. And through his use of dog-whistle politics, Nixon legitimized and popularized views about low-income urban African Americans that differed entirely from those that activist city workers in Baltimore communicated through their advocacy of community participation, neighborhood-based service delivery, and wealth redistribution. With Nixon's views in ascendance, the sustainability of Baltimore's largely federally funded antipoverty efforts grew increasingly uncertain. The context made the stakes in Baltimore's 1971 mayoral election very high. To the next mayor would fall the delicate job of determining how to allocate limited local resources to three important yet competing tasks: fighting poverty, combating depopulation, and attracting new businesses, corporate taxpayers, and jobs to the city. The workers needed someone who shared their goals and appreciated the urgency of their efforts.

"Father-Knows-Best" Governance: The Election of William Donald Schaefer

The 1971 mayoral election in Baltimore generated considerable excitement. Activist city workers were not the only constituency with a lot at stake. Many Black city residents were determined to follow in the footsteps of residents of Newark, New Jersey; Cleveland, Ohio; and Gary, Indiana, and elect an African American mayor. The goal became plausible when the city's sitting mayor, Thomas D'Alesandro III, announced he would not seek reelection or endorse a successor. His decision raised hopes among African Americans, who made up almost half of the city's population, although less than 40 percent of registered voters. As had typically been the case in Baltimore, the Democratic primary would determine the outcome of the race. George L. Russell, a former judge appointed city solicitor by D'Alesandro, was the first to announce his candidacy. As city solicitor, Russell held the highest post in the city government ever occupied by an African American. He entered the race with considerable support from both influential African Americans and whites and made unity the theme of his campaign.[25]

Eventually William Donald Schaefer, the white sitting president of the city council, and Clarence Mitchell III also became serious contenders. Schaefer had sixteen years of political experience in city office and enjoyed strong ties with behind-the-scenes politicos. Mitchell was serving his second term in the State Senate. His considerable name recognition was the product of his family's prominent history—his mother, Juanita Mitchell, and grandmother Lillie May Jackson, had run the city and state chapters of the NAACP for thirty-five years; his father, Clarence Mitchell, was the national NAACP's chief lobbyist in Washington, DC; and his uncle Parren Mitchell, had served as the director of the CAA before becoming the state's first Black representative in the U.S. Congress. Candidate Mitchell had also established his own reputation as a leader in the city as the result of his participation in sit-ins during the 1960s.[26]

Despite his imprimatur, many in the city's Black establishment considered Mitchell the spoiler. They may have been right. Mitchell lacked Russell's experience, credentials, and connections, and his entry into the campaign eroded the chances of the more seasoned Black contender. On the campaign trail, Russell and Mitchell spent considerable time attacking each other, which undermined Russell's unity theme. Meanwhile, Schaefer largely stayed out of the fray and rallied white and some African American supporters. Prior to the election, the *Afro-American* endorsed Russell and pled with readers to make a strong showing at the polls. The effort was to little avail. Black turnout was lower than it could have been, and Schaefer soundly defeated his opponents; even Russell's and Mitchell's combined vote totals failed to equal the support Schaefer amassed. Russell was the undisputed winner of the Black vote, but that was not enough. Importantly, five Black candidates did win city council seats. They were significantly outnumbered by the thirteen whites who won the remaining positions.[27] Schaefer's victory and the persistent underrepresentation of African Americans on the council meant that Black workers' influence within, and especially at the helm of, city agencies remained a critical source of Black political power in the city.

Although the white vote won Schaefer the election, he was certainly no race-baiter along the lines of Nixon and Agnew. During his political career, Schaefer was publicly critical of Black nationalists, and he had stayed on the fringes during the city's many civil rights battles, which doubtlessly appealed to many white city voters. But Schaefer also attracted African American supporters. In fact, he won more Black votes than did Mitchell.[28] Schaefer was a staunch advocate of neighborhood associations, which attracted African Americans and whites alike. Moreover, like the two Black candidates, Schaefer was a Baltimore native. When he was seven years old, his parents had moved to a row house in a west-side neighborhood called the Hill. With the exception of the years he spent in the military during World War II, he had continued to reside in his childhood home. As an adult, he shared quarters with his mother Tululu, living with her until her death in 1983. The demography of the Hill changed during the years the Schaefers lived there. By the 1970s, what had once been an exclusively white neighborhood had become home to large numbers of African Americans. Schaefer's decision to remain in the Hill as most of its white residents left no doubt won him a measure of credibility among some African Americans.[29]

As a council member, Schaefer had also compiled a decent voting record on issues of concern to Black communities. His record had won him the endorsement of both Juanita and Clarence Mitchell in 1967 when Schaefer had run for city council president, a position filled by a citywide election. Thus the modest support he received from African Americans during the 1971 election was not entirely surprising. And the new mayor's popularity among Black voters increased with time. He garnered between 70 percent and 80 percent of African Americans' votes during the three subsequent mayoral elections—winning even when challenged by a Black contender. He certainly had numerous run-ins with the city's African American leaders. Yet Black support would also help Schaefer win Maryland's gubernatorial race in 1987, a victory that finally forced him to vacate his home in the Hill and move to Annapolis.[30]

As mayor, Schaefer became the greatest booster the city had ever known. He was also an assiduous micromanager. He was known to prowl Baltimore's neighborhoods in his Pontiac, seeking out broken streetlights and abandoned cars. The next work day, department heads could expect a to-do list on their desks and a follow-up call a few days later to make sure the problems had been solved. Although unequalled in his devotion to the city, he was also a relentless and sometimes patronizing patrician who observers critically described as adopting a "father-knows-best" approach to governance.[31] "I believe I know my City better than anyone else and that includes the federal government, the state government and neighborhood groups which know their problems well, but cannot be expected to fully comprehend the totality of the issues and problems with which a city is faced," Schaefer declared.[32] On the whole, he expected no more from his staff and municipal employees than he was willing to give himself.

Despite his obvious dedication to the city and its residents, Schaefer was not a leader who shared the ambitions of activist antipoverty and human services workers. Although he did not oppose redistributive remedies to poverty, he prioritized efforts to stem white flight and to attract new businesses to the city—even when the efforts came at the expense of services for the poor. The exodus of human and corporate taxpayers from Baltimore was of tremendous concern to Schaefer. Unlike most cities in the United States, Baltimore was not located within a county but was instead its own jurisdiction. As a result, the city did not benefit from tax revenue paid by those who lived in its suburbs. Baltimore also suffered higher rates of unemployment than the surrounding counties and was home to large numbers of poor and elderly residents. The demographics of the city were reflected in low yields from income taxes. The year Schaefer took office, Baltimore's income tax revenue generated $33.38 per capita while neighboring Baltimore County, using the same tax rate, generated $62.50 per capita. Depopulation and deindustrialization cost the city not just income-tax but also property-tax revenue. To compensate for its low tax yields, the city asked for more from its remaining property owners than suburbanites had to pay. In 1970, the tax rate in Baltimore per $100 of property value was $2.01 higher than in the city's wealthier fringes. The relatively high property-tax burden fueled white flight, which worsened the city's revenue problems.[33]

To combat the situation, Schaefer began creating programs to respond to the frustration of outer-city residents who had felt neglected during the 1960s, when federal and city resources seemed aimed only at the inner city. Schaefer's attention to the outer city strengthened his political base, but the mayor also agreed with many of its residents that a myopic focus on antipoverty efforts could not effectively solve the city's problems. Schaefer believed scarce municipal resources were best used salvaging neighborhoods in danger of decline and maintaining those in good health. He disagreed with those who would concentrate resources on the monumental task of resuscitating areas of Baltimore already ravaged by poverty. He also prioritized attracting new businesses to the city. His was a triage strategy not unlike those under way in other cities that were hemorrhaging working- and middle-class white residents, corporate taxpayers, and jobs.[34] It did not endear him to those either inside or outside of the government who were angered by the racial and economic status quo of the city. The policies of the Nixon administration, however, reinforced Schaefer's agenda—and in some ways even compelled it.

"Removing the Foundation Stone of the International Monetary System": Nixon and the Global Economy

Schaefer became the mayor of Baltimore as momentous changes were under way regarding the organization of the global economy. And although not necessarily issues that sparked a lot of interest in the city, the macroeconomic policy decisions that Nixon made during the early 1970s had grave implications for Baltimore. In an effort to preserve the dominance of the United States in the global economy during a moment when that hegemony seemed imperiled, Nixon pursued policies detrimental to both the economic health of deindustrializing cities such as Baltimore and the job prospects of the often predominantly African American residents of those cities. The president replaced multilateral economic agreements premised on the Keynesian consensus of the mid-twentieth century with unilateral decisions that helped to forge the neoliberal economic order of the late twentieth and early twenty-first centuries. To be sure, Nixon took only the first steps in a process that his successors in the White House continued. Nevertheless, his role in dismantling the Bretton Woods system that had governed the global economy since the end of World War II and reorienting the global economy in accordance with free-market principles dramatically changed the course of history. It also gravely diminished the prospects that Baltimore or any other city would win the War on Poverty.

When Nixon took office, the Bretton Woods system was poised on the brink of collapse. That system, which political scientist John Ruggie describes as imbued with "embedded liberalism," had helped to resuscitate global trade after World War II and had also accommodated the welfare states and commitments to full employment that many participating nations had promised their citizens.[35] The source of stability of the Bretton Woods system was the

American dollar, which was pegged to a fixed value of gold. The very serious problem that Nixon faced was that the U.S. Treasury did not have anywhere near enough gold to cover all of the dollars in global circulation. Americans had spent far more—on military alliances, foreign investments, hot and cold Cold War ventures, imports, international aid, and even tourism—than they could possibly back up with gold, and the fear of a run on the dollar had been tormenting U.S. Treasury secretaries for years. Johnson had addressed the problem by imposing capital controls and limits on the flow of currency across borders and implementing other stop-gap measures. But he left to his successor the monumental task of salvaging the system of international cooperation on which so many around the world depended.[36]

Ultimately Nixon opted to replace rather than repair the Bretton Woods system, a unilateral move that astounded U.S. allies and trading partners. "At the stroke of a pen, or more factually, in one brief TV broadcast, Mr. Nixon removed the foundation stone of the international monetary system. The result is monetary chaos and uncertainty," observed one economist with alarm.[37] Although he initially closed the gold window only temporarily, ultimately the president opted not to restore the earlier system. Instead he allowed the value of the dollar to float, the policy preference of renowned monetarist economist Milton Friedman, who had many acolytes in the Nixon White House, including George Shultz, Donald Rumsfeld, and Dick Cheney. In the service of trade liberalization, Friedman and like-minded advisers also endorsed the elimination of capital controls—the policy option Johnson had recently taken and that nations around the world used to limit potentially destabilizing foreign investment or disinvestment. Nixon adopted that proposal as well, and as the administration negotiated the terms of the new floating currency system with its trading partners, it pressed them to also abandon capital controls. Within a few years, Nixon had laid a foundation for the neoliberal macroeconomic regime that would replace Bretton Woods.[38]

The changes Nixon introduced had profound consequences, most of which emerged over time and were reinforced by subsequent presidents. In the increasingly unrestrained free-market global economy that Nixon and his advisers began building, the steps that governments could be called upon to take to conform to neoliberal prescriptions would come at the cost of measures intended to ease poverty and redistribute wealth. Moreover, in already deindustrializing cities like Baltimore, the elimination of capital controls worsened vulnerability to capital flight and thus job losses. The changes also increased pressure on urban executives such as Schaefer to adopt austere local budgets and pursue other policies intended to make their locales attractive to investors. In addition, the elimination of capital controls contributed to making credit markets increasingly competitive, and poor cities often found it difficult to secure funding for local projects.[39] In Baltimore, the changes had dire implications for the agendas of activist municipal workers, whose bold ambitions for fighting poverty relied on generous public spending.

"The Most Exciting, Fiscally Sound Port City on the Atlantic": Austerity in Baltimore

As an elected official in a city that for decades had relied in large measure on both the tax revenue and jobs generated by manufacturers, Schaefer faced the daunting challenge of managing Baltimore's economic health within a global economy increasingly characterized by capital mobility. An oil embargo and the recession and inflation of the early 1970s worsened the city's problems. Fiscal strain created pressure on elected officials to practice austerity. So too did the need to demonstrate fiscal health to woo potential investors to the city. Schaefer willingly accommodated the economic imperatives. He kept a tight lid on spending, cutting municipal jobs and services to keep the city budget in the Black. He also adopted two practices that locally elected officials nationally would soon find increasingly hard to avoid and that indicate the corporate sector's growing influence over urban affairs. He closely monitored Baltimore's credit rating and pursued austerity to improve it, and he worked with state officials to create tax incentives intended to keep businesses in or lure them to the city.[40]

Mayors in other U.S. cities responded differently to the fiscal challenges. Many executives in deindustrializing or cash-strapped cities with stronger liberal-labor coalitions than existed in Baltimore defied the new fiscal pressures in an effort to defend public services and jobs. In the process, they racked up considerable debt burdens. Even as capital flight cost cities revenue that had earlier helped cover the cost of local services, the elected officials nevertheless opted not to compel residents with low incomes or city workers, whose incomes generally trailed those of their counterparts in the private sector, to take the hit for the economic changes. American cities, such as New York, Detroit, Philadelphia, and Washington, DC, soon found it difficult to meet their debt obligations. In response, financial institutions and credit-rating agencies denied the cities credit or downgraded their credit-rating status, making it difficult for elected officials to secure additional loans or sell bonds. The situation led observers on the political left to argue that the conservative financial industry was using its influence over lending practices to discipline cities with liberal leaderships by punishing those who did not practice austerity.[41]

The charge had a particularly large number of adherents in New York City. Its financial crisis came to a head during the mid-1970s, when the municipal government teetered on the brink of default but could not secure additional credit. In October 1975, Standard and Poor's, one of the nation's top two credit-rating agencies, dropped New York City's credit rating twice, and municipal officials could not find new sources of credit. The federal government offered no relief. Nixon's successor, President Gerald Ford; Ford's chief of staff, Donald Rumsfeld; and other policy advisers were determined to teach New York and cities in general a lesson on the imperative of fiscal "responsibility," and they refused to provide federal relief. Only intense domestic and international pressure from those concerned about the dire ramifications for the health of the global economy of a New York City bankruptcy led the president to relent. Nevertheless, ultimately, the proponents of austerity got their way in New York when an unelected Emergency Financial Control Board was created to oversee fiscal affairs, and residents lost the ability to direct the way their taxes were spent.[42]

No such dramatic showdowns occurred in Baltimore. As a result of what the *Baltimore Sun* described as Schaefer's "Spartan" fiscal policies, during the early 1970s the city had just over a third of New York's per capita debt, making it one of the least indebted of the nation's largest cities.[43] During the mid-1970s, Moody's Investor Service rewarded Schaefer's austerity by raising the city's credit rating from A to A-1. Aware that Baltimore was competing for investors with similarly downtrodden cities as well as with Sunbelt upstarts, the city's boosters hoped the improved rating would give Baltimore an edge. They celebrated the A-1 status in a twelve-page advertisement in *Forbes*. In the hopes of attracting investors, they enthusiastically if unpoetically dubbed Baltimore "the most exciting, fiscally sound port city on the Atlantic." In a not-so-subtle reference to the financial straits of northern and midwestern rivals, the ad noted that Baltimore's fiscal health allowed it to "offer a host of advantages that our sister cities may not be in a position to offer." Among those advantages were "industrial revenue bonds; State loans for building construction and equipment; State loan guarantees for construction and equipment; Tax exemption on equipment and machinery; Foreign trade zone (proposed); Tax exemption on manufacturers' inventories; sales tax exemption on new equipment; Tax exemption on manufacturing materials; Accelerated depreciation of industrial equipment; [and] Free employee training."[44] Preying on the weakness of competitor cities rather than finding common cause with urban mayors facing similar fiscal pressures, Schafer had boldly entered what some feared would become a race to the bottom in terms of incentives that elected officials of already cash-strapped cities felt compelled to offer to potential investors.

Schaefer's attention to Baltimore's credit rating and effort to lure investors with tax abatements were practices that municipal officials across the nation found increasingly hard to resist in their quest to keep their cities financially viable. Both, however, created pressure on elected officials to prioritize business over local concerns. As antipoverty workers in Baltimore could easily attest, particularly vulnerable to neglect were the costly human-services needs of residents with low incomes. The situation was not entirely new. Private credit-rating agencies had existed in the United States since the early twentieth century. Their judgments concerning the creditworthiness of localities grew in importance, however, during an era of increasing capital mobility. Critics certainly protested the influence unelected agents from elite private firms were able to wield over local policy-making. But once mayors such as Schaefer entered the tax-abatement game, elected officials debating policy options in similarly downtrodden cities had to remain ever mindful of market imperatives.[45]

Meanwhile, tax abatements eliminated one of corporations' historic fiduciary obligations: a degree of responsibility both for the infrastructure needed by their businesses, such as roads and firefighting forces, and for the human services that nurtured their current and future workforces, such as hospitals and schools. Nevertheless, despite pressing need for tax revenue and faced with rising and debilitating unemployment rates, elected officials such as Schaefer responded to intense competition for global capital by attempting to entice potential employers with tax breaks. As a result, as urban-planning scholar Peter S. Fisher argues, absent leadership and planning in Washington, DC, to protect manufacturing jobs, federal, state, and local tax incentives became the "American version of industrial policy."[46] The incentives also, however, shifted the burden for paying for infrastructure and services increasingly onto the shoulders of taxpaying city residents. Meanwhile, though conservatives leveled many criticisms against cities and their liberal and supposedly profligate elected officials during the 1970s, tax abatements, a significant source of revenue loss that worsened cities' fiscal problems, never received the opprobrium aimed at welfare spending and wage increases won through union negotiations for city employees.[47]

Since Schaefer was the mayor of a rust-belt city, his attention to keeping businesses and taxpaying residents in the city and his efforts to attract new ones certainly made sense. At the same time, however, activist city workers and community leaders worried about the unmet and pressing needs of low-income residents. It hardly took an MBA to connect fiscal "health" with unmet need in cities with high poverty rates. But Schaefer was undeterred. Confronted with the toll that white flight and deindustrialization were taking on Baltimore's tax base, he responded with belt-tightening. Rewarded for his efforts with a strong city credit rating from the financial community, Schaefer pressed his advantage over competitor cities suffering fiscal crises. In the meantime, he saddled the city with two new sources of austerity pressures. Fiscal "responsibility" was necessary to maintain Baltimore's credit rating, and new businesses were excused from some taxes, which failed to relieve city residents of already comparatively high property tax rates during an era of rising prices. Residents of Baltimore entrusted Schaefer with the task of effectively balancing competing demands for city resources. From the vantage point of workers in the city's antipoverty and human-services agencies, he was neglecting important constituents. Their agencies and the low-income residents they served paid a steep price for the mayor's commitment to austerity. But their ability to effectively combat the new municipal priorities was diminishing. Nixon's domestic policies were eroding their influence within the city government and strengthening the authority of the mayor's.

CHAPTER 6

"The Hell-Raising Period Is Over"

New Federalism in Baltimore

In 1973, when Maude S. Harvey was appointed the director of the Baltimore Department of Social Services (DSS), she became the first Black woman in the city's history to run a municipal agency. She also became the first African American to run DSS and one of very few women in a top leadership post in the municipal government. Born in 1918, Harvey had worked her way up through the ranks of DSS during a career that spanned nearly three decades, so she certainly knew the welfare system and its problems well. "The nation's priority," she noted, based on experience, "does not seem to be people."[1] While some complained that the welfare rolls were too long, Harvey countered that they were not long enough. Many people who qualified for benefits and services remained outside of the system and needed to be brought in, she believed. In addition, she noted that a sizable population of city residents did not officially qualify for assistance but were nevertheless in dire need of help that she felt her agency should provide. The likelihood that things would change for the better, she knew, was slim. "People believe everyone can pull themselves up by their bootstraps when some people don't even have boots," she protested, echoing the words of Martin Luther King.[2] Greed was the problem, she concluded. Miserly state and federal spending on Aid to Families with Dependent Children and other means-tested programs confined many people to poverty and had also created a "welfare mess" that frustrated everyone, she explained.[3] During her stint as director, Harvey did what she could to correct the problems. She oversaw the continuing decentralization of DSS, worked to expand service delivery, lobbied on behalf of the Food Stamps program, and testified in the State House to improve welfare programming.[4]

Ultimately, however, Harvey achieved fewer of her goals than she would have liked. Even as she accepted the directorship of DSS, she knew that negotiations were under way to transfer DSS employees out of the municipal government and into the Maryland state workforce. In what was clearly a bid to tame the activist DSS staff, state officials had offered to cover Baltimore's welfare tab in exchange for changing the status of the workers. Harvey described the transfer, which both public and private social-service providers in the city adamantly opposed, as an effort by state officials to gain the "power to manipulate" 2,600 municipal employees. She also predicted that in her position as director, she would soon become little more than a "figurehead."[5] Worse, by shifting control over Baltimore's DSS to Annapolis, state officials were robbing not only Harvey but all city residents of the limited leverage they had over how the municipal agency responded to local poverty.

Harvey was hardly unique among Black women in Baltimore's municipal workforce who believed that the nation's welfare system was flawed and that antipoverty efforts were inadequate. She was also not the only African American and woman serving as a public official who found her authority and influence in the city severely diminished during the 1970s, when officials on the federal, state, and local levels took steps to contain the activism that had exploded in cities like Baltimore during the 1960s. In Harvey's case, behind-the-scenes wheeling and dealing culminated in the transfer of DSS employees to the state civil service, over which African Americans and Baltimore residents had little authority. In other instances, municipal agency heads who remained in the city's workforce lost influence as a result of federal-level policy changes that Richard Nixon implemented in order to diminish the power of liberals in Congress, shrink the size of the federal government, and return power on the local level back to elected officials. New Federalism, Nixon's signature domestic policy, was an attempt to reorganize the way that the federal government transferred funds to states and localities. Rather than as categorical grants earmarked for specific purposes and sent to public agencies, the president proposed that federal funds should be repackaged, often as block grants, and sent to elected officials to use with considerable discretion. In other words, he aimed to reduce the kinds of grants that had gone to Parren Mitchell in Baltimore's Community Action Agency and create new grants that would go to such mayors as William Donald Schaefer, who did not tend to be advocates of community participation or harsh critics of the status quo. Leaders of national civil rights organizations and labor unions led the battle against New Federalism but met with only limited success.

In Baltimore, New Federalism, in combination with cuts Nixon made to the War on Poverty, shifted power relations within the municipal government. Antipoverty and human-services workers, among whom African Americans and women were increasingly well-represented, saw their authority decline, while predominantly white and male elected officials gained influence. The change made it difficult for activist municipal employees to either achieve their objectives or challenge the mayor's commitment to austerity and growing faith in the power of commercial revitalization to solve the city's problems. The influence of antipoverty and human-services workers declined at the same time that Baltimore's law enforcement agencies saw their economic fortunes improve. Nixon's commitment to law-and-order remedies to urban problems and disinvestment from the Great Society meant that police officers began to replace social workers as the first responders to urban poverty. The change represented a shift in what or whom was perceived as the enemy in cities. The War on Poverty had targeted economic insecurity. The war on crime would eventually become a war on urban African Americans.

Public-sector unions closely monitored the impacts of policy shifts in Baltimore. And the unions fiercely challenged the mayor's willingness to sacrifice the well-being of city workers and residents for an improved business climate. Strikes by municipal employees won important policy changes and wage concessions during the mid-1970s. Distorted national media coverage of one local strike, however, damaged the prestige of the public-sector labor movement at a time when growing numbers of Americans increasingly viewed not only low-income urban African Americans but also government unions and their members as drains on the national economy. Gains only recently won by municipal employees and their unions proved very fragile during the Nixon years.

"Local Control" or White Control?
Nixon's Domestic Agenda

During the early 1970s, as activist municipal employees in antipoverty agencies and human-services departments in Baltimore continued to press for redistributive responses to economic injustice, the influence they wielded over policy-making and the city's agenda was under assault. Nixon's major domestic policy innovation, New Federalism, imperiled their direct access to federal funds, which earlier had provided them with a measure of independence from locally elected officials who did not share their ambitions. Nixon offered an overview of his New Federalism proposal during his 1971 State of the Union address. General revenue sharing (GRS) was one of its hallmarks. The president proposed transferring a portion of the money the federal government collected in taxes to states and localities where it could be used at the discretion of elected officials. He aimed to encourage policy innovation outside of Washington and reduce red tape and bureaucracy, he explained. He also had motivations that he did not mention. He wanted to bolster the authority of elected officials in cities in the wake of the protest movements of the tumultuous 1960s, and he relished derailing the policy agenda of congressional liberals.[6]

Nixon made some of his unspoken intentions clear in his address by using the dog-whistle politics he had honed on the campaign trail. He explained that revenue sharing was intended to replace "present narrow-purpose aid programs," in other words, the grants that had sent antipoverty funds to cities and often to African Americans. Further, revenue sharing would diminish the authority over policy-making of the "bureaucratic elite in Washington," meaning liberals who supposedly favored African Americans and the poor over the white silent majority. Alternatively, revenue sharing would provide relief to "homeowners and wage-earners," again meaning whites.[7] And it would restore "local," which also meant white, control over decision-making. (Southern segregationists might have used the phrase "states' rights" rather than "local control," but they certainly knew what Nixon meant.) Without so much as mentioning race, Nixon promised to overhaul the funding mechanisms that had enabled service providers to launch the War on Poverty and in Baltimore had given African Americans a voice in local policy-making. Simultaneously, his dog-whistle rhetoric erroneously implied that African Americans fell outside of the category of wage-earning homeowners and that the interests of Nixon's voters were at odds with those of people with low incomes.

To add insult to injury, Nixon offered a paean to local control that entirely neglected the history of African Americans who had endured slavery and then a century of government-sanctioned Jim Crow segregation and exploitation that had only recently been tempered by federal civil rights legislation. The president expounded, "The idea that . . . you cannot trust local governments is really a contention that you cannot trust people to govern themselves. This notion is completely foreign to the American experience. Local government is the government closest to the people, it is most responsive to the individual person. It is people's government in a far more intimate way than the Government in Washington can ever be."[8] Contrary to his populist rhetoric, however, revenue sharing was partly an effort to undermine the actual democratization of local decision-making that occurred during the 1960s when African Americans and residents with low incomes in cities such as Baltimore had actually gained some formal influence over policy-making. To be sure, there were legitimate ideological and practical issues at stake in debates over federalism. But Nixon foreclosed honest conversations concerning the level at which governmental decision-making should occur by ignoring racism and invoking white victimhood and identity politics.

Not surprisingly, GRS quickly won the bipartisan endorsement of the members of the national organizations that represented states, localities, and their elected officials, such as the National League of Cities, the Council of State Governments, the U.S. Conference of Mayors, and the National Governors Association. Their members embraced GRS for three reasons. First, they believed that the federal distribution of categorical grants robbed them of control over policy-making on fiscal matters in their jurisdictions while empowering federal administrators. Second, they worried that categorical grants gave the directors of local public agencies unwarranted control over resources. And finally, many disliked the community participation mandates associated with some grants, which empowered the very citizens in localities who were often the least satisfied with the political status quo. In sum, elected officials anticipated the GRS would reconcentrate authority in their offices.[9]

The most vocal opponents of New Federalism on the national level were leaders from civil rights organizations and the labor movement. NAACP executive director Roy Wilkins cautioned, "It ought to be remembered that the whole fight of Black Americans for 70 years has been for federal legislation, federal executive action and federal court decisions precisely because many of the individual states grievously shortchanged them."[10] Labor leaders contended that New Federalism would enable elected officials to evade federal equal-opportunity provisions, labor-standards laws, and other regulations required of recipients of categorical grants. In testimony before the Committee on Ways and Means, Andrew Biemiller of the AFL-CIO derided Nixon's initiative as "no-strings, no-standards, and no-supervision revenue sharing."[11] Critics also worried that New Federalism would undermine community participation in decision-making. Further, they argued that the initiative would disperse across multiple jurisdictions, including wealthy districts, federal funds that should have been targeted at areas with high concentrations of poverty.[12] And even revenue that made it to struggling cities would not necessarily be used to fight poverty. "You can't make me believe that the localities which get the money are going to use it for the poor," protested Maryland's congressional representative Parren Mitchell, who as the former director of Baltimore's Community Action Agency was intimately familiar with the obstinacy of locally elected officials when it came to funding anti-poverty efforts. Mitchell also found it unlikely that elected officials, especially southerners, were going to use the money on behalf of Black people.[13]

Notably absent from the anti-GRS coalition was AFSCME. The public-sector union's leaders predicted that Nixon's initiative would be a boon for many of their members and supported the measure. When AFSCME president Jerry Wurf testified on GRS before the Senate's Finance Committee, however, he was mindful of the threat it posed to a targeted war on poverty and said as much. "Funds must be allocated to those jurisdictions which have the most serious fiscal difficulties," he urged.[14] Nevertheless, as was the case on other important policy matters during the 1970s, including most notably liberal efforts to secure full-employment legislation, government workers' interests put them at odds with those pursuing the social and economic justice agenda more fully embraced by civil rights organizations and some unions representing private-sector workers.

Despite the opposition from civil rights and many labor leaders, as well as the reluctance of some members of Congress to weaken their own authority over policy-making, GRS became law. Urban advocates did succeed in ensuring that local- rather than state-level officials received the lion's share of GRS funds. The new iteration of intergovernmental aid only transferred one-third of allocated federal funds to states, while local governments shared the rest, and ultimately, GRS only accounted for about 5 percent of state and local budgets. When paired with decreases in federal spending on the War on Poverty, however, the change had profound implications for power relations in cities that disadvantaged African Americans.[15]

Opponents had greater success in limiting the second type of revenue sharing that Nixon proposed. Through the use of special revenue sharing, Nixon planned to consolidate multiple categorical grants into block grants with loose policy directives. This represented an important, although not unprecedented, departure from past practices. Categorical grants, which had risen in number during Johnson's War on Poverty, were the primary means the federal government used to redistribute federal dollars to states and localities. Critics on the right and left legitimately charged that the grants were in some cases redundant and also the source of considerable red tape. They also necessitated a sizable bureaucracy on the federal and local levels. Additionally, categorical grants could preclude policy innovation outside of Washington, DC. Mindful of the problems, Johnson had funded the Model Cities program in a block grant–like fashion in order to provide flexibility to those actively engaged in local antipoverty efforts. Despite their flaws, however, categorical grants were the source of the independence from elected officials that antipoverty and human-services workers capitalized on in cities such as Baltimore as they fought the war on poverty.

Conservative elected officials in Washington were keenly aware that the method that the federal government used to transfer money to states and localities had significant implications for local power dynamics. They also knew that liberals and increasingly African Americans were particularly politically influential in the nation's cities. In fact, conservatives, including both Republicans and southern Democrats, had already used that knowledge strategically during the late 1960s when Congress was debating the response the federal government should take to growing concerns about crime. As part of the deliberations over the Omnibus Crime Control and Safe Streets Act of 1968, conservatives succeeded in replacing with a block grant smaller grants that the Johnson administration had proposed sending to local law enforcement agencies. They also made the block grants available only to state-level officials and prohibited the distribution of the funds to any agency with ties to the Office of Economic Opportunity, which oversaw the War on Poverty. By so doing, they used a funding mechanism to place authority over the nation's burgeoning war on crime firmly in the hands of the white and largely conservative governors and outside of the purview of the agencies in which African Americans had gained the most influence. By calling for block grants and targeting them at elected officials during the early 1970s, in other words, Nixon was not reinventing the wheel.[16]

Civil rights and other liberal activists appreciated what was going on and opposed special revenue sharing. They opposed efforts to reduce congressional oversight of the use of federal funds and to enhance the power of state and local elected officials. They met with some success. Nixon initially proposed six block grants, but only the Comprehensive Employment and Training Act of 1973 (CETA) and the Housing and Community Development Act of 1974, which created Community Development Block Grants (CDBGs), became policy. Gerald Ford had replaced Nixon as president by the time CETA made it through Congress. Ford was also in office when Congress passed Title XX of the Social Security Act in 1975. A block grant–type program, Title XX allowed states that had already qualified for federal support for social services programming to receive the funds as block grants.[17]

Although AFSCME officials had not opposed most of Nixon's New Federalism, they were very wary of CETA. It replaced job training–related categorical grants and also mandated some job creation in the public sector. The leaders of government workers' unions were understandably alarmed by the introduction of special categories of public-sector jobs. AFSCME officials were especially concerned because their membership rolls already included many at or near the bottom of government pay scales. They worried that CETA workers might be assigned tasks regularly performed by full-time government employees, who could in turn be eliminated. They were also concerned that the presence of workers employed on terms less favorable than those whose compensation was determined by collective bargaining could force rollbacks in hard-won wages and benefits packages. The use of the government as an employer of last resort, an idea that had many progressive supporters, worried AFSCME officials because of their members' vulnerability.

In the long run, the creation of CETA and other block grants certainly did not entirely transform American domestic policy. Categorical grants remained the primary way the federal government transferred funds to states and localities, and the Nixon and Ford administrations created fewer block grants than they proposed. In addition, during their years in office, Nixon and Ford committed more federal resources to grant-in-aid programs than had previous presidents. And contrary to the concerns of revenue-sharing critics, the regulations governing the use of federal funds also increased—at least during the administrations of the two presidents. Nevertheless, the practice of distributing intergovernmental revenue as block grants became a tool that conservative elected officials on the federal level continued to use to target revenue at their like-minded counterparts on the local, or more often state, level and to exclude African Americans and liberals from influence over policy-making and implementation.

In Baltimore, New Federalism threatened in three key ways gains African Americans had only recently achieved. First, it contributed to undermining the nation's War on Poverty. Both types of revenue sharing diffused among many localities with varying degrees of need funds that might have been directed entirely toward antipoverty efforts. Moreover, because population counts figured into the formulas used to determine a locality's appropriation, older cities with declining populations stood to lose funding while suburbs and Sunbelt cities with expanding populations gained.[18] Second, federally mandated community participation fell victim to New Federalism. In a booklet on GRS and civil rights, for example, officials explained, "While it is the responsibility of local government officials to make the *final* determination of where and how revenue sharing funds will be used in the community, *it is the residents of the community who have the responsibility to inform their elected officials of their needs and desires*" (emphasis in the original). Residents were encouraged to influence decisions by educating themselves, organizing citizen committees, meeting with officials, and "writing letters to the editors of local newspapers."[19] Third, New Federalism altered power relations between elected officials and those at the helm of public agencies and departments. Categorical grants distributed by the federal government were earmarked for specific uses. When the federal government had allocated resources to antipoverty efforts, they had given administrators of human-services programs a measure of security that their agencies would be funded regardless of the priorities of local- or state-level elected officials. GRS upended this dynamic.[20] In cities such as Baltimore, the authority that African Americans and women had gained in the municipal government during the 1960s was concentrated in agencies that relied on War on Poverty–related categorical grants, whereas the officials who controlled budget-making were almost entirely white and male. The shift in policy that Nixon introduced eroded the authority and independence of those government officials most sensitive to the concerns of African Americans and poor people and who tended to be advocates of a strong welfare state.

"Occasioned by Cutbacks in Federal Spending": The War on the War on Poverty

In Baltimore, Nixon's New Federalism made it difficult for antipoverty activists and human-services providers to pursue their policy priorities. It also hampered their efforts to counter Schaefer's agenda and temper his commitment to austerity. The workers' enhanced influence over the municipal agenda during the mid-1960s had enabled them to compel city officials to move away from a near single-minded focus on downtown commercial revitalization, a goal that local business leaders affiliated with the Greater Baltimore Committee had secured from the city council during the 1950s. To be sure, fighting poverty directly and fighting it via private-sector job creation were hardly mutually exclusive. Few in the city, including activist municipal workers, rejected all commercial revitalization efforts. Residents needed jobs and expected that the private sector would be the major source of many of them. And the mayor and leaders in the business community did not oppose all redistributive poverty-fighting strategies. Yet many antipoverty and human-services workers as well as other local activists felt the mayor's priorities were skewed too far in favor of private interests. And Nixon's New Federalism further tipped the scales to his advantage. In turn, administrators of antipoverty agencies and human-services departments became competitors who had to vie against one another for a share of the municipal budget and federal revenue-sharing funds.

Even before the advent of New Federalism, Baltimore's City Charter already imbued the mayor with considerable authority over the municipal budget. The document enabled the mayor to nominate all municipal department heads, including the director of the Department of Finance. The Department of Finance drafted the city's annual budget and then presented it to the Board of Estimates for review. The board had five members, including the mayor and two of his appointees. With an almost guaranteed majority on every vote, the mayor could easily tailor the budget to suit his agenda. From the Board of Estimates, the budget, called the Ordinance of Estimates, moved to the city council. Baltimore's charter, however, only empowered the council to reduce budget allocations; the members could not increase funding for any department or program. As a result of this executive-dominated system, control over fiscal matters, as over city management, rested firmly in the office of the mayor. Nixon's New Federalism enhanced the power of the position. Schaefer used his considerable authority over appointments and the budget to combat dissension in the municipal workforce, bolster his political base, and advance his business-friendly agenda.[21]

The Community Action Agency was an easy target for Schaefer. By the early 1970s, the CAA was no longer the source of activism and rebellion it once had been. In 1968, following the city council's refusal to appoint Walter Carter to the agency's top post, activist antipoverty workers had shifted their energies to Baltimore's new Model Cities program. After a subsequent CAA director was indicted for fraud, which hardly raised the popularity of the agency in and around Baltimore, Mayor D'Alesandro and the city council appointed African American Lenwood Ivey to the top post.[22] While committed to relieving poverty, Ivey was not an enthusiast of community participation. As he later explained, he suspected that federal policy makers may have intentionally required community participation in order to make antipoverty ventures fail and Black people look incompetent. Putting residents without the requisite skills in positions of authority was hardly a recipe for success, he argued.[23] In the early 1970s, as the head of the CAA, he declared the "hell raising period . . . over."[24] He prioritized service provisions over community mobilization and largely abandoned the agency's effort to fundamentally redistribute power in the city.[25]

Meanwhile, some transplanted CAA activists in the Model Cities program and their coworkers tried to use that agency to prolong the hell-raising period. They were led by William Sykes, the program's director; Elva Edwards, an African American social worker who began her career at the CAA; and the activist members of the Model Cities Policy Steering Board.[26] Increasingly, however, the Model Cities' staff found themselves diverting energy they had earlier committed to community mobilization to efforts intended simply to save their agency in the face of federal funding cuts. The staff of the CAA faced similar pressures. In early 1972, Sykes sent a memo to Model Cities' project directors requesting "that priority be given to grantsmanship" so that they might find alternatives to the federal funding on which the agency had relied.[27] A year later, Sykes announced imminent "expenditure controls," "staff reductions," and "increased workloads" for those spared the pain of a pink slip. "It will take a cooperative effort on the part of all of us if we are to survive this period of transition during which the degree of federal commitment to the kinds of activities supported by Model Cities is tested," he reported.[28]

Sykes and Ivey lobbied in Congress and the Maryland General Assembly largely unsuccessfully to secure replacement funding for their agencies. They did, however, win Schaefer to the cause of preserving an antipoverty agency in Baltimore. Although the mayor prioritized improving Baltimore's business climate, as an executive in a struggling rust-belt city, he hardly opposed fighting poverty head on—especially if he was in charge of the money and staffing. As a result, even as CAAs across the nation closed their doors permanently, Schaefer worked with Ivey and Sykes to find ways to maintain some of the services provided by their agencies. In 1974, the CAA and the Model Cities program merged to become the Urban Services Agency (USA), a new division of the city government. The outcome was a victory given the dismal fate of many antipoverty agencies elsewhere. Thereafter, however, and as evidence of their fading independence, USA administrators, like the heads of other human services, were often compelled to compete for resources in annual budgeting contests.[29]

Theoretically, GRS and block-grant money could have compensated for the loss of federal antipoverty funds, an arrangement antipoverty activists appear to have endorsed. The mayor and his advisers, however, did not adopt that approach. Robert Embry, the white administrator of the Department of Housing and Community Development, was among them. So too was Mark K. Joseph, the city's white development coordinator. "The new [antipoverty] group both as an agency and its citizen advisory group should *not* be the agency which is charged with setting priorities for either revenue sharing or for special revenue sharing," Joseph argued (emphasis in the original).[30] On community participation in the new agency, the two advisers also had similar views. Embry recommended that the mayor disband the Community Action Commission and Model Cities Steering Board and proposed that the administrator of the new agency be accountable only to the mayor. Joseph concurred. "We may want some citizen involvement," he conceded, "but I would not see a heavy emphasis on it."[31]

Schaefer's advisers largely won the day. Between 1975 and 1980, Schaefer directed 18 percent of the almost $200 million Baltimore received in CDBG funds to USA. While the figure was higher than the share of CDBG funds that elected officials in other jurisdictions allocated to human services, it also reflected Schaefer's decision not to invest in the War on Poverty as enthusiastically as he pursued commercial revitalization. Ultimately, the funding USA received was considerably lower than the combined budgets the CAA and Model Cities would have enjoyed had they been supported at 1960s levels. Antipoverty advocates did succeed in winning a citizen's advisory board for USA. The director of the agency, however, answered only to the mayor and was not accountable to the board. And Schaefer chose the relatively conservative Ivey to head the agency. Longtime antipoverty worker Edwards became the agency's deputy director. In her new post, Edwards joined a small but growing number of Black women who were winning leadership positions in the municipal government during the 1970s. The victories multiplied, however, as antipoverty and human-services agencies lost both clout and independence.

The appointment of African Americans to top municipal posts, moreover, did not necessarily correspond with activist leadership. In fact, Evelyn Burrell, an original member of the Model Cities board, argued that some high-ranking African American municipal officials were themselves culpable in the loss of momentum of the War on Poverty in Baltimore. Disunity resulted, she explained, when "Black people, mostly Black males" won influential positions and "just back[ed] off and stop[ped] pushing."[32] No doubt she was right. Schaefer was hardly inclined to appoint agency heads who were likely to challenge his power and agenda. Simultaneously, however, New Federalism and the defunding of the War on Poverty undermined community participation and eviscerated the strength and independence of antipoverty agencies.

The staff of the Department of Health also found themselves competitors in battles over revenue-sharing funds and the municipal budget. By the early 1970s, the health department could claim some important achievements. The city's African American infant mortality rate had declined and was approaching the white rate. Maternal deaths and tuberculosis cases were at an all-time low. Although cases of lead poisoning had risen, the consequence of the city's extensive stock of dilapidated housing, rat bites were at an all-time low. New nutrition programs for the elderly were also making a dent in public health figures.[33] Officials at the health department were quick to point out that some of the improvements were the consequence of "many social and economic factors."[34] But the positive health statistics also "reflect[ed] the improved utilization of Baltimore's expanded medical services," which had grown under the guidance of community residents and in accord with the neighborhood-based service delivery model.[35]

Efforts to make additional improvements stalled, however. "Cutbacks of federal funding" were part of the problem, according to health officials.[36] So too was the inability of the officials to secure replacement resources from Schaefer's budget and cache of revenue-sharing funds. During the early 1970s, the department operated five decentralized facilities but scaled back the number of services they had planned to provide. Primary care was one such casualty, despite the critical need for that service occasioned by the declining number of private providers in the city. Community engagement in health care planning was an additional casualty. In keeping with the spirit of the 1960s, the health department had created citizens' councils in an effort to democratize decision-making. Researchers studying Baltimore's decentralization efforts in 1974, however, discovered that residents had begun to lose interest in the councils as their recommendations could not be matched with funding sources. To remedy the situation, the researchers suggested the mayor allocate GRS or CDBG funds to the councils. City officials responded that those funds had already been "committed."[37]

While the control that Nixon's New Federalism transferred to Schaefer enabled him to constrain the independence and ambitions of antipoverty warriors and municipal human-services providers, the mayor used his power to make appointments, using political cunning and good old-fashioned patronage to eliminate the staff of the Department of Education as a source of organized opposition to his authority. He moved slowly and with stealth, as he had to evade considerable opposition from Black activists. During the late 1960s, African Americans had launched a campaign to win control of the school system, which served a growing percentage of Black students as white parents increasingly sought private or suburban alternatives for their children's education. In 1971, intense pressure by Black city residents and leaders led the members of the school board to select Ronald Patterson as the district's new superintendent. Patterson quickly earned the ire of many whites, including Schaefer, by attempting to eliminate patronage-hiring in the department and by replacing some high-ranking white administrators with African Americans. He also worked cooperatively with Black leaders who many whites considered "militants," pushed for desegregation and community control, and partnered with outspoken critics of the mayor. Not surprisingly, Schaefer wanted him out. He also wanted to be able to use the school system to achieve political ends.

It took several years, but Schaefer ultimately achieved his goal. By 1975, Schaefer had appointed three African American supporters to the school board and had the votes to oust the activist superintendent.[38] Thereafter, the mayor firmly clamped down on dissension within the Department of Education. As Schaefer's biographer C. Fraser Smith, explains, "Control over the schools was given over to African Americans as their inviolate pool of patronage."[39] Black Baltimore did not receive free rein over the system, however. Scholar Kenneth Wong observes that although the Department of Education became the city's "Black agency" and was consistently headed by local African American administrators, "central office school administrators critical of the [Schaefer] administration were either demoted or transferred." What is more, Wong reports, "Not infrequently, school resources were allocated in a politicized manner to serve as a warning to dissenters at the school building level."[40]

Maude Harvey and her staff at the DSS also saw their independence and influence undermined during the first half of the 1970s. Early in the decade, Maryland officials offered to cover for Baltimore the portion of welfare costs that state law required local governments to pay. In exchange, state officials wanted to transfer Baltimore's DSS employees into the state civil service. Opposition to the proposal in the city was immediate. Critics suspected that the move was intended to tame the activism of DSS employees.[41] Benjamin Davis, the executive director of the Maryland Chapter of Social Workers, explained with frustration that his members were superficially stereotyped as "bleeding hearts who are too permissive."[42] Baltimore was home to about 70 percent of Maryland's welfare recipients, and critics throughout the state blamed the city's welfare workers for the large and expensive caseload.[43] Criticism was sharpest in the state's most conservative areas: Western Maryland, the Eastern Shore, and some of Baltimore's suburbs. Staunchly conservative Republican state senator Robert E. Bauman, a founding member of both the Young Americans for Freedom and the American Conservative Unions who later represented Marylanders in the House of Representatives, raged against the "negative attitude" among welfare workers, who he believed pandered to the poor.[44] The widespread belief that DSS employees enrolled "ineligibles" or "cheats" for AFDC and Food Stamps motivated Maryland's elected officials to propose the takeover of the Baltimore DSS.

Welfare workers and members of DSS's citizen advisory board fought the change as did AFSCME and the Maryland Conference of Social Workers. They defended the integrity of DSS workers and argued that local control over the agency made it adaptable to specific circumstances in Baltimore. Mindful that the Maryland governor's willingness to waive Baltimore's welfare expenses would prove tempting to Schaefer, Maurice Harmon, who was the DSS director when the change was proposed, wrote a letter to one of the mayor's key advisers. "I recognize the fiscal plight of local government and believe there should be increased federal and state assistance in these programs, but feel we should not abdicate whatever little control still remains with the City," he argued.[45] The Conference of Social Workers concurred. "Urban welfare needs cannot be satisfied by further alienation of the city's citizens from the social services system," the group argued.[46] Eventually, however, the change proved inevitable. Reading the tea leaves, Harmon accepted a position in the Maryland DSS, anticipating that he might be "able to do more for the City from the State level."[47] The move at least assured Baltimore's welfare recipients and DSS employees an advocate on the state level—for the time being. Schaefer eventually replaced Harmon with Harvey, whose appointment as the first African American woman to run a municipal agency was symbolic but whose stature in the municipal government soon diminished.

By the mid-1970s, Baltimore's antipoverty and human-services workers had lost much of the independence they had briefly enjoyed. During the 1960s and early 1970s, the agencies had served as sites of opposition to local, state, and federal legislators whose actions imperiled the nation's fragile welfare state. They had also been a source of policy innovation and improvement as the largely female and African American staffs of the agencies had used their positions within that state in efforts to direct the course of public policy and make municipal services more accessible, useful, and accountable to poor residents. Antipoverty and human-services providers prioritized an urban agenda that served as a counter to the business-friendly solutions of the Schaefer administration. Nixon's New Federalism bolstered the mayor's authority while undermining the independence of the agencies. Baltimore's mayor accelerated the change as he worked to consolidate his power. The waning independence of the agencies eroded the ability of the staffs to demand that city leaders attend to the pressing concerns of residents with low incomes.

While antipoverty and human-services workers saw their influence and resources decline, another group of city workers, the predominantly white men who worked in law enforcement, saw the economic fortunes of their departments improve. On the campaign trail, Nixon had made clear his commitment to using the criminal justice system rather than antipoverty agencies to tame crime and solve urban problems. "If the conviction rate were doubled in this country, it would do more to eliminate crime in the future than a quadrupling of the funds for any governmental war on poverty," he contended.[48] Once in office, the "law-and-order" president wholeheartedly prosecuted the war on crime, particularly in low-income urban areas populated by African Americans. There, as historian Elizabeth Hinton argues, federal anticrime funds enabled law enforcement agencies to extend their operations deeply into neighborhoods and public housing complexes. Nixon also launched a war on drugs that criminalized drug users and led to significant increases in arrests, and he overhauled the American prison system, building hundreds of new jails. As Hinton explains, Nixon began putting in place the legislation and infrastructure that ultimately led to the crisis of mass incarceration of the late twentieth century.[49]

In Baltimore on Nixon's watch, the number of drug arrests grew dramatically. In 1966, the city had made 430 arrests on drug charges. By 1972, the number was 4,500. Notably, however, arrests related to heroin use, the supposed scourge that prompted the war on drugs, were in decline. In actuality, most drug arrests involved marijuana use.[50] At the end of 1973, when the arrest rate was still on the rise, for every one arrest on a heroin charge, four were arrested for marijuana. The tremendous increase led Schaefer's drug-abuse adviser to advocate marijuana decriminalization.[51] Meanwhile during the early 1970s, the city received more than $20 million in federal anticrime funds. With the sanction of state as well as local officials, the Baltimore City Police Department used the revenue and other resources to increase the size of the force, the density of officers assigned to "high-crime" areas, and the level of security in public housing. The funds paid for some drug-use prevention and also for additional patrol cars, high-end walkie-talkies, computerization, and helicopters. As the influence of Baltimore's antipoverty warriors waned during the early 1970s, city residents, primarily those in African American neighborhoods, experienced an expanded police presence both on the ground and in the air. The blare of police sirens, the crackle of walkie-talkies, the whirl of helicopter blades, and the glare of searchlights became standard fare in the city as the War on Poverty began to give way to the war on crime and drugs.[52]

"Money for Everything Except What's Really Needed": Public-Sector Unions Respond

Even as the independence and influence of employees in municipal agencies waned, public-sector unions remained an important source of power for workers and of opposition to Schaefer's austerity and commercially oriented revitalization agenda. Union-led fights with the mayor were battles in larger contests over how the nation should respond to changes in the patterns of global capitalism that were the sources of economic decline in cities such as Baltimore; they were also part of ongoing disputes over how to effectively respond to racial and economic injustice. Among public-sector union leaders and members, those questions were raised directly and also articulated indirectly in widespread anger at low wages that failed to keep pace with rising inflation, poor working conditions, and municipal policies and practices that demeaned the dignity and professionalism of city workers and in some cases precluded them from providing the high quality of services they believed city residents deserved. Strikes in Baltimore in 1974 concerning such issues attracted teachers, sanitation workers, police officers, and other municipal employees in addition to local and national union officials. Many city residents evinced sympathy for the workers' problems, despite considerable inconveniences created by the strikes and reluctance among many taxpayers to see tax rates increased. National news coverage of the Baltimore strikes revealed little of the local nuance, however. Instead, much of the national coverage presented a city besieged by self-serving unionists, representations that conservative opponents of government unions capitalized on to promote their cause. In Baltimore, striking city employees won some of their demands and demonstrated the growing clout of their unions in municipal affairs.

Coverage of the strikes outside of the city, however, helped fuel national animosity toward public-sector unions.

During the early 1970s, collective-bargaining negotiations between the city and its public-sector unions were annual reruns of a familiar drama. As negotiations got under way, Schaefer would threaten that unions' wage demands would force the layoffs of thousands of city workers. The unions would counter that the city was holding out, hinting that the mayor had access to resources he was hiding from underpaid and overworked employees to use for other purposes. If you can find it in the budget, you can have it, the mayor would retort, making available the city's Ordinance of Estimates for union perusal. And the wrangling would continue until the city and unions settled on terms that typically included raises that failed to keep pace with inflation and fringe benefits intended to partially compensate for the slow growth in wages.[53]

But 1974 proved an exception. That year, a month-long strike by Baltimore's public-school teachers and a two-week-long strike initiated by sanitation workers signaled widespread discontent. The teachers' strike was called by the Public School Teachers Association in February and supported to varying extents by the Baltimore Teachers Union and AFSCME. PSTA represented teachers; BTU represented teacher aides; and AFSCME represented other employees of the school system such as cafeteria workers. The strike began in early February, when teachers announced they had "had it" with salaries that lagged well behind those in most other jurisdictions in Maryland, unmanageably large class sizes, inadequate teaching materials, deteriorating school buildings, and other working conditions that prevented them from providing Baltimore's children with a quality education.[54] According to a survey by the *Baltimore Sun*, between 85 percent and 90 percent of the city's 8,400 teachers participated in the strike.[55]

The teachers' strike enjoyed widespread community support—even if some complained privately of inconveniences and worried about the toll it took on their children's education. Parents, otherwise bitterly divided over the use of busing to desegregate the city schools, supported the teachers across racial and economic lines. "The problems of the teachers are the problems of the community," proclaimed Nathan C. Irby Jr., the president of the Parent-Teacher Association of Samuel Chase Elementary School.[56] Parents also made incisive observations when assessing the strike's causes and legitimacy. Dorothy E. Lane connected the teachers' concerns to Schaefer's downtown revitalization priorities. Referencing deliberations under way regarding the possible construction of a new professional sports complex, for example, she commented, "It seems to me they can find money for everything except for what's really needed."[57] And Anne Gresser addressed the state of Maryland's culpability in the low salaries earned by Baltimore teachers.[58] Meanwhile, the Public Schools Administrators and Supervisors Association also supported the strike.[59]

Despite the considerable public support, the strike's resolution ultimately disappointed many. The discontent stemmed from division among and within the unions representing employees of the school system and a degree of political naivete on the part of PSTA. The teachers did win two significant concessions: raises larger than the city originally proposed and an official commitment to smaller class sizes. Had expectations among strikers not risen so high, the settlement could have counted as a small victory. To many, however, especially those in BTU, it seemed a capitulation. Members from that union wanted the strikers to secure commitments from the governor of Maryland and the state's General Assembly to improve urban education. Reliance on local taxes to fund city schools perpetuated racialized patterns of economic injustice because the city simply could not afford what wealthier districts could, the advocates argued. Their objective became a demand of the teachers too late in the negotiations, however, which produced considerable frustration that an important opportunity had been squandered. The remedy for resolving gross funding disparities among educational jurisdictions in Maryland had to come from the statehouse, BTU representatives argued but striking teachers realized only belatedly.[60]

The two-week strike waged in 1974 by AFSCME-affiliated workers started as a wildcat action during a heat wave in July. A group of sanitation workers dissatisfied with a contract their fellow AFSCME members voted to accept independently walked off the job. The sanitation workers had just cause for their anger. The year of the strike, Baltimore's sanitation workers ranked twenty-sixth out of thirty-one cities with populations over four hundred thousand in starting salaries and maximum wage rates. The workers were also angry about dangerous working conditions and a demeaning absenteeism policy the city had recently implemented. "They don't care nothing about you," complained sanitation worker Leroy Anderson about city officials.[61] After failing to convince the wildcat strikers to return to work, AFSCME officials Ray Clarke and Ernie Crofoot had little choice but to endorse the strike and try to make the most of it. They coordinated walkouts by additional blue-collar workers, including school janitors, prison guards, and sewer, parks, dog-pound, zoo, and highway workers. As in 1968, few women participated in the strike. AFSCME's female members remained largely segregated in caretaking jobs, and Clarke worried the strike would quickly lose public support if school and hospital employees abandoned children and ailing patients.[62]

As workers walked the picket line, officials from AFSCME International scrutinized Baltimore's budget in search of sources for larger concessions than the city was offering. Their findings confirmed their frustration with the mayor's priorities. As one analyst noted, the municipal budget was "tilted heavily in favor of capital expenditures [such as a highway project] as opposed to operating expenditures [which could be a source of raises]."[63] "Such a set of expenditure priorities," he had earlier noted, "is clearly geared to the more affluent commuters and not to low income inner city residents."[64] Beyond the bias, however, he found little fat in Schaefer's budget and concluded that additional revenue would have to come from the state.[65] Schaefer's priorities were skewed, AFSCME officials believed, but if the mayor was holding out, they could not determine how.

As the strike wore on, negotiations between the city and an AFSCME-affiliated police union stalled over the question of raises. Disgruntled police officers initiated a workplace protest campaign. They completed lost property reports for such items as pennies that they found on the street and issued tickets—to the mayor, among others—for the most minor of parking and traffic infractions. When their actions yielded reprisals rather than concessions, a group of Baltimore's officers—about half—joined the AFSCME strike. The addition of police officers in a strike that already included prison guards raised the stakes dramatically in AFSCME's showdown with Schaefer; strikes by law enforcement were controversial and potentially dangerous. According to the *New York Times*, the Baltimore officers' five-day strike became the most significant labor protest to date by police in a major city since the Boston strike of 1919.[66]

Despite the heaps of stinking trash that began to accumulate in Baltimore's streets during the strike and the fear occasioned by the police officers' walkout, many city residents sympathized with the strikers. To be sure, some agreed with one outraged resident who fumed, "They're making enough money. I'm paying enough taxes for now for what these cats are doing."[67] More, however, agreed with Warrington E. Coates. Coates lived with his grandmother in a low-income and predominantly African American neighborhood in West Baltimore, where the strike plunged sanitary conditions from "bad to worse," according to one local journalist. "The rats have taken over. I can't even sit here on my back porch. There's no use in washing it down.

I try to grow flowers.... But it's ridiculous," his grandmother Helen Coates complained during the strike. Nevertheless, she and many of her neighbors agreed with her grandson, who showed empathy for the workers. "[Schaefer] should give them what they want. It's a dirty job right from the start. Who the hell wants to pick up garbage?" he asked. Many residents held city and state officials rather than low-wage sanitation workers responsible for conditions in their neighborhood.[68]

Police officers won empathy as well—despite an evening of looting, which occurred the first night after the officers went on strike. Thereafter, the presence of state police sent to Baltimore by Maryland governor Marvin Mandel (but whom Wurf wished in retrospect AFSCME had thought to request) largely restored order. To be sure, the early chaos occasioned by the strike enflamed local racial prejudices and reinforced white fears of Black urban lawlessness. The white wife of one merchant whose carpet business was raided on the first night of the police strike—and who had been put out of business following the looting that occurred in the city after the assassination of Martin Luther King—angrily declared her intention to relocate to "a safer part of the city—an all-white area." But anger at looters did not necessarily mean anger at police. When asked by a reporter who was to blame for the strike, another merchant replied, "I don't know, I don't know. I think police deserve a raise, but where they're going to get it? I don't know—they can't raise taxes."[69] Some African Americans also expressed support for the police officers' cause even as there was no love lost between many Black residents and the police department. In reference to the first six months of 1974, the editorial board of the *Afro-American* wrote, "We have had enough Black marks against the police this year, what with the corruption trials and convictions, the continued reports of police brutality by citizens, even during the strike period. And not to mention the department's Black mark on its continued failure to hire and upgrade Black officers on an equitable basis and in proportion to the population."[70] Yet the editors nonetheless described a "sympathetic mood" for the city's strikers and urged that officials "compromise" with the police.[71]

In the end, strikers won very significant concessions from Schaefer, an indication of AFSCME's growing influence in the city. But they also suffered reprisals that mitigated their victory. Although the mayor earlier had claimed "no money," nonuniformed AFSCME members won a hefty raise, more than 20 percent for some, which would be distributed in increments over a two-year period.[72] The amount was considerably higher than the 5.5 percent raise the city and workers had agreed on two weeks earlier. The city also agreed to fully fund workers' health insurance. In addition, the union and city agreed to refer the unpopular absenteeism policy in the sanitation department to arbitration, and the mayor, disingenuously it later turned out, promised not to carry out reprisals against strike participants. Even as he announced the strike's settlement, however, the mayor added that the cost of the raises would be made up as needed in cuts to city services and layoffs—which he said would be concentrated in the sanitation department. He forcefully made the point that the strike's settlement compelled only a reallocation of revenue; raises for some meant job losses for others. And in the months that followed, Schaefer kept tabs on which workers suffered the effects of the layoffs with the likely intention of punishing those accountable for the strike.[73]

The police officers also won wage concessions as well as reprisals. Baltimore's police commissioner Donald Pomerleau took charge of disciplining his officers. Appointed by the governor, Pomerleau was a notoriously intimidating figure suspected of keeping J. Edgar Hoover–like files on the "who's who" of Baltimore. During the strike, the conservative commissioner took a hard line. "I sense that the moral fiber of this country has been deteriorating rapidly," Pomerleau declared. He then announced "that there will be no general amnesty for those police officers who have failed their responsibility to the public."[74] Pomerleau followed through on his pledge. Despite a no-reprisals promise from Maryland's Democratic governor, the commissioner fired, suspended, or demoted 170 patrolmen and officers. Following the strike, the police union also lost its exclusive bargaining rights with the city and its dues check-off privilege. The harsh punishments alarmed AFSCME's Wurf, who personally intervened on behalf of the officers, to no avail. The layoffs of both sanitation workers and police officers had a chilling effect on the city's public-sector labor movement. Although the union could legitimately call the strikes victories and the concessions AFSCME members won were a tribute to their union's power, workers also learned to take Schaefer's threats seriously that raises and layoffs were reciprocal.[75]

Although residents of the city largely took the strike in stride, its depiction in the national media suggested a city under siege. An article originating with the *Washington Post* that appeared in national newspapers on July 9, even before police officers joined the strike, opened with the alarmist news that the Baltimore strike was nearing "potentially crippling proportions."[76] Four days later, while prison guards were outside picketing, a group of juvenile offenders briefly held hostage four replacement guards. Adult prisoners, members of the jail's inmate council, were helping to quell the disturbance when nonstriking police officers arrived on the scene. Bedlam ensued. Rejecting an offer of help by picketing guards, the officers barged past them and into the jail, where they unleashed their police dogs—on the inmates who were defending the replacement guards. "A lot of innocent inmates got hurt," explained prison nurse Joan Wendler, who said nurses treated several for dog bites.[77] National media accounts missed most of the subtleties of the event. In a front-page article taken from the Associated Press titled "Police Storm Baltimore Jail, Freeing Hostages Taken During Strike by Guards," the *New York Times* quoted a Baltimore police officer: "We hit the door and we did what we had to. It was a hell of a job."[78] The reality was more complicated than the officer—and the newspaper—reported.

National news magazines also depicted Baltimore as ravaged by callous and self-interested municipal workers. The AFSCME sanitation strike coincided with an unfortunately timed announcement by the Baltimore Promotion Council that it was undertaking a $40,000 advertising campaign intended to attract tourists to the city. Baltimore was dubbed "Charm City, USA" in the campaign's marketing materials. Mindful of the tons of garbage strewn throughout Baltimore's streets when they made their announcement, the promoters hedged their bets. They invited tourists to come to Charm City— "when we are ready to receive visitors."[79] (The announcement was made by the executive vice president of a local advertising firm that clearly was in the midst of a spate of bad luck. It had also just launched an antilittering campaign in the city. "It was just beginning to catch on before we had this strike on our hands," Schaefer mused regretfully.[80]) Not surprisingly, the press could not resist poking fun at the city's new moniker. *Time* covered the strike fairly accurately but under the headline "Chaos in Charm City." *Newsweek*'s coverage in an article titled "Trash City," however, fed antiunion sentiments, leading even the editors of the *Baltimore Sun* to complain of a "grossly exaggerated account of Baltimore's troubles."[81]

Conservatives intent on delegitimizing public-sector unions exploited the dramatic coverage of the Baltimore strike and a rift that emerged between Wurf and Mandel. As part of the strike's resolution, AFSCME had secured the governor's pledge that striking police officers would not suffer reprisals. When the governor refused to force Pomerleau to reinstate officers he had fired, Wurf and other labor leaders were outraged and withheld their endorsement of the governor, who was in the midst of a reelection campaign. Mandel did not give in, and in August, he made a statement to the press in which he said that during the strike Wurf had "warned [him] that Baltimore

City would burn to the ground unless the City gave in to his demands."[82] For the rest of his life, Wurf denied having made the comment. And Mandel's get-tough posturing likely won him votes in the election. Nevertheless, an ardent opponent of public-sector unions, former *Newsweek* editor and cofounder of the *National Review* Ralph de Toledano, alluded to the statement in the title of his 1975 diatribe against public-sector unions, *Let Our Cities Burn*. Conservative senator Jesse Helms authored the foreword of the book, and future president Ronald Reagan, warning that "forced unionization of public employees threatens to replace elected officials with an undemocratic 'private government,'" described it as "*must* reading."[83] The momentum de Toledano and other conservatives helped to build against public-sector unionization contributed to undermining ongoing efforts by AFSCME to win passage of the National Public Employee Relations Act, which was intended to extend union rights to all government workers. It also contributed to the national erosion of the public's support for public-sector unions.[84]

By the mid-1970s, AFSCME had never been as strong—or as vulnerable. The union's membership continued to grow during the Nixon and Ford years, and collective bargaining narrowed the gap that separated the wages of public- and private-sector workers. As the private-sector labor movement continued to decline, the public-sector movement, powered by large numbers of African Americans and women, increased in clout and stature. Meanwhile, in Baltimore, AFSCME served as an important source of constraint on the Schaefer administration—a reminder that the mayor's austerity measures that came at the expense of public services and jobs would not go unchallenged. Yet the forces that had already begun to undermine the independence of Baltimore's antipoverty and human-services workers also presented grave challenges to public-sector unions. Mounting hostility to antipoverty efforts, welfare, human-services providers, and public-sector unions jeopardized significant gains African Americans had only recently secured in Baltimore. Not surprisingly, AFSCME leaders as well as many African Americans and urban residents nationwide hoped a Democrat in the White House would provide some relief.

CHAPTER 7

"Polishing the Apple While the Core Rots"

Carter and the Cities

"Is Baltimore trying to kid someone?" asked the editors of the *Afro-American* in early 1977. The Commission on Governmental Efficiency and Economy, a division of the city's Chamber of Commerce, had recently authored a study comparing Baltimore to ten other municipalities. Charm City ranked first, the study's authors reported with enthusiasm, in "financial standing." Mayor William Donald Schaefer's commitment to austerity and to making the city attractive to investors was working. But the *Afro-American* editors were more concerned about the city's ranking on other indicators. In the category of "social health," Baltimore had come in ninth. And it ranked tenth in "educational level per capita." So what was there to celebrate, the editors wondered? The city's business climate was important but hardly more so than the well-being of the population. "Baltimore officials go on building monuments to our shortsightedness and gambling away the welfare and best interest of city residents," the editors protested. Municipal officials did not have their priorities straight. It was time to stop "polishing the outside of the apple while the core rots," the editors charged.[1]

As Baltimore's Black leaders had been arguing for decades, access to better jobs was key to improving conditions in the city's core. And given the success African Americans had had opening the public sector to Black workers and the importance of that sector to African American communities, the *Afro*'s editors wanted to build on the record. Black workers already filled many of the city's lowest-paid positions; they needed more of the better jobs. And it just did not make sense that white suburbanites held so many high-paying posts. The Baltimore Civil Service needed to limit municipal employment to city residents, the editors argued. Philadelphia and Chicago already had residency requirements for municipal employment, and the policy had withstood scrutiny by the courts on the grounds that locals have a vested interest in the quality of their public services. With both jobs and better services at stake, the editors were frustrated that Baltimore voters had recently rejected a residency-requirement proposal—and angered that election officials had buried the measure deep in a lengthy ballot where only the most diligent and persistent were likely to find it. Without the requirement, taxpayers in Baltimore continued to play "Santa Claus to the wealthier suburbs" and their mostly white residents, the editors argued.[2] And city dwellers who actually lived in Baltimore's core had to compete for jobs with those who elected not to make Baltimore their home.

During the mid-1970s, as mounting inflation and unemployment eroded national economic conditions—and Baltimore officials continued to pursue economic "health" by practicing austerity and sacrificing the actual health of residents—fights over public-sector employment remained highly politicized. The residency requirement was but one front in an ongoing battle over the racial makeup of the municipal workforce and its leadership. In the deindustrializing city, public-sector jobs provided a critical source of stable employment. They had also become a bedrock of the city's Black middle and working classes. Meanwhile, many African Americans remained skeptical that whites would provide Black communities with high-quality services. Black representation in the municipal workforce, particularly in leadership roles, was required to ensure that Black concerns were addressed and that African Americans were involved in decision-making. Although they had been largely overlooked during previous battles over municipal employment, women, both Black and white, also began demanding greater representation in positions of authority. In addition, they pressed both the city and their unions for changes to hiring and other employment practices that perpetuated their disadvantage in the municipal bureaucracy and led to earnings that significantly trailed men's. The fights were about fairness, and they were also critical to the economic well-being of the city's Black communities, which relied heavily on women's public-sector incomes and were thus especially hard hit by gender bias.

Shrinking budgets hindered efforts to further diversify the municipal workforce, improve the terms and conditions of government employment, and use the state to combat pressing urban problems. And although many in Baltimore had hoped that Democrat Jimmy Carter's election to the presidency in 1976 would be a source of relief, they were sorely disappointed. Flummoxed by the perplexing challenge of the nation's economic woes when he entered office, the president's faith in the power of the government to solve problems deteriorated during his term. Ultimately, he turned to conservative remedies to combat inflation, even though he was aware they would worsen unemployment. In so doing, as historian Judith Stein has argued, he lent the weight of the federal government to advancing the economic interests of the nation's financial sector, which produced wealth but not a lot of jobs, at the expense of the industrial sector, which produced both goods and jobs.[3] Carter's policies increased hardship in the nation's struggling cities and contributed to shaping the neoliberal global world order that Nixon had started to build. At the same time, the increasingly conservative steps Carter took to fight economic problems limited the domestic policies he could pursue to address poverty and other urban ills. The approach Carter's administration ultimately adopted to stem decline in distressed cities—the funding of public-private partnerships—enhanced the power in municipal affairs of the advocates of trickle-down commercial revitalization efforts. National labor and civil rights leaders proposed liberal alternatives to Carter's conservative policies to limited avail. The federal policy changes were blows to workers in Baltimore's antipoverty and human-services agencies whose increased influence in the city government during the 1960s had given them the opportunity to shift the municipal agenda away from a myopic focus on commercial revitalization and toward what they called human renewal. During the Carter years, the workers and their unions lost ground in their efforts to ensure that city officials remain responsive to the pressing needs of residents with low incomes.

"A Greater Mix in People Who Make Decisions": Affirmative Action in Baltimore

During the early 1970s, Richard Nixon's New Federalism had been an intentional revocation of the independence and influence of activist antipoverty workers and human-services providers in the nation's struggling cities. By concentrating considerable control over federal resources in the hands of elected officials, the Republican president had diluted the power of African Americans and women in the municipal government. The change hardly stopped Black leaders from demanding top municipal jobs for African Americans. Administrative positions remained a critical source of influence over local policy-making in a city in which Black residents continued to be underrepresented in elected offices. During the second half of the 1970s, African

American leaders continued to diligently monitor municipal hiring practices and repeatedly pressed Schaefer to appoint Black candidates to top positions. They wanted to maintain African Americans' influence over antipoverty and human-services agencies, but they also sought leadership posts in more powerful divisions of the government, such as the Department of Finance. On both fronts, they met with frustration.

In 1976, Maude Harvey announced her retirement. James Chavis, a Black assistant professor at the University of Maryland's School of Social Work and Community Planning, was one of three finalists for the position. Chavis had many years of service with the DSS and had earlier worked for the city's Community Action Agency and had been the director of the Neighborhood Youth Corps. Ultimately, however, Schaefer selected another finalist, Kalman "Buzzy" Hettleman, for the job. Hettleman was a lawyer whose experience included a stint with the national Office of Economic Opportunity's Legal Services division and several years as the director of the Consumer Law Center of Baltimore's Legal Aid Bureau.[4] Although no stranger to issues concerning poverty, Hettleman was a white candidate and, according to the *Afro-American*, a "Schaefer pal" who owed no allegiance to Black communities. The paper's editors complained that the appointment reflected the city's "white buddy buddy arrangement," which continuously impeded Black advancement.[5]

Less than two months later, Black leaders had further cause for anger. Baltimore's white finance director, Charles Benton, had two open positions in his department. The Department of Finance wielded considerable authority over the important task of budget-making and was also, in the words of the editors of the *Afro-American*, "one of the more lily-white sections" of the city government. The city's Metro Democratic Organization, an influential Black-run political club, had recently and publicly appealed to the mayor for more powerful spots for African Americans in the city government. At least one position in the Department of Finance would indicate that the white power structure of Baltimore took Black people seriously. Nevertheless, Benton filled both positions with whites. The *Afro-American* editors called the move a "face slap," and Raymond V. Haysbert, of the Metro Democratic Organization observed about the mayor, "It seems that he simply doesn't have any respect for us."[6] African Americans in Baltimore certainly did not hold uniform views on public policy or financial matters, nor did Black city residents expect that any single African American could represent all Black perspectives. Nevertheless, African Americans wanted to see individuals with a level of awareness of and accountability to Black communities in positions of authority. They wanted Black people to play a meaningful role in municipal decision-making. Schaefer and his senior staff appeared indifferent to their concerns.

The pressure that African Americans applied on the mayor was somewhat effective, however. In 1976, following years of pressure, Schaefer finally adopted an affirmative action plan for the city. Shortly thereafter, he also selected a new personnel director who was actually likely to implement it. The hire was a victory for the city's Black leaders and also for women, both Black and white, who had begun to protest more forcefully their own exclusion from influential positions and the discrimination they faced in the municipal bureaucracy. Schaefer chose Hilda Ford, an African American New Yorker, to run the city's personnel department. During the War on Poverty and while she was in New York, Ford had run the nation's largest Youth Opportunity Center. She had also overseen the community involvement efforts undertaken by the New York State Employment Service and worked as the assistant director of the Career Opportunities Division in the civil service department. In other words, she was precisely the kind of candidate Black and feminist leaders wanted at the helm of Baltimore's civil service department, a body that civil rights leaders had been criticizing as racist for decades.[7] Ford would not have authority over the municipal budget, but she could make improvements to the city's employment practices.

Ford's hire drew criticism from some white city officials. Hyman Pressman, the comptroller, complained that Ford was not a city native. But while African American leaders tended to favor a residency requirement for municipal employees, they were more than prepared to make an exception in Ford's case. As Verda F. Welcome, an African American state senator, explained to Pressman in a letter that was published in the *Afro-American*, "Instead of deploring this choice of a qualified woman because she gained her experience elsewhere, perhaps you should deplore the fact that Baltimore City has given so few women, particularly Black women, the opportunity to advance up the career ladder so that they qualify to hold such a position."[8] Welcome and many others in Baltimore hoped that Ford's hire meant that past discriminatory practices were going to change.

And change was certainly needed. African Americans and women, and Black women in particular, had made important gains in municipal employment, largely in antipoverty and human-services agencies and low-wage support positions. Government jobs had compared favorably to the informal, low-wage jobs into which many Black workers had earlier been concentrated. But it was now the mid-1970s. African Americans expected and wanted better jobs and more influence. Yet they remained largely excluded from positions of power. In 1977, shortly before Ford assumed her post, members of the Community Relations Commission released a study that attended not only to race-based but also to sex-based inequities in the municipal workforce. It showed that white men held seventy-six of the city's eighty-six top-paying jobs. White women occupied seven and Black men three of the remaining ten. Black women, who were the most numerous demographic in the municipal workforce, were not correspondingly represented in well-paying and influential positions. And Black men were not doing much better. In addition, outside of the Department of Education, only 25 percent of African Americans compared to 60 percent of whites earned more than $10,000 a year. And although Black workers made up the majority of the noneducation municipal workforce, many of their positions were federally funded, including vulnerable CETA jobs, whereas whites held over 60 percent of the city's noneducation jobs financed by municipal revenue. Women as a group, meanwhile, made up most of the city's clerical workforce, but beyond that they were well-represented only in health, education, and welfare agencies. Less than 30 percent of women earned salaries over $10,000 a year.[9] Ford had her work cut out for her.

Despite the tough economic times, Ford arrived in Baltimore determined to implement equal opportunity in the municipal workforce and move people generally excluded from positions of leadership into those jobs. She was also aware that her ambitions generated anxiety and anger among those who benefited from the status quo. "We live in a society dominated by white males and white male egos and images. There is a certain resistance to changing the habits and patterns which have perpetuated this domination," she explained. Nevertheless, she was prepared to make such changes. "That is not to say that people will be excluded," she added. "It simply means we will have a greater mix in the kinds of people who make decisions."[10] To achieve her goals, Ford pursued multiple strategies. She took affirmative action by instituting hiring procedures that expanded the pool of candidates from which supervisors could choose when filling vacancies. And she was a particularly strong advocate on behalf of women. She conducted a major study of municipal clerical jobs and instituted a reclassification plan that resulted in wage increases for many. The change also created career ladders over some formerly dead-end jobs and moved the city's clerical salaries closer to local prevailing wages. Baltimore Working Women, an organization that advocated on behalf of clerical workers and monitored municipal employment practices, lauded the changes. In addition, Ford held management workshops for women to encourage them to seek advanced positions, and she urged Schaefer to pursue calls from municipal employees for child-care services and other initiatives that would help them balance work and family obligations.[11]

Baltimore's civil service department was not alone in attempting to improve the employment status of women during the second half of the 1970s. Under pressure from women in its international union and probably local pressure as well, the predominantly male AFSCME leaders in Maryland also increased the attention they paid to issues of gender equity. The American Federation of Government Employees, which represented the predominantly female staff of the Social Security Administration—headquartered just outside of Baltimore—as well as other unions representing federal employees in and around Baltimore, undertook similar efforts. Organizations representing employees of the state of Maryland continued to lack official recognition, but they nonetheless advocated on behalf of their members and made gender-related demands.[12]

AFSCME's efforts on behalf of gender equity were particularly noteworthy. During the early 1970s female staffers at AFSCME pushed AFSCME International to take seriously the fact that its membership included hundreds of thousands of women. The staffers pressed the union to take a strong stand opposing sex discrimination and to establish a committee tasked with addressing women's concerns. Shortly thereafter, the International began to encourage its locals to address during contract negotiations such issues as maternity leave, child care, and gender-related inequities in fringe-benefits packages. The International also encouraged local unions to establish women's committees and to consider the potential family obligations of women workers during organizing drives. In addition, women in the International and among the rank and file as well reminded the union of its need to clean its own house. By the mid-1970s, few women held positions of authority within the union. Feminists in AFSCME urged their male counterparts to encourage women to seek leadership positions and to include women on bargaining committees. Additionally, they pushed for more job-training opportunities for women and for AFSCME leaders to work with state and local government officials to create job ladders that would open opportunities for low-wage women workers.[13]

In Maryland, local AFSCME officials adopted a number of the recommendations coming from the International. In fact, Ernie Crofoot served as the vice chair on the International's first women's committee and gained a sense of women's frustrations firsthand. Among the most aggressive actions Maryland locals took on behalf of women were investments in training programs and the creation of job ladders. These changes were of particular significance to African American women, who were concentrated at the bottom of most hierarchies. For hospital workers, AFSCME created training programs that enabled workers to advance from aides to nurses. The union built negotiated routes to advancement out of formerly dead-end jobs in the Department of Social Services as well. AFSCME officials also pressured the state and local governments to enforce equal-pay legislation. Over time, many bureaucracies had created sex-specific job titles for workers who performed essentially the same functions. The problem was pervasive in the custodial field, and AFSCME's leaders combated the inequity and also encouraged women to seek so-called male positions because they offered more opportunity for advancement and better pay. Meanwhile, the number of women in the leadership of AFSCME locals and on bargaining committees began to increase, including in Baltimore. The changes proved a source of pride even for some old-school AFSCME leaders. Well after he retired, Ray Clarke considered the opportunities AFSCME created for women the most important contribution the union and he personally had made to the city.[14]

Successful efforts by the staff of the CRC, Ford, and the leaders and members of public-sector unions to improve the status of women as a group and of African American men in the municipal workforce enhanced the value of public-sector employment in the city's otherwise deeply troubled economy. And the changes were profoundly important for Black women. In 1970, nearly a third of employed African American women in Baltimore held a job on the local, state, or federal level. By 1980, nearly 40 percent did. (The corresponding figures for Black men were 21 percent and 28 percent.)[15] In a city plagued by structural male unemployment, improvements to Black women's status in public-sector jobs were a matter of justice and also tremendously important to the economic health of African American families and communities. Attempts to make further improvements, however, were hampered rather than helped by the Democratic president that Black Baltimore had helped to elect in 1976.

"Poor and Working Americans Will Be the Prime Victims": Carter's Battle Against Inflation

Following the neglect of urban problems during the Nixon and Ford years, many in Baltimore had hoped that President Jimmy Carter would be a source of relief. On the campaign trail, the candidate had made enthusiastic promises to city residents. He had also proclaimed, "When I finish my term, I want Black people to say that I did more for them in my Presidency than any President in their lifetimes."[16] Despite healthy skepticism, many African Americans were willing to give him a chance. Nationally, Black voters were critical to Carter's victory. And even in Baltimore, where Carter also garnered a lot of white support, Black city voters alone had given him the margin he needed to win Maryland's electoral college votes. "Our Vote Did It," proclaimed a banner headline in the *Afro-American*, and articles described the intensive voter registration and get-out-the-vote drives, which included free transportation to the polls and babysitting services.[17] But following the victory, Black leaders lost little time before getting down to business. Expectations of the president were high. As Parren Mitchell commented, "We must now seek the rewards for our efforts" in the form of appointments to positions of authority in the federal government and policies helpful to African Americans.[18] National civil rights leader Jesse Jackson, one of the new president's early supporters, expressed the same sentiment but more poetically: "We selected him, elected him and now must collect from him."[19]

Initially, Carter did try to respond to the concerns of his party's traditional base. On assuming office, however, he inherited an economic crisis of both perplexing and alarming dimensions. Stagflation, the term coined to describe the phenomenon, combined rising unemployment and mounting inflation. The pairing defied conventional economic fixes; policies often used to lower unemployment tended to increase inflation, and remedies to counter inflation tended to worsen unemployment. Nevertheless, in keeping with the expectations of his core constituencies, Carter initially prioritized the battle against unemployment. As he had argued while accepting his party's presidential nomination, "We simply cannot check inflation by keeping people out of work."[20] He raised the minimum wage and passed a stimulus package intended to combat unemployment. Meanwhile, he also appointed record numbers of women and African Americans to positions in his administration. Patricia Roberts Harris, for example, became the secretary of the Department of Housing and Urban Development (HUD), making her the first African American women to hold a cabinet position and a key player in the direction of the nation's urban policies.[21]

Regarding cities, the president attempted to follow through on his campaign promise for innovation by appointing a group of advisers to come up with a bold urban plan. He also directed a greater concentration of national resources to poor cities. By so doing, his administration responded to concerns that the distribution of Community Development Block Grants spread resources too thinly across jurisdictions with grossly divergent levels of need instead of concentrating them in cities with the most urgent problems. Federal officials revised the regulations governing the distribution of block grants so that they targeted poor cities. And in 1977, the administration used CETA funds to create 425,000 public-sector jobs.[22]

Observers in Baltimore lauded the change in CDBG policy, hoping that increased funding for the city would help to combat pressing problems. Early indications were positive. Carter's increased investment in CETA enabled the city to hire almost two thousand new workers. Under the leadership of Marion Pines, a white woman who led the Mayor's Office of Manpower Resources, Baltimore's CETA program had become a national model. Researchers found that the program's participants had high and enduring employment rates even though the program nationally achieved more mixed results.[23] The success of the program, the Baltimore staff believed, demonstrated the positive results municipal agencies could produce if provided resources and a federal commitment. CETA training and job experience programs were far from perfect. Women, for example, often acquired skills likely to lead to low-wage service positions. Nevertheless, both male and female workers gained needed résumé-building experience, and those who won jobs often made important contributions to the city. As Pines explained, "We are providing some valuable services to low income communities through our training and work experience programs. Daycare for working mothers, health care for homebound elderly persons, the weatherization of old homes, and the renovation of vacant houses provides real employment skills for CETA participants *and much needed services to our communities*" (emphasis in the original).[24] Carter's move was a first step in the right direction—but he urgently needed to do more. In 1977, at just one of Baltimore's manpower centers, employees typically arrived at work on the days that they accepted CETA applications to find fifty to a hundred job seekers waiting outside their doors.[25]

Leaders of the nation's liberal establishment, including representatives from civil rights organizations and labor unions, believed they had solutions for the nation's ills that Carter should pursue. Plans had been under way since before the presidential election to secure a full-employment law from Congress. Full employment had been a policy objective of Franklin Roosevelt, and it was also a practice in place in many European nations. The United States, however, had yet to commit the full power of the federal government to guaranteeing its citizens jobs. Given the high rates of unemployment during the mid-1970s, along with other political calculations, the timing seemed perfect for a renewed campaign for full-employment legislation, many activists believed. Meanwhile, liberals also advocated for a host of other reforms to fight unemployment, including stimulus spending and a higher tax rate for the wealthiest, and labor leaders called for a national industrial plan. Unifying their demands was the conviction that even as the nation reeled simultaneously from high unemployment and inflation rates, the need for jobs was the more pressing national problem.[26]

Carter, a self-described centrist, was not a ready convert to the liberal policy proposals. He had won the presidency when public mistrust of government was high. Stagflation, the nation's defeat in Vietnam, the Watergate scandal, and Ford's decision to pardon Nixon for any crimes he may have committed in office convinced many Americans that elected officials in Washington did not know what they were doing and could not be trusted. In an election year when a popular bumper sticker suggested "Don't Vote; It Only Encourages Them," Carter's status as a Washington outsider held much appeal. During his campaign, although Carter certainly made promises, he also made his lack of name recognition rather than specific political proposals a selling point. Whereas Nixon had assiduously cultivated racial and other resentments among middle- and working-class whites to win the presidency, Carter relied on disdain for the political status quo to win votes. In fact, Carter did not even use the label "liberal" to describe himself.[27]

In office, as the nation's economic conditions worsened, Carter came under pressure not only from the left but also from the right to pursue specific policy proposals. Throughout his term, conservatives, such as economist Alan Greenspan, persistently demanded that Carter prioritize the battle against inflation rather than unemployment to combat the nation's economic woes. An oil shock during the late 1970s worsened the nation's economic troubles and intensified the urgency of the pleas for action. The U.S. automobile industry, once the symbol of American prosperity and strength, verged on the brink of collapse, and financial markets, the source of much new wealth in the postindustrial economy, also took a huge hit. If the status of the United States in the global economy had appeared bleak during Nixon's watch, Carter confronted an even gloomier reality. Many of the president's most trusted economic advisers subscribed to Keynesianism, but stagflation seemed to defy both their economic models and policy prescriptions. Meanwhile, conservative economists proffered neoliberal solutions they promised would bring inflation under control.[28]

Among the remedies conservative economists proposed were fiscal restraint, tax cuts, and deregulation. The supply-side solutions were intended to stabilize the marketplace by reducing federal intervention and concentrating capital in the hands of elites, who the economists agreed could put it to its most productive uses and thus stimulate economic growth. To combat inflation, the economists asserted that only a severe contraction of the nation's money supply would cure the problem. The remedy would also strengthen the dollar and help revive the currency in global markets, a vital step in the effort to reassert U.S. hegemony overseas. Keynesians balked at the monetarist remedy, which would inevitably spark recession and drive up unemployment. The nation's workers, they argued, should not pay the highest price for economic recovery. But the sun was setting on the Keynesians' reign as the neoliberal era continued to dawn.[29]

In the face of mounting pressure to combat inflation, which came not only from ideologues but also from a wide range of Americans concerned about rising prices, Carter began adopting some of the policy recommendations of conservative economists. As the president's priorities started to shift from fighting unemployment to combating inflation, he and his staff began replacing calls for social-welfare and job-producing initiatives with endorsements of balanced budgets. Indicative of the change, during a speech in Baltimore in 1978, Carter probably surprised many in his audience of Democrats when he enthused that his policy achievements included tax cuts, reducing the deficit, deregulation, "put[ting] the 'free' back into our free enterprise system," and "get[ting] the government's nose out of the business of the people."[30] Though in town to stump for a Democrat, the president sounded like a Republican. Moreover, his policies and inflation-fighting strategies were recipes sure to increase unemployment and hardship in the very city where he was speaking. In response to his disappointing track record, many of Carter's former supporters quickly became outspoken critics. "It is unjust to impose on the poor and on minorities the burden of achieving price stability in this country," Vernon Jordan of the National Urban League charged.[31]

Certainly there were no pain-free solutions to the economic problems the nation faced. Parren Mitchell, who had served as the head of Baltimore's Community Action Agency before becoming the city's first Black congressional representative and then a founder of the Congressional Black Caucus, knew that well. During the late 1970s, Mitchell chaired the House Domestic Monetary Policy Subcommittee and signed off on some of the unemployment-inducing anti-inflation strategies that Carter pursued. And he did so while painfully aware that Carter's strategies would benefit elite interests more than those of regular Americans and come at a particularly steep price for many of his African American and low-income constituents in Baltimore.[32] Carter's inflation-fighting remedies privileged the interests of those on Wall Street and came at the expense of those on Main Street. They also proved disastrous in the nation's struggling cities that already had high unemployment rates.

While the anti-inflation efforts Carter pursued during the first half of his term cost urban residents social welfare measures and other reforms they had hoped for, the draconian strategies he sanctioned in 1979 and 1980 created far worse problems. In response to intensifying pressure, Carter took the dramatic step of enhancing the authority of the unelected members of the Federal Reserve Board, those who carried out the nation's monetary policies by controlling the volume of dollars in circulation. During the post–World War II period, the ambition of full employment had generally guided the Fed's policies. Moreover, its influence over the nation's macroeconomic-policy priorities had been secondary to that of Congress's. Carter veered sharply from precedent. In 1979, he appointed Paul Volcker to the helm of the Federal Reserve. Previously Volcker had headed the New York Federal Reserve and served in the Department of the Treasury under Presidents Kennedy, Johnson, and Nixon. He had earned his Wall Street credentials as an economist at Chase Manhattan Bank, and he was also well-known in elite financial circles globally. Volcker was a Democrat, an inflation hawk, and a prominent member of the banking establishment. He was Wall Street's preferred man for the job, and his appointment represented a Carter concession to powerful banking interests, who wanted a sympathetic economist to tame inflation regardless of the employment costs or dire implications for residents in struggling cities. Under Volcker's stewardship, which extended into the Reagan years, the Federal Reserve aggressively combated inflation. His remedies proved very costly. Although they ultimately helped to reduce inflation, they also plunged the country into the worst recession since the Great Depression and drove the unemployment rate into the double digits.[33]

The Volcker years at the Fed marked a significant turning point in the history of the institution and had long-term as well as immediate implications for residents of rust-belt cities such as Baltimore. Even after inflation later abated, constraining it—rather than maximizing employment and wages—remained the priority of the members of the Federal Reserve. The change buoyed the fortunes of the nation's financial sector and investor class but came at the expense of the nation's manufacturing sector and American workers, including those in deindustrializing cities. Fortunes to be made on Wall Street, insulated by the Fed's anti-inflation commitment, made investment in industry in the United States less appealing by comparison, especially in the context of the liberalizing global economy. Carter's appointee to the Fed, in other words, contributed significantly to what scholars have called the financialization of the American economy. Economic activity in the realm of finance, insurance, and real estate soon eclipsed manufacturing as the engine of the American economy, which would often compel nationally elected officials to defer to the demands of elite interests over the needs of average citizens. Nixon had abandoned the Bretton Woods system and begun building its free market–oriented replacement. Carter's contribution to the new neoliberal world order was a reordering of American macroeconomic priorities in a manner that privileged financial interests. The changes did not bode well for jobless and low-income residents in Baltimore.[34]

Not surprisingly, liberals responded in outrage to both the Volcker appointment and Carter's policy concessions. In 1980, William Lucy, the secretary-treasurer of AFSCME International, described a political landscape that was in the midst of dramatic transformation. "We currently have a Democratic administration, elected largely by labor and minorities, pursuing pro-business economic policies—high interest rates, scarce money and cutbacks in public spending for human services. . . . Poor and working Americans will be the prime victims," he predicted.[35] Carter's policy decisions represented significant departures from the macroeconomic strategies the Democratic Party had pursued since the 1930s. From the New Deal onward, the party had engaged in a very delicate balancing act. Democrats pursued measures that advanced profit-making and corporate interests. They simultaneously maintained a measure of commitment to wealth redistribution and considered themselves the caretakers of the nation's workers and welfare state. During the late 1970s, Carter turned his party sharply to the right. His policy choices and commitments made it difficult for many Americans to remember that the Democratic Party had once fancied itself the champion of the people and a foe of the forces of unrestrained capitalism. The Democrats seemed to have switched teams.

The ramifications of Carter's macroeconomic policies in Baltimore were devastating. At the end of the 1970s, the city had the second highest African American unemployment rate in the country, surpassed only by Philadelphia. The U.S. Bureau of Labor Statistics reported the unemployment rate for Black workers in Baltimore at 18 percent, a figure that had climbed from

15 percent in 1977 and was four times higher than the white rate. An economist with the labor bureau hypothesized that the high Black unemployment figure in Baltimore resulted from the large number of African Americans who were actively seeking jobs. Federal officials did not include the "discouraged," individuals who lacked work but were not in the job market, in unemployment calculations. Employees of the Mayor's Office of Manpower Resources thought the economist was right. Job training and work experience that they provided, they believed, had convinced formerly discouraged African American workers in the city to seek jobs. But the job seekers graduated into Baltimore's depressed labor market. And if employment prospects for Black workers were bad in 1979, as Mitchell correctly predicted, things were only going to "get worse."[36] For a man who wanted "Black people to say that [he] did more for them . . . than any President in their lifetimes," Carter proved a tremendous disappointment.[37]

"A Collision Course": Carter's Urban Plan

The urban policies that Carter pursued also evinced a betrayal of earlier ideals of the Democratic Party. At the beginning of his presidency, Carter had created a task force charged with breathing life into the bold urban agenda he had promised but not specified as a candidate. The macroeconomic strategies he adopted to fight inflation, however, severely constrained the options its members could realistically consider, and they made little headway for over a year. "We are on a collision course between the demands of the urban constituency and the demands for a balanced budget," one high-ranking official at the Department of Housing and Urban Development told the *New York Times* in 1977. Another anonymous administration official noted, "We're in a pretty tight box politically. We've got a real problem with the people who put this President in office." In early 1978, word leaked that the urban policy task force was considering proposing targeted commercial redevelopment programming to the exclusion of social welfare programs as their major initiative. The people who put the president in office reacted with anger, and even Harris, the secretary of HUD, expressed misgivings. Given ongoing deindustrialization and the tight credit squeeze, which prevented cities from easily securing funds for capital improvements, few urban advocates opposed commercial development initiatives categorically. But Harris echoed the concerns of many when she worried that White House staffers and other federal officials were pressuring the urban advisers to forgo social welfare initiatives entirely. "Let us remember," she cautioned, "that economic development is not the penicillin for urban decay, if at the same time there are no hospitals, no low-cost housing and no decent transportation."[38]

The leaders of the National Urban League (NUL) were more than ready to supply the task force with an aggressive urban policy plan. By the mid-1970s, the NUL was over a decade removed from its earlier history as the voice of moderation within the civil rights movement. Under the leadership of Whitney Young Jr., who became the organization's president in 1961, the NUL had become increasingly politically active, joining the nation's other leading civil rights organizations in assertively demanding increased federal commitments to both racial and economic justice. Vernon Jordan Jr., who succeeded Young as the organization's executive director in 1972, shared his predecessor's commitment to a broad progressive agenda. In fact, during the second half of the 1970s, Jordan helped the NUL to become one of the nation's most prominent civil rights organizations—and a source of sharp criticism of the Carter administration. During the 1960s, Young had proposed that the Johnson administration create an "urban Marshall plan." The original Marshall Plan, the more than $13 billion that the United States committed to helping rebuild Europe following World War II, had been remarkably successful. Surely the United States should make a similar commitment to its own cities, Young reasoned. Jordan resurrected the idea and pressed Carter to commit $50 billion to urban aid. Civil rights leaders also weighed in on the form urban aid should take. Aware of the difficulties many cities faced attracting and retaining businesses, they acknowledged the need for grant programs aimed at facilitating physical renewal and encouraging private investment. They also, however, considered social welfare initiatives indispensable. "The connection between economic incentives and social programs is crucial," one leader argued. "You can't plan one side without the other."[39] Jordan also cautioned against a one-sided approach. "The way to save cities isn't to abandon them to the mercies of speculators. The cities will be revitalized through programs that help the poor, preserve and improve their neighborhoods and ensure their participation in decisions that affect their lives."[40] Overall, full-employment legislation, affirmative action, and a much stronger social safety net—in addition to programs that incentivized private investment in cities—were the ingredients needed to effectively combat urban poverty, civil rights activists argued.[41]

Officials from AFSCME International, whose members included many in the nation's struggling cities, also had policy recommendations for Carter.

Although the union's leaders tended to share the progressive agenda of civil rights leaders, their contribution to the urban policy debate largely focused on economic formulas needed to maintain service delivery. To help poor cities better weather the vagaries of the business cycle, they advocated for countercyclical federal aid. Union officials also urged the federal government to use the power it wielded over the distribution of intergovernmental revenue to compel state and local governments to adopt more progressive tax structures to fund public services. In addition, AFSCME advocated that state governments redistribute tax revenue from richer to poorer jurisdictions to fund services. To combat unemployment in struggling cities, AFSCME leaders favored urban economic development programs and stimulus spending to encourage private-sector job growth. In addition, despite their suspicion of what they called "make-work schemes," which they feared would result from the adoption of full-employment legislation and which they believed would threaten hard-won gains they had achieved for their members through collective bargaining, they did also endorse limited and targeted public-sector job creation.[42]

The debates on the federal level concerning the appropriate balance to be sought in urban planning between commercial revitalization projects and social-welfare initiatives mirrored battles well under way in Baltimore. Moreover, individuals seasoned in the trenches of Baltimore figured prominently in the national conversations. Not only had Mitchell moved from leading his city's War on Poverty to championing full-employment legislation and affirmative action in Congress; he was also leading attempts in that body to redirect resources within the federal budget toward HUD and the Department of Health, Education, and Welfare. Simultaneously, another Baltimore native worked toward a different goal. Robert C. Embry Jr., the former director of Baltimore's Department of Housing and Community Development and a driving force behind his hometown's ongoing commercial revitalization efforts, was the chair of Carter's urban policy task force.[43]

During a campaign stop in Baltimore, then presidential candidate Carter had been favorably impressed by the downtown redevelopment efforts under way in the city. Although antipoverty workers had gotten the city to move beyond brick-and-mortar responses to poverty, commercial revitalization had continued apace in the city during the 1960s and 1970s. From his post at the helm of Housing and Community Development, Embry had played a significant role in the efforts. Much of the responsibility for balancing the city's commitment to commercial revitalization and neighborhood concerns had fallen to Embry after he assumed the directorship in 1968. He evinced a genuine empathy for residents of the city's poor communities. During the 1960s, he acceded to the demands of public-housing activists for resident participation in decision-making. He also led efforts to include residents in housing-related decision-making on the national level. During the early 1970s, however, Embry's commitment to community participation seemed to wane. As the city consolidated into a single entity its Community Action Agency and Model Cities program, Embry advised the mayor to abolish the advisory boards of the older agencies, even though they were the only bodies in the city government in which African American women and people with low incomes held significant influence. He urged the mayor instead to make the director of the new antipoverty agency accountable only to the mayor. As Embry's confidence in War on Poverty–era strategies dimmed, his enthusiasm for public-private redevelopment ventures persisted. He worked in collaboration with the leadership of the Greater Baltimore Committee, an influential organization of business executives committed to revitalizing the city's downtown commercial district. Embry's skillful management of public-private initiatives in Baltimore piqued Carter's interest, and on winning the White House, Carter invited Embry to serve as assistant secretary of HUD. Embry arrived in Washington hoping to help other cities adopt some of Baltimore's commercial revitalization strategies.[44]

The urban policy task force that Embry chaired concluded its deliberations in early 1978, and in March, Carter unveiled his urban program. Although the policy advisers had added a small budget for social-welfare initiatives, the thrust of the $10.4 billion two-year program was trickle-down economic redevelopment. In his National Urban Policy Message to the Congress, Carter explained that his goal was to "combin[e] the resources of Federal, State and local government, and us[e] them as a lever to involve the even greater strength of our private economy to conserve and strengthen our cities and communities."[45] To that end, the administration created Urban Development Action Grants (UDAGs), which made available federal funds to stimulate private investment in distressed cities. Although the law did not initially state that the funds had to be used exclusively for commercial development, HUD's selection process typically limited them to that purpose. Both cities and investors could qualify for support once investors committed to a viable project, which could be anything from an industrial park to a shopping mall.[46]

In addition to introducing UDAGs, the Carter administration also directed the Economic Development Agency, created during the mid-1960s as part of the Johnson administration's assault on rural poverty, to make available to struggling cities funds for commercial enterprises. Further, the administration loosened restrictions on the use of CDBG money so the funds could be used to help cities attract new businesses. To be sure, poor cities were in desperate need of investors. Nevertheless, as the task force's early critics had warned, enticements for investors could hardly stand alone as an adequate solution to the nation's severe urban problems. Ultimately, however, Carter's concern with inflation—and his willingness to sacrifice the aspirations of the poor and unemployed in pursuit of stabilizing the dollar—prevented him from doing more for cities and eventually led him to do less. In early 1979, Jordan of the NUL reported, "This year we are reduced to trying to preserve the few and relatively meager [urban and social welfare] programs currently in existence."[47] And the prospects of low-income urban residents for relief from the federal government only grew bleaker. By the end of his term, Carter had cut overall federal aid to cities.[48] Having prioritized the battle against inflation over combating unemployment, the Democratic president introduced Baltimore and other city residents to trickle-down economics before the Reagan revolution even began.

Certainly, Carter was not the only one to blame. Liberals also faulted Congress, including a fresh crop of New Democrats who did not aspire to the redistributive aspirations of New Dealers. Although Mitchell had himself been elected as a party outsider in 1970, he derided fellow Democrats voted into office in and after 1974 for "abandon[ing] this great liberal reform" and blithely falling into line with more conservative critics of government.[49] Meanwhile, Jordan, outraged that Democrats in Congress weakened both full-employment efforts and Carter's evolving urban program, charged that Congress had become "a negative force in the country" instrumental in the "national backlash against the poor and minorities.... Today ... we see the formation of a new negativism in America that calls for a weak, passive government, indifference to the plight of the poor and abandonment of affirmative action.... People are not merely saying no to higher taxes and inflation; they are saying no to inclusion of black and brown people into the mainstream."[50] From the vantage point of those still committed to the earlier ideals of their party, Democrats in both the White House and Congress were moving the party and the nation in the wrong direction.

In early 1977, shortly before Carter took the oath of office, the editors of the *Afro-American* had complained of locally elected officials who were more concerned with Baltimore's attractiveness to investors than to the well-being of its citizens. They had urged the city's leaders to attend to problems at the city's core instead of "polishing the outside of the apple."[51] They, along with other Black leaders, also had relentlessly pressed the mayor for positions of authority for African Americans in the municipal government so that representatives of Black Baltimore could play a role in setting the city's priorities and determining its revitalization strategies. Carter, a Democratic president who Black Baltimore contributed to electing, did not help the city's African American leaders move toward their goals. To be sure, African Americans and white women made gains in public-sector employment, and both the city's personnel director and government unions had improved some of the terms and conditions enjoyed by many workers. But stagflation had wreaked havoc on the local economy, and Carter's attempts to tame inflation came at the cost of municipal job freezes, layoffs, service reductions, and worsening unemployment rates. Moreover, the president's macroeconomic policies further dimmed prospects that the city's manufacturing sector could make a recovery. The policies had also largely limited his urban advisers to recommendations weighted heavily in favor of apple-polishing revitalization strategies. But not everyone in Baltimore was disappointed with Carter's urban plan. The city's mayor, for one, could think of quite a number of ways to use UDAGs and the other public-private funds Carter had made available to struggling cities.

CHAPTER 8

"A Tourist Town at the Expense of the Poor"

The Making of Two Baltimores

On a warm, sunny day in July 1981, Baltimore's mayor, outfitted in a yellow-and-red-striped Victorian bathing suit and sporting a straw hat, stood on the edge of a seal tank beside his city's newly built national aquarium. The mayor had already dropped rubber duckies into the water and was preparing to follow them in. He descended a set of underwater stairs until all that remained for the few hundred reporters and spectators to see was his hat floating on the water. After he resurfaced, the mayor swam to some rocks, making way for the tank's rightful inhabitants. Released by their attendants, a group of seals slowly scooted down a runway to join the mayor in their new home. As the seals swam around "Hizhonor," the audience could not help being charmed by Charm City's quirky mayor. And as they looked up from the spectacle to glance around the inner harbor that the aquarium bordered, few could fail to be impressed by recent dramatic changes. Looking southwest across the tip of the harbor, reporters sent by local, national, and even international news outlets could see the Maryland Science Center, built some five years earlier to attract visitors to the waterfront. Spectators looking to the west of the seal tank and past a new high-rise World Trade Center glimpsed the mast of the city's historic all-sail Civil War navy ship docked at a new marina. Next to the ship and just north of the Science Center, the two glass pavilions of Baltimore's Harborplace mall, designed by nationally renowned developer James Rouse, hugged the harbor's edge. Attached to one of the pavilions by a pedestrian walkway was the recently opened Hyatt Regency hotel. And just beyond the hotel was a new convention center, which city officials hoped would attract increased business now that the mayor's swim with the seals was going to put Baltimore on the map.[1]

Baltimore's waterfront had changed considerably during the less than ten years that Mayor William Donald Schaefer had been in office. And Schaefer had presided over the harbor's facelift with enthusiasm. He and his staff labored with the same degree of dedication and passion that had fueled the city's antipoverty and human-services workers in their efforts to combat economic insecurity during the 1960s and early 1970s. In fact, the mayor and his advisers understood the waterfront projects as a type of antipoverty initiative. By attracting tourists and businesses to Baltimore, the mayor hoped to jumpstart the economy of his deindustrializing city and generate revenue that would reverse decline and eventually trickle down to low-income residents. The strategy was one also pursued by other executives in rust-belt cities. Schaefer proved particularly masterful at the approach for two main reasons. First, like the antipoverty warriors, he was adept at securing federal grants to pursue his projects—for like Baltimore's War on Poverty, much of the city's commercial redevelopment was paid for with federal dollars. And second, but this time unlike the city's antipoverty warriors, who had worked hard to bring city residents into the political process, Schaefer deliberately limited the number of people who participated in redevelopment-related decision-making in order to accommodate the expectations of the business community. By so doing, he may have cinched deals the city otherwise would have lost. He also, however, denied city residents a role in determining how their city responded to deindustrialization and globalization and largely excluded African Americans from opportunities to share in the entrepreneurial opportunities that redevelopment opened.

Jimmy Carter's UDAGs subsidized much of Baltimore's redevelopment. The Democratic president was far less generous when it came to funding social welfare measures, however. As a result, the city's predominantly African American and female antipoverty and human-services workers found their resources, efficacy, and influence in municipal affairs further eroded—as the flow of federal funding for anticrime measures continued to increase the presence of law enforcement in low-income neighborhoods. During much of the 1960s and early 1970s, activist public-service providers had played important roles in battles over how the city should respond to poverty and other urban problems. President Richard Nixon's New Federalism and then Carter's UDAGs shifted power and federal resources into the hands of predominantly white and male elected officials. Local decision-making still mattered and could have countered the shift to the right on the national level, but Schaefer's notorious "Father-Knows-Best" approach to governance, fierce commitment to austerity, enthusiasm for commercial redevelopment, and inattention to African Americans' aspirations helped to forge the deep race- and class-based divides that grew to characterize postindustrial Baltimore.

Meanwhile, public service providers and recipients and the leaders of government unions continued to call attention to the human costs of the mayor's agenda and the president's conservative macroeconomic policies. Increasingly, however, they found themselves scapegoated for the nation's economic woes by conservative politicians, angry taxpayers, and a growing number of Democrats. In Baltimore, welfare workers continued to come under the fiercest scrutiny, and officials subjected their department to repeated inquiries and investigations. As in other struggling cities, African American women were overrepresented among both welfare workers and recipients. In a political context in which conservatives intent on discrediting redistributive responses to poverty and rolling back civil rights legislation continued to press dogwhistle claims that associated urban African Americans with criminality both on the street and in welfare offices, indictments of Black welfare-service providers, government employees more generally, and public-sector unions reinforced the claims. Meanwhile, cuts to public services compelled women in their roles as family caretakers to attempt to compensate with their own labor. Leaders of AFSCME defended both their members and the essential services they provided, but they faced a powerful foe as the New Right launched an aggressive assault on the regulatory state, the workers who staffed it, and collective bargaining in the public sector.

"Tourism? It Was Like Working for a Crazy Person": The Baltimore Renaissance

While Carter's macroeconomic and domestic policies did not bode well for the city's poor residents and job seekers, the president's public-private programs were greeted with considerable fanfare in the mayor's office. City officials had long partnered with members of the business community on urban planning, and Schaefer was an enthusiast of the downtown revitalization efforts jointly undertaken by the Greater Baltimore Committee and the city. In fact, Schaefer ultimately proved even more ambitious than many of his corporate collaborators when it came to downtown development. While many of his revitalization plans targeted keeping factories in or attracting them to the city, Schaefer also appreciated the folly of trying to rebuild Baltimore using blueprints from its industrial heyday. The city needed to forge its postindustrial future. During the early 1960s, city voters had approved bonds to support the revitalization of 240 acres around the city's inner harbor. The long-term plans for the waterfront included commercial, residential, and recreational development. By the end of the 1960s, the project was under way, but investor confidence failed to materialize. Few private firms stepped up to gamble on Baltimore's port, scared off perhaps by the dead fish that floated on the scummy surface of the harbor or the colonies of rats that made the city's waterfront their home. And that is when Schaefer had become mayor. Perennially optimistic about Baltimore's future, the mayor imagined possibilities for the harbor beyond those proposed by the Greater Baltimore Committee. "Tourism?" one city employee remembers thinking incredulously when the mayor touted the idea at a civic breakfast. "It was like working for a crazy person."[2]

Schaefer's ideas may have seemed outlandish to city natives who could hardly imagine rusting Baltimore as a destination point for out-of-towners, but they mayor knew he had to innovate. As federal interest in cities plummeted during the 1970s, urban executives realized that they were being left to fend for themselves in a global economy characterized by destabilizing capital mobility and competitive credit markets. The changes led to a shift in the responsibilities of local executives. As scholar David Harvey explains, rather than simply being managers of cities, mayors began to assume the role of entrepreneur.[3] Business interests with a stake in the commercial viability of city centers often encouraged the change and the opportunity to make city governments more attentive to their needs. In Baltimore, Schaefer enthusiastically embraced the role of entrepreneur, convinced that trickle-down remedies were an important solution to his city's problems. Tourism was a cornerstone of his entrepreneurial agenda.[4]

As Schaefer embarked on his campaign to transform Baltimore's waterfront into a tourist attraction, he garnered a young and enthusiastic group of staffers committed to his agenda. So dedicated were some that they were eventually dubbed the "Kool-Aid drinkers," a reference to the devotees of cult figure Jim Jones who committed group suicide in Jonestown, Guyana, in 1978.[5] The mayor's financial officers also stood ready to help. In addition, the mayor also had an influential ally in Baltimore native Robert Embry, the assistant secretary of HUD, who had previously coordinated Baltimore's commercial revitalization projects. Baltimore was well-served by having an advocate with influence over the distribution of UDAGs. Although some national observers complained that Embry favored his hometown, his supporters joked that he was actually quite fair; he doled out UDAGs fifty-fifty—half for Baltimore and half for the nation's other cities.[6]

Carter's public-private partnership grants enabled Baltimore officials to realize many redevelopment projects. By 1981, the city had received $37 million in UDAGs and $50 million from the Economic Development Administration. Some of the federal funding did support development projects in neighborhoods. The city also used the aid to support industrial interests. General Motors, which was one of the few remaining large manufacturing employers in the city, had little trouble convincing officials that what was good for GM was good for Baltimore. A $9 million UDAG enabled the corporation to expand its local production facilities. Most noteworthy, however, city and business leaders used considerable federal funds to reinvigorate the Greater Baltimore Committee harbor renewal plan and move it in the direction of tourism. A $10 million UDAG helped the city secure a glitzy waterfront Hyatt Regency hotel, which became a magnet for the harbor redevelopment that followed. In addition, $1.5 million from the Economic Development Administration helped cover the costs of the aquarium. Federal as well as state revenue also helped subsidize the convention center, the dock for the city's historic navy warship, the science center, shoreline landscaping, and a marina. The combination of intergovernmental revenue and Schaefer's boosterism created what would soon provoke marvel as the Baltimore renaissance.[7]

Flush with various forms of development funds earmarked for public-private ventures, Schaefer sought an efficient method of distributing the revenue and overseeing the city's development projects. He was reluctant, however, to relinquish to the democratic process authority over the delicate and sometimes time-sensitive business of deal-making. Schaefer believed that if the city was going to achieve its downtown metamorphosis, municipal representatives were going to have to move with the rapid rhythms of the business world rather than the plodding tempo compelled by city politics. Referenda took time and required city administrators to defend priorities citizens might not share. And city council debate could produce contract riders requiring developers to hire union workers or minority contractors—requirements that might squelch a deal with a firm that could quite easily turn to another more accommodating downtrodden city. With those concerns in mind, Schaefer adopted the antithesis of the decision-making mechanism War on Poverty advocates had embraced. Whereas they had endeavored to bring people into the political process, Schaefer pursued minimal feasible community participation. He created a network of quasi-public corporations to handle deal-making and project management. Because they were public, the corporations had the legal authority to exercise eminent domain to amass land and distribute public resources. Because the corporations were also private, however, they could avoid federal regulations that mandated public disclosure, competitive bidding, and affirmative action.[8]

By the early 1980s, Schaefer had created between thirty and forty quasi-public corporations, such as the Baltimore Development Corporation and Charles Center–Inner Harbor Management, Inc. The most controversial of the corporations was the Baltimore City Trustees Loan and Guarantee Program, which served as the city's development bank. The mayor appointed two trustees to run the outfit. One was Charles Benton, the city's finance director. During the 1960s, Benton had been relentlessly suspicious of the ways African Americans who ran the city's antipoverty agencies disbursed federal funds. He frequently charged mismanagement and called for audits. Ironically, considering his espoused devotion to probity, Benton demonstrated considerable flexibility in the way he managed federal funds for redevelopment. As journalist C. Fraser Smith explains, "If he finagled the books, taking money that had been voted for one purpose and washing it bureaucratically for use in another project, or engaging in minor league arbitraging, investing federal government money and taking the interest for local uses, a prohibited practice, he knew how to retrace his steps or how to have those steps blessed by Schaefer and the Board of Estimates."[9] Benton and a second trustee, Frank Baker of the Monumental Life Company, worked almost entirely free from public scrutiny, creatively packaging public funds, including UDAGs and CDBGs, to firms willing to invest in the city if offered adequate incentives. Between 1976, when the bank opened, and 1986, when Schaefer shut it down to avoid uncomfortable questions during his bid for the governorship of Maryland, the city trustees brokered $500 million in development deals, some of which were risky enough that traditional bankers would have balked. Some, although certainly not all, of the development funds went into Baltimore's new postindustrial skyline and harbor redevelopment. And while many of the projects met with success, others flopped. According to calculations by Joan Jacobson, a reporter for the *Baltimore Sun*, by 1992 the city had either written off or did not expect repayment on fifty loans with a total value of about $60 million.[10]

Most people in the city knew nothing of Baltimore's trustees and quasi-public corporations until 1980 when a series of exposé articles in the *Baltimore Sun* by Smith introduced residents to their "shadow government." Many responded with outrage at what they saw as a subversion of democracy.

AfroAmerican columnist and city activist Madeline Murphy protested the mayor's willingness to "pander to business interests at the expense of basic programs" and complained of "corporations cynically developed to circumvent the will of the people."[11] Resident L. H. Kohlman wondered how Baltimore could find funds for hotel developers but not for textbooks for students in the city's public schools. The editors of the *Baltimore Sun* protested as well. "Ours is supposed to be a government of checks and balances. But in the part of the government run by trustees as a private corporation that seems to mean only blank checks and bank balances," they complained.[12] Others expressed alarm that the city council was being circumvented and wondered if the City Charter could accommodate such questionable practices. (It did, a judge later determined.)[13] Meanwhile, Frances Froelicher, the founder of Baltimore's Citizens Planning and Housing Association who had known Schaefer for years, attributed the mayor's use of the secretive corporations to conceit. She surmised that the mayor "feels he doesn't want to be bothered with citizens' committees because he has listened to all that in the past. He is in power right now and he wants to accomplish what he has wanted to accomplish all these years."[14]

Members of the city council also expressed shock at the revelation that they had been largely excluded from economic planning in their city. For quite some time, the council had not been much of a match for Schaefer. The mayor had multiple acolytes in the eighteen-member body, and only a few others occasionally dared to seriously challenge him. Meanwhile, during the late 1970s, the body suffered from weak leadership, which Schaefer easily exploited. From 1971 to 1982, the council's president was Walter Orlinsky. Although Schaefer and Orlinsky had once been running mates, by the late 1970s they rarely agreed. In fact, as a *Sun* reporter explained in 1978, the mayor and the city council president "quite thoroughly detest[ed] one another, [did] not speak to one another, and bad mouth[ed] one another at every opportunity."[15] Meanwhile, Orlinsky often exercised ineffective control during council meetings, which sometimes deteriorated into chaos.[16]

Schaefer did have one particularly outspoken critic on the city council. In 1979, Kweisi Mfume won a seat representing the city's majority African American Fourth District. Unlike many of the city's other Black elected officials, Mfume, born Frizzell Gray in 1948, had a working-class rather than a middle-class background. Following the death of his mother, he dropped out of high school and eventually spent more time on street corners than he later viewed prudent. A chance encounter with Parren Mitchell helped lead

Mfume to take his life more seriously. He returned to school and became increasingly politically active. African American Vietnam War veterans, his fellow members of the Black Student Union at the Community College of Baltimore County, "the Pan-Africanists, the Panthers, and the Black Muslims" helped to shape his political perspectives, he recalls.[17] His anger about the status of African Americans in the United States intensified. "We were a people chronically and institutionally disenfranchised, feeding off the scraps of the educational system, the job market, and any other channels leading to a life of dignity," he remembers realizing.[18] As a result, he worried, "heroin, illiteracy, and low self-esteem had a choke hold on the ghetto. While some were making it out, others were trapped for life."[19] Ultimately, Mfume completed a bachelor's degree at Morgan State University and a graduate degree at Johns Hopkins University. And at age thirty, his indignation at the state of urban affairs led him to seek a seat on the city council, which he narrowly won. He remained in the position until 1986, when he was elected to the U.S. House of Representatives, where he rose to become the chair of the Congressional Black Caucus. He left Congress in 1996 to assume the presidency of the NAACP, a position he held until 2004.[20]

In Baltimore in the late 1970s, Mfume used a radio program for which he was the disc jockey to criticize Schaefer's inattention to Black Baltimore, and he repeated his concerns on the campaign trail. Then as a council member, he made access to public-sector jobs for African Americans and women, the appointment of African Americans to municipal boards and commissions, and open housing his top priorities. But when it came to countering Schaefer in city politics, as *Baltimore Sun* columnist Mike Bowler opined in a 1980 piece titled "Our Impotent City Council," Mfume and another newcomer to the council were a breath of fresh air but "too little, too late."[21] So successful had Schaefer become at passing the parts of his agenda that he actually submitted to the council that it alarmed even his own supporters. Council member Clarence "Du" Burns, for example, who became the city's first African American city council president and then mayor when Schaefer moved to the governor's mansion, complained, "There are no checks and balances whatsoever.... We should not be just a rubber stamp."[22] But clearly even a rubber stamp had not been enough for the mayor, council members realized following the "shadow government" exposé. Many responded in anger, even as their fear of Schaefer's penchant for seeking retribution largely led them to comment to the media anonymously. "I understand the need for progress ...," one contended, "[but] it's that old question of whether it's better to have a democracy or a benevolent dictator." Willing to go on the record, council member Mary Pat Clarke concurred. "Democracy is a very messy process, but it works," she argued.[23]

In response to the criticism, Schaefer, known more for boosterism than eloquence, defended his actions as in the best interest of Baltimore. "When you manage a city and you come up with innovative ideas, there's always the possibility of a higher echelon overcoming the innovative thing you're trying to do. The trustees are needed in my mind to find innovative ways to do things that you couldn't do if you didn't have the flexibility of the trustees," the mayor explained. The decisions of the trustees did require the approval of the members of the Board of Estimates, he added, referencing a five-member body on which he served alongside two of his appointees. And the proceedings of the Board of Estimates were public records, so nothing was done in total secrecy, he asserted. The trustees were simply needed for the sake of expediting decision-making. "Speed and flexibility are an asset. If you've ever tried to get through some government red tape, if you've ever tried to get through all the bureaucracy, you can see the need for the ability to move. . . . That's one of the reasons why the city of Baltimore is known for its innovative ideas. We move. And the time to move is now, not two or three or four or five years from now," he argued.[24] According to Schaefer, the ends his administration was achieving justified the means; democracy was simply too slow.

The mayor, whose herculean efforts to redevelop the city had attracted national and international attention, was not without defenders both inside and outside of the city. "We should be grateful to Mr. Schaefer," city resident John Miklos contended, "for having the will and stamina to see the city grow from a deteriorating mess toward a beautiful masterpiece."[25] After all, supporters argued, Schaefer was meeting with success. Much to the amazement of many locals, out-of-towners were starting to get off of Interstate 95 and come to Baltimore—and not just out of desperation for a gas station or restroom. They actually wanted to visit the city. Many in the business community were thrilled with Schaefer's results regardless of the maneuvering he used. Was anything similar happening in Cleveland or Chicago, real estate developer James A. Ulmer III demanded to know? "In this day of rapid change and increasing competition among cities and regions for a limited supply of jobs and money, it is essential that a municipality be run with as much intelligence, imagination and competitiveness as any private business," he argued.[26] City development officials also defended the quasi-public management system. "I think corporations appreciate being able to work with us because we're here to smooth the way," one development official explained to the *New York Times* in 1984. "It's not like trying to deal with a government agency. We're very entrepreneurial. We think government is a business."[27] Perhaps the most ringing endorsement of the shadow government came from the U.S. Conference of Mayors. In the early 1980s, the organization studied Baltimore's trustee system and in a report subtitled "How Your City Can Make Use of Baltimore's Approach to Creative Financing for Economic Development" recommended the system for emulation.[28] Following a decade during which many mayors had been disciplined to prioritize raising credit ratings over solving local problems and felt compelled to negotiate tax abatements to attract employers despite pressing needs for revenue, democratic decision-making apparently seemed expendable as well.

Although many in the city expressed at least a measure of concern about the trustee system, the sentiment did not indicate an overall rejection of Schaefer's agenda. Even the mayor's critics knew something had to be done to commercially redevelop the city. When compelled by law to bring a decision concerning revitalization to the voters, such as when he wanted to float a bond, Schaefer typically won the day. Meanwhile, his many supporters thought Schaefer's ideas were terrific and the mayor himself the best thing that had happened to Baltimore since Francis Scott Key wrote "The Star-Spangled Banner." And critics quickly learned the danger of opposing the renaissance. Mfume reports that his constituents paid in public services for his decisions to buck the mayor.[29] And a neighborhood group in South Baltimore was denied CDBG funds for two years because members publicly criticized Schaefer's priorities.[30] There were no easy solutions to the complex urban problems the mayor had to tackle. But by subverting the democratic process and punishing critics, Schaefer denied residents the opportunity to explore alternatives and voice concerns.

Despite his multiple efforts to quell dissent, some Schaefer critics did make their views known. Parren Mitchell derisively dubbed the aquarium "the fish tank" and anticipated that the attraction would be a place "where our unemployed city workers can go to look at fish they can't eat."[31] (Of course, that was before the city announced the aquarium's steep admission prices, which foreclosed attendance even for many locals with full-time jobs.) Welfare rights activists found it unfathomable that the city would even consider building an aquarium given widespread poverty, and leaders of the Baltimore Welfare Rights Organization pledged to picket the proposed waterfront shopping mall.[32] The leaders of AFSCME and the Classified Municipal Employees

Association, a union that represented about 4,500 of the city's white-collar workers, also criticized Schaefer's downtown projects. Sensitive to the critique that its members' wages were a burden to city taxpayers, AFSCME leaders called attention to the tremendous municipal revenue losses represented by tax abatements extended to encourage harbor revitalization. A 1977 union poster protested Schaefer's use of corporate welfare by querying the wisdom of granting "$2.5 million in property tax breaks for luxury high-rise apartment operators and three downtown hotels" when the city desperately needed services.[33] Similarly, a columnist in CMEA's monthly newsletter argued that Schaefer's attention to downtown projects came at the expense of the poor and complained of "hotels receiving enormous tax breaks [and] funds being shifted from social programs and 'loaned' to commercial interests."[34]

Public-sector union leaders also expressed concerns about the toll tax abatements and austerity took on the size of the municipal workforce. Government employees composed a significant portion of the city's working population, and their incomes were vital to the local economy. Yet an article in a 1978 CMEA newsletter complained of "city employees being layed-off [sic] and denied a decent wage" while the city was wheeling and dealing over the harbor's revitalization.[35] Unionized government jobs were more important to the city's residents than the low-wage service jobs a tourism industry would create, public-sector union critics contended, yet municipal workers were being sacrificed. In addition, many worried that poorly paid service positions in tourism were inadequate replacements for the unionized manufacturing jobs the city was still losing. As Henry Koellein Jr., the president of the Metropolitan Council of the AFL-CIO, argued, "We just can't make it on fast food and hotels ... because you can't replace 2000 steel workers and 2000 shipyard workers, who are making $8, $10, $12 an hour with 2000 or 4000 fast food, hotel, or restaurant employees, or office employees, who are making minimum wage to $5 an hour, because your tax base is eroding."[36] If new businesses got tax abatements, city residents had low-paying jobs, and the federal government was cutting back on urban aid, how could Baltimore pay for critical public services?

Schaefer's use of incentives to encourage gentrification in the harbor area and other neighborhoods and his seeming indifference to those moderate- and low-income residents displaced by revitalization further angered activists. During the second half of the 1970s, the largely white, middle-class, back-to-the-city movement produced an unanticipated pool of potential municipal taxpayers. Schaefer wooed some to Baltimore with "homesteading" initiatives, such as houses that could be purchased for a dollar and came with low-interest credit opportunities.[37] Meanwhile, although Baltimore did have a program for renovating housing for residents with low incomes, the pace of construction was frustratingly slow. A 1976 housing survey by the U.S. Bureau of the Census had revealed that more than 50 percent of housing occupied by African American renters in the city had structural deficiencies. In 1978, twelve thousand families were on the waiting list for public housing, and seven thousand were on the waiting list for rental assistance.[38] Yet the city was subsidizing luxury and middle-class housing. Angry residents joined or formed organizations, such as the Citywide Coalition Against Displacement and Communities Organized to Improve Life, Inc.[39] And one particularly frustrated group of twenty-five women joined by activist Ralph Moore staged a sit-in at the Department of Housing and Community Development to protest rodent infestations, shoddy construction, and broken furnaces. As Moore explained to a reporter following the protest, "The ladies can see the need for revitalizing the city and firming up the tax base, but they do not want to see Baltimore become a tourist town at the expense of the poor."[40]

Meanwhile, when Schaefer's deal-making did occur in public, African American leaders such as Mitchell sought at least some concessions for Black Baltimore. By the mid-1970s, Mitchell had come to embrace Black wealth creation as the most feasible, if not his preferred, path to African American economic advancement. As he later explained with evident disappointment, "I call economic empowerment the second phase of the civil rights movement because whether we like it or not, that's what runs this country."[41] In 1976 while in Congress, Mitchell succeeded in adding an amendment to a public-works program that compelled states and localities seeking federal contracts to set aside 10 percent for minority-owned firms, and he continued to pursue similar ends throughout his career. In Baltimore, Mitchell as well as other Black leaders wanted to make sure that African Americans received a share of the wealth-generating contracts downtown redevelopment entailed. To secure the aquarium venture, political pressure led Schaefer to pledge on the pages of the *Afro-American* that Black workers would be included during all stages of the projects.[42] In addition, Mitchell and the influential Interdenominational Ministerial Alliance initially refused to endorse Harborplace, creating pressure that led the city to eventually agreed to mandate set-asides for minority contractors. The concessions were significant but infrequent since so much deal-making happened behind closed doors.[43]

African American Maryland state legislators, particularly those representing Baltimore, also attempted to use their leverage on behalf of Black city residents. In one instance, they threatened to block bond bills the mayor needed to get through the State House unless he agreed to a 25 percent set-aside for minority contractors and pledged to appoint to municipal boards and commissions an equal number of African Americans and whites. At the time, Black representation on the bodies was only 24 percent, even though African Americans made up more than 50 percent of the population. Although the legislators ultimately backed away from their threat, the mayor did agree to increase set-asides and minority appointments.[44]

African American leaders' success at winning concessions from the mayor when his initiatives were deliberated publicly indicates that Baltimore's redevelopment efforts that were negotiated secretively could and probably would have unfolded differently had the mayor used the democratic process. Because of the covert decision-making approach Schaefer adopted, however, Black leaders, as well as the leaders of other interest groups in the city, such as organized labor, women, and welfare recipients, did not have the opportunity to forge deals advantageous to their constituents. Similarly, Baltimore residents and members of the city council did not have the chance to attempt to win some of the agreements brokered with investors in other cities. In San Francisco, for example, those developing office spaces larger than 50,000 square feet were required to make contributions for housing, day care, and transportation services. Boston officials required downtown developers to contribute to housing initiatives and to hire local workers, and the Chicago city government had plans to contractually link center city and neighborhood redevelopment.[45] Schaefer worried that Baltimore would have missed deals had he not circumvented the city council, and perhaps he was right. The city might have gained, however, a tourism industry and central business district that came a little less at the expense of residents, services, and the poor. Instead, as scholar Marc Levine explained about the mid-1980s, because of the infrastructure and public services costs the city incurred to maintain the redeveloped downtown area, "Baltimore annually absorb[ed] around $17 million *more* in city expenditures than it generate[d] in municipal revenue" (emphasis in the original).[46] City residents were footing a hefty bill for private-sector profit-making. Meanwhile, African American entrepreneurs largely had been left by the wayside. Investigators from the U.S. Commission on Civil Rights assessing revitalization in Baltimore concluded that "except for deliberate and race conscious efforts, minority participation in the economic development of the city was negligible."[47] African Americans had been excluded from most of the wealth-generating potential of downtown revitalization, and city residents had lost opportunities to make Baltimore's new corporate residents more accountable to local needs.[48]

"Further Cuts Would Render Most Programs Useless": Service Providers During the Carter Years

As the Carter administration subsidized considerable commercial revitalization, workers in antipoverty and human-services agencies struggled to respond to mounting need with shrinking budgets. Spending cuts on the federal, state, and municipal levels left workers with fewer resources to counter problems that Carter's anti-inflation strategies were worsening. Economic hardship compelled low-income women in their roles as caregivers to intensify the unpaid labor they put into keeping their families safe. The task of compensating for lost services often fell to them. Meanwhile, the Carter administration continued to fund the growth of the carceral state, and law enforcement increased its reach into poor and predominantly African American neighborhoods, which were simultaneously losing social services outposts. Some employees in antipoverty and human-services agencies, as well as some African Americans in other administrative positions, continued to serve as the conscience of the city and publicly challenged the wisdom of Baltimore's reliance on trickle-down antipoverty remedies. But antipoverty and human-services workers increasingly found themselves the targets of intensifying public hostility as growing numbers both locally and nationally identified them as a source of the nation's economic woes.

During the second half of the 1970s, Baltimore's public-sector workers received small budgets to solve big problems. Over the course of the decade, more than a quarter of the city's white population left, an exodus of about 134,000 people. Median income dropped along with the revenue the city could collect from income taxes. Similarly, because many who left the city had been homeowners, the pool of those from whom the city could collect property taxes declined as well—as the number of abandoned properties grew. Simultaneously, deindustrialization cost the city both tax revenue and tens of thousands of jobs. By 1978, nearly a quarter of the population lived in substandard housing, most of which was concentrated in African American neighborhoods, and the number of residents receiving welfare was on the rise even though the city's population was shrinking. An AFDC check for a family of four left the family at 52 percent of the poverty rate, and the addition of Food Stamps to their resources raised them to only 69 percent of the poverty level. The director of the Baltimore Department of Social Services described the benefits as "grossly inadequate," and the editors of the *Baltimore Sun* warned it was "a bad time to be hungry" in the city.[49] In 1979, following nearly a decade of inflation, welfare recipients did not even receive the income the state had determined ten years earlier to be the minimum required simply for subsistence.[50]

In response to fiscal constraints, Baltimore's elected officials and agency administrators spent the late 1970s perpetually trying to balance the valid yet often conflicting concerns of service recipients in obvious and dire need of assistance; taxpayers, whose yearly tax rates surpassed those in surrounding suburbs; and public employees whose earnings were critical to their families' and communities' well-being and the city's remaining tax base. Despite shared hardship, residents with low incomes faced the most severe challenges. Regardless, between 1977 and 1980, as inflation drove up prices and unemployment soared, the city reduced by a quarter its contribution to the budget of the Urban Services Agency, the unit into which the Community Action Agency and the Model Cities program had been merged. It was hard to fight poverty with bare-bones budgets. By 1980, Lenwood Ivey, the director of USA, was pleading for his budget to be restored simply to its 1977 level. "I have already cut staff substantially in all programs. Further cuts would render most programs useless," he wrote to the mayor.[51]

Meanwhile, on the state level, periodic cuts culminated in large budget reductions in 1980, a recession year. The Maryland Departments of Health, Social Services, and Education each took a sizable hit. Administrators in all of the departments attempted to mitigate the effect of the cuts on service delivery with hiring freezes. The solution, while probably the most humane, was nonetheless a source of deep frustration to the city's growing pool of job seekers. And in some cases, both layoffs and service reductions followed budget cuts. Baltimore, home to between 65 percent and 70 percent of Maryland's low-income residents, suffered the brunt of the state's cuts, local officials alleged. As the Carter years came to an end, the city was eliminating services by laying off workers who provided home-based care for elderly residents and those with disabilities, day care, legal services, social services in public housing facilities, and support services for battered spouses and single parents. Meanwhile, some sanitation trucks lay idle following layoffs that affected about two hundred workers, and officials in the Department of Parks and Recreation were trying to decide which playgrounds and public pools to close.[52]

The reduced availability of services during a time of rising prices took a toll on all residents, but women with low incomes, among whom African Americans were overrepresented, paid a particularly significant price. In 1979, Elrae Singletary, a recipient of AFDC, had taken to cooking meals for her four children from scratch to avoid the expense of ready-made food. She also mixed powdered milk with regular milk and replaced shampoo with bar soap to cut down on expenses. Mary Turner, another AFDC recipient, likewise struggled with food costs. In response, she tried to keep on hand a constant stock of potatoes and other inexpensive staples to feed her children. Both women also exerted considerable effort to keep their families secure in inadequate housing. During the winter, Singletary taped plastic garbage bags over her windows to keep out the cold. She also waged unrelenting warfare against roaches and mice, and she perpetually worried about the health of her children, whom she was reluctant to allow to play outdoors because of the mounds of garbage that attracted rats in the yards of nearby abandoned homes. Turner launched a similarly unsuccessful battle against winter's chill. She tried to compensate for cracks in her walls and insufficient funds to pay for fuel by nestling her two children in front of her oven. Her efforts kept her children warm but landed her with an exorbitant utilities bill. Worse, she contracted pneumonia and spent three days recovering in the hospital.[53] Reductions in city services made even more challenging the lives of families struggling to get by and added to the responsibilities of women, who attempted to personally fill service gaps.

While antipoverty and human-services providers attempted to maintain maximum programming on threadbare budgets and low-income women endeavored to make up for lost services, those engaged in crime control fared better. As historian Elizabeth Hinton argues, during the 1970s, federal investment in anticrime efforts meant that the criminal justice system filled voids left by disinvestment in the War on Poverty.[54] Among the Carter administration's contributions to the burgeoning carceral state was the Urban Initiatives Anti-Crime Program. With the initiative, the administration attempted to shift away from the law-and-order, boots-on-the-ground approach of the Nixon administration and toward a supposedly more community-directed and social services–inclusive crime-control strategy. The Department of Housing and Urban Development rather than the Department of Justice oversaw the program, which transferred funds directly to cities rather than to states and incorporated the element of resident participation. Despite the changes, however, fighting crime rather than poverty was the objective, and the initiative enabled the continued construction of a vast law-enforcement infrastructure in low-income Black neighborhoods.

In Baltimore, municipal officials used federal anticrime funds to purchase cameras, intercom systems, and bulletproof security-guard stations in public housing units populated almost exclusively by low-income African Americans. The efforts were intended to beef up security—and surveillance.[55] Meanwhile, community participation included having residents serve as tenant security aides. A decade earlier, the Johnson administration had provided funding that enabled Baltimore residents with low incomes to earn a paycheck for providing services that directly combated poverty. During the Carter years, federal grants paid public-housing residents to police their neighbors. Certainly, security and crime gravely concerned public-housing residents. A survey conducted following the implementation of Carter's urban anticrime initiatives, however, revealed that most believed that security had gotten worse instead of better.[56]

Amid the changes, the tight grip Schaefer kept on power and his close scrutiny of staffing decisions largely quelled dissent in city agencies. "Mr. Schaefer's greatest personality failing in office is an autocratic instinct that attracts sycophants and brands others as enemies," opined the editors of the *Baltimore Sun*.[57] Nevertheless, some agency heads did voice opposition to the nation's miserly wealth-redistribution efforts and the city's increasing reliance on trickle-down strategies to fight poverty. They often directed their ire toward state and federal officials rather than at the mayor. Kalman Hettleman, the white director of the Department of Social Services, complained about the inadequacy of the funds the state made available to aid the poor. "What is missing in Maryland is a commitment to provide even a minimal, fair share of state resources and wealth for social service programs," he argued.[58] More pointedly, Quentin Lawson, the city's director of human resources and one of the few African Americans in the mayor's cabinet, protested that President Carter's urban commercial revitalization priorities neglected the needs of the people. The government had "traditionally emphasized . . . programs in physical development," Lawson noted. What was needed was an equal commitment to a "human service plan."[59] The critiques of state legislators and the president—but, circumspectly, usually not of the mayor—were echoed by other municipal employees.[60]

Despite the assertions of protest, austerity took a toll on antipoverty and human-services agencies. In a context characterized by considerable job insecurity, many municipal workers found it difficult to sustain the spirit of defiance that had earlier characterized some in their agencies. In 1979, infighting in a community-based agency led the editors of the *Afro-American* to urge workers to stop "squabbl[ing] over 10 jelly beans while downtown diverts the real riches elsewhere."[61] Meanwhile, funding cuts also eroded fragile solidarities between service recipients and providers that had emerged in some cases during the 1960s and early 1970s.[62] Echoes of past advocacy did continue, but antipoverty and human-services workers lacked the capacity to mobilize the masses as some of their predecessors once had.[63] Nixon, Carter, and Schaefer had rescinded the resources and the independence service providers needed to launch protests against budget austerity and local and national priorities that no longer included the poor.

Making matters worse, the antipoverty and human-services workers found themselves under increasingly withering public scrutiny. The negative attention was hardly new. War on Poverty warriors had weathered it since the 1960s, and welfare workers and other service providers had taken hits during the first half of the 1970s. But at the end of the decade, the hostility intensified. Workers were caricatured locally as well as nationally as the inefficient, lazy, and overpaid staff of the "giant bureaucracy which is dominating our lives," in the words of one woman from Baltimore's suburbs.[64] As had been the case through the 1970s, employees of DSS, who, like their clients were predominantly Black women, were denigrated and investigated the most. Federal officials, state's attorneys, welfare-fraud investigators (who, along with child-support collectors, were among the few members of the DSS staff to see their numbers grow during the Carter years), and the Baltimore grand jury kept poverty-related service providers under close scrutiny. As *Baltimore Sun* reporter Sharon Dickman noted with empathy in 1977, "Fighting poverty lacks the glamour it had in the 1960s."[65]

Discoveries of wrongdoing in welfare-related agencies were sometimes greeted by officials with barely concealed delight. In 1977, an investigation by federal prosecutors uncovered that in Detroit and Chicago there existed among municipal employees some former welfare recipients who were still receiving benefits checks that should have been terminated. "We're hitting two for two," proclaimed a U.S. attorney with apparent enthusiasm that presumptions of malfeasance had been confirmed.[66] Despite the lack of proximity or clear relevance of the fraud cases to Baltimore, the *Sun* dispatched a reporter to cover the local angle and included a story on it on the front page. Not surprisingly, the journalist found that federal investigators in Maryland were "extremely interested" and appeared ready to launch their own local probe.[67] In a separate case the following year, "deadwood," "inept," "poorly-trained," "careless," "appalling," and "inexcusable" were among the adjectives used in a *Sun* article that described the findings of a Baltimore grand jury's recent investigation of DSS.[68] The agency's director, Hettleman, protested as exaggerated and distracting claims of rampant inefficiency and abuse. Members of his staff made a large number of paperwork errors and had to do better, he conceded, but cases of actual fraud were rare.[69] The outraged enthusiasm among officials for launching politically popular investigations into suspected wrongdoing in social services agencies and the broad brushes used to describe DSS employees demeaned workers, who were predominantly African American women, and communicated to them that they were not trusted to do their jobs honestly or effectively.

The level of public mistrust and anger directed at antipoverty and DSS workers during the late 1970s far exceeded the ordinary frustration typically engendered by bureaucracy and governmental inefficiency. That is because it was fueled by the same dog-whistled animosity that had helped to put Richard Nixon in the White House. As arrest rates in Baltimore rapidly rose in response to the nation's wars on crime and drugs, few officials questioned the integrity of police officers or the wisdom of new legislation that was ensnaring so many in the criminal justice system, even on minor charges. If anything, they heralded a job well done. Conversely, increases in the numbers of people receiving welfare drew harsh critiques, legal inquiries, and accusations of fraud. Welfare workers were not lauded for providing the needy with relief but instead were indicted along with so-called welfare "cheats" as supposed coconspirators in efforts to defraud the government and rob taxpayers of hard-earned dollars. The contrast in the responses to law-enforcement agents and welfare workers reflected an expectation on the part of many whites of Black criminality, an expectation with deep roots in the nation's history but that was also a product of recent efforts by conservatives to criminalize urban African Americans. Black women, who made up many of the foot soldiers in the nation's redistributive responses to poverty, were convenient prey to those intent on discrediting the liberal welfare state and derailing the enforcement of civil rights legislation.

"Threat to All Public Employees, Threat to All Public Services": AFSCME Defends the Welfare State

Dog-whistle indictments of antipoverty and welfare workers helped to pave the way for an assault on the public-sector workforce writ large during the late 1970s. Certainly, conservative opponents of the regulatory state had been critical of governmental inefficiency and waste for decades. And the New Right's fetishization of the free market also rendered much of the public sector suspect. Meanwhile, stagflation exacerbated popular frustrations over taxes, which provoked calls for smaller government. Yet critiques of antipoverty and welfare workers—and probably also the continuing movement of African Americans into the government workforce—contributed to the notion that public-sector workers were drains on the national economy. So too did mounting anger at public-sector unions. The attacks took the form of tax revolts and calls for the privatization of public services.

During the second half of the twentieth century, the United States underwent a sea change in popular opinion regarding government workers. At midcentury, many American parents urged their children to apply for a government post, which often promised stable hours and a pension on retirement. Views were different during the late 1970s. As civil rights leader and Congress of Racial Equality founder James Farmer noted, "It has become high political fashion in recent years for candidates to run against 'government,' to vilify public employees as public leeches." The changes worried Farmer, who by the Carter years had become the director of the Coalition of American Public Employees, an organization founded by AFSCME.[70] And although the charges originated with conservatives, Democrats were proving increasingly willing to score political points with voters by championing government downsizing. Carter also joined in the fray. In October 1978, he proposed as reforms "slash[ing]" hiring in the federal government and shrinking the federal workforce.[71] The pledge signaled to the general public and those in state and local government that public-sector employees were expendable.

Anger with public-sector unions also undermined confidence in government workers. Although many Americans had sympathized with the AFSCME-affiliated Memphis sanitation workers with whom Marin Luther King had marched in 1968, within a decade many viewed the leaders of government unions as greedy rabble-rousers responsible for or associated with fiscal crisis and urban unrest. And as historian Joseph McCartin astutely notes, Democratic mayors facing fiscal crises were some of the first to face off against AFSCME. During the late 1970s, it became politically popular to woo voters with promises to take a tough stance against public-sector unions and the specter of higher taxes.[72]

AFSCME leaders defended their members against what they called the "slanders of public workers' inefficiency and incompetence."[73] They also championed the vital public services the workers provided. At a million members strong, AFSCME became the largest union in the AFL-CIO in 1978. The union's president, Jerry Wurf, and the secretary-treasurer, Bill Lucy, were outraged by what they identified as an aggressive reassertion of corporate and elite power over public policy during the 1970s, which they believed fueled calls for smaller government.[74] Many in AFSCME's rank and file occupied the lowest positions in government hierarchies. The union prided itself on its success in raising the bottom of many governments' pay scales and providing low-wage workers not only with fringe benefits and workplace protections but also upward mobility through training programs and career ladders. The union represented large numbers of women and workers of color, and the jobs they defended were invaluable to the economic security of many families and communities. So too were public services the workers provided, and AFSCME officials connected and fiercely defended both. Simultaneously, they defended collective bargaining in the public sector and their own legitimacy.[75]

AFSCME officials connected critiques of public-sector unions to wider campaigns to weaken the American labor movement. The late 1970s was a challenging period for organized labor. Manufacturers' quest to save on labor costs fueled the continuing deindustrialization of what was becoming the rust belt. The changes eroded the strength of industrial unions, earlier the lifeblood of the labor movement.[76] Meanwhile, as historian Lane Windham argues, private-sector employers in the nation's growing service sector were defiantly—and sometimes illegally—resisting unionization campaigns that would have extended union protection to workers previously ignored by the leaders of industrial unions. At the same time, Carter, who as president served as the standard-bearer for the Democratic Party, failed to back labor-law reform that would have made union organizing easier. All the while, a new antiunion consultancy industry, which would help employers fight off union drives, was gaining steam.[77] AFSCME leaders' efforts to defend their union and its members were not going to be easy.

To be sure, public-sector union leaders sometimes provided their critics with legitimate grounds for frustration. In keeping with practices widespread in both public- and private-sector unions, AFSCME leaders defended their members in termination disputes even when the members' actions were seemingly indefensible. Moreover, union officials often categorically resisted government downsizing and the contracting out to the private sector services previously provided by the government—even in instances when such practices might have eliminated inefficiencies or otherwise served the common good. AFSCME undeniably had a vested interest in "big government," which union leaders largely continued to understand as a labor-movement victory— the source of regulations and services critical to the public welfare and a healthy democracy. And they described themselves and their members as the guardians of the American welfare state. Certainly, their claims might have been better received had their local leaderships more consistently engaged in coalition-building and sought partnerships with the recipients and users of public services. Nevertheless, they accurately identified anti–public sector union rhetoric as a strategy in a larger campaign to erode the social safety net, undermine organized labor as a whole, and shift resources up the economic ladder. And they were gravely disappointed that so many failed to appreciate their significance.[78]

Yet many did. Anger at the government, its workers, and their unions manifested itself most starkly in suburban tax revolts and mounting enthusiasm for privatization, which included transferring government functions to the private sector. AFSCME fiercely combated both. In 1978, California voters passed Proposition 13, which imposed limits on government spending by capping property taxes. The measure alarmed but did not surprise Wurf. The AFSCME leader had been anticipating such a "Threat to All Public Employees, Threat to All Public Services" for some time.[79] In response, the union worked in states across the country to prevent similar campaigns from meeting with success. In addition, they continued to press elected officials for more progressive taxing formulas, which would shift more of the burden for funding public services to those with the highest incomes and off the shoulders of those of more modest means.

Meanwhile, AFSCME officials bitterly opposed the practice of contracting out, which they equated with putting up a "government for sale" sign, and warned that such arrangements promoted corruption and graft. As an AFSCME representative argued, "Some of the leaders of the anti-public employee chorus are businessmen who are trying to get their hands on more government dollars through lucrative contracts."[80] AFSCME leaders pointed out that the practice of contracting out circumvented merit-system reforms that many governments had adopted nearly a century earlier to prevent politicians from using access to government resources to reward campaign contributors and amass power. Inflated contracts, political kickbacks, and price-fixing could result when the government invited the private sector to play a role in service provision, AFSCME leaders insisted. Indeed, as union leaders pointedly reminded Americans, former Maryland governor and U.S.

vice president Spiro Agnew had recently resigned from the Nixon administration in disgrace as a consequence of his involvement in such chicanery. Contracting out also contributed to diluting civic culture because decision-making fell to unelected consultants rather than citizens. Service provision became the domain of those potentially more attentive to profit margins than the public's welfare. While the business model served an important role in American society, its principles were not applicable to all dimensions of public life, government union leaders warned.[81]

"Poverty on Its Fringes": The Efficacy of Tourism

AFSCME leaders' spirited defense of American welfare liberalism and government workers hardly reversed the course of national events or the direction of urban planning in Baltimore. A momentous political realignment was under way in the United States, and Schaefer had a clear vision for his city's postindustrial revitalization. And bolstered by financial assistance from the federal and state governments and the business savvy of his trustees, the mayor executed his plans with limited interference. The results were undeniably impressive. The city's waterfront redevelopment was a commercial success. In 1981, Harborplace, the Rouse-designed mall, attracted eighteen million, more people than visited Disneyland the same year.[82] But the economic benefits did not trickle down in the manner Schaefer had suggested they would. Residents may have gotten a psychological reward as a result of Baltimore's facelift, but the best-paying jobs, researchers soon found, went to suburban commuters even as city taxpayers took the hit for infrastructure costs. Meanwhile, during the 1970s, the poverty rate increased in the vast majority of the city's poorest neighborhoods.[83] Rising income inequality led some to start speaking of the existence of not one but "two Baltimores—one Black and poor, the other white and largely well off."[84] The claim was not entirely accurate. Baltimore had sizable African American working- and middle-class populations, among whom public-sector employees were numerous. Nevertheless, at the bottom of the economic ladder, race and class were becoming indistinguishable. And as the mayor's critics noted, trickle-down remedies to urban poverty did little to solve the problem.

Western High School student Felicia Willett was one such critic. In 1979, she wrote to Schaefer, "I would like to know why, when the city wanted to build the project for the Inner Harbor, the city managed to find a few million dollars for it. There are people who are starving, living in homes without heat, and people living in homes with [more] roaches and rats than the number of people living in the house. Mr. Mayor, I know the Harbor is important to the growth of the city but the people should also be considered."[85] The mayor replied to Willett as he did to the many others who expressed similar frustrations. He argued that downtown redevelopment reflected not necessarily his personal policy preference but the efforts of entrepreneurs and officials in Annapolis and Washington, DC. "Many of the improvements in the Inner harbor are not the result of City funds," the mayor explained. "A very large percentage of the monies spent is the result of private investments and the City's ability to successfully lobby for specific state and federal grants, that were in many incidents, earmarked to assist in the development of the kinds of improvements realized in the harbor."[86]

The mayor's defense was true but did not tell the whole story. Carter had steered his party sharply to the right. He pursued macroeconomic policies best suited to the interests of Wall Street, and he responded to urban problems by subsidizing trickle-down solutions. Baltimore was hardly in a position to forge its own path independent of outside aid, so the mayor pursued public-private partnerships. But that had also been his preference. And he had adopted commercial revitalization strategies while subverting the democratic process. By so doing, he robbed city residents and city council members of opportunities to at least consider alternatives or negotiate deals that served public as well as private ends. Quickly it became apparent that Carter's and Schaefer's trickle-down remedies were inadequate solutions to the city's urgent and in some cases worsening problems. On the same day that Schaefer took his acclaimed dip with the seals at the city's new harbor-front aquarium, an opinion piece in the *Evening Sun* by a former public-school counselor expressed a view not unlike Willett's. Certainly Baltimore's downtown renaissance was a boon to a city plagued by decades of deindustrialization, depopulation, and decline. "But," Leon Lerner wrote, "can it not be said that the enormous success of Harborplace is diminished by the poverty on its fringes?"[87]

CHAPTER 9

"A Revolving Door for Impoverished People"

Reaganomics and American Cities

"The reactions in Maryland are predictable: Reagan's crushing defeat of Carter draws cheers in the suburbs and moans in the city," read a headline in a Baltimore newspaper following the presidential election in 1980.[1] "Reagan's Victory: Are We Doomed?" the *Afro-American* asked more pointedly. For Baltimore City Council member Kweisi Mfume, the future definitely did not look bright for African Americans. Just as whites had rescinded on promises made to Black people following the end of slavery and the Reconstruction era, so too did they seemed intent on rolling back recent civil rights gains. Both Mfume and Maryland congressional representative Parren Mitchell pointed to Ronald Reagan's invocation of states' rights on the campaign trail and worried that it had served as a rallying cry for reactionary white voters.[2] And it hardly required elected office to appreciate the implications of Reagan's economic agenda for Black Baltimoreans, who by 1980 made up 55 percent of the city's population.[3] "I think Reagan is going to be against Black people," predicted Phyllis Allen, a resident of east Baltimore. "He's going to cut out a lot of funding for social welfare programs. He was talking about taking away medical assistance from poor people. And when people get sick, how are they going to pay the bills?"[4] Many of the city's antipoverty and human-services providers shared Allen's fears. Reagan's frequent characterization of the poorest Americans as drains on the national economy communicated clearly that these public agencies and the critical services they provided would not soon be better funded.

Meanwhile, although Baltimore's mayor William Donald Schaefer noted with circumspection only that he was "very disappointed" following the election, he too had significant cause for concern; federal aid for commercial revitalization was also on the line.[5] The new president had given all urban dwellers reason to worry. "I think one of the problems today with the cities is federal aid," Reagan had charged during a presidential debate, invoking the logic about the detrimental consequences of "handouts" that he also applied to welfare.[6] The sentiment implicated distressed cities in their entirety in the narrative of criminality that conservatives also used to describe Black protest, urban African Americans more generally, public-sector unions, and government workers, especially welfare providers. In Baltimore, where many believed that one of the biggest problems the city faced was insufficient federal aid to relieve poverty and decline, Reagan's views were not widely shared. Maryland was one of the six states that Jimmy Carter won in the 1980 election, and Baltimore voters were critical to that outcome; nearly three-quarters of them supported the incumbent despite their frustrations with him.[7] Carter's defeat presaged an era of even greater cuts to redistributive antipoverty efforts and urban aid than the rightward-swinging Democrat himself had introduced. Reagan's election also made strange bedfellows out of elected officials in Baltimore, African American leaders, and public service providers and their unions, who found their interests aligned when fighting Reaganomics even as they continued to disagree on policy matters at home.

Although largely unpopular among Baltimore's residents, Reagan's agenda held considerable appeal for many outside of the city. His calls for smaller government excited corporate and business interests hungry for regulatory and tax relief. It also heartened a growing number of white middle- and working-class Americans who felt that the federal government had done little for them in recent years while their tax dollars subsidized a bloated bureaucracy and welfare programs for those they believed were too lazy to get a job—and often imagined to be people of color. As Baltimore's Black leaders noted, Reagan stoked the hostility. He also used coded references to welfare fraud and called for tougher crime policies as he sought votes. Although not the only source of his popularity, Reagan's use of dog-whistle politics helped him attract disenchanted white Democrats to his ticket and win the White House. So too did his repeated assertions about government inefficiency and waste, which also had echoes of racial bias. Once in office, the president got to work implementing his neoliberal agenda both at home and abroad. Both efforts had dire implications for the predominantly African American and female antipoverty and human-services providers in Baltimore, the predominantly African American and female clients they served, and the direction of the city's economy.

But municipal service providers—and their counterparts in the private sector—did not surrender to Reaganomics without a fight. Mere opposition, they knew, would not be enough. They also had to work together to mitigate the effects on vulnerable residents of impending budget cuts. Meanwhile, Schaefer did Baltimore proud during repeated trips to Washington, DC, where he implored Congress to preserve targeted federal aid for struggling cities. At the same time, leaders of national civil rights and feminist organizations launched a fierce defense of the welfare state, even as they remained mindful of the ways the nation's supposedly universal welfare programs had often poorly served their constituents. And public-sector unions adamantly advocated on behalf of both government services and the workers who provided them. On the ground in Baltimore, as service providers moved forward with their plans, some also attempted to rekindle the solidarity activist municipal employees had once shared with low-income residents. For public service providers and recipients, however, Reagan proved a grave threat. Government jobs and critical services were on the line, and the only part of the government Reagan seemed enthusiastic about growing was the criminal justice system.

"Government Is the Problem": Reaganomics at Home and Abroad

Following Reagan's election, antipoverty and human-services workers in Baltimore—both independently and under the aegis of their unions—began planning their resistance. They called for a strong, unified response from public and private service providers, the board members of their multiple agencies, low-income residents, and members of grassroots civic and religious organizations. USA staffers charged that "[spending] reductions in many program levels and [the] elimination of others will impact the heaviest on the poor, the elderly and minorities, those already suffering the most from inflation and unemployment" and urged members of those groups to join forces in protesting.[8] Likewise, Samuel Banks, the coordinator of social studies instruction in the Baltimore City Public Schools, argued, "Each day, it becomes painfully evident that Baltimore's Black majority and the poor will have to coalesce for their mutual survival. No salvation or relief is to be found in President Reagan's supply-side economics."[9]

The Baltimore workers had just cause for concern. Although Carter's economic and domestic policies paved the way for the Reagan revolution, the incoming president did not struggle as Carter had while weighing the interests of the needy against the needs of the wealthy; the Republican's allegiance to the wealthy was never in doubt. It was their ingenuity and business acumen that Reagan believed could be mobilized to revitalize the American economy and restore the United States to the position of strength and prestige in the global economy it once commanded. He wanted federal lawmakers to facilitate the process by maximizing the business community's access to capital, eliminating regulation, and reducing obstacles to free trade. Reagan was also fiercely anticommunist, and he intended to use his time in office to best the Soviet Union in the Cold War and prove capitalism the superior economic system.

To achieve his goals, Reagan pledged to spend liberally on the military but also to cut taxes. He planned to make up the difference in the federal budget by reducing the roles performed by and cost of the government. As he argued in his first inaugural speech, "Government is not the solution to our problem; government is the problem."[10] He favored fiscal austerity on nonmilitary matters, transferred to the private sector functions previously performed by the government, and decreased union strength and influence. And he was a particularly staunch opponent of many social welfare programs. His administration justified service and entitlement cuts by arguing that wealth redistribution disincentivized work and had engendered a culture of poverty and dependency among the poor. Inflation remained high when Reagan entered office, and the president sanctioned the continuation of the Federal Reserve's tight monetary policy, an approach consistent with conservative economic doctrine popular at the time even if it was also the cause of recession and high rates of unemployment.[11]

Although conservatism had a long history in the United States, Reagan's strident free-market antistatism had not been evident in the White House for a long time. The Republican was able to move the center of American politics to the political right by using a host of strategies. As he campaigned, he courted evangelical Christians, whose numbers had grown in recent years; espoused "family values"; boldly denounced communism; and adapted his messaging to correspond with specifically regional politics and concerns. To win supporters and erode confidence in the welfare state, he also employed the logic of Nixon's "Southern strategy," using racism to court white voters.

The two issues Reagan most frequently invoked to stoke racial animus were welfare and crime. He referenced both without specifically mentioning race but nonetheless communicated the belief that low-income African Americans were a major source of the nation's and their own problems. His use of the tactic was not new. During his campaign for the presidency in 1976, Reagan repeatedly told the story of a woman in Illinois who was supposedly milking the system to the tune of $150,000. "She used 80 names, 15 telephone numbers to collect food stamps, Social Security, veterans' benefits for four nonexistent deceased veteran husbands, as well as welfare," Reagan claimed.[12] Although the candidate never directly said that the woman he was referring to was African American, he relied on his audience members to use popular stereotypes to fill in that detail. And he continued to invoke racialized welfare-queen rhetoric during his subsequent presidential bids as well. By intentionally associating Aid to Families with Dependent Children and other entitlement programs with Black women and exaggerating the generosity of the benefits, the length of time recipients generally received them, and the level of fraud associated with the programs, Reagan endeavored to undermine faith in the concept of wealth redistribution and grow his base among white voters.[13]

Reagan also had a history of manipulating fears of crime and supposed Black male criminality. In one instance in which he was discussing crime as a gubernatorial candidate in California in 1966, he contended that "every day the jungle comes a little closer."[14] And he also invoked the specter of the mythical Black male rapist, a trope that gained currency in the popular discourse to justify lynching and the resurgence of white supremacy after the Civil War. Reagan warned that the nation's streets were becoming unsafe for "our women," suggesting that white women were increasingly vulnerable to assaults by Black men.[15] Although he largely transitioned to law-and-order and tough-on-crime rhetoric while on the campaign trail in 1980, the racial implications of his anticrime messages were clear. And even more aggressively than Nixon, he proposed solving the supposed problems by reducing funding for social welfare programs and bolstering the power of the criminal justice system.[16]

While the president's positions on the welfare state and criminal justice alarmed many service providers and recipients in Baltimore, his critical stance on federal aid to cities was of particular concern to Schaefer. Reagan argued that assistance to economically distressed cities distorted market forces. Shortly after the new president assumed office, the *Evening Sun* noted, "It is clear that the way in which the Reagan administration will address [urban problems is] . . . not with direct federal grants for urban renewal, model cities, neighborhood grants and all the Great Society programs, but with maximum utilization of the private sector."[17] His laissez-faire approach to urban affairs seemed likely to make even Carter's public-private partnership programs appear progressive by comparison. Although Carter had advocated trickle-down approaches to poverty alleviation, his administration at least targeted aid at distressed cities. In contrast, in *The President's National Urban Policy Report*, the Reagan administration argued that programs such as Carter's—and those of Nixon as well—"had the unintended effect of channeling credit to less competitive firms. The private market is more efficient than Federal program administrators in allocating dollars among alternative uses."[18] In other words, the administration proposed that distressed cities go it alone in their redevelopment efforts. "While the Federal Government concentrates on establishing the conditions for increasing rates of growth in the gross national product, State and local governments will find it is in their interests to concentrate on increasing their attractiveness to potential investors, residents and visitors," Reagan's urban policy report concluded.[19] Accordingly, the president's budget director David Stockman aimed to eliminate Nixon's general revenue sharing and Community Development Block Grants and also Carter's Urban Development Action Grants.[20] Many policy makers assumed that UDAGs would be safe from Reagan budget cuts because, as one federal administrator commented, "It's such a Republican-type program."[21] But Schaefer and other elected officials felt nervous. Ultimately, the threatened and then eventual loss of redistributed wealth from the federal government compelled elected officials in cities such as Baltimore to intensify austerity efforts and increase their reliance on race-to-the-bottom strategies such as the issuance of tax abatements, which further cost municipalities revenue needed to fund services.

As Reagan worked to cut or eliminate programs that gave cities like Baltimore a slight edge in national and international competitions for investors and credit, he also promoted global free trade. The combination did not bode well for the city. Although his administration occasionally supported protectionist measures intended to shield specific U.S. industries from foreign competition, Reagan officials more typically strove to open markets. Administration officials also used the United States' influence in the World Bank and the International Monetary Fund to compel leaders in other nations to conform their economies to the emerging neoliberal world order.[22] Most notably, officials in the international lending agencies began compelling compliance with a host of neoliberal policy prescriptions that became known as the Washington Consensus in negotiations with leaders from the Global South whose countries had high debt burdens. The resulting agreements, called structural adjustment programs, required nations to undertake many of the austerity measures elected officials in struggling American cities had begun adopting a decade earlier. Just as fiscal crises and debt served as the leverage banks and elected officials used to compel structural adjustment at home, so they powered efforts to reorient the global economy.

The global macroeconomic regime that Nixon, Carter, and Reagan did much to create did not bode well for job seekers in Baltimore. Deindustrialization was well under way in the city by the 1980s, but as historian Judith Stein argues, American presidents' failure to pursue an industrial policy to protect the nation's manufacturing interests followed by pursuit of a renewed American hegemony via financialization led them to promote wealth production over capital production.[23] But while wealth production could create big profits, it was not a source of the solid, working-class jobs that capital production could create and that Baltimore needed to relieve unemployment. Macroeconomic decisions made by U.S. presidents hamstrung the nation's industrial sector and made a manufacturing comeback in such cities as Baltimore nearly impossible. Simultaneously, the decisions began to cost the nation its welfare state and proved a dire threat to the public service providers who staffed it and the many low-income Americans who needed it. In deindustrializing Baltimore, where Black men already suffered high jobless rates due in large part to the decline in manufacturing jobs, the city's predominantly African American and female public service providers and their clients were also about to take a big hit.

"Would You Come to Baltimore?" Schaefer Defends the Cities

Reagan's policy achievements did not come without a fight, and Baltimore's Mayor Schaefer helped lead the charge. Unwilling to stand idly by while the new president eliminated government programs that he considered critical to his city, Schaefer distinguished himself among urban elected officials in the nation by very publicly and repeatedly calling attention to the implications of Reaganomics for the nation's struggling cities. In 1981, the *Washington Post* described Schaefer as "stalk[ing] the halls of the U.S. Capitol, pleading with one congressional committee after another to reject proposed federal cuts in a wide range of urban programs."[24] During his visits to the Capitol, Schaefer vociferously championed those Carter initiatives that had funded Baltimore's renaissance. But he also attempted to portray the human face of urban life and the toll that cuts in social welfare spending would have on people in his city.

Distressed cities simply could not go it alone in a global, free-market economy, the mayor argued to whatever congressional committee would listen. They were home to a disproportionate share of the nation's poor citizens and could not independently generate the revenue needed to meet local needs. He offered his own city as a case in point. During the early 1980s, Baltimore residents made up 17 percent of Maryland's population yet housed 60 percent of the state's residents with low incomes. By comparison, 15 percent of the state's population—but only 5 percent of Maryland's poor residents—lived in neighboring Baltimore County. The concentration of poor people in Baltimore meant that the city yielded little in comparison to nearby suburbs on the piggyback income tax Maryland law permitted county-level or equivalent governments to assess. During the early 1980s, Baltimore collected $99 per person from its income tax revenue while Baltimore County's coffers grew by $179 per person. Minimal changes to property tax rates also produced significantly different revenue streams. A one-cent property-tax hike in Baltimore earned the city 68 cents per person, while the same rate increase in Baltimore County produced double the city's return.[25]

Yet Baltimore had serious need for tax dollars. The city's shrinking population and industrial base had not diminished the need for costly municipal services. Although the total number of residents had declined since the end of World War II, Baltimore's acreage and infrastructure had not. As an older city, many of Baltimore's houses were coated in lead paint, which was costly to remove. Lead poisoning caused learning difficulties that the city's public school system had to address. Suburban commuters also drove up the bills for road maintenance and traffic planning. High numbers of residents living in poverty created the need for expensive municipal services as well. Homelessness, hunger, and the problem of drug addiction—which had not yet been acknowledged but was about to explode in the city following the popularization of crack cocaine, for example—gave rise to the need for public programs in less demand in wealthier jurisdictions. In other words, the city's costly urban problems persisted, and in some cases worsened, even as its population and tax base declined.[26]

During his trips to Washington, Schaefer tried to describe conditions in his city to compel sympathy and federal support. It was not an easy job, and the mayor rued his need to appear hat in hand in front of multiple congressional committees. "It is not very nice for me to come over to tell you about the problems of Baltimore," Schaefer confessed to the Joint Economic Committee. "We are, in a way, a very proud city. We're proud of what we've been able to accomplish with federal help, with state help, and with our own initiative. So now I continually come over in a way on the defensive to tell you the difficulties that we're having."[27] In keeping with his faith in commercial revitalization strategies, Schaefer was particularly concerned about the fate of UDAGs. He anticipated that Reagan would view the grants with suspicion and consider Baltimore a UDAG queen. And he was right; some in Reagan's administration did view Baltimore as an example of liberal, federal, urban "giveaways" run amok. Richard Williamson, the assistant to the president for intergovernmental affairs, revealed an imprecise knowledge of geography but a firm commitment to Reaganomics when he complained that Schaefer had received so much money from the Carter administration that "Baltimore is about to sink into the [Chesapeake] bay."[28]

Schaefer desperately feared the loss of the UDAGs because other cuts in federal spending would lead cities to rely even more heavily than they already did on private-sector growth. Clearly not a radical, Schaefer nonetheless acknowledged that Baltimore's business community could not possibly compensate for reduced federal aid. And without UDAGs, the city's ability to attract investment would further dim. As it was, the governments of Baltimore and Maryland already offered many potential investors considerable tax relief for setting up shop in the city. It was hard to imagine what additional incentives could be granted. Baltimore needed UDAGs to give it an edge over other jurisdictions—both domestically and globally. As the mayor asked of the members of the Joint Economic Committee, "If you were going to locate an industry, would you come to Baltimore where all the problems are or would you go to an area where there are very few problems? And that's something that really concerns me. Where would you locate?"[29]

Schaefer was also alarmed that Reagan was proposing a new iteration of New Federalism. Nixon's New Federalism had disarmed antipoverty warriors by sending federal aid to elected city officials. Reagan, however, intended to send intergovernmental resources to states rather than local governments. The mayor anticipated that his city would not do well fighting for resources in Maryland's State House. Baltimore could effectively solve its problems if assisted with federal resources and provided them directly, he told the Joint Economic Committee. "But when the money is pulled away and when the state really doesn't understand the plight of a city like ours and where I go down [to Annapolis] and I tell them 'the poor,' and the answer is, 'They're your poor.' Well, they're not my poor. I think they are everyone's poor, and I think we must take some cognizance of the fact that the city where the poor are located need special consideration. I don't want to preach but I get just a little concerned about what is happening in our cities."[30] Local- rather than state-level elected officials needed the authority to distribute federal funds to combat urban problems, Schaefer told the nation's lawmakers.[31]

Although Schaefer most frequently defended federal funding for commercial revitalization during his D.C. trips, he also called attention to the implications for those in his city of the administration's plan to consolidate categorical grants for social welfare concerns into block grants and cut overall spending. One plan, he explained as an example, involved merging twenty-six health-related grants into two block grants. Policy makers contended that the reconfiguration would lower administrative costs and justify a funding cut of 25 percent. Schaefer adamantly disagreed and translated the funding reductions into their human costs. Displaying charts painstakingly created by hand by his staffers, the mayor explained that in Baltimore, a 25 percent reduction in funding would result in "1,100 fewer youth, 2,900 adults and 500 drinking drivers losing access to alcohol programs; 2,500 people not being served by mental health programs; 600 pregnant adults and 600 pregnant teenagers not receiving maternal and infant care (increasing infant mortality); . . . fewer code enforcers for rat eradication programs; 3,600 students who won't be immunized; and 6,000 fewer children than in the past tested for lead poisoning."[32] In other words, the mayor argued, "The assurance that a 25% reduction of federal expenditures will not hurt local delivery units is simplistic and uncritical."[33]

Although his impact on federal policy remained to be seen, back in Baltimore, Schaefer's battles against Reagan's budget axe won him tremendous accolades. Even those who regarded the mayor's local policy priorities with suspicion and considered him an unreliable ally in the fight for racial justice lent their praise. John B. Ferron, the African American director of the city's Community Relations Commission, who had long been critical of the mayor's tepid commitment to affirmative action, was among those who penned cards or letters of thanks. "Though we have occasionally disagreed on some matters in the past . . . my primary purpose for writing, Mr. Mayor, is to share with you my intensified respect and admiration for you as the top executive in the City of Baltimore . . . especially in view of the fact that you appear to be the one person on the national level who has the courage to challenge the new order of priorities set by the National Administration."[34] Additional fan mail piled up at city hall from grateful residents proud that their quirky mayor had gone to bat for Baltimore and the nation's other struggling cities.[35]

"A Revolving Door for Impoverished People": The Liberal Response to Reaganomics

While Schaefer distinguished himself among mayors with his public opposition to the administration's proposals, seasoned activists also protested the new president's agenda. Many of the organizations that took the lead in combating Reaganomics had also protested Nixon's New Federalism and pressed Carter to prioritize the battle against unemployment over concerns with inflation. The leadership of the National Urban League was especially vocal among the civil rights advocates who challenged the new president. Organized labor mounted a resistance, in which those at the helm of AFSCME played a major role. Reagan's effort to redefine the role of government threatened both the union's members and the vital public services they provided. And representatives from feminist and women's organizations also protested much of the president's agenda and warned of its many dire implications for women.

Vernon Jordan, the president of the NUL, and other officials from his organization combated Reaganomics in both congressional testimony and appeals to the general public. Decades of federal policies had contributed significantly to undermining the economic viability of the nation's older cities, Jordan repeatedly argued. Most significantly, postwar government housing programs and incentive policies that enhanced the commercial viability and competitiveness of suburban and Sunbelt regions had promoted the outmigration of people and jobs from cities. Fiercely policed residential segregation in combination with employment discrimination prevented African Americans from following the jobs. Given the federal government's role in subsidizing economic development in the Sunbelt, Reagan's hands-off approach to the rust belt struck NUL leaders as particularly duplicitous.[36] Moreover, a bipartisan report by the Joint Economic Committee predicted that the president's first budget request was likely to stimulate business activity in areas already experiencing growth. The report's authors explained, "Tax proposals to promote investment will generally reinforce current regional and urban growth trends, since they, on balance, favor new investment over investment in older structures."[37] Despite his free-market rhetoric, in other words, the president's economic policies were inherently geographically biased and detrimental to the areas in which many African Americans were concentrated, NUL officials protested.[38]

Making matters worse, according to leaders of the NUL, the Reagan administration proposed cutting social welfare programs and entitlements that helped to alleviate the urban poverty that the federal government's Sunbelt bias had played a role in creating. During the 1960s, Great Society initiatives had relieved poverty in American cities. As a result, even as the weight of federal largesse had benefited the Sunbelt, the government had at least sent struggling cities antipoverty funds—and the results had been impressive, according to Maudine Cooper, the vice president of the NUL. "Two-thirds of the Black underclass were lifted from poverty between 1967 and 1975, primarily as a result of government programs," she argued.[39] Reductions in federal spending on the programs, in combination with federal policies that continued to disadvantage the rust belt, spelled disaster for African Americans in the nation's distressed cities, NUL officials warned. "Present federal efforts may construct a revolving door for impoverished people seeking access to this nation's economic mainstream," Cooper cautioned.[40]

The new president's method for achieving reductions in federal funding for social welfare programs also alarmed the NUL leadership. As Schaefer also mentioned in his testimony, Reagan's New Federalism differed from Nixon's in two important ways. First, the new president argued that consolidating categorical grants into block grants justified significant spending reductions because administrative costs would be reduced. Second, while Congress and other pressure groups had compelled Nixon to send the bulk of his repackaged intergovernmental aid to localities, Reagan intended to direct federal resources to state governments. The NUL condemned the revival of states' rights and protested funding formulas that transferred federal revenue to the state rather than the local level.[41] As an alternative to Reagan's agenda, NUL leaders reprised their demands from the Carter years. "The only way, and it cannot be stressed too strongly—the only way—to limit federal social programs is to implement full employment with jobs for all who want to work," Jordan urged. "To suppose that simply unshackling the private sector is going to create jobs for all is a myth. The federal government will still have to shape its tax and regulatory policies in a way that encourages job creation where it is most needed, and not, as at present, in a way that drains jobs from our industrial heartlands to other regions or other countries."[42]

AFSCME leaders offered an equally biting critique of the president's agenda. They denounced Reaganomics as a sham predicated on demeaning stereotypes of public service providers and recipients that was intended to shift money and power up the economic ladder. Following the 1980 election, they announced "a multi-pronged campaign to save public services and jobs from President Reagan's budgetary butcher knife."[43] The union was an important organizer of Solidarity Day, a march on Washington, DC, in September 1981 to oppose Reagan's agenda and to protest his recent decision to fire striking unionized federal employees. The march attracted at least two hundred thousand and possibly as many as half a million protesters. The AFL-CIO, of which AFSCME was a member, was the major force behind the march, which attracted the endorsement and participation of civil rights, feminist, and multiple other groups.[44] AFSCME also sent lobbyists to visit Congress members, participated in coalitions fighting Reagan's agenda, and rallied members to vigorously protest the new president's policies. In addition, AFSCME leaders voiced their concerns about the perils of Reaganomics in congressional testimony, speeches, television interviews, and union-produced films. Rather than an entity that served the people, AFSCME secretary-treasurer William Lucy warned, the president's backers would turn the government into a power protecting the privileges of elites. Jerry Wurf, the union's president until his untimely death in December 1981, argued that "corporate America, the new masters of the federal government," was demanding reductions in spending on social programs to reduce its tax burden.[45] Wurf also warned, however, that "tax breaks for the rich do little to create jobs. The money just ends up in the pockets of the wealthy like it always has in the past."[46]

Public-sector workers and low-income service recipients were among the groups that would pay the highest price for the reassertion of corporate power, AFSCME leaders asserted. "You don't need a calculator to figure out why the federal budget is so important to AFSCME members. A federal budget that cuts aid to state and local governments spells disaster for us and public services everywhere," AFSCME's assistant public policy director Marcia Caprio explained.[47] Since the 1970s, AFSCME officials had been attempting to make the case that the cause of its members and the well-being of service recipients were inextricable. They pressed the point during the 1980s and also joined feminist leaders in identifying the gendered implications for women of Reaganomics. As Lucy explained, "Many [women] would lose their jobs and others on unemployment and welfare programs would see their already meager benefits slashed or wiped out."[48] Lucy was also concerned about the prospects of low-income women who depended on government services and worked government-subsidized jobs. Proposed cuts to spending on CETA, which provided federal funds for jobs and job training, would disproportionately impact women, many of whom were heads of households. AFSCME certainly had been a reluctant supporter of CETA. Nevertheless, union officials could empathize that CETA cuts, along with reductions of spending on day-care programs, "[spelled] disaster for thousands of women who for a brief time could see a glimmer of hope."[49]

Union officials also worried that the public-sector workers most likely to lose their jobs were often staunch advocates for the poor. In an article in the *Public Employee*, AFSCME's monthly newspaper, the union's staff challenged Reagan's assertion that he championed "family values." "In our opinion, the people really supporting the family have been the workers—especially AFSMCE members—who see the family firsthand: AFSCME workers who process unemployment forms, who provide day care, who counsel the distressed and nurse the ill. AFSMCE members who, on their own, collect food for the hungry, contribute money for heating bills, make a home for neglected and abused children, give of their time without making cruel judgments," the paper's staff countered.[50] In 1982, the union recommended Congress adopt a stimulus plan to jump-start the economy. The union advocated increased government spending on public health, transportation, and employment and training to create jobs and combat poverty. And they remained insistent that wealthy Americans should be taxed to foot the cost of the programs they proposed.[51]

The leaders of feminist organizations were also among those who staunchly challenged Reagan's proposed policies. The National Organization for Women was one of the sponsoring organizations of Solidarity Day, and the organization's president, Eleanor Smeal, joined nationally prominent leaders from the labor and civil rights movements in leading the historic march and addressing participants from the platform at the event's concluding rally. Smeal's inclusion among Solidarity Day's top leaders shows the gains feminists had made in integrating some women's issues into the national liberal agenda. That success did not necessarily translate into winning policy outcomes to their liking during the Reagan years, however.

The increasing feminization of poverty was an issue of considerable concern to many leaders of women's organizations during the 1980s, and they repeatedly called attention to the role Reaganomics played in exacerbating women's economic insecurity. In 1981, representatives from a broad range of organizations formed the Coalition on Women and the Budget to assess the implications for women of Reagan's proposals. In their 1984 report, which was endorsed by close to eighty organizations, they argued the president had compelled "inequality of sacrifice" from the American people.⁵² Women suffered disproportionately as a result of the president's budget cuts, they charged. Reductions in federal spending on AFDC; Food Stamps; the Women, Infants and Children program; legal services; child nutrition; and housing were particularly devastating, and the coalition members raised the alarm that additional proposed cuts would again fall disproportionately on women. In general, national feminist leaders were less consistent than those at the helm of public-sector labor unions at identifying federal spending cuts as a source of job insecurity for women, who were overrepresented in government employment. The Coalition on Women and the Budget, which included both AFSCME and the advocacy group Federally Employed Women, did note, however, the toll Reaganomics had taken on women in the federal workforce and warned that additional budget cuts imperiled the jobs and security of many others.⁵³

In opposition to Reaganomics, feminist leaders expressed a deep commitment to an activist and interventionist federal government, which they felt was indispensable in the quest for gender equality. Ultimately, however, many continued to insist that access to fairly remunerated paid employment was women's best option for economic independence, and a defense of the critical economic importance of women's unpaid caretaking work did not figure prominently on their agenda. Thus, during the Reagan years, as feminists firmly advocated on behalf of the social safety net and the increased provision of social services, they pressed even more forcefully for measures that would improve women's status in the labor market. They called for efforts to reduce the wage gap between men and women, demanded job-training programs, argued in favor of affirmative action and equal opportunity, advocated for increased access to child care, and supported additional programs that accommodated working women's child-rearing roles. Feminist leaders also denounced the stereotyping of poor women as "welfare queens" and advocated for improvement of the AFDC program.⁵⁴

"We Are Going to Hurt and Hurt Badly": Workers in Baltimore Protest Government Cuts

As national civil rights, labor, and feminist leaders protested Reaganomics in Washington, government service providers and their unions in Baltimore mounted their own resistance. Some in municipal agencies tried to revive the solidarity with city residents with low incomes that had existed in the 1960s and early 1970s but that had weakened considerably during a long decade of austerity, budget cuts, and dashed expectations. City workers also joined forces with civic and religious organizations and attempted to partner as well with those in the local nonprofit social services sector, which was also often dependent on government funds. Public-sector workers protested Reaganomics to defend their own jobs and protect the economic security of their families. In Baltimore's troubled labor market, the government workforce remained a critically important source of stable employment and had become a vital niche for African Americans and Black women in particular. But the workers' fight was not only self-serving. Their defenses of their agencies and the services they provided reflected a deep commitment to a set of principles about fairness, racial and economic justice, and women's rights that had been evident in various forms since the 1960s.

Protests during the Reagan years were not as well choreographed, ambitious, or optimistic as the spirited battles of the 1960s and early 1970s had been; the reassertion of corporate power over public policy, the shift of the nation's political discourse to the right, and Schaefer's strategic appointment of accommodating allies to key leadership positions had taken their toll. Nevertheless, in response to Reaganomics, service workers in many city agencies pulled out tattered playbooks that had provided many of the protest strategies used earlier, and public-sector unions used their institutional power to support their members and defend the social safety net. The fights over Reaganomics in Baltimore, although grounded in local and national issues, were iterations of the larger fights emerging globally over the legitimacy of neoliberalism and the toll it was taking on the poor. And women, among them many public services providers and recipients, were prominent in the battles.

To rally service recipients and others to the cause of protecting the welfare state, service providers decoded the language the Reagan administration used to describe its agenda. The workers worried that Reagan's talk of New Federalism and bureaucratic waste obscured in jargon the president's actual intention to cut programs that helped poor people. The Reagan administration was attempting to gut the welfare state, officials from local- and state-level human-services departments explained. Staffers at the Urban Services Agency, the city's antipoverty agency, created a fact sheet that they distributed to residents that spelled out the implications of New Federalism for familiar War on Poverty programs: "[The] Reagan administration will end 40 programs, including the Community Services Administration which funds CAA, the Legal Services Corporation which funds Legal Aid, and low-Income Energy assistance which provides fuel assistance. They will take funds proposed for these and reduce the total by 20–25% and send this amount to the states in the form of block grants," the staffers warned.[55] Meanwhile, Ruth Massinga, the African American director of the city's Department of Social Services, which was being renamed the Department of Human Resources, protested as false the administration's assertion that budget reductions would not lead to service losses. "It is Reagan mythology that 25 percent [of costs] is due to administrative overhead. None of us have administrative fat. It makes a pretty speech, but in reality, we are going to hurt and hurt badly," she argued.[56]

State-level officials in human-services agencies also joined the battle. "This is not only an economic but an ideological assault on every social welfare program in the state," argued Kalman R. Hettleman, Maryland's secretary of human resources.[57] Dr. Charles R. Buck Jr., Maryland's secretary of the Department of Health and Mental Hygiene, agreed. He described the contention that block grants would increase state-level control over programming and resources as "in many ways . . . a sham."[58] Instead, he asserted, "Under the guise of flexibility, they are cutting services to people who really need them giving us [on the state level] the responsibility of saying no to these people." Hettleman concurred, adding that Reagan's "so-called block grants" were "ill-disguised reductions in funding."[59]

Local- and state-level public-sector union officials, especially those affiliated with AFSCME, also vociferously critiqued the president's agenda. Not surprisingly, AFSCME officials repeated for local audiences and media outlets many of the same talking points asserted by national-level leaders. Ernie Crofoot, the executive director of AFSCME Council 67, asserted his union's concern that the nation's wealthiest were not paying their fair share in taxes. "Reagan makes certain that his actions benefit business and industry while pulling ever more from the pockets and purses of the taxpayers. Pass the buck back to business . . . where it belongs," he argued.[60] Meanwhile, Raymond Clarke, the president of AFSCME Local 44, was stoically unapologetic in his defense of gains his union had won for low-wage workers.[61] Laura Moseley, an African American eligibility supervisor in the income maintenance program of the Department of Human Resources and an elected official in AFSCME, reiterated the point that social service providers were some of the nation's fiercest defenders of the welfare state because they saw firsthand the devastating consequences of economic injustice. "These people need money to keep a roof over their heads, food in their stomachs, and clothes on their backs— just the bare necessities to keep body and soul together," she worried.[62] In response to Reaganomics, public-sector workers in the city mounted a fierce defense of their members, their members' clients, and the vital public services the government provided.

Meanwhile, public service providers and their allies took action independently of their unions. Replicating a strategy often used during the heyday of the civil rights movement, they held a mass meeting to plan a course of action. Ultimately, the group adopted a two-pronged strategy. They agreed to engage in direct protest to oppose funding reductions. Simultaneously, they pledged to work together to coordinate service delivery in order to mitigate the effects of the president's imminent budget cuts on those most in need. If they planned carefully, they hoped, they could attempt to ensure that services cut in one agency remained available at others.[63]

As part of their direct-action campaigns, public-sector workers attempted to build coalitions. Some, including Rachel Wohl of USA and AFSCME member Linda Thompson, participated in the local planning committee for Solidarity Day. The organizers wanted to send the president a clear message. "The key point of this march is to show Reagan that he does not have a mandate to cut social programs," Thompson explained.[64] Members of the committee held dozens of meetings with community groups and won endorsements of the march from many area churches and organizations, including the Interdenominational Ministerial Alliance and the Baltimore NAACP.[65] African Americans often did not need much convincing to protest the president's agenda. As local NAACP official George Bunton explained, "Black people were against Reagan from the beginning, but now whites are waking up."[66] AFSCME officials in and around the city as well as other representatives of organized labor also played important roles in local planning efforts for the national march. And many city workers and their allies were among the thousands from the Baltimore area who helped to fill the hundreds of buses hired to transport protesters to the demonstration. Moreover, following the Washington, DC, event, AFSCME leaders in Maryland sponsored a second Solidarity Day—this time in Annapolis—to pressure state-level officials to do what they could to mitigate federal budget cuts.[67] In addition to planning and participating in demonstrations, public service providers and their allies also met with their congressional representatives to express their concerns, wrote angry letters to state and federal lawmakers, testified in defense of federal welfare spending, implored state officials for relief, continued to politicize and work in conjunction with service recipients, and joined local, state, and national campaigns against Reagan's policies.[68]

At the same time, service providers took steps to help soften the blow budget cuts would have on the residents they served. Following changes in the eligibility requirements for federal entitlement programs, staff members at the Department of Human Resources created a checklist for AFDC recipients to use to determine if they would be impacted by cuts and worked with them to develop survival strategies. Meanwhile, as the author of an article in the newsletter of the Department of Human Resources explained in 1981, "Cuts of this magnitude will require radical changes in the service delivery system."[69] As some had earlier pledged, public and private service providers worked cooperatively. By considering the state's entire landscape of social services, public service providers attempted to limit service reductions in their agencies to those programs that might be available elsewhere from charities and other nonprofit organizations.[70] Ultimately, however, they could not fully compensate for the effects of the cuts, and service elimination proved inevitable. In 1981, for example, Department of Human Resources administrators realized that their commitment to maintaining programming for teenage mothers meant that services for the elderly would take a big hit. They hoped that volunteer organizations and the Office on the Aging would be able to compensate, but they could not be sure. At the same time, to make the best use of remaining resources, Massinga, the director of Baltimore's welfare services, recycled a strategy from the community-participation days. She brought her agency's clients into decision-making conversations. Unlike during the 1960s, however, in the Reagan era, discussions involved not what antipoverty efforts to pursue but instead which to eliminate.[71]

National- and local-level protest against Reaganomics met with some success. Opposition to Reagan's agenda emboldened congressional Democrats to act as a restraint against the president's budget axe when they could. And the president himself proved willing to sacrifice ideology for pragmatism in some instances. Nevertheless, Reagan successfully reoriented the federal government away from midcentury liberal priorities. Tax cuts in 1981 and 1986 collectively reduced the highest U.S. income tax rate from 70 percent to 28 percent, and the president also reduced the level of funds the government redistributed to poor individuals and the distressed cities where many of them lived, thereby shifting wealth up the economic ladder. The Omnibus Budget Reconciliation Act of 1981 eliminated four hundred thousand from the AFDC rolls and reduced the benefits of hundreds of thousands of other recipients largely by changing eligibility requirements. Ultimately, spending on AFDC was cut by $1 billion, or 12 percent. Federal spending on the

Food Stamp Program dropped by 13 percent, and administration officials cut child-care services even as they attempted to compel low-income women to seek paid employment. Ultimately, few social welfare programs were spared.[72]

Struggling cities fared poorly as well. During the Reagan years, intergovernmental aid fell by 38 percent. In 1982, Reagan eliminated more than a hundred categorical grants by combining close to sixty programs into nine block grants and cutting others entirely. The administration also reduced federal oversight over the use of the funds and sent intergovernmental aid to state-level rather than municipal-level officials. Reagan reduced targeted aid to cities as well, and programs on which Baltimore had come to depend took a particular hit. The administration cut funding for CDBGs by 20 percent; in 1986, it discontinued GRS; and in 1988, the administration eliminated the UDAG program. Overall, just between 1981 and 1984, federal aid to cities fell by almost 20 percent, and by 1989, it had dropped by an additional 14 percent.[73] During the 1980s, the federal government largely abandoned struggling cities in the increasingly competitive global economy.

As had been the case during the Nixon and Carter years, one group of government workers did see the economic fortunes of their agencies brighten. Federal spending on anticrime measures, and specifically on drug-related crime enforcement, increased significantly, a boon to those in the fields of law enforcement and criminal justice, although not necessarily always for public-sector workers given the increasingly popular practice of outsourcing. In 1982, Reagan announced that he was launching a War on Drugs. Funding for antidrug initiatives carried out by the Federal Bureau of Investigation, the Department of Defense, and the Drug Enforcement Agency mushroomed during the years that followed. At the same time, funding for drug-use prevention and rehabilitation plummeted. Between 1981 and 1984, the administration reduced the budget of the National Institute on Drug Abuse from $274 million to $57 million, and the Department of Education lost $11 million in antidrug funds.[74] The War on Drugs was to be fought by the staffs of criminal-justice rather than human-services agencies. The president launched his war on drugs at a time when public concern about drug use was actually quite low and a few years before the use of crack cocaine became an urgent crisis in many of the nation's cities, including Baltimore. Reagan officials soon seized on the rising use of crack, however, to justify the War on Drugs and to press for additional punitive legislation, such as the Anti-Drug Abuse Act of 1986. The law included mandatory minimum sentencing guidelines, which restricted the ability of judges to consider extenuating circumstances in drug cases. It also penalized crack cocaine–related offenses far more harshly than those involving powder cocaine, the form of the narcotic typically favored by whites.[75]

Reagan contracted spending on welfare, rehabilitation, and other human services and simultaneously eliminated or reduced federal grants for urban programs that distressed cities used to attract investors and potential taxpayers. He thus pulled the rug out from under the feet of Baltimore residents with low incomes and made it more difficult for the city to lure new businesses and jobs. Meanwhile, he dramatically increased federal support for law enforcement and instituted racially biased antidrug policies. Not surprisingly, in Baltimore, the results were devastating job losses in the public sector, worsening poverty rates in the city's already poor neighborhoods, and the tragedy of the crisis of mass incarceration. As Baltimore's army of predominantly Black and female social service providers had been arguing since Reagan won the election, the implications of his policies for their city were catastrophic.

CHAPTER 10

"There's Tragedy on Both Sides of the Layoffs"

Privatization and the Urban Crisis

In March 1986, more than seventy workers from Baltimore's Urban Services Agency and their union representatives marched on city hall to protest a decision by their agency's head to lay off twenty-one employees. Although small in numbers, the layoffs followed a series of cuts that had already shrunk the antipoverty agency's staff by a crippling two-thirds in five years. The March layoffs were also particularly poignant. Many of those who lost their jobs were African American women who were veterans of the city's War on Poverty. They were low-level, direct-service providers, and some had grown up in the communities in which they worked. During their demonstration at city hall, the workers expressed concern about their clients' uncertain futures. As one woman later explained about her program, which was being eliminated as a result of budget cuts, "We handle families that have multiple problems such as eviction proceedings, lack of food, truancy among young people, teenage pregnancy, a whole host of difficulties. . . . I don't know what some of our clients are going to do once we close the cases."[1] The workers had good cause to worry about their own futures as well. As Ronald "R. B." Jones of the *Afro-American* reminded readers, "There is tragedy on both sides of . . . the layoffs."[2] The women left unemployed by the cuts faced dismal job prospects in postindustrial Baltimore, and their clients, among the most vulnerable in the city, were left to provide themselves or do without services the state earlier guaranteed its citizens.

The implications of the Reagan revolution for African Americans in Baltimore were multiple and dire. For over a decade, Republican politicians had been recklessly touting dog-whistle claims that suggested that urban African Americans were prone to criminality and that cities with large Black populations were dangerous and corrupt. "Law-and-order" and "welfare queen" rhetoric, in combination with a revival of states' rights and assaults on the public sector as bloated and inefficient, imperiled gains that Baltimore's civil rights activists had worked decades to achieve. For much of the twentieth century, Black leaders in the city had pursued three important goals. To challenge white supremacy and enhance the lives of Black city residents, they sought to increase African Americans' political influence, enhance the job prospects of Black workers, and improve the quality of services available to African American residents. Reagan's agenda threatened gains that had been made on all three fronts. The Republican introduced his own version of New Federalism, which differed from Richard Nixon's in that it involved the transfer of federal resources to elected officials at the state rather than the local level. The change shifted power over affairs in Baltimore away from African Americans and toward predominantly white, male officials in Annapolis. New Federalism meant that important decisions concerning Baltimore's future would be made in the State House, where African Americans had considerably less political influence than they had in the city.

Reaganomics, meanwhile, did not bode well for Black public-sector workers, the mainstay of the city's African American middle and working classes. By 1980, nearly 40 percent of employed Black women and close to 30 percent of employed Black men in Baltimore worked for the federal, state, or municipal government, and most of them worked for the city.[3] Reagan's neoliberal macroeconomic policies wreaked havoc on the public sector, shrinking a source of employment—and of influence over public policy—of vital importance to the economic health of Black communities. Moreover, the concentration of federal-level budget cuts in the human services hit hardest at those government agencies in which African American women had made the most substantial job gains.

Simultaneously, the president launched the War on Drugs. As human-services workers watched their numbers and influence decrease, the fortunes of the predominantly white and male Baltimore Police Department increased. Arrest rates soared as officers cracked down on drug use in the city, and African American men were ensnared disproportionately, even though drug-use rates among Blacks and whites in Maryland were similar. The crisis of mass incarceration, long in the making, was under way. Meanwhile, reductions in funding for social welfare programs and public services rent holes in the social safety net that disproportionately impacted women, who bore gendered responsibilities for family caretaking. Women were forced to provide themselves, do without, or find alternative sources of services that recently had been available from the state. The president's neoliberal policies, in other words, often required that women absorb into the domestic sphere—and provide without compensation—services the government had earlier paid for and thus implicitly acknowledged as economic activity. The savings to taxpayers were shifted up the economic ladder. During the 1980s, the policies of the Reagan administration entrenched an ongoing urban crisis in Baltimore that only two decades earlier had shown signs of easing.

"The States Proved Themselves Unfair in the Past": Reagan and Black Political Power

Reagan's reassertion of states' rights while on the campaign trail angered and worried the nation's and Baltimore's African American leaders—for good reason. Once in office, the president's adoption of New Federalism weakened Black political influence over policy-making. During the presidency of Lyndon Johnson, Black Baltimore had gained unprecedented influence in the municipal government as they secured jobs and leadership posts in the city government and positions on boards and advisory committees. The categorical grants the federal government sent to municipal agencies provided city employees, such as those waging the War on Poverty, an important level of independence from white elected officials. Conservatives had noticed and responded. In the name of restoring "local control," Nixon used his version of New Federalism to shift influence over federal revenue streams from municipal agencies to elected officials, who in Baltimore remained predominantly white and male. Carter further eroded the power of African Americans within municipal agencies by cutting urban spending and subsidizing public-private partnerships. Over the years, however, African Americans increased their representation on the city council and secured municipal jobs outside of their historical base in antipoverty and human-services agencies. As their local power was growing, Reagan again moved power just beyond their grasp. In accord with his New Federalism, important decisions that affected the city's future would be made not in municipal offices or even in city hall but instead in the statehouse. The city's Black leaders identified the usurpation of power under way. And they anticipated its likely outcomes on government programs critical to the well-being of African Americans. As the editors of the *Afro American*, recalling Maryland's long and not too distant history of Jim Crow, reminded their readers in a piece on New Federalism, "The states proved themselves inefficient and unfair in operating those programs in the past."[4]

The change in the method the federal government used to distribute intergovernmental revenue occurred at a moment when Baltimore was already struggling to defend itself in Annapolis. Some Maryland suburbanites, inspired by the 1978 California tax revolt, favored imposing tax caps to limit government spending. Worried Baltimore officials calculated that if a measure like California's Proposition 13 passed in Maryland, the city would lose close to $137 million in revenue. They kept close tabs on tax initiatives not only on the state level but also on the county level. They were particularly attentive to the political leanings of elected officials in the Maryland suburbs that bordered Washington, DC. Population numbers there were on the rise, while Baltimore's was continuing to fall. As a result, voters in the D.C. suburbs were becoming the heavyweights in Maryland politics. Ultimately, a tax-cap initiative did pass in Prince George's County, located just outside of the nation's capital. Voters in neighboring Montgomery County defeated a similar measure, however, and fortunately for Baltimore, tax-revolt fever did not become contagious in Maryland.[5]

The task of Baltimore's delegation to the State House nonetheless remained daunting. The representatives had to counter a white backlash against welfare expenditures as well as suburban and rural suspicions of urban profligacy. During the 1970s, under Schaefer's crafty stewardship, Baltimore had done fairly well when making requests of state officials. At the end of the decade, however, the goodwill of representatives from nonurban jurisdictions had begun to wear thin. To promote literacy in the city, local boosters had dubbed Baltimore the "City That Reads." A Montgomery County representative proposed the "city of greed" as a more suitable moniker.[6] Although the D.C. suburbs had been growing in population for some time, it was only during the early 1980s that officials from these jurisdictions finally began to appreciate their ability to challenge legislation from the city. The *Sun* acknowledged the shift warily in an article that warned Baltimore residents that Montgomery County, for one, was "shed[ding] its weakling image in state politics" and "get[ting] rid of [its] 'kick me' sign."[7] To counter hostility toward the city from officials from elsewhere in the state, Janet Hoffman, Baltimore's chief lobbyist in Annapolis, organized tours of the city for state legislators. Elected officials enjoyed a harbor cruise, which provided them with a stunning view of the city's new aquarium, Harborplace mall, Hyatt Regency hotel, and other waterfront attractions. The delegation also visited a city housing project.

Having shown the legislators both the productive uses to which the city put intergovernmental funding and the severe need for antipoverty relief, Baltimore officials hoped for sympathy votes in Annapolis.[8]

Baltimore's need for allies increased significantly in 1983. Because of depopulation, the size of the delegation Baltimore sent to Annapolis had shrunk over the preceding decades. During the early 1980s, state-level reapportionment further reduced the number of elected officials city residents could send to the State House. In 1983, Baltimore residents voted into office six fewer delegates and three fewer senators than they had in the previous election. A worried city paper described the congressional delegation as "the weakest in recent memory" because of its small size.[9] Yet the delegates and senators shouldered the weighty responsibility of defending Baltimore's need for a disproportionate share of the state's resources. And because of Reagan's New Federalism and cuts to welfare and urban funding, the city's dependency on its small delegation was tremendous. Baltimore's status in Annapolis was not entirely bleak; the likelihood that Schaefer would win the state's next governor's race incentivized political support for his requests. Despite his gallant stand against Reaganomics in the halls of Congress, however, the mayor's trickle-down revitalization priorities were inconsistent with the policy preferences of those who favored more direct responses to poverty, including many in the city's human-services agencies. Their influence over decision-making in the city had declined considerably, however. A lot had changed since the optimistic days of the mid-1960s, when the federal government had boldly confronted racism and discrimination with civil rights legislation, launched a War on Poverty, sent federal aid earmarked for antipoverty efforts directly to those in the trenches, and mandated maximum feasible community participation in decision-making.[10]

"Residents Still Need Help Whether People Are Laid Off or Not": Reagan and Job Losses

As Reagan's New Federalism robbed city residents of influence over local agenda-setting, the president's budget-cutting had a second major consequence in Baltimore. It compelled significant downsizing in the public sector. Building on public antipathy toward public-sector workers that Reagan also reinforced, cuts occurred at all levels of government. And since Baltimore was home to municipal, state, and federal employees, the pain was felt widely. City employees were the first to see their numbers decline. Staffing reductions in some agencies were already under way when Reagan took office. Then, between 1981 and 1986, the city's grant revenue fell from $220 million to $124 million. Additional reductions in intergovernmental funding cut even more deeply. Overall, according to the Johns Hopkins Center for Metropolitan Planning and Research, the city lost $569 million in revenue for its 1982, 1983, and 1984 budgets collectively.[11] In a city in which poverty was on the rise, and only a third earned enough to pay taxes, the cuts were devastating. As they had for decades, Baltimore's elected officials worried that a property tax increase to offset the revenue losses would only increase the movement of taxpaying residents out of the city. Instead, officials increased rates for many public services. Tuition went up at the community college, and officials even tried to raise money by increasing parking-meter fees. Ultimately, however, lawmakers had no option but to eliminate jobs and services. The loss of some positions was probably warranted. Like all bureaucracies, the Baltimore municipal government had its share of inefficiencies. But Reaganomics compelled dramatic cuts that hardly could be described as fat-trimming. Between 1980 and 1990, the city government reduced its workforce by 18,400 positions, a loss of 37 percent.[12]

Municipal job cuts took a toll on workers across the city government, but they had a particularly significant impact on African American women. By the early 1980s, African Americans as a group made up more than 55 percent of municipal employees. Black women alone were close to 40 percent of the total workforce, and as had been the case since the early 1970s, they outnumbered Black men, white men, and white women. They represented nearly 70 percent of the city's minority employees and almost two-thirds of the female full-time classified workforce. And they were concentrated and had gained the most influence in the very agencies where Reagan's budget reductions cut the most deeply.[13] Ultimately, it is impossible to determine the precise number of Black women—or men—in the municipal workforce whose jobs were affected by Reaganomics. City officials used attrition in addition to layoffs to achieve staffing reductions; in many cases, they simply did not refill positions left vacant by employees' departures. In such cases, job seekers rather than jobholders took the hit. Moreover, some lost government posts but became private-sector workers when their agencies or the services they provided were privatized and shifted out of the government. In such cases, workers may have lost fringe benefits associated with public-sector employment, but they at least kept their jobs. Other city workers, however, joined the ranks of the unemployed.

The first workers in Baltimore to feel the bite of federal cuts were those receiving jobs or training through CETA programs. Shortly after taking office, Reagan eliminated the jobs-creation mandate in CETA and cut overall funding for training. By October 1981, 2,531 workers in Baltimore had been laid off. The cuts also resulted in 1,300 fewer spots in general training programs and 6,500 fewer employment and training positions for young people in a city in which 43,000 adults and 25,000 youth were unemployed. The loss of the training and employment programs interrupted a record of accomplishment that had won the city's CETA program a national reputation for quality.[14] The terminations had additional implications. Some of those who lost their positions had provided critical services because of the strategic use to which Baltimore officials put some CETA funds; they had created jobs that not only eased unemployment but also alleviated urban problems. For the two years before she lost her job, African American former health department employee Pat Green had worked for the city inspecting houses for lead paint. She was one member of a larger army of city workers attempting to combat the very serious problem of lead-paint poisoning among children. Green was given a week's notice before being laid off. She then collected unemployment insurance for as long as she could as she searched in vain for a new job. The $408 a month she received did not go far as she attempted to provide for four teenagers and a grandchild. "I knew there were going to be changes when the new administration took over," she reflected about Reagan's election, "but I never thought I'd see the day when I had to resort to feeding my family hot dogs and beans every day, and then having to explain why. I'm in debt way up over my head . . . my credit is bad . . . all thanks to President Reagan. He's living in style and comfort, while I'm living in pure hell."[15] And CETA funding cuts did not impact program participants alone. By 1984, the Mayor's Office of Manpower Resources, which coordinated CETA as well as other jobs-related programs and had a majority African American and female staff, had lost almost a thousand positions.[16]

Job losses at USA also cost residents critical services and jobs. Maxine Garland-Bey, an African American service provider, had been with the agency for seventeen years when she was laid off. Despite a decade of disinvestment in the War on Poverty, she remained committed to the cause. She had a reputation for working through lunch and for ending her workday by delivering surplus food to community centers that serviced the elderly. Evelina Ryce, who also lost her job, was also a dedicated antipoverty warrior. She had been nominated by the residents she served for "Baltimore Is Best" awards on multiple occasions and won twice before she was laid off. "It is with real regret that I must abolish your position," the director of USA, Lenwood Ivey, wrote to her in 1983. "The need to do this is through no fault of your own, but is a direct result of reduced funding."[17] And as USA's budget shrank through the 1980s, the job toll rose. By 1986, the agency had merely a third the number of employees it had had when Reagan entered office. And then came the cuts that prompted workers and their union officials to protest at city hall. Sallie Williams, an African American AFSCME official, was an organizer of the rally. A former nurse and an AFSCME member since 1968, she had moved full-time into the public-sector labor movement during the early 1970s and gained a reputation as a staunch defender of gender equity.[18] In the face of layoffs compelled by budget cuts, however, there was little she could do.

Those who lost their jobs at USA expressed deep concern for the clients they would no longer be able to support. Although caricatured in conservative rhetoric as barely more trustworthy than the so-called "welfare queens" they served, antipoverty workers knew well the critical roles they played in their clients' lives. As one worker explained, "We cut through the red tape that sometimes keeps people from getting help. We get a lot of referrals from other agencies because we really follow our cases through. Sometimes on our own time."[19] Some USA employees, such as Veronica Johnson, demonstrated their commitment even after they lost their jobs. "Even though I'm not working now I do some volunteer work to help some of my residents who are elderly or unable to get around well," she explained. "The residents still need help whether people are laid off or not."[20] Ultimately, funding cuts all but decimated USA. In addition to layoffs, the agency consolidated several day-care centers and closed some food distribution sites. By August 1986, Clarence Blount, an African American state legislator who had begun serving as the commissioner of the Community Action Agency in 1968 and who had continued his service as the director of the USA board into the 1980s, described with sadness and frustration the antipoverty agency's utility in Baltimore following years of budget cuts. "Of course [USA] doesn't do enough. It isn't supposed to do a lot. It can't do a lot. Urban Services is nothing more than a toothpick for a problem which requires a shovel. But what are you supposed to do? Throw out the toothpick?"[21]

While antipoverty and human-services providers took some of the hardest hits during the 1980s, few departments were spared the pain of staff reductions. Layoffs, however, were not the primary way that the city reduced its workforce. More often, city administrators simply abolished rather than filled vacant positions. Baltimore's 1984 budget estimate included 125 layoffs but eliminated more than four times as many positions through attrition. Downsizing via attrition rarely made headlines and mercifully spared current employees the pain of a pink slip. It also, however, increased the workloads of those who remained and took a toll on service delivery.[22] In 1984, when the city failed to fill positions previously held by workers who provided chore services for the elderly, for example, older residents simply lost the needed help. Downsizing through attrition was also alarming for the city's large pool of job seekers. And although benevolent because it spared current employees their jobs, it was a very unsystematic method of achieving governmental efficiency—a supposed goal of the Reagan administration.

Baltimore's elected officials also responded to fiscal pressures by privatizing city services. In 1982, for example, the city handed over the management of its public hospital to the Johns Hopkins Hospital, an arrangement made permanent in 1984. The move may have boded well for the quality of health care available to city residents; the hospital was internationally renowned. In the local Black community, however, it was known by many as "the Plantation." Located in the midst of neighborhoods with predominantly African American and in many cases also low-income residents, the hospital had hardly been a model neighbor. Rumors that they might be abducted by hospital officials for experimental purposes had led some who grew up in the city to fear the institution.[23] Meanwhile, its growth over the years had displaced many locals, who complained of unkept promises of relocation assistance. The hospital's record for minority hiring and promotion was also far from stellar. Four years after it acquired the public hospital, although about 40 percent of its workforce was African American, only about 15 percent of its managerial and professional staff was Black, according to the *Baltimore Sun*.[24] Raymond V. Haysbert, the African American chief executive of the Black-owned Parks Sausages Company, a local firm with $28 million in annual sales, believed the institution failed to do all it could to promote Black economic advancement. "As the largest private employer, Johns Hopkins could turn the whole damn city around," he declared.[25] At the very least, he argued, the institution could hire more African Americans for influential positions and create some role models for the city's youth.[26]

From the perspective of hospital workers, the ramifications of the privatization deal were unclear. The city brokered an agreement with the hospital that guaranteed its employees their jobs—for six months. The workers were also to remain represented by their union, although some hospital employees were themselves unionized. Yet all of the employees of the city facility, including the 40 percent who were African American women, lost their status as municipal employees. The change was significant. As the demographics of the municipal government and hospital workforces demonstrate, Black political power was not as effective at combating discrimination in the private sector as it was in the public sector. As *Afro-American* reporter Gerald C. Horne cautioned, "Those who appoint or help set the standards for hiring public sector employees can be voted in and out of office. Those who appoint and set standards for private sector employees are voted in and out by shareholders and boards of directors—where Black representation is near nil."[27]

The contraction of the city government's workforce by more than a third eliminated jobs that had been an important source of income for thousands of families in Baltimore. The job losses were particularly significant for African Americans. Certainly discrimination and inequities persisted in the municipal workforce. Female city employees earned considerably less than their male counterparts, and Black women held a disproportionate share of the city's lowest-paid jobs. To protest ongoing discrimination, in 1983, the NAACP filed a complaint against the city with the U.S. Justice Department's Civil Rights Division.[28] Yet despite persistent problems, African American women and men had made important strides in the public sector. And Hilda Ford, the city's African American personnel director, defended the progress her department had made against critiques launched by political opponents of the mayor. During the 1970s, she had made significant changes among those responsible for doing the hiring for Baltimore, and African American and female representation had increased. Between 1976 and 1983, the percentage of the city's workforce from historically underrepresented groups had increased from 45 percent to 56 percent. The change had come, Ford noted pointedly, despite an overall decline in the number of city employees. In addition, she observed, African Americans managed almost 50 percent of the city's operating budget, and Black and white women as a group controlled a third of the budget. About 22 percent of the city's female workforce earned $25,000 or more per year, which Ford compared favorably to the national figure of 8 percent. In addition, the gap between male and female earnings was lower in the municipal system than it was nationally. Municipal jobs offered other advantages as well. Unionized city employees earned health insurance, pensions, and additional fringe benefits that many private-sector employers in Baltimore did not provide. What is more, Ford, AFSCME, and the city's other public-sector unions had improved the working conditions and promotional opportunities of city workers, including women.[29] The municipal civil service certainly had its problems, but there were real advantages to be had by working for the city as well. Reaganomics meant that city jobs were available to thousands fewer than had only recently been the case. Reagan's budget cuts sliced deeply into Baltimore's Black working- and middle-class communities.

Fear of Being "Reaganized": State and Federal Employees Take a Hit

Municipal workers were not the only government employees in Baltimore affected by government downsizing. Employees of the state of Maryland, including many who lived in the city, also worried about being "Reaganized," as the *Afro-American* dubbed the public-sector downsizing phenomenon.[30] Theoretically, the president's New Federalism boded well for state-level public employees because administration officials shifted to them some government functions formerly performed elsewhere. State officials, however, had immediately recognized that they would nevertheless take a hit because of Reagan's dramatic reductions in overall spending. "We've told [Governor Harry Hughes] the block grants mean that he gets more and more flexibility to do less and less," Maryland official Bill Benton explained.[31] After the president proposed his first budget, Maryland officials projected a $215 million reduction in federal funds for the state. In response, in June 1981, Maryland's personnel secretary, Theodore Thornton Jr., announced the state was reducing its workforce by 1,800.[32] As on the municipal level, some cuts to the public workforce may have been warranted. Funding reductions by the Reagan administration, however, were the consequence of the ideological conviction that all levels of government were bloated and thus did not reflect careful and measured consideration of the actual needs of Maryland residents and taxpayers.

The prospect of layoffs created anxiety among all state workers, but fear ran especially high in human-services agencies, where Reagan's cuts were likely to strike the deepest. Welfare workers anticipated that they would be targets. Schaefer's desire to eliminate rebels from the municipal civil service is one reason he had agreed to transfer the workers from the city's to the state's employ. In June 1981, more than 2,000 employees of the Department of Social Services met in Baltimore to discuss their prospects and plan their response. Defiantly, many refused to be divided. They took a tally, and a majority of the staff agreed that if proposed cuts came to pass, they would pursue a "shared lay-off" plan proposed by their director, George Musgrove. They decided to adopt a four-day work week and accept 20 percent reductions in pay, benefits, and leave time in order to prevent an estimated 255 of their fellow workers from being terminated.[33]

Black state employees felt particularly vulnerable to job losses. Overall, African Americans were not as well represented in the state workforce as they were in the Baltimore city government. Nevertheless, a study by the Maryland Commission for Women, which did not include men, found that by the end of the 1970s, minority women, most of whom were African American, made up 20 percent of Maryland's employees. They had offices not only in Annapolis but throughout the state, and many lived and worked in Baltimore. Black women were concentrated in the lowest job grades in the state civil service, and race- and gender-based discrimination help to explain why. By the late 1970s, African Americans as a group held 57 percent of the state's service and maintenance jobs and 46 percent of paraprofessional positions but only 8 percent of administrative posts. Remarkably, however, given the state's long record of discriminatory hiring, Black women were approaching income parity with white women. The earnings of both Black and white women, however, fell well below those of white men. Black women earned on average $600 less per year than white women, close to $1,700 less than Black men, and a staggering $5,000 less per year than white men. In 1983, at the same time that they took the city to task, frustration with salary discrepancies and the difficulties African Americans experienced when seeking promotions in the state system led the Baltimore NAACP to file a complaint with the U.S. Justice Department.[34] Despite ongoing concerns about inequities, however, Black leaders knew state jobs were critical to the economic health of many families and communities, and they were determined to prevent African American workers from suffering disproportionately from layoffs.

Pete Rawlings and John Douglass, African American state legislators from Baltimore, were among those who took the lead in a campaign to press Governor Hughes to consider equity issues when making decisions about job cuts. Shortly after Thornton announced the state's decision to cut its workforce, a group of more than twenty African American legislators and community leaders met with the governor to offer proposals intended to save Black jobs. The leaders explained that many Black workers lacked seniority in the state system because of the legacy of employment discrimination. Rawlings and Douglass also explained that African American job losses would have tragic ripple effects in the state's Black communities. As *Afro-American* reporter Sue Williams recounted, they "estimated that as much as $20 million could be lost, not only in terms of actual workdays missed, but in terms of the reduction of goods and services purchased by Blacks from Blacks."[35] To prevent proposed employment reductions from reversing recent gains by African Americans and women, the leaders urged the governor to be proactive. Some proposed awarding African American employees credit for four extra years of service so that Black workers would not be penalized for past discriminatory hiring practices by layoff calculations that considered seniority. The governor pledged to establish guidelines concerning terminations and to send progress reports to the state's Congressional Black Caucus. "We shall make every reasonable effort to protect the gains of our affirmative action programs against the threat posed by the Reagan cutbacks," he promised.[36]

Nevertheless, while the Maryland state workforce did not suffer the high staffing reductions experienced by the city, changes that did occur had worrisome implications for African Americans and women. In 1984, state officials announced that Maryland had lost a total of $825 million in federal support. Maryland ranked among the top ten states in the country that experienced the most severe cuts in funding for general education, special education, health resources, health services, urban mass transit, and several other programs. Job cuts were unavoidable. During the early 1980s, the state reduced its workforce by about 6 percent. Ultimately, the reductions did not prove permanent but did lead to worrisome employment trends. By 1987, however, the overall number of state workers had rebounded and was about 4,300 higher than it had been in 1982. The growth resulted, however, largely from the use of part-time workers, those who typically do not enjoy the security and fringe benefits associated with full-time employment. In 1987, the state employed 3,000 fewer full-time workers than it had five years earlier. Meanwhile, state workers employed in hospitals saw their numbers decline by more than 4,400, probably largely as the result of the Reagan administration's effort to deinstitutionalize people with disabilities. One division of the state government did experience growth, however. Reflecting the law-and-order priorities of the Reagan administration, the number of corrections officers grew by more than 1,800. While education and health care suffered cuts, the jails and prisons were still hiring.[37]

Job losses also impacted federal workers in Baltimore. The Social Security Administration's headquarters and its satellite offices supplied the majority of Baltimore's federal jobs. The agency long had been a source of coveted employment in the city's African American communities, and civil rights activists had been monitoring its civil services practices for decades. By the 1980s, the agency was one of the state's largest employers, and it remained a critical source of jobs for African Americans in Baltimore. Because the Reagan administration entered the White House pledging to shrink the federal workforce, employees of the agency had good cause to worry about the security of their jobs. Tensions mounted in late 1981, when the *Baltimore Sun* reported an alarming trend: "Minority group members and women who have attained high-paying administrative jobs in government are losing them at a high rate in President Reagan's drive to reduce the size of the federal work force."[38] And cuts did not affect only top-level employees. The *Sun* noted that across the board "minority group members are 50 percent more likely to lose their jobs than whites."[39] Maryland representative Michael D. Barnes explained what many in Baltimore had feared: members of minority groups were experiencing particularly high job losses because they were concentrated in health, education, and welfare agencies. Lonis Ballard, of the national organization Blacks in Government, argued, "The Administration has shown, in its Economic Recovery Plan, little concern for the severe impact of the personnel reductions on the lives of Federal Employees."[40] And Lynn Revo-Cohen, a representative from the organization Federally Employed Women, worried that the job losses would "decimate the gains by women and minorities."[41]

Although early cuts in the federal workforce evoked sympathy from Baltimore residents, few felt the full reverberations of downsizing until 1985. It was then that the Reagan administration announced its determination to cut SSA's national workforce of close to eighty thousand by about nineteen thousand jobs. Administration officials had concluded on the basis of a commissioned study that SSA had grown bloated. Moreover, they argued that agency staff made insufficient use of computer technology, the use of which could make redundant large numbers of employees. Others familiar with the internal organization of SSA adamantly disagreed that its staff was too large. It "sounds pretty ridiculous to me," commented Robert Ball, who had been the commissioner of SSA from 1962 to 1973. He explained that the operating expenses for SSA came out of the payroll deduction tax and that only one-and-a-half cents of each dollar went for administrative costs. In fact, given how effectively SSA officials used limited resources, Ball argued, the government should actually increase the agency's staff and make them more accessible to the public.[42]

The American Federation of Government Employees, which represented many Social Security employees, also fiercely protested the proposed cuts. The largest local of the union in the country was in Baltimore, and its leadership played a leading role in fighting job losses.[43] They faced a formidable opponent in Reagan, who was hardly a fan of public-sector unions or organized labor more broadly. During his first year in office, he fired eleven thousand striking members of the Professional Air Traffic Controllers Organization and refused to allow any to be reemployed by the Federal Aviation Administration. The union members had been engaged in an illegal work stoppage and had also rebuffed earlier efforts by the administration to reach an agreement. Nevertheless, Reagan's move was out of step with those of his predecessors in the White House, who also had been confronted by illegal strikes by federal workers and who had chosen to negotiate. Reagan's forceful and unequivocal response to the strikers set the tone for his presidency. After his confrontation with the air traffic controllers union, he worked steadily to undermine the influence and past gains of federal unions.[44] In such a context, AFGE had limited success fighting the downsizing at SSA. The federation was able to save two thousand jobs, however, and they won an extension of the timeline during which the staffing reductions would occur.[45]

As the negotiations between AFGE and the federal government played out, the SSA staff braced for painful changes. Prior to downsizing, about 70 percent of SSA's national workforce was female, and minority women made up almost a third of SSA's employees, the result of equal-opportunity battles that had increased their representation from 22 percent in 1970. In the Baltimore region, SSA employed about 20,000 workers, an invaluable contribution to the depressed local economy. In the end, staffing reductions shrank the national workforce of the SSA by 18 percent between 1983 and 1989, at a cost of 13,500 jobs. Headquarters suffered a disproportionate share of the agency's national job losses. In the end, downsizing was achieved through attrition, which spared employees the pain of layoffs but further dimming the prospects of job seekers. Meanwhile, many remaining employees found their workloads increased as they compensated for short-staffing, which in turn doubtlessly frustrated those seeking the agency's services. As in other agencies, downsizing eroded capacity, which the advocates of small government could use to further deride the public sector. Simultaneously, downsizing also imperiled the ability of the SSA to achieve its equal opportunity goals. As Barbara Sledge, the director of SSA's equal opportunity office, explained in 1984, "The problems facing the EO [equal opportunity] program at SSA today are difficult ones. This agency is getting smaller, and we won't have the opportunity to make the same rate of progress we made in the past, when the agency was growing."[46]

Job losses at Social Security in combination with those that occurred on the state and municipal levels jeopardized important economic gains African Americans, and particularly Black women, had secured over the previous two decades. Since the 1960s, public-sector jobs at all levels of government had helped many middle- and working-class African American families become homeowners and send children to college. Even as popular rhetoric suggested that most urban African Americans were unemployed and on welfare, unionized government jobs had provided for many Black workers some of the security that unionized industrial jobs had earlier extended to whites. The public-sector gains were especially important given the limited access many African Americans in Baltimore had to alternative opportunities for upward mobility. In other cities with large Black populations, particularly those with African American mayors, the sources of the Black middle class tended to be more diverse than was the case in Baltimore. Elected officials elsewhere were more intentional about opening opportunities for Black wealth creation than Schaefer had been.[47] In Baltimore, not only had the city not practiced affirmative action as early and as aggressively as it could have, but African Americans were also largely kept on the sidelines of the city's commercial revitalization efforts. As the U.S. Commission on Civil Rights concluded after conducting an investigation on the matter, "Minority economic development has not been a priority in Baltimore City."[48] The neglect accounted for the "comparatively minimal level of minority participation in the city's redevelopment."[49] Stymied in significant ways from pursuing alternative paths to economic security, African Americans at least had created a refuge in government workforces. Then came Reaganomics, which contracted the very sector of the economy that had become critical to Black upward mobility and economic security.

The contraction of government workforces had additional implications. The public sector had also been important to city residents who did not pursue long-term careers in the government but instead used public-sector employment as a launching pad into the private sector. As a witness explained to the U.S. Commission on Civil Rights during a hearing in Baltimore in 1981, the government workforce had become "very critical for minorities at the entry level."[50] It enabled workers to establish an employment history and thus served as a stepping-stone to future jobs. Fewer government posts meant fewer stepping-stones into the mainstream economy.

The dramatic contraction of the public sector during the Reagan years worsened conditions that had already produced heart-wrenching scenes in Baltimore. In 1980, the SSA had listed openings for seventy-five entry-level positions. Twenty-six thousand people applied for the coveted spots. A year later, officials with the U.S. Post Office sparked a second avalanche of applications when they announced they would be offering an exam for mail handlers. Word spread like wildfire, and fifteen thousand people applied for a shot at the jobs. Journalists from the *Afro-American* described with clear sadness both demonstrations of the dim odds faced by the city's job seekers. The paper also made a gloomy prediction. Thousands would likely again participate in yet another futile exercise in job-hunting; the Post Office was preparing to open several labor-custodial positions.[51]

The contraction of the public sector, and particularly of municipal human-services agencies, had another important ramification. From their posts in government offices, many African American women and men had played important roles in shaping public policy and improving the delivery of human services. By the mid-1970s, the influence of human-services workers over policy had begun to wane in response to shifts in federal urban policy. Nevertheless, through the decade, and especially as Schaefer attempted to mobilize city and federal resources behind Baltimore's downtown commercial renaissance, many city and state human-services workers served as advocates of residents with low incomes within the government bureaucracy. They became the conscience of the city and limited the extent to which the champions of commercial redevelopment could neglect the concerns of the poor. Reaganomics contracted the size of agencies from which African Americans and others had historically attempted to call attention to pressing urban problems and serve as a counterweight to the advocates of trickle-down urban revitalization.

"If We Could Get These People Help": The War on Drugs in Baltimore

In the wake of downsizing in municipal human-services departments and considerable investment in the War on Drugs, law enforcement officials increasingly became first responders to urban poverty. It was a job for which they were not trained nor, given their line of work, particularly well suited; despite past efforts at community policing, their relationship with many in Baltimore's Black neighborhoods remained antagonistic. In 1982, following Reagan's declaration of the war, the enforcement of drug laws became a local policing priority. During the mid-1980s, local officials estimated that there were about thirty thousand users of opiates in the city.[52] And although crack cocaine use became a problem in a few large cities at that time, it was not yet particularly prevalent in Baltimore. Opiate abuse caused many of the city's drug-related problems. Few users could afford their habits independently, so many turned to crime. Others, including children, who dealers began to recruit during the era because of the lighter sentencing they received in the criminal justice system, took up hustling in the drug trade in pursuit of cash. By 1988, about 55 percent of crime in the city was linked to drugs.[53]

Given the clear relationship between drug use and crime, many in Baltimore, including some in law enforcement, identified addiction treatment as the most commonsensical response. "If we could get these people help, we'd be ahead of the game," commented Captain Joseph Newman, the chief of the Baltimore Police Department's Narcotics Task Force.[54] But help was frustratingly hard to find. A year after the president launched the War on Drugs, budget cuts had cost spots in local treatment centers, and stints on waiting lists could last from weeks to months. There were sixteen state-funded programs for drug addiction, and all were full beyond capacity.[55] Due to increasing demand over the years that followed, by the late 1980s, drug treatment had become "big business," according to one official in Maryland—but only for those with means or who had good health insurance.[56] A two-tiered system had emerged. "There's one tier for those with money, and a second tier for those without," the official explained.[57] And those on the second tier had a hard time getting help; funding for treatment had not kept up with increases in enforcement.

The city did engage in drug-use prevention and education. In 1983, the Narcotics Task Force had a staff of three dedicated to the task, and they averaged about forty presentations a month. One officer minced no words, especially when talking to youth, who were vulnerable to recruitment efforts by drug dealers. "A lot of you are going to end up in jail. Some of you are going to wind up dead," Detective Charlie Smith stated bluntly to a group of junior high school students.[58] For years, the Baltimore Police Department had been dispatching "Officer Friendly" to elementary school classrooms to improve community–police relations, and the practice continued during the 1980s. But following two decades of law-and-order criminal justice policies and in the wake of the increasing scourge of addiction and its attendant problem of crime, some determined that by middle school, children needed tough love. Meanwhile, community groups also engaged in drug-use prevention and education. "People are tired of having their neighborhoods taken over," explained social worker Addie Key, who was a cofounder of Neighborhood Action Coalition.[59] The group encouraged parent groups and community organizations to sponsor recreational activities for young people. The city's provision of such services had declined precipitously over the past decade, so residents had to fill in.[60]

Ultimately, waiting lists for treatment and community education proved an inadequate defense against the city's burgeoning drug market, which in some instances was becoming a source of needed employment for those left out of or unwanted in the mainstream economy. And treatment and prevention were local rather than federal priorities. Two decades of wars on crime and drugs had already provided considerable infrastructure and some of the manpower that were preconditions for the crisis of mass incarceration. Reagan increased federal resources for policing and also imposed mandatory sentencing requirements that were marred by racial bias. In 1983, police were responding to drug use in the city with three times the number of resources they had had two years earlier, and the city's arrest rates quickly rose. Between 1984 and 1988, arrests involving heroin or cocaine more than doubled.[61] And although Black and white drug-use rates were reportedly similar in Maryland, African American men were arrested at a much higher rate than white men. The police targeted open-air drug markets rather than fraternity parties or other private venues where white drug use was more prevalent. Ultimately, between 1979 and 2003, the Black male prison population in the state increased by more than 370 percent.[62] And though it was too soon to see that long-term trend in the late 1980s, it was not too hard to predict it. Since the civil rights era, conservatives had been drumming up fears of Black criminality to roll back civil rights gains and later also to discredit the welfare state. The crisis of mass incarceration was the culmination of those efforts.

"Watching Their Children's Every Move": Reaganomics and Gendered Caretaking

The crisis of mass incarceration unfolded in Baltimore at the same time that the Reagan administration was tightening eligibility requirements for entitlement benefits and reducing spending on social welfare. The ramifications for Black women, particularly those with low incomes and among the working poor, were perilous. By the early 1980s, Baltimore had one of the highest percentages of residents living in poverty in the nation, and the numbers were growing.[63] Because women often served as the caretakers of their families, it typically fell to them to manage and attempt to compensate for economic insecurity. In the wake of Reaganomics, many intensified their own caretaking work to stretch family budgets and meet pressing needs. During the War on Poverty, the federal government had funded a range of programs—in nutrition, health care, recreation, and sanitation, for example—that eased the responsibilities women bore for caring for their families. During the 1970s and 1980s, federal funding for the programs diminished, leaving women with the option of stepping up to fill the void or watching their families do without.

Cuts to entitlement benefits and public housing had devastating implications for many in Baltimore. In November 1981, about 18,000 city residents were eliminated from the AFDC rolls, and almost 16,500 had their monthly benefits reduced. In addition, 10,000 were dropped from the Food Stamp Program, and 69,500 learned they would be receiving smaller allotments. Meanwhile, although Baltimore had 45,000 residents on waiting lists for public housing and the projected wait time was five years, the city's funding from the Department of Housing and Urban Development was also cut. As a consequence, the city's 58,000 recipients of subsidized housing were required to pay 30 percent rather than 25 percent of their incomes for housing. John A. McCauley, the city's deputy commissioner for public housing, expressed alarm at the change. "People will simply use the income that used to go to buy food, clothing or medicine and pay the extra rent. While 5 percent doesn't sound like much, to a family on welfare, an extra $10 to $15 makes all the difference," he worried.[64] Simultaneously, Maryland's funding for unemployment insurance dropped by $10 million even as the Volcker recession increased the numbers of the jobless.[65] Although Congress later restored some of the lost benefits, the cuts intensified economic insecurity and hardship.

The Reagan administration also reduced federal funding for social service programs provided by states and localities. Title XX of the Social Security Act, from which Maryland received 70 percent of its funds for social services, was cut by 20 percent. The reduction affected both income maintenance programs and other vital services. Although reverberations would be felt throughout the state, "Baltimore's poor will bear the brunt of the cutbacks," a newspaper reporter predicted.[66] Allotments for fuel assistance plummeted by $7.5 million. In December 1981, as city residents braced for winter, Richard Aull, the head of Baltimore's weatherization program, reported that his agency would be serving only half the number of residents it normally helped. What is more, he would no longer be offering furnace-cleaning and related services. Simultaneously, funds to support the community-services activities sponsored by antipoverty agencies dropped by $200,000. Among the consequences providers anticipated was longer waits for day-care service. The reductions in welfare and social services spending compounded problems caused by cuts in federal funding for education, health, urban mass transit, legal aid, jobs and training, and other vital programs. At the start of the 1980s, Baltimore depended for more than half of its budget on intergovernmental sources of revenue. By November 1981, Reagan's budget cuts had already cost the city $70 million. By 1983, the city had not only eliminated jobs but had also cut municipal services by 25 percent, and by 1989, Baltimore's expenditures per year were 36 percent lower than they had been in 1975.[67] To be sure, the population of the city had continued to decline, which reduced some need for services. Yet the persistence and worsening of some urban problems—and the expensive infrastructure obligations in commercially revitalized portions of the city—carried big price tags.

Women paid a particularly high cost for budget cuts because of the effort it took to compensate for the lost services. Reduced spending on weatherization and nutrition programs, for example, exacerbated hardship that had already worsened for many during the Carter years, when mothers such as Elrae Singletary and Mary Turner had taken to feeding their families a handful of inexpensive staples. Cuts in the Food Stamp Program, on which one in four Baltimore residents depended in 1981, and nutrition programs, which provided ninety thousand students with lunch every school day, intensified women's struggles to feed their families. When the school year started in September, increases in the cost of subsidized lunches had pushed six thousand children out of the program.[68] The funding cuts sent increasing numbers of women to food pantries and soup kitchens, increasing the time, effort, and stress associated with food preparation. The cuts were particularly devastating for those who had jobs that paid wages that did not lift them out of poverty. Food charities staggered under the weight of increased need. "Soup kitchens are overcrowded. And those who administer the programs are having trouble doing their jobs because of layoffs, low morale and high turnover," the *Baltimore Sun* reported in December.[69] The end of the recession eased hardship for some but did not restore benefits and services.

Cuts to other service programs also increased women's gendered caretaking responsibilities. Poverty continued to limit many to the city's most dilapidated housing. Reductions in funding for public housing and housing-related programs, fuel assistance, sanitation services, and municipal rat and other pest-eradication efforts intensified the challenges women faced as they tried to keep their families healthy and safe. Many found that even the most diligent housekeeping could not prevent windows from leaking, lead paint from peeling, and germs and illness from spreading. Decreased spending on housing sometimes led to tragedy. In 1983, Bob Cheeks, the executive director of the Welfare Rights Organization, told Mayor Schaefer that a broken elevator in a public housing high-rise had delayed a mother who was rushing to seek medical attention for her sick infant. The delay, Cheeks charged, cost the child his life. He blamed Schaefer for the death because the mayor's "single-minded focus to build hotels, restaurant, shops, and housing for the rich" had come at the expense of "the concerns of the poor."[70] Schaefer had certainly prioritized downtown development. But two years earlier, Reagan had halved federal spending on public housing, which may also have accounted for the broken elevator.[71]

While most mothers who faced health care emergencies did not suffer the tremendous loss experienced by the high-rise resident, federal cuts in spending on health compelled women to attempt to compensate at home. The Reagan administration's decision to tighten eligibility requirements for Medicaid only worsened the problem. Meanwhile, CETA layoffs cost many health providers their jobs and service recipients needed help. The cuts imperiled the ongoing efforts of the city's public health nurses and aides in the Department of Health to battle not only lead-paint poisoning but other serious health problems. With fewer public health programs available, women with limited means often had no choice but to assume responsibilities for caring for ill family members who would have been better served by professional health care providers. The task of tending to the sick could prove particularly challenging when women provided care for elderly relatives. During the early 1980s, the poverty rate in the United States among African American elderly was triple that for whites in the same age group. Conditions for the elderly had actually improved in Baltimore during the 1960s and 1970s, due in large part to the efforts of activists and social service providers. Reaganomics jeopardized the gains. In 1981, an elderly African American man attending a small rally in Annapolis to protest budget cuts, whispered his concern to a reporter. "Things had been getting better for old folks for a while. Now I'm afraid that everything will go back to the way it was," he said.[72]

Meanwhile, locally provided subsidized day-care services, which had never been adequate, became more expensive and harder to access. One day-care center in northwestern Baltimore saw its fees more than triple. Staff and family members responded to the cuts by helping children served by the agency write protest letters to both Reagan and Maryland's governor.[73] Reagan's policies also reduced funding available for municipal parks, recreation programs, libraries, and museums, making child care all the more difficult.[74] By January 1984, the Department of Parks and Recreation was laying off employees for the fourth time in two years and seeking volunteers to mow grass and trim bushes. Funds for special services for teenagers and money for summer camps were also cut.[75] Fewer public spaces and programs were available to young people just as conditions in many neighborhoods deteriorated due to lost services and the burgeoning drug trade, rendering them increasingly unfit for play and increasing the need for adult supervision. The city's inadequate provision of recreational spaces was a grave concern for Shelia Rhyne. In a letter to the *Baltimore Afro-American* she explained, "My youngest son has been hospitalized with a torn tendon in his hand from glass in the yard surrounding the building. Why do the low to middle class people have to live in projects where they must watch their children's every move because they don't know whether their children will be killed, raped or God knows what else?"[76]

Women protested the cuts in ways other than letter-writing but encountered significant obstacles. One woman who sought a legal remedy to her concerns turned to Legal Aid—but then learned that the agency's staff had been shrunk from 125 to 107 lawyers. As a result, she received nothing more than sympathetic advice, which included the suggestion that she take a course to learn her rights. Women also worked collectively to protest the economic changes under way. In 1981, the Baltimore Welfare Rights Organization filed a successful class-action suit against the state for terminating AFDC benefits without providing recipients sufficient warning. But the victory only restored benefits for a single month.[77] High-rise public-housing residents also worked together. Following the death of the infant whose mother had been stymied by the broken elevator on her way to the hospital, a group founded MOM, an organization of mothers united to "Save Our Children from High Rise Housing."[78] Even collectively, however, it was impossible for women with low incomes to repair the damage to the social safety net wrought by Reaganomics.

CONCLUSION

In 1988, Kurt Schmoke, Baltimore's first elected African American mayor, made a bold proposal to the U.S. Conference of Mayors and then to a House Committee of the U.S. Senate. The wars on crime and drugs were clearly not working, he noted. As a result, he urged that the nation face up to the failure of drug prohibition policies and decriminalize the possession of narcotics. "We have spent nearly 75 years and untold billions of dollars trying to square the circle, and inevitably we have failed," he observed, referring to the period since the nation first passed federal antinarcotic legislation. But prohibition had reduced neither crime nor addiction. To shift gears, drug addiction should be treated as a medical rather than a law-enforcement problem, Schmoke reasoned, and he advocated for "a measured and carefully implemented program of drug decriminalization." The response to his proposal was not the rigorous debate he had hoped for. In a context in which Republicans had wielded dog-whistle claims about urban crime for decades to win political power and in which their "soft-on-crime" taunts kept many Democrats on the defensive, meaningful consideration of alternative approaches to dealing with crime and addiction was not an option. As the *New York Times* reported at the time, the likelihood of his proposal meeting with success was "nil."[1] So Schmoke took the "small steps" he could in Baltimore to implement "drug medicalization."[2]

Schmoke was not the only person in Baltimore with innovative ideas about how to try and solve some of the city's most pressing problems. During the 1990s, in response to concerns raised by economically strapped, though employed, city residents, members of the community- and faith-based organization Baltimoreans United in Leadership Development (BUILD) launched a campaign to compel the major players in the city's downtown tourism industry to pay their workers a living wage. Many of the employers were the recipients of considerable subsidies from the federal, state, and local governments, and BUILD members believed such largesse should at least be met with jobs that elevated workers out of poverty.[3] AFSCME joined and strongly supported the campaign. The effort pitted predominantly African American activists, such as Blacka Wright, a hotel housekeeper, against Schmoke, who, despite his bold stance against the War on Drugs, was continuing former mayor William Donald Schaefer's efforts to revitalize the city's troubled economy with tourism.[4]

Meanwhile, AFSCME officials and the other city activists were also alarmed by the ongoing privatization of municipal services. Unionized public-sector jobs were disappearing, but the new private-sector positions that sometimes replaced them often paid less than and lacked the security and benefits of government posts. Valerie Bell, who worked as a cleaner in a Baltimore public school—but who received her paycheck from a private company that contracted with the city—called the situation "plain old city-sponsored poverty."[5] Bell was involved in the newly formed Solidarity Sponsoring Committee, which was attempting to bring the concerns of low-wage service workers to the city's attention. Ultimately, the activists, while maintaining pressure on the city on multiple fronts, targeted their living-wage efforts at securing an ordinance that would apply specifically to companies with municipal contracts. As AFSCME area director Kimberlee Keller argued, "This is the new American workforce—contingent, temporary, part-time, low-wage workers doing what in many cases used to be decent jobs. This is the most direct possible way to address the problem of poverty in the city."[6]

The nascent efforts in Baltimore anticipated the increasingly important role public-sector unions, often working in partnership with faith-based and other community organizations, came to play in battles over economic justice in the twenty-first century. And successes in some of those battles help to explain why government unions nationwide became the target of intensifying conservative animosity. Baltimore's workers played an important role. In 1994, their campaign for an ordinance met with success, and Baltimore became the first city in the nation with a living-wage law. The city's low-wage workers had struck a blow against privatization. Like Schmoke's efforts to treat drug addiction as a medical issue, the living-wage law was a small step; it applied only to a subset of the city's workers. But its supporters considered it a step in the right direction.[7] What is more, the Baltimore activists' success sparked living-wage movements in other cities—and eventually also on the state level. Such was the case in Maryland, which in 2007 became the first state in the nation to require a living wage for those employed under state contracts.[8]

Efforts in Baltimore to interrupt the crisis of mass incarceration, compassionately respond to addiction, meaningfully raise the wages of those in the working poor, and resist the contracting out of public-service provisions cut against the grain of much national policy-making during the late twentieth and early twenty-first centuries. During the 1970s and 1980s, elected officials on the federal level had introduced a range of macroeconomic and domestic policies that produced a momentum that proved hard to stop. And in the wake of the Reagan revolution, not only did most Republicans remain staunchly tough on crime and firmly hostile to redistributive antipoverty efforts, the supposedly bloated public sector, and government unions, Democrats increasingly took similar stances as well. To be sure, concern with crime, welfare, the size of the government, and collective bargaining in the public sector had multiple sources. Nevertheless, they were all inextricably connected to discourses that emerged or gained prominence during the late 1960s and 1970s, linked Blackness with criminality, and rendered African American working people invisible or suspect. In an effort to win political power after decades of Democratic dominance—and also to roll back civil rights legislation—Republican politicians and strategists had fomented and courted racism. The rhetoric they used to discredit liberalism described struggling cities like Baltimore as overpopulated with African American "thugs," "welfare queens," and incompetent civil servants who were represented by greedy union officials. Conservative discourse identified those groups as culpable in the nation's economic woes and charged them with driving up the tax burdens of an entirely separate group: the "hardworking" Americans, who were presumed to be white. The message proved persuasive to many voters and helped to turn the tide in American politics away from Democrats, who in turn grew more conservative, and toward Republicans, who also grew more conservative.

Democrats had hardly been mere bystanders as struggling cities and their populations were denigrated. Even in Democratic strongholds, showdowns with public-sector unions and calls for smaller government often had proven politically popular—but pitted Democratic voters against those most in need of public services and also against government employees. Meanwhile, on the federal level, the party certainly had played a role in the construction of the carceral state. And Democrats and Republicans alike had acceded to conservative and elite pressure and pursued policies that largely institutionalized the logic of neoliberalism within the governing structures of the national and global economies. Members of both parties had also presided over the financialization of the American economy. Policy-making during the 1970s and 1980s that favored Wall Street over Main Street, and even more so over Martin Luther King Boulevard, dealt a grave blow to American manufacturers at the cost of jobs and also tax revenue that could have alleviated fiscal crises. In addition, trickle-down economics, achieved in part through generous tax cuts for the wealthiest, starved governments of the revenue they needed to pay for public services and the workers who provided them. The age of austerity ensued and was felt particularly urgently in struggling cities with large populations of low-income residents that depended not only on locally generated tax revenue but also on aid from the state and the federal governments. But calls by urban residents for federal relief were rebuffed with logic crafted in the 1960s and 1970s—that poverty in cities was self-inflicted and often the consequence of supposed Black criminality. The dynamic continued into the twenty-first century with devastating implications for Baltimore.

Despite the changes, during the decades following the Reagan years, the public sector remained a critical, if vulnerable, job niche for African Americans and Black women in particular, in both Baltimore and the nation more generally.[9] In the city in 2000, African American women made up 45 percent of residents who worked for the federal, state, or local government, a figure that had risen from 42 percent in 1980 and from 12 percent in 1950. Meanwhile, Black men composed 25 percent of government workers, a proportion that had hovered around that number since 1970 but that had been only 10 percent in 1950. At the new century's dawn, African Americans made up about 65 percent of Baltimore's population but 70 percent of its government workers. Even so, the persistence of Black workers' public-sector job niche masked persistent problems. In 2000, almost eighteen thousand fewer Black women and nearly thirteen thousand fewer Black men who lived in Baltimore had government jobs than had been the case two decades earlier.[10] In addition to government downsizing, some of which may have been justified by the shrinking size of the city's population, the decline likely reflected Black flight from the city. During the 1990s, the number of Black Baltimore residents declined for the first time.[11] Despite the demographic changes, however, there was no disguising the steep price public-sector workers were paying for neoliberal forms of governance. But though downsizing cut deeply and discrimination persisted, Black workers' ongoing overrepresentation in unionized government employment remained critical to the economic health of the city's African American communities—a reason why AFSMCE and other local activists defended it so fiercely.

African Americans' public-sector job niche and Black individuals' rise within government workforces had not come easily, and the job gains had required vigilant monitoring. Civil rights advocates of the 1950s and 1960s had fought hard in Washington, D.C., and on the state and local levels to open government jobs to Black workers. African Americans' public-sector job niche represents a critical, although largely unheralded, achievement of post–World War II civil rights activists as well as those who followed them and defended and built on their successes. In addition, Black women's ongoing overrepresentation within the public sector—and prominence in human-services agencies—helps to explain the vital economic roles that they have played in their families and communities and reflects the tremendous level of public service they have contributed to the nation.

Baltimore's twenty-first-century public-sector unions also represent an enduring legacy of dedicated Black activists, who led and participated in both the Baltimore Teachers Union and AFSCME during the tumultuous 1960s, when the city granted the organizations recognition. And as indicated by AFSCME's involvement in the city's living-wage campaign, some public-sector unions rekindled their activist roots in the late twentieth century. In 1990, Glenard "Glen" S. Middleton Sr., the African American president of the largest AFSCME local in Baltimore, also became the executive director of the union in Maryland. Under his leadership, AFSCME expanded its focus well beyond its members' bread-and-butter issues. During the late twentieth and early twenty-first centuries, the union partnered with BUILD, the Interdenominational Ministerial Alliance, the Association of Community Organizations for Reform Now (ACORN), and other activist groups to press for a range of progressive changes in the city.[12] On Middleton's watch, in addition to defending its own member and their jobs, AFSCME has weighed in on national labor-law issues, attempted to organize part-time and low-wage private-sector workers, and endeavored to keep city residents' attention focused on the steep price they pay for costly tax abatements for corporate interests.[13] In a nation in which many continue to associate distressed cities such as Baltimore with crime, welfare, and dysfunction, Middleton paints a more accurate picture of much of Baltimore's population: "We are the working poor."[14] And the BTU and its parent association, the American Federation of Teachers, have also remained involved in local and state politics, where they are fierce defenders of quality public education.[15] The continuing vitality of the public-sector labor movement in Baltimore, even in the face of serious, ongoing attacks, reflects the energy and dedication of its leadership and largely female and predominantly African American rank and file. Moreover, the resilience of public-sector unions nationwide demonstrates the continuing faith many in the nation's new working class have in the power of collective bargaining and the utility of unions in the quest for economic and social justice.

But even as African Americans' public-sector jobs niche and public-sector unions symbolize simultaneously the achievements of past Black activism and the possibility of a brighter future, the challenges facing Baltimore remain both numerous and dire. Ironically, it has often fallen to Black elected officials to respond to the repercussions of decades of federal policies that have had devastating impacts on struggling cities. In Baltimore, by the late twentieth century, African Americans had significantly increased their political influence in municipal affairs. Since 1987, all but one of the city's mayors have been Black, and although Martin O'Malley, the lone white mayor, ultimately served two terms, his initial 1999 victory surprised many. African Americans also increased their representation on the city council and have held many of the top posts in the municipal government, including within and at the helm of the Baltimore Police Department.[16] Black leaders, in other words, took over the reins of local political, though not economic, power just in time to confront—and be blamed by conservatives for—serious urban problems that they may have contributed to perpetuating but certainly had not created. As a result, battle lines that had once pitted African American residents against white officials became more complicated, and class in addition to race increasingly divided city politics. Presiding over Baltimore during the late twentieth and early twenty-first centuries has hardly been easy. The shrinking tax base could not cover the cost of needed public services, even though municipal tax rates remained far higher than elsewhere in the state, and poverty has deepened in the city's poorest and highly segregated African American neighborhoods.[17] As Schmoke learned when he proposed drug decriminalization, the ability of locally elected officials to innovate was limited by nationally elected politicians, who have pursued policies that are informed by and continued to reinforce the notion that urban poverty is the product of Black dysfunction and that African American city residents must be disciplined by either the criminal justice system or the rigors of the free market.

As scholars such as Michelle Alexander have argued, in the realm of criminal justice, American presidents of the late twentieth and early twenty-first centuries contributed to escalating the crisis of mass incarceration and perpetuating the criminalization of Black people.[18] During the 1980s and 1990s, Republicans wielded "soft-on-crime" taunts like bludgeons to discredit their Democratic opponents.[19] And Democrat Bill Clinton, who won the presidency in 1992, attempted to rebut the critique with the Violent Crime Control and Law Enforcement Act of 1994, which exacerbated the mass incarceration crisis.[20] Even Barack Obama, the nation's first African American president, who expressed deep concern about the racially biased carceral state, found it difficult to interrupt the crisis and the ongoing criminalization of Black urban communities.[21]

While federal—and also state—policies were preconditions for the crisis of mass incarceration, local policing practices procured the bodies that filled the cells. During the late 1980s and 1990s, Schmoke, who served three terms as mayor, attempted to implement on a small scale his addiction medicalization plans. They proved no match, however, for the crack epidemic that exploded in the city and was concentrated in its poorest and most heavily policed neighborhoods. "It was like an entirely new economy had begun to replace the manufacturing one that was in tatters. This was the new economy," explains journalist Sabrina Tavernise.[22] The illicit drug trade became a source of needed employment for some and a source of escape for many others, and it remained so even after the crack epidemic eased. By the end of the twentieth century, residents' fear of crime and drugs helped O'Malley win the mayor's office. The candidate promised to bring New York City's zero-tolerance policing strategy to Baltimore. The result was not what many in Black Baltimore had had in mind. "Let me think when they started arresting everybody. Well, I'm gonna say—how about in the late '90s?" quipped city resident Davetta Parker, whose African American son was stopped by the police on multiple occasions.[23]

During the late twentieth and early twenty-first centuries, the Baltimore Police Department (BPD) shouldered incredibly difficult responsibilities. In a city with an inadequate array of social services and in which the proliferation of low-wage jobs and unemployment remained major problems, police officers were tasked with more than crime control. Nevertheless, zero tolerance proved catastrophic. Unconstitutional policing in low-income, African American neighborhoods was hardly new, but it became fairly standard following the adoption of zero tolerance. As the U.S. Department of Justice later determined, "As part of this strategy, BPD leadership pressured officers to increase the number of arrests and to 'clear corners,' whether or not the officers observed criminal activity. The result was a massive increase in the quantity of arrests—but a corresponding decline in quality."[24] The 2016 report confirmed what many Black city residents had long known—that they had been systematically detained, searched, and arrested—and in some cases brutalized or killed—by the police simply for being Black and in a particular neighborhood. Sheila Dixon, the first woman and second African American to be elected mayor of Baltimore, succeeded O'Malley and discontinued zero-tolerance policing.[25] Nevertheless, abusive policing practices persisted, and in 2006, the American Civil Liberties Union and the NAACP sued the BPD.[26] And according to many observers in Baltimore, the city's history of unconstitutional policing is probably what led Freddie Gray to run from the police in 2015 during an encounter that ultimately led to his death.[27]

Scholars and activists, including Alexander and those in Baltimore who protested the death of Freddie Gray, have met with success in drawing national attention to the crisis of mass incarceration and its implications for the voting rights, economic opportunities, and quality of life of the disproportionately African American men ensnared in the criminal justice system. In some states, including Maryland, the prison population is declining.[28] Nevertheless, the year Gray died, Baltimore had a larger percentage of its residents incarcerated than did such cities as New York and Philadelphia, and its inmate population was one of the largest in the nation.[29] Thirty years after Schmoke pointed out that the wars on drugs and crime had failed, the nation has yet to embrace an alternative response. The persistence of the destructive wars despite their devastating consequences reflects their continuing utility in justifying a broader racist, antiurban narrative that conservatives rely on to sustain the confidence of many white conservative voters in neoliberal economics and forms of governance.

Just as the wars on drugs and crime reinforced and perpetuated notions of Black criminality, federal welfare policies and the language elected officials used to discuss them did so as well. In 1996, Clinton ended welfare as Americans knew it when he signed the Personal Responsibility and Work Opportunity Act. Even the title of the legislation communicated the rebuke that mothers living in poverty lacked a work ethic. The law replaced Aid to Families with Dependent Children, an entitlement that guaranteed qualifying recipients a cash benefit, with Temporary Aid to Needy Families (TANF), a block grant that sent federal funds to officials on the state level to disburse. As during the Reagan years, the method of distributing intergovernmental revenue limited the ability of representatives of low-income Baltimoreans to influence how the funds were used. Moreover, the legislation and welfare-related measures that followed during the administration of George W. Bush promoted remedies to poverty, such as marriage incentives, that perpetuated the notion that economic insecurity was principally the result of poor decision-making by individuals. And as had been the case for decades, the justification for reducing wealth redistribution was a presumed criminality and dysfunction on the part of the poor.[30] By the Obama years, such logic had been so firmly ingrained that Republicans introduced a new dog whistle: "Food Stamp president." The descriptor was not a compliment intended to describe an elected official attempting to alleviate hunger and jump-start the economy during a severe economic downturn. Instead, it was an insult meant to communicate that the nation's first Black president was dispersing "handouts" to undeserving African Americans.[31]

Ultimately, TANF compelled or enabled some women to move permanently into the labor force. But despite some constraints, the legislation also gave elected officials the authority to divert TANF revenue to purposes tangential to poverty relief. Within less than two decades, the erosion of the social safety net contributed to plunging millions, including one in five single mothers nationally, into dire poverty: existence on $2.00 or less per day.[32] Meanwhile, "block granting" remained a strategy of choice among Republicans hoping to further shrink the welfare state. And though conservative efforts to turn programs such as Medicaid into block grants have not met with success, they have often kept Democrats on the defensive. In addition, block granting continues to pose a particularly pernicious threat to African Americans in Baltimore, whose electoral representation in the Maryland State House has continued to dwindle in accord with the city's shrinking population.

Black women in Baltimore were among those who paid a steep price for the elimination of welfare. In Maryland, the number of people receiving public assistance dropped sharply following the adoption of TANF, although the decline was slower in the city than elsewhere.[33] Some women expressed gratitude that the legislation helped prepare them for entry into the mainstream economy.[34] But even for enthusiasts, Baltimore's postindustrial job market hardly provided many with pathways for upward mobility, particularly for those who lacked a college degree. And that was a reality already well-known to many former AFDC recipients who, like most welfare recipients nationwide, had already been moving in and out of the labor force.[35] Many postindustrial jobs in Baltimore that were filled by city residents, as opposed to suburbanites, and by African Americans were service positions that did not pay a living wage. Between 1980 and 2007 in the Baltimore metropolitan region, job creation in low-wage industries rose by 63 percent, while job growth in middle-income and high-income industries increased by only 36 percent and 10 percent, respectively.[36] And according to a 2018 study commissioned by the Associated Black Charities, the region's African Americans were "concentrated in low-wage industries and occupations."[37] Patterns evident in the metropolitan area were even more pronounced when considering the city alone, where health care and education were major sources of employment. A report by the Baltimore Black Worker Center that was based on the 2010 Census found that while African American women made up 61 percent of the city's female workforce, they filled 71 percent of female, low-wage jobs.[38] Former welfare recipients who exercised "personal responsibility" and secured a "work opportunity" nevertheless found it difficult to move out of poverty.

Meanwhile, marriage promotion smacked not only of patriarchy and heteronormativity but also of willed ignorance of the actual job prospects of low-income Black men in cities like Baltimore. In the early twenty-first century, the unionized heavy manufacturing sector, which had long been dominated by white men, was issuing death knells. The 2005 closure of Baltimore's GM plant and the 2012 final shuttering of Bethlehem Steel at Sparrows Point were cases in point.[39] American presidents had failed to protect the nation's industrial sector. Nor had they effectively used the power of the government to create meaningful alternative employment options and strengthen the hand of workers and unions.[40]

The economic reorientation of the city's economy had produced winners in addition to losers. The city's financial industry was an obvious beneficiary. In fact, its executives, including those at the helm of such Baltimore-born firms as Legg Mason and T. Rowe Price, had worked hard over the years to make the city, Maryland, and the nation more business friendly.[41] And some Black and white blue-collar workers enjoyed a bit of a surge as a result of liberalized global trade. Having been retooled to accommodate super-sized container ships that bring manufactured products and other goods to the United States from Asia, during the 2010s, Baltimore's port became one of the busiest on the East Coast. The development boosted the fortunes of some of the area's unionized longshoremen, who had seen their fortunes and numbers decline decades earlier.[42] But while the profits to be made in asset, wealth, and investment management in glistening downtown skyscrapers may have boosted the foot traffic in new boutiques, coffeehouses, and luxury waterfront condominium complexes in downtown Baltimore, they provided limited relief to local unemployment. Moreover, few living in the shadows of the city's abandoned factories could fully celebrate the tens of millions of tons of goods, including automobiles and steel, that passed through the expanded port—but had been manufactured somewhere else.

In Baltimore's early twenty-first-century postindustrial labor market, Black men, like Black women, were overrepresented in low-wage jobs. In 2010, African

American men were 51 percent of the city's male workforce but 62 percent of its male low-wage workers. When combined with the figures for Black women, almost 55 percent of African American workers earned low wages as compared to 29 percent of whites.[43] Baltimore's postindustrial economy relied on an army of low-wage workers, who were disproportionately Black and predominantly female. The statistics indicated that neoliberal solutions to poverty, which emphasized only work and marriage, were unrealistic paths to economic security. The contraction of the social safety net was a tactic of social control that provided area employers with low labor costs. And although the employment trends in Baltimore mirrored those evident in other struggling cities, they were the product of local urban planning in addition to federal policymaking. Their concentration in low-wage employment in combination with higher than average unemployment rates led to an African American median income in Baltimore that was 54 percent of that of whites, a figure that was worse than the differential had been during the mid-1950s in Jim Crow Baltimore.[44]

As had long been the case, economic hardship took a particularly high toll on women, to whom the care of family members frequently fell. Food insecurity was one of multiple manifestations of poverty with gendered implications. A 2015 study of the city revealed that the mere act of food shopping remained a logistical challenge for many. One in four city residents—and one in three children—lived in a food desert. The statistics were brought to life by the many women who could regularly be seen lugging grocery bags or pushing shopping carts in Baltimore's low-income neighborhoods. "It's really hard to find good meals. The prices are so high. You really need to stretch your buck," commented Bernice Matthews, who had a family of four to feed in a food desert. Reflective of the extent to which neoliberal solutions had come to dominate local problem-solving, the city's mayor, Stephanie Rawlings-Blake, proposed offering tax breaks to grocery stores.[45] Meanwhile, life in substandard housing also remained a perennial source of labor for many low-income women compelled to stave off vermin and the cold to keep their families safe. And though the mayor sold some city-owned parking lots to secure the funds to address the problem, municipal parks had not seen many improvements since the 1960s and 1970s.[46]

Black public-sector workers were hardly immune from or unaware of the problems facing other African Americans in Baltimore. And while unionization provided even low-wage Black government employees greater security than many of their private-sector counterparts, the threat of being downsized or privatized often loomed large. Despite the austere times, many workers continued to do their part to keep their agencies responsive to the needs of residents. Mindful that the city had rolled back social services but that residents still needed help, in the 2010s, Baltimore's public librarians innovated. They used grant funding to bring in graduate students from the University of Maryland School of Social Work to assist patrons. The program met with early success. Within its first few weeks, one social worker had helped a woman she had found crying over a computer keyboard apply for disability assistance. And a graduate student was proud to report that she had found a homeless mother and child a place to stay.[47]

Despite the important contributions of government workers, elected officials often spoke of them as if they were expendable. Republican Newt Gingrich's 1994 Contract with America called for downsizing the federal government based on a presumption of waste and inefficiency. And a year into his presidency, Clinton bragged about having already decreased the number of federal workers by a hundred thousand—a declaration he felt no compunction to qualify with assurances that the cuts had been judicious.[48] Across party lines, candidates for national office and American presidents often curried favor with voters by pledging to shrink the federal workforce. On face value, the proposition was counterintuitive; as the nation's population grew, the number of federal workers might reasonably have been expected to rise to accommodate increased demand for public services. That the promise of downsizing nevertheless remained popular signals the extent to which the narrative associating public-sector workers with inefficiency and waste continued to inform American politics. And although elected officials did not typically invoke race in their denigrations of government workers, the overrepresentation of African Americans in the public sector meant that they were disproportionately—and perhaps also conveniently—the targets of the dismissive rhetoric. By the late twentieth century, such rhetoric could be quite extreme. In 1995, conservative syndicated columnist George Will endorsed the notion that the nation's wealth was being siphoned "to support vast bureaucracies of social-service providers."[49] And in 2011, an editor of the *National Review*, a conservative publication, wrote of "public-sector cartels ... choking off economic growth."[50]

In Baltimore, public-sector downsizing was not typically announced with the same level of glee that was evident in Washington. The municipal government remained a critical local employer, and AFSCME and other activist groups monitored privatization practices carefully. Although Clinton spoke enthusiastically of cutting tens of thousands of federal posts, activists in Baltimore worried about each municipal job loss—mindful of the person, family, and community that might be affected. But downsizing proved inevitable given the city's shrinking population and tax base, national indifference to cities, and ongoing pressures to cultivate an inviting business climate. Within his first five years in office, Schmoke eliminated 4,000 city government jobs. He added to that total in 1993, when he closed the Urban Services Agency, the city's antipoverty agency that had been formed in the 1970s when the Community Action Agency and Model Cities program had merged.[51] By the late twentieth century, USA was only a shadow of the earlier activist agencies. Nevertheless, USA still had committed workers. Among those displaced by the closure were two employees who had forestalled 1,800 evictions the previous year in a city with a mounting eviction crisis.[52] Government officials also continued to contract out public services. During the late 1990s, Lockheed Martin, the world's largest defense contractor, was tracking down so-called deadbeat dads in Baltimore. It was also lobbying the state legislature to win for itself, a private corporation, the authority to garner parents' wages without a court order.[53] Downsizing and privatization continued into the twenty-first century, further imperiling both a job niche vital to African American workers and the quality of services available to city residents.

As they had since the 1970s, AFSCME and other public-sector unions fiercely defended their members, the vital services they provided, and the principle that the government had obligations to its citizens that should not be compromised by the introduction of the profit motive. An explicitly anti–public sector union campaign led by conservatives hampered their efforts. During the late twentieth and early twenty-first centuries, Democrats' tepid support for federal legislation that might have revitalized the labor movement sometimes made it seem that they had lost sight of the importance of unions to their electoral successes. Republicans, however, had not. And many targeted government unions, which had grown in influence in the labor movement as the number of organized private-sector workers had declined.

Conservatives critiqued public-sector unions for driving up the cost of government, having undue influence over public policy, and serving as roadblocks to privatization efforts. The animosity had been building since the late 1960s, but it began making national headlines in the 2010s. During that decade, Republican governors in several states introduced legislation intended to roll back government unions' collective-bargaining rights. The American Legislative Exchange Council (ALEC), an influential conservative group composed of Republican lawmakers and business interests, spearheaded the efforts. In several states, the effort met with success, and a dramatic showdown in Wisconsin between Governor Scott Walker and public-sector unions, in particular, attracted considerable attention.[54] ALEC and the wealthy Koch brothers, who bankrolled many conservative campaigns, also backed an effort by the National Right to Work organization to use the courts to curtail the power of public-sector unions.[55] That effort met with success in 2018, when the conservative majority on the U.S. Supreme Court reversed its own precedent and in the case *Janus v. AFSCME Council 31* ruled that public-sector unions could not collect a fee from government workers who were nonunion members but who nevertheless benefited from collectively bargained contracts. The ruling had potentially grave implications for the coffers of government unions. "Powerful corporate interests," argued one AFSCME official, were "out to eliminate unions from the American economic and political land-scape because they want to be able to call all the shots."[56]

The ramifications of the *Janus* decision in Maryland, which had labor laws that the ruling invalidated, were not immediately apparent. But public-sector labor leaders in Baltimore were precisely those whom conservative activists were hoping to disempower. The leaders were unapologetic advocates of economic justice who were willing to take on an adversary that AFSCME described as including "privatizers, deregulators, tax-cutters, people who want to turn back the clock on racial justice and women's equality, and selfish people at the helm of corporations."[57] Middleton of AFSCME had been in the fight for decades and had a lengthy track record of advocating on behalf of his members, other low-income workers, and progressive causes in the city. Meanwhile, "the radical teachers' movement [had come] to Baltimore," according to the *Nation*. A contingent within BTU had founded Baltimore Movement of Rank-and-File Educators, a group with counterparts in such cities as Chicago, New York, and Philadelphia that were intentionally attempting to use teachers' unions to promote social justice causes. And the group was vying for increased influence within the BTU.[58] Conservatives' concerns about public-sector workers and their unions were coming true.

Advocates of public-sector unions such as those in Baltimore counter their critics by defending the multiple and critical roles organized labor plays. While conservatives such as political scientist Daniel DiSalvo argue that public-sector workers have to join "the real world" and accept the deteriorating labor standards that increasingly define the private sector, public-sector union officials argue that they are fighting on behalf of all workers to maintain a high bar, one that Martin Luther King once described as preserving the dignity of labor.[59] And while critics such as political scientist Terry Moe argue that government unions gain too much power over public policy, public-sector union leaders describe themselves as defenders of democratic decision-making. The unions, advocates argue, protect the public from those who would commodify government-service provision and sell it in the private sector, where decisions are made behind closed doors.[60] As AFSCME officials explain, public-sector unions and their critics are locked in a "battle for the country's soul, over its basic values," and "the stakes are high."[61]

The stakes were definitely high in Baltimore. For just as the city's late twentieth- and early twenty-first-century labor market reflected the neoliberal orientation of the national and global economies, local patterns of governance did as well. Schmoke won his first bid for mayor in part on the critique that his predecessors had paid too much attention to downtown at the expense of neighborhood concerns. Nevertheless, he and his successors hardly abandoned and could ill afford to neglect the city's tourism industry, other commercial revitalization efforts, and the neoliberal imperatives that mayors act like entrepreneurs. In a context characterized by intense national and global competition for investors, Baltimore's elected officials had to keep the city attractive to businesses. Thus, like Schaefer, they sacrificed the health of the population for the economic health—as measured in metrics such as credit ratings—of the city. They also continued the practice of deal-making. During the 1970s, with federal and state support, Schaefer had incentivized investment in Baltimore's renaissance with generous tax abatements, and developers continued to expect no less. The city continued to broker arrangements such as payment-in-lieu-of-taxes agreements, which forgave property-tax obligations, sometimes for twenty years, in exchange for a lower fee and which were intended to compensate developers simply for choosing Baltimore for their profit-making ventures. Although elected officials undertook redevelopment projects in neighborhoods, including in those with large low-income populations, downtown commercial ventures were far more numerous.[62]

Schmoke also pursued and his successor secured from the state the authority to negotiate tax increment financing (TIF), a controversial and risky development strategy.[63] In typical TIF agreements, which were not necessarily tax relief but which were often negotiated along with abatements, municipalities agreed to float a bond—and thus take on financial risk—to fund infrastructure and site development on "blighted" land. The projected taxes to be garnered from the improved area minus the value of the taxes that the undeveloped area would have generated were supposed to cover the cost of the bond. In 1980, the Maryland General Assembly allowed its jurisdictions to negotiate TIF agreements. Schaefer, who was in the throes of the controversy surrounding his "shadow government" and its secretive redevelopment dealmaking, had Baltimore excluded from the legislation. He believed that TIFs, which did not require voter approval, could become giveaways to developers. Moreover, he worried that TIFs would create conflict among neighborhoods because only some would benefit directly from the deals.[64] Despite Schaefer's uncharacteristic caution—but largely because he had set the standard for Baltimore that job creation was enough and that any additional fiduciary obligations a developer might have to the city were negotiable—his successors sought to add to their toolbox the development-luring incentive.

During the late twentieth- and early twenty-first centuries, the Baltimore Development Corporation (BDC), a public-private body, brokered most of the city's payment-in-lieu-of-taxes and TIF agreements and other development deals, which were then sent to the mayor and city council for approval. The product of the merger of the multiple public-private deal-making entities that Schaefer had created and older development-oriented boards, BDC was created in the wake of the shadow government controversy, when many were alarmed that critical decision-making regarding the city's future was happening behind closed doors. Though the result of calls for greater transparency, BDC also shrouded its work in secrecy. In fact, it took a lawsuit that was settled in 2006 to compel the body to comply with Maryland's open-meetings law. Even thereafter, BDC, which was regarded locally as an advocate for developers, continued to thwart public scrutiny of its deal-making.[65] In stark contrast to the days of the War on Poverty, when the federal government had mandated maximum community participation in decision-making, the minimal public involvement in deal-making that had become standard fare during the Schaefer years remained the norm in Baltimore.

City activists, however, including the leaders of local public-sector unions, grew increasingly frustrated with business as usual. Protest often followed the negotiations of TIFs and other incentive agreements, particularly those that further subsidized downtown.[66] In a city in which in 2000 nearly 40 percent of families with children lived at or below the poverty line, it seemed unconscionable that wealthy developers received tax breaks.[67] In 2016, the issue of corporate welfare came to a head. BDC had completed the negotiation of a TIF with the Sagamore Development Corporation, which was owned by Kevin Plank, who also owned the transnational apparel and footwear company Under Armour. Sagamore had proposed creating a massive multiuse complex in South Baltimore that would include housing, retail, and the global corporate headquarters of Under Armour, whose 2016 revenue was $4.8 billion.[68] In addition to the TIF, the deal was contingent on the receipt of tax credits valued at close to $760 million.[69] According to activists, the city's mayor was "fast-tracking" the TIF, which at the time was valued at $658.6 million, a figure that far exceeded the city's previous development deals.[70] "The swift process prevents and limits the opportunity of citizens to understand what this deal is all about and what its [financial] implications are for the long term," charged Madeline Wright, the director of the Maryland Consumer Rights Coalition. She and the leaders of multiple other organizations, including AFSCME, the AFT, and BUILD held a rally in front of city hall to slow things down.[71]

Among the opponents of the Port Covington TIF, the American Civil Liberties Union was particularly vocal. The group called the project "financially and socially irresponsible" and argued that it would "further entrench segregation in an already hypersegregated city, and impose those costs on the predominantly African American residents and taxpayers of the City, while the benefits will largely accrue to a future workforce and population that is by design, predominantly white, affluent, and not currently residing in Baltimore City."[72] The argument resonated with many residents and set off a months-long, spirited debate about the ethics and utility of neoliberal urban planning in Baltimore. Ultimately, the pressure from activists produced some results. Sagamore entered into an agreement that promised an economic return to the predominantly African American neighborhoods that would be affected. The developer also negotiated with the activist organizations. The deliberations resulted in a Community Benefits Agreement, which included modest concessions on such issues as the construction of low-income housing and the hiring of city workers. Many of the TIF's critics remained unwavering in their opposition. But perhaps motivated by pragmatism, BUILD endorsed the agreement, which its leaders described as "unprecedented."[73] The influential group's approval gave members of the city council cover to vote in favor of the TIF.[74]

While the Community Benefits Agreement made the Port Covington TIF a better deal for city residents than the original proposal had been, even those activists who endorsed passage doubtlessly knew that it was not a meaningful solution to the city's immediate and urgent problems. As they had for decades, residents largely shared the belief that commercial development was critical to the city's revitalization. But as activist public-sector workers from the 1960s and 1970s—such as Parren Mitchell and his staff of antipoverty warriors and Maude Harvey and her staff of client advocates—had argued, physical renewal had to be paired with what they called at the time human renewal, which required wealth redistribution, job creation, democratic decision-making, quality public services, and affirmative action. During the 1970s and 1980s, however, as American presidents had forged a neoliberal future for the nation and shifted wealth up the economic ladder, they contracted the sources of revenue needed to fund human renewal. And they helped to justify subsequent cuts to the welfare state with the claim that redistributed aid that ended up in cities such as Baltimore had been squandered on the city's African American population, which was supposedly made up largely of criminals and welfare queens and also of inefficient public-sector workers who were represented by tax-grubbing union officials. Federal-level policy-making during the late twentieth and early twenty-first centuries reinforced the logic that African American urban residents were the enemy. The false claims obscured the price that Black residents of cities like Baltimore paid in services, jobs, and opportunity for neoliberal policies that shifted wealth out of their neighborhoods and up the economic ladder.

NOTES

Introduction

1. "Freddie Gray Death Sparks Huge Protest in Baltimore," *CBS Evening News*, posted April 25, 2015, https://www.youtube.com/watch?v=0Zjbour3dIw.
2. "Tawanda Jones Wages Long Fight for Justice in Baltimore," *CBS Baltimore*, November 14, 2015, https://baltimore.cbslocal.com/2015/11/14/tawanda-jones-wages-long-fight-for-justice-in-baltimore/.
3. Jon Swaine, "Freddie Gray Funeral: 'Most of Us Knew a Lot of Freddie Grays. Too Many,'" *Guardian*, April 27, 2015, https://www.theguardian.com/us-news/2015/apr/27/freddie-gray-funeral-most-of-us-knew-a-lot-of-freddie-grays-too-many.
4. Swaine, "Freddie Gray Funeral."
5. Lawrence Brown, "Two Baltimores: The White L vs. the Black Butterfly," *Baltimore Sun* (hereafter *Sun*), June 28, 2016, https://www.baltimoresun.com/citypaper/bcpnews-two-baltimores-the-white-l-vs-the-black-butterfly-20160628-htmlstory.html.
6. Elizabeth Ponsot and Daniel Costa-Roberts, "Life in Freddie Gray's Neighborhood by the Numbers," *PBS News Hour*, aired May 2, 2015, https://www.pbs.org/newshour/nation/learn-statistics-life-freddie-grays-baltimore-neighborhood; and Yvonne Wenger, "Incomplete Healing," *Sun*, May 10, 2015, 1, 24.
7. Baltimore Community Relations Commission (hereafter CRC), "Survey of Employment in City Government—1977" (Baltimore: CRC, 1977).
8. Lane Windham, *Knocking on Labor's Door: Union Organizing in the 1970s and the Roots of the New Economic Divide* (Chapel Hill: University of North Carolina Press, 2017).
9. Jefferson Cowie, *Stayin' Alive: The 1970s and the Last Days of the Working Class* (New York: New Press, 2012).
10. Bart Landry, *The New Black Middle Class* (Berkeley: University of California Press, 1988).
11. William Julius Wilson, *The Truly Disadvantaged: The Inner City, the Underclass, and Public Policy* (Chicago: University of Chicago Press, 1987); Wilson, *When Work Disappears: The World of the New Urban Poor* (New York: Vintage, 1996); and Thomas Sugrue, *The Origins of the Urban Crisis: Race and Inequality in Postwar Detroit* (Princeton, NJ: Princeton University Press, 1996).
12. Michael Katz, Mark Stern, and Jamie Fader, "The New African American Inequality," *Journal of American History* 92, no. 1 (June 2005): 75–108.
13. Ian Haney López, *Dog Whistle Politics: How Coded Racial Appeals Have Reinvented Racism and Wrecked the Middle Class* (New York: Oxford University Press, 2015).
14. Jon Shelton, *Teacher Strike! Public Education and the Making of a New American Political Order* (Urbana-Champaign: University of Illinois Press, 2017); and Nelson Lichtenstein and

Elizabeth Shermer, *The Right and Labor in America: Politics, Ideology and Imagination* (Philadelphia: University of Pennsylvania Press, 2016).

15. Ralph de Toledano, *Let Our Cities Burn* (New York: Arlington House, 1975).

16. Elizabeth Hinton, *From the War on Poverty to the War on Crime: The Making of Mass Incarceration in America* (Cambridge, MA: Harvard University Press, 2016), 19; and Marisa Chappell, *The War on Welfare: Family, Poverty, and Politics in Modern America* (Philadelphia: University of Pennsylvania Press, 2012).

17. Judith Stein, *Pivotal Decade: How the United States Traded Factories for Finance in the Seventies* (New Haven, CT: Yale University Press, 2011).

18. Timothy Conlan, *From New Federalism to Devolution: Twenty Five Years of Intergovernmental Reform* (Washington, DC: Brookings Institution Press, 1998); Dennis Judd and Todd Swanstrom, *City Politics: Private Power and Public Money* (New York: HarperCollins College Publishers, 1994); Robert Thomas, "National-Local Relations and the City's Dilemma," *Annals of the American Academy of Political and Social Science* 509, no. 1 (May 1990): 115; and Deil Wright, "Policy Shifts in the Politics and Administration of Intergovernmental Relations, 1930s–1990s," *Annals of the American Academy of Political and Social Science* 509, no. 1 (May 1990): 60–72.

19. Joseph McCartin, "'Fire the Hell out of Them': Sanitation Workers' Struggles and the Normalization of the Striker Replacement Strategy in the 1970s," *Labor* 2 (2005): 67–92; and Shelton, *Teacher Strike!*

20. Fred Barbash, "Analysis: Welfare Mess Lies in Faulty Paper-Pushings, Miscast Workers," *Sun*, November 12, 1971, C9.

21. David Harvey, "From Managerialism to Entrepreneurialism: The Transformation in Urban Governance in Late Capitalism," *Geografiska Annaler* 71, no. 1 (1989): 3–17.

22. "Baltimore: New Breed of City," *Forbes*, September 16, 1976, advertisement, p. 8.

23. C. Fraser Smith, "Some Council Members Shocked," *Sun*, April 21, 1980, A1; and Smith, "Two Trustees and a $100 Million Bank Skirt the Restrictions of City Government," *Sun*, April 13, 1980, A1.

24. Madeline Murphy, "Rumpelstiltskin, What's Next," *Baltimore Afro-American* (hereafter *Afro*), May 3, 1980, 4; and Richard Hula, "The Two Baltimores," in *Leadership and Urban Regeneration: Cities in North America and Europe*, ed. Dennis Judd and Michael Parkinson (Newbury Park, CA: Sage, 1990).

25. Marc Levine, "A Nation of Hamburger Flippers," *Sun*, July 31, 1994, E1, E4.

26. Vernon Jordan Jr., "The New Regionalism," *To Be Equal* (January 21, 1981), Folder "(A-Z) Reagan, Ronald (President Elect)," box 423, Schaefer Papers (hereafter SP), Baltimore Records Group 9 (hereafter 9), Baltimore City Archive (hereafter BCA).

27. Coalition on Women and the Budget, "Inequality of Sacrifice: The Impact of the Reagan Budget on Women" (Washington, DC: Coalition on Women and the Budget, 1984).

28. "Proposition 13: Threat to All Public Employees, Threat to All Public Services," *Public Employee* (July 1978): 1.

29. Michelle Alexander, *The New Jim Crow: Mass Incarceration in the Age of Colorblindness* (New York: New Press, 2010).

30. Michael Katz, *The Price of Citizenship* (Philadelphia: University of Pennsylvania Press, 2008).

Chapter 1

1. James P. Connolly, "Baltimore Area Looks to Boom Times in '51: Surplus Labor Already Sought Outside State," *New York Times*, January 2, 1951, 66.

2. Bertha Brown and Gina Butler [pseudonyms], interview with Jane Berger, Baltimore, December 17, 2005.

3. Apral Smith, "Love and Sacrifice for the Sake of the Family," undergraduate student video project, n.d., Coppin State University, Baltimore. At the start of the 1950s, the U.S. Bureau of Labor Statistics declared $3,800 the necessary minimum income needed to sustain an urban family. Two years later, the median nonwhite income in Baltimore was $2,600, indicating that well over half the Black population was significantly below the necessary minimum. Maryland Commission on Interracial Problems and Relations (hereafter MCIPR), *An American City in Transition: The Baltimore Community Self-Survey of Inter-Group Relations* ([Baltimore]: MCIPR, 1955), 30, 32.

4. C. Fraser Smith, *Here Lies Jim Crow: Civil Rights in Maryland* (Baltimore: Johns Hopkins University Press, 2012).

5. David Terry, "'Tramping for Justice': The Dismantling of Jim Crow in Baltimore, 1942–1954" (PhD dissertation, Howard University, 2002), 20.

6. Sherry H. Olson, *Baltimore: The Building of an American City* (Baltimore: Johns Hopkins University Press, 1980), 239–240; and Carroll Williams, "Bethlehem Plant Here Tops World," *Sun*, February 26, 1958, 26.

7. Quoted in Ira De A. Reid, *The Negro Community of Baltimore: A Social Survey* (Baltimore: National Urban League, 1934), 38.

8. Jo Ann Argersinger, *Toward a New Deal in Baltimore* (Chapel Hill: University of North Carolina Press, 1988); and Roderick Ryon, "Ambiguous Legacy: Baltimore Blacks and the CIO, 1936–1941," *Journal of Negro History* 65, no. 1 (Winter 1980): 18–33.

9. U.S. Department of Census, *1940 Census of Population*, vol. 2 (Washington, DC: U.S. Government Printing Office, 1943), 577; and U.S. Department of Census, *United States Census of Population—1950, Census Tract Statistics: Baltimore, Maryland and Adjacent Area* (Washington, DC: U.S. Government Printing Office, 1952).

10. Letter to Mayor Theodore R. McKeldin from Thomas J. S. Waxter, November 10, 1944, folder T10, box 259, 22 McKeldin Papers, 9, BCA.

11. Argersinger, *New Deal*, 12; David Milobsky, "Power from the Pulpit: Baltimore's African-American Clergy, 1950–1970," *Maryland Historical Magazine* 89, no. 3 (Fall 1994): 275–289; and Harold McDougall, *Black Baltimore: A New Theory of Community* (Philadelphia: Temple University Press, 1993).

12. Hayward Farrar, *The Baltimore Afro-American, 1892–1950* (Westport, CT: Greenwood, 1998).

13. Sandy Shoemaker, "'We Shall Overcome, Someday': The Equal Rights Movement in Baltimore, 1935–1942," *Maryland Historical Magazine* 89 (Fall 1994): 261–273.

14. "Dr. Lillie M. Jackson—Great American," *Baltimore CRC Newsletter*, October–November 1969, folder CRC, box 550, 26, 9, BCA.

15. John Salmund, *"My Mind Set on Freedom": A History of the Civil Rights Movement* (Chicago: Ivan R. Dee, 1998), 88.

16. Enolia McMillan, interviewed by Richard Richardson, April 6, 1976, Governor Theodore McKeldin–Dr. Lillie May Jackson Project (hereafter McKeldin-Jackson Project), Maryland Historical Society, Baltimore (hereafter MHS).

17. Clarence M. Mitchell Jr., interviewed by Leroy Graham, July 29 and August 3, 1976, McKeldin-Jackson Project, MHS. See also Lillie M. Jackson to John Morsell, June 22, 1959, and "Biographical Sketch of Dr. Lillie M. Jackson," folder "Baltimore, Maryland, July–Dec. 1959," NAACP Branch Files, 1940–1955, Library of Congress, Washington, DC (hereafter LOC).

18. "Biographical Record: Juanita Jackson Mitchell," n.d., folder 1, box, 2, collection 7, National Council of Negro Women Archive, Washington, DC; Juanita Jackson Mitchell, interviewed by Leroy Graham, July 29, 1976, and August 3, 1976, McKeldin-Jackson Project, MHS; and Denton Watson, *Lion in the Lobby: Clarence Mitchell, Jr.'s Struggle for the Passage of Civil Rights Laws* (Lanham, MD: University Press of America, 2002).

19. "Juanita Jackson Mitchell," *Sun*, February 5, 2007, http://www.baltimoresun.com/features/bal-blackhistory-juanita-story.html.

20. Quoted in Olson, *Baltimore*, 368–369.

21. Evelyn T. Burrell, interviewed by Susan Conwell, June 25, 1976, McKeldin-Jackson Project, MHS; Editorial, "Let Freedom Ring," *Afro*, May 2, 1942, 4; B. M. Phillips, "2,000 Join in March on Md. Capitol," *Afro*, May 2, 1942, 1–2; "C-P, Transit Co. Officials Rebuff TWE Committee," *Afro*, March 13, 1944, 1; "Transit Co. Hit at NAACP Meeting," *Afro*, June 19, 1945, 1; "Pratt Library Case Won: Supreme Court Refuses Review," *Afro*, October 9, 1945, 1; "Some of the Accomplishments of the Baltimore Branch of the NAACP," multiple years, folder "Baltimore, Maryland, 1945,"NAACP Branch Files, 1940–1955, LOC; Editorial, "Police School a Help," *Afro*, January 1, 1944, 4; and Smith, *Here Lies Jim Crow*.

22. Fred Rasmussen and Dewitt Bliss, "Troy Brailey, Champion for Civil Rights, Dies at 78," *Sun*, October 7, 1994, 11B.

23. Ralph Pearson, "The National Urban League Comes to Baltimore," *Maryland Historical Magazine* 70 (Winter 1977): 530–538; Nancy Weiss, *The National Urban League, 1910–1940* (New York: Oxford University Press, 1974), 67–68; Amy Bentley, "Wages of War: The Shifting Landscape of Race and Gender in World War II Baltimore," *Maryland Historical Magazine* 88 (Winter 1993): 423.

24. "Leader Dies While Honors Being Set," *Afro*, February 14, 1970, 1.

25. Smith, *Here Lies Jim Crow*.

26. James Patterson, *Grand Expectations* (New York: Oxford University Press, 1996), 58; and Judith Stein, *Running Steel, Running America: Race, Economic Policy and the Decline of Liberalism* (Chapel Hill: University of North Carolina Press, 1998).

27. Desmond King, *Actively Seeking Work? The Politics of Unemployment and Welfare Policy in the United States and Britain* (Chicago: University of Chicago Press, 1995); Robert Lieberman, *Shifting the Color Line: Race and the American Welfare State* (Cambridge, MA: Harvard University Press, 1998); Ira Katznelson, *When Affirmative Action Was White: An Untold History of Racial Inequality in Twentieth-Century America* (New York: W. W. Norton, 2005); and Jill Quadagno, *The Color of Welfare: How Racism Undermined the War on Poverty* (New York: Oxford University Press, 1994).

28. "NAACP Wires President, Urging Permanent FEPC," *Afro*, November 21, 1944; "NAACP Carries FEPC Fight to Washington," and "6 Maryland Congressmen Seen by Associated Groups on FEPC," newspaper articles, n.d., folder "Baltimore, Maryland, 1946," NAACP Branch Files, 1940–1955, LOC; "Plea Made for Crusade for FEPC Legislation," *Afro*, January 19, 1946, 1–2; and Dona Cooper Hamilton and Charles V. Hamilton, *The Dual Agenda: Race and Social Welfare Policies of Civil Right Organizations* (New York: Columbia University Press, 1997), 54–55.

29. Editorial, "Full Employment Possible," *Afro*, August 21, 1945, 4.

30. "Report of NAACP Labor Department at the 38th Annual Conference in Washington, D.C.," June 26, 1947, folder "Baltimore, Maryland, 1947," NAACP Branch Files, 1940–1955, NAACP Papers, LOC; Watson, *Lion in the Lobby*, 152–156.

31. Warren M. Banner, *A Review of the Program and Activities of the Baltimore Urban League and a Brief Analysis of Conditions in the Community Which It Serves* (New York: National Urban League, October–November 1949), 45, 150.

32. Banner, *Review*, 45, 150. The Baltimore Urban League noted that African Americans were concentrated in the lowest four pay grades.

33. "Baltimore Steelworkers Remember," in *The Baltimore Book: New Views of Local History*, ed. Elizabeth Fee, Linda Shopes, and Linda Zeidman (Philadelphia: Temple University Press, 1991), 178.

34. Mark Reutter, *Making Steel: Sparrows Point and the Rise and Ruin of American Industrial Might* (Urbana-Champaign: University of Illinois Press, 2005); and Karen Olson, *Wives of Steel: Voices of Women from Sparrows Point Steelworking Communities* (University Park: Pennsylvania State University Press, 2012).

35. Banner, *Review*, 16–17.

36. "Annual Report of Branch Activities—1951," [1952], and "Annual Report of Branch Activities—1952," [1953], folder "Baltimore, Maryland, 1953," NAACP Branch Files, 1940–1955, Baltimore, LOC.

37. Margaret L. Callcott, *The Negro in Maryland Politics, 1870–1912* (Baltimore: Johns Hopkins University Press, 1969), 101–138; and Argersinger, *New Deal*, 13–16.

38. "FEPC for Baltimore," *Afro*, March 13, 1954, 17.

39. Matthew Countryman, *Up South: Civil Rights and Black Power in Philadelphia* (Philadelphia: University of Pennsylvania Press, 2006).

40. Shirley Kyle, "FEPC Hearings Set for Tuesday, 1 p.m.," *Afro*, April 24, 1954, 1, 7; and "Council Chambers Packed at FEPC Hearings," *Afro*, May 1, 1954, 28.

41. Shirley Kyle, "Tidbits," *Afro*, June 19, 1954, 17.

42. Verda Welcome, as told to James M. Abraham, *Verda Welcome: My Life and Times* (Englewood Cliffs, NJ: Henry House, 1991), 42.

43. Editorial, "Another Step Forward," *Afro*, April 7, 1956, 4.

44. Editorial, "Time for Action," *Afro*, May 18, 1957, 4.

45. Quoted in Olson, *Wives of Steel*, 105. See also MCIPR, *American City in Transition*, 72.

46. Quoted in Olson, *Wives of Steel*, 73.

47. MCIPR, *American City in Transition*, 61, 68; and Kenneth Durr, *Behind the Backlash: White Working-Class Politics in Baltimore, 1940–1980* (Chapel Hill: University of North Carolina Press, 2003), 80.

48. MCIPR, *American City in Transition*, 72.

49. *Toward Equality: Baltimore's Progress Report* (Baltimore: Sidney Hollander Foundation, 1960), 63–64.

50. MCIPR, *American City in Transition*, 30–33, 67–68, 72, 76.

51. John C. Schmidt, "Negro Unemployment—What City Businessmen Are Doing About It," *Sun*, September 27, 1964, D1. See also Hammer and Company Associates, "Economic Report on the Baltimore Region," October 1964, 4–11, Department of Legislative Reference, City Hall, Baltimore; and Sugrue, *Origins of the Urban Crisis*.

52. Hammer and Company, "Economic Report," 5.

53. Callcott, *Negro in Maryland Politics*, 82–83; Durr, *Behind the Backlash*, 58; and Hammer and Company, "Economic Report," 4–7, 81.

54. Kweisi Mfume, with Ron Stodghill II, *No Free Ride: From the Mean Streets to the Mainstream* (New York: Ballantine, 1996), 19.

55. Quoted in Stephen Tuck, *We Ain't What We Ought to Be* (Cambridge, MA: Harvard University Press, 2011), 184; and "Houston Calls Wagner-Lewis Bill a 'Sieve': Workers Would Drop Through Its Holes, Says NAACP Man," *Afro*, February 16, 1935, 6.

56. Welcome, *Verda Welcome*, 28.

57. Paula Giddings, *When and Where I Enter: The Impact of Black Women on Race and Sex in America* (New York: W. Morrow, 1984); Darlene Clarke Hine, Wilma King, and Linda Reed, eds., *We Specialize in the Wholly Impossible: A Reader in Black Women's History* (New York: New York University Press, 1995); and Nancy Folbre, *The Invisible Heart: Economics and Family Values* (New York: New Press, 2001).

58. Lizbeth Cohen, *A Consumers' Republic: The Politics of Mass Consumption in Postwar America* (New York: Vintage, 2003); and Melvin Oliver and Thomas Shapiro, *Black Wealth/White Wealth* (New York: Routledge, 1995).

59. Banner, *Review*, 197–198; and MCIPR, *American City in Transition*, 46, 49–50.

60. "Mother Rescuers Fight for More Welfare Help," *Afro*, July 2, 1966 in Rhonda Y. Williams, "We're Tired of Being Treated Like Dogs: Poor Women and Power Politics in Black Baltimore," *Journal of Black Studies and Research* 31 (2001), 31–41.

61. The *Afro-American* began conducting clean block campaigns in 1935. See, for example, "37 Clean Block Captains to Receive Personal Gifts," *Afro*, September 18, 1945, 23. See also Daniel Wilner et al., *The Housing Environment and Family Life: A Longitudinal Study of the Effects of Housing on Morbidity and Mental Health* (Baltimore: Johns Hopkins University Press, 1962), 76, 88, 110, 243; and Rhonda Williams, *The Politics of Public Housing: Black Women's Struggles Against Urban Inequality* (New York: Oxford University Press, 2004).

62. "School Board Faces Court Action: Citizens Condemn Segregation Here," *Afro*, June 8, 1963, 1. See also Banner, *Review*, 145.

63. Terry, "Tramping," 260–267.

64. *One Hundred and Thirty-Sixth Annual Report of the Department of Health, 1950* (Baltimore: City of Baltimore, 1950), 348, 350, 377–379, 384.

65. During the postwar years, Maryland was exceptional in that it was one of only two states that provided subsidized medical assistance to some of its neediest residents. Ida Merriam and Laura Rosen, "Medical Care for Needy Persons in Maryland," *Social Security Bulletin* 18, no. 11 (November 1955): 10–16.

66. Callcott, *Negro in Maryland Politics*, 151; "Interracial Report Given," *Sun*, March 26, 1954, 10; "Urge All Social Agencies to Adopt Desegregation," *Afro*, March 24, 1956, 32; and "Dixon Proposes Ban on Racial, Creed Bar," *Evening Sun*, October 29, 1957, 44.

67. Jacqueline Jones, *Labor of Love, Labor of Sorrow: Black Women, Work and the Family from Slavery to the Present* (New York: Vintage, 1986).

Chapter 2

1. "Goodman Wants EEOC to Start on City Jobs: Feels Some Bypass City Merit Lists," *Afro*, January 23, 1960, 32.

2. Editorial, "A Good Starting Point," *Afro*, October 27, 1956, 4.

3. "City Hall Job Slip Is Showing," *Afro*, February 6, 1960, 1, 5.

4. Editorial, "City Job Picture," *Afro*, February 6, 1960, 4.

5. James Patterson, *Freedom Is Not Enough: The Moynihan Report and America's Struggle over Black Family Life* (New York: Basic, 2012).

6. Patterson, *Freedom*.

7. Quoted in Watson, *Lion in the Lobby*, 453.
8. "Biggest Day in Baltimore!" *Afro*, September 24, 1960, 1.
9. "Vote Registration Drive Moves into High Gear," *Afro*, August 6, 1960, 5; "Hip, Hip Hurrah!" *Afro*, October 1, 1960, 4; "It's Official Now 106,306 Eligible to Vote Nov. 8," *Afro*, October 22, 1960, 1; and "It's Kennedy: AFRO's Choice for President," *Afro*, October 29, 1960, 1.
10. "166 AFRO Precincts Give Nixon 24%," *Afro*, November 12, 1960, 1; and Louis Lautier, "Colored Vote Called Margin of Victory," *Afro*, November 12, 1960, 8.
11. Lyndon Johnson, "Annual Message to Congress on the State of the Union," January 8, 1964, LBJ Presidential Library, Austin, TX, http://www.lbjlib.utexas.edu/johnson/archives.hom/speeches.hom/640108.asp.
12. Lyndon Johnson, "Remarks at the University of Michigan (May 22, 1964)," in *Lyndon B. Johnson and American Liberalism*, ed. Bruce Schulman (Boston: St. Martin's, 1995), 174–176.
13. Stein, *Pivotal Decade*.
14. Sugrue, *Origins of the Urban Crisis*.
15. Durr, *Behind the Backlash*, 199; Nancy MacLean, *Freedom Is Not Enough: The Opening of the American Workplace* (Cambridge, MA: Harvard University Press, 2008); and Stein, *Running Steel, Running America*.
16. U.S. Department of Labor, *The Negro Family: The Case for National Action* (Washington, DC: U.S. Government Printing Office, 1965).
17. Patterson, *Freedom*.
18. Chappell, *War on Welfare*; and Robert Self, *All in the Family: The Realignment of American Democracy Since the 1960s* (New York: Hill and Wang, 2013).
19. Julie Gallagher, *Black Women in New York City Politics* (Urbana-Champaign: University of Illinois Press, 2014).
20. Judd and Swanstrom, *City Politics*, 123; and John Mollenkopf, *The Contested City* (Princeton, NJ: Princeton University Press, 1983), 83.
21. Emily Lieb, "'White Man's Lane': Hollowing Out the Highway Ghetto in Baltimore," in *Baltimore '68: Riots and Rebirth in an American City*, ed. Jessica Elfenbien, Elizabeth Nix, and Thomas Hollowack (Philadelphia: Temple University Press, 2011), 51–69; Nicholas Dagen Bloom, *Merchant of Illusion: James Rouse, America's Salesman of the Businessman's Utopia* (Columbus: Ohio State University Press, 2004); Marc V. Levine, "Downtown Redevelopment as an Urban Growth Strategy: A Critical Appraisal of the Baltimore Renaissance," *Journal of Urban Affairs* 9, no. 2 (1987): 107.
22. Health and Welfare Council of the Baltimore Area, Inc., *Social Welfare Planning in Baltimore City* (Baltimore: Health and Welfare Council of the Baltimore Area, 1966), 9; and Theodore McKeldin to Thomas S. Nichols, August 18, 1964, folder "316. Poverty," box 414, 25, 9, BCA.
23. Reverend Herbert O. Edwards to Harold C. Edelston, February 1, 1964, folder "Human Renewal Program 207," box 395, 25, 9, BCA.
24. Melvin G. Roy to Theodore McKeldin, March 12, 1964, folder "316. Poverty," box 414, 25, 9, BCA.
25. Walter T. Dixon to Theodore McKeldin, May 21, 1964, folder "Human Renewal Program 207," box 395, 25, 9, BCA; "Itemized Budget, a Plan for Action on the Problems of Baltimore's Disadvantaged People," December 1964, and Theodore McKeldin to R. Sargent Shriver, November 25, 1964, folder "107 Community Action Commission Anti-Poverty Program (4)," box 378, 25, 9, BCA.
26. "Poverty Plan for City Rapped," *Sun*, December 12, 1964, 32.

27. "Anti-Poverty Plan Backed," *Sun*, December 18, 1964, 31.

28. Robert E. Hinton Jr., "Negro Leadership," *Sun*, December 19, 1964, 12.

29. Quadagno, *Color of Welfare*.

30. "Four Negros in Council," *Sun*, November 7, 1967, A1; and Welcome, *Verda Welcome*, 110–113.

31. Peter Bachrach and Morton Baratz, *Power and Poverty: Theory and Practice* (London: Oxford University Press, 1970), 183, 195; and Frank L. Stanley Jr. to Whitney M. Young Jr., March 17, 1965, folder "Admin 1965, Baltimore, Maryland, BUL," box 62, series I, National Urban League Part II, Library of Congress.

32. Ray Abrams, "Why Anti-Poverty Fight Lags," *Afro*, November 20, 1965, C2; and Ronnie Goldberg, "The Politics of Local Government in Baltimore," in *Power and Poverty*, ed. Bachrach and Baratz, 119, 180.

33. "Lively Joins Local 44 Field Staff; Predicts Victory Here," *Afro*, December 7, 1968: 20.

34. Quoted in Bachrach and Baratz, *Power and Poverty*, 175.

35. Quoted in Bachrach and Baratz, *Power and Poverty*, 175–176.

36. Quoted in Allan Matusow, *The Unraveling of America: A History of Liberalism in the 1960s* (New York: Harper & Row, 1984), 246.

37. Theodore McKeldin to R. Sargent Shriver Jr., November 26, 1965, and "News Release," November 27, 1965, folder "107. Community Action Commission Community Action Poverty Program (1)," box 377, 25, 9, BCA.

38. Frank L. Stanley Jr. to Whitney M. Young Jr., March 17, 1965, folder "Admin 1965, Baltimore, Maryland, BUL," box 62, series I, National Urban League Part II, Library of Congress; and Bachrach and Baratz, *Power and Poverty*, 183, 195.

39. Community Action Commission, "Minutes of Meeting," October 5, 1965, folder "107 Community Action Commission Anti-Poverty Program (2)," box 377, 25, 9, BCA; Michael Stetz, "War Stories: A History of the Urban Services Agency," *City Paper*, August 1, 1986, folder "(Dept.) Urban Services Agency," box 940, SP, 9, BCA; and Williams, *Politics of Public Housing*, 162.

40. "2nd Member Sought for Welfare Board," *Afro*, May 14, 1963, 20; and "A First: Public Housing Delegates to Meet Thursday," *Afro*, October 1, 1968, 14.

41. Quoted in Williams, *Politics of Public Housing*, 171.

42. "2nd Member," 20; "A First," 14; and "Model Cities Feud," *Sun*, May 28, 1968, C14.

43. Kay Mills, "City Advancing Toward Community Schools," *Evening Sun*, December 4, 1967, B1.

44. "Mother Rescuers Fight for More Welfare Help," *Afro*, July 2, 1966.

45. "Recommendations to the Mayor—Civil Rights Coalition Boards and Commissions," January 9, 1968, folder "348 Civil Rights," box 495, 26 McKeldin Papers (hereafter 26), 9, BCA.

46. Charlotte Minton to Thomas D'Alesandro, September 4, 1969, folder "270. Department of Public Welfare (2)," box 486, 26, 9, BCA.

47. "Mother Rescuers." See also Williams, *Politics of Public Housing*, 194.

48. Michael Katz and Mark Stern, *One Nation Divisible: What America Was and What It Is Becoming* (New York: Russell Sage Foundation, 2008).

49. U.S. Department of Commerce, Bureau of the Census, *Census of Governments, 1962, Vol. 3, No. 2, Compendium of Public Employment* (Washington, DC: U.S. Government Printing Office, 1963), 222; and U.S. Department of Commerce, Bureau of the Census, *Census of Governments, 1967, Vol. 3, No. 2, Compendium of Public Employment* (Washington, DC: U.S. Government Printing Office, 1969), 238.

50. Levine, "Downtown Redevelopment," 116.

51. See, for example, "Rec Dept. Bypasses Employee," *Afro*, March 19, 1960, 1; and "Then What Is It?" *Afro*, April 2, 1960, 4.

52. "Municipal Notices," *Sun*, March 2, 1964, 35.

53. "City Employment Practices—Some Recommendations," *Baltimore CRC Newsletter*, February–March 1967, 2, folder "McK BCRC (2)," box 363, 25, 9, BCA; and CRC, "Survey—1977," i.

54. Alan Lupo, "'Why Us?' for CORE Target, Officials Ask," *Evening Sun*, April 15, 1966, D20.

55. "Minutes of the Mayor's Task Force for Equal Rights Employment Subcommittee Meeting, Programs to Achieve Equality in Employment," September 8, 1966, folder "387 Employment Committee, Mayor's Task Force on Equal Rights," box 502, MP, 9, BCA.

56. "Minutes of the Task Force," September 8, 1966, and Mayor's Task Force for Equal Rights, "Minutes," March 20, 1967, April 28, 1967, and June 30, 1967, folder "1963–1967 Mayor McKeldin," box 16, 4, 7, BCA. See also "Schmidt Denies Bias on Force," *Sun*, April 20, 1968, 21; and Alan Lupo, "C.O.R.E. Asks Transfer of White City Foremen," *Evening Sun*, July 19, 1966, B6.

57. Adam Spiegel, "Mayor Seeing Streamlined City Charter," *Evening Sun*, December 16, 1967, 18.

58. Leon Sachs to Thomas D'Alesandro III, December 26, 1967, with "Recommendations Designed to Overcome Imbalance in Negro Municipal Employment," folder "449. Mayor's Advisory Committee on the CSC," box 512, 26, 9, BCA.

59. Spiegel, "Mayor," 18.

60. "Julian Hits Dixon, Urges Heavy Vote," *Afro*, September 5, 1967, 16; Baltimore City Council, *Journal of Proceedings of City Council of Baltimore at the Session of 1967–1971, Second Councilmanic Year, December, 1968–December, 1969* (Baltimore: Baltimore City Council, [n.d.]), 820; and "Many City Workers Live Outside," *Sunday Sun*, March 14, 1971, C4.

61. James Griffin to G. V. Walters, June 7, 1966; G. V Walters to James Griffin, June 13, 1966; and Lawrence Ageloff to Bernard Werner, July 19, 1966, all folder "369 CORE," box 199, 26, 9, BCA; Juanita Jackson Mitchell to Theodore McKeldin, August 16, 1966, folder "329 Black and White (1)," box 492, 26, 9, BCA; Thomas J. Murphy to Norman P. Ramsey, July 1967, folder "1967 General Correspondence (2)," box 9, 6, 7, BCA; David L. Glen to F. Pierce Linaweaver, September 29, 1969, folder "362 CRC (3)," box 498, 26, 9, BCA; and CRC, "Problems, Solutions and Gains," n.d., folder "362 CRC (2)," box 498, 26, 9, BCA.

62. CRC, "Survey—1977," i.

63. U.S. Department of Commerce, *1970 Census of the Population, Vol. 1: Characteristics of the Population, Part 22, Maryland* (Washington, DC: U.S. Government Printing Office, 1973), 212, 347; and CRC, "Survey—1977," i.

64. Nancy Naples, *Grassroots Warriors: Activist Mothering, Community Work and the War on Poverty* (New York: Routledge, 1998).

65. Lee Lassiter, "Welfare: Reform or Revolt—'Income, Dignity, Democracy,'" *Baltimore News-American* (hereafter *News-American*), May 1, 1969, folder "Social Welfare," Maryland Room, Vertical Files, Enoch Pratt Free Library, Baltimore (hereafter MR, VF, EPFL).

66. Cleveland A. Chandler and Mainstream Associates, "Study of Equal Employment Opportunity in the Baltimore Metropolitan Area, Interim Report I," July 28, 1967, 4, folder "Baltimore Community Relations Commission (2)," box 363, 25, 9, BCA.

67. Williams, *Politics of Public Housing*, 164.

68. Robert Blake, "Provident Head Quits, Joins City Hospitals," *Evening Sun*, March 27, 1964, B12; Chandler and Mainstream, "Study of Equal Employment," 8; "Pinderhughes Named: 3 Appointed to School Posts," *Afro*, July 23, 1968, 1; Stephen J. Lynton, "Model Cities Funds Called Insufficient by Miss Lazarus," *Sun*, May 21, 1968, C9; and "Ewing Acting Head of Giant BURHA," *Afro*, October 10, 1967, 1.

69. "George L. Russell, Jr.—Biography," Maryland State Archives, Annapolis, http://msa.maryland.gov/megafile/msa/speccol/sc3500/sc3520/011500/011548/html/11548bio.html; and Adam Speigel, "Linaweaver Named to Works Department," *Evening Sun*, December 19, 1967, B28.

70. David Ahearn, "Women Wield Little Power at City Hall," *News-American*, November 11, 1969, folder "Officials and Employees-Baltimore-1960-," MR, VF, EPFL; "BURHA Names 2 Project Managers," *Afro*, May 21, 1963, 20; Corinne E. Hammett, "Community School Idea Steams Ahead," *News-American*, November 24, 1968, folder "Education-Baltimore 1955–1969," MR, VF, EPFL; Marguerite Campbell to Maurice Harmon, May 26, 1971, folder "270 Department of Welfare (1)," box 486, 26, 9, BCA; "Mrs. Ferguson Named Service Coordinator," *Afro*, October 29, 1968, 7.

71. Bureau of the Census, *Census of Governments, 1962, 1967, 1972, Vol. 3, No. 2, Compendium of Public Employment* (Washington, DC: U.S. Government Printing Office, 1963, 1969, 1974).

72. Jerome W. Mondesire, "Rise in Black City Workers Slowed to 1.1%, Report Shows," *Sun*, April 18, 1974, C2.

73. Maryland Commission on Interracial Problems and Relations, "Survey of Non-White Employees, Summary Report on a Decade in Race Relations," [1964], Maryland State Archives, Annapolis.

74. "100 Stage March on SS Building at Woodlawn," *Afro*, May 28, 1964, 1. See also "Few Top $$ for Tan PO Employees," *Afro*, May 21, 1963, 1–2; Furman Templeton and Clarence Mitchell III, "An Open Letter to SSA Employees," *Afro*, May 23, 1964; Dr. Lillie May Jackson to Lyndon Johnson, August 20, 1963, and Robert M. Ball to Lillie May Jackson, August 24, 1963; Ralph Matthews Jr., "Can Social Security Clean House in 90 Days?" *News-American*, September 1963; all folder "PE-6-3-1 1963 Vc's," box 292, RG 47, Social Security Papers, National Archives, College Park, MD.

75. "At Social Security: Bob Johnson Thrives on Helping People in Need," *Afro*, March 18, 1969, 5.

76. Department of Commerce, *1970 Census of Population*, 212, 347.

77. Lynn C. Burbridge, "The Reliance of African American Women on Government and Third Sector Employment," *American Economic Review* 84, no. 2 (May 1994): 104.

Chapter 3

1. Jewell Chambers, "CAA Sets War on Poverty War Foes," *Afro*, October 24, 1967, 28; and "1,000 Rally in Protest of Cuts in Poverty War Funds," *Afro*, November 7, 1967, 24.

2. Stephen J. Lynton, 'Poverty Fighters Take Off for March on Capitol," *Sun*, November 13, 1967, C20, C9.

3. "Poverty Marchers Return, Assured Protest Was Noted," *Sun*, November 15, 1967, C6, C24.

4. Jewell Chambers, "Poverty Marchers Protesting Cuts," *Afro*, November 14, 1967, 1–2; and "Poverty Marchers Return."

5. Any Zanoni, "'Working on Many Levels': A History of Second Wave Feminism in Baltimore" (unpublished MA thesis, University of Maryland, Baltimore County, 2013).

6. Peter J. Koper, "Emerging Force: 'Student Power,'" *Afro*, May 4, 1968, 4; and Matthew Crenson, *Baltimore: A Political History* (Baltimore: Johns Hopkins University Press, 2017).

7. Quoted in Stetz, "War Stories."

8. Judd and Swanstrom, *City Politics*.

9. Fredrick P. McGehan, "City Agency on Nutrition Is Requested," *Sun*, October, 15, 1968, C7; and "City's Public Health Plans Called Confusing, Inefficient," *Sun*, December 13, 1968, C24, C12.

10. Health and Welfare Council of Baltimore Area, *Social Welfare Planning in Baltimore City*, 11.

11. Jon C. Teaford, *The Rough Road to Renaissance: Urban Revitalization in America, 1940–1985* (Baltimore: Johns Hopkins University Press, 1990), 183.

12. "Poverty War's Peril Described," *Sun*, November 29, 1967, C8.

13. "Mitchell, Parren James," History, Art, and Archives, U.S. House of Representatives, http://history.house.gov/People/Detail?id=18367.

14. Abrams, "Why Anti-Poverty," C2.

15. "CAA Goes for Tighter Control," *Afro*, November 6, 1965, 1, B6.

16. "CAA Goes for Tighter Control," 1.

17. Michael Ollove, Jerry Bembry, Abby Karp, David Simon, and Martin C. Evans, "Black in America: Moses Allen's Pride Inspires Progeny," *Sun*, April 7, 1988, A12.

18. R. B. Jones, "Urban Services Reassigns Family Services Workers," *Afro*, March 29, 1986, 2.

19. Quoted in Williams, *Politics of Public Housing*, 163–164.

20. CAA, "Community Action Agency of Baltimore City: Summary Program Report," January 1968, 15, folder "355 Community Action Agency (2)," box 497, 26, 9, BCA; Virginia Lee, Celestine Johnson, and Lloyd Taylor to Director, December 2, 1965, and Sanitation Committee to Jacob Bonnett, n.d., folder "107 CAC Community Action Poverty Program," box 377, 25, 9, BCA; and "1969 AFRO Honor Roll," *Afro*, March 7, 1970, 15.

21. "Mitchell Scores Neglect of Involvement of the Poor," *Afro*, May 14, 1968, 28.

22. Daniel Drosdoff, "Anti-Poverty Staff Runs Rally," *Sun*, February 7, 1967, C22.

23. Max Johnson, "Self-Help Program Wins Approval After Amendments," *Afro*, February 18, 1967, 14.

24. Johnson, "Self-Help Program," 14. In a bid to win Black votes, three white political candidates advertised their previous support for Self-Help Housing in the *Afro-American*. "Our Fight for Civil Rights *Is a Matter of Record!*" *Afro*, August 5, 1967, 8 (emphasis in the original).

25. Stetz, "War Stories."

26. Stephen J. Lynton, 'Model Cities Funds Called Insufficient by Miss Lazarus," *Sun*, May 21, 1968, C9; "Model Cities Feud Goes On," *Sun*, May 28, 1968, C14; and Stetz, "War Stories."

27. "'Awards' Meeting," *Afro*, April 16, 1955, 14; and Melody Holmes, "Pearl Cole Brackett, 83, Rose Through the School System," *Sun*, August 18, 2000, http://articles.baltimoresun.com/2000-08-18/news/0008180034_1_brackett-baltimore-school-baltimore-chapter.

28. Corinne E. Hammett, "Community School Idea Steams Ahead," *News-American*, November 24, 1968, folder "Education-Baltimore 1955–1969," MR, VF, EPFL.

29. Hammett, "Community School"; and James D. Dilts, "Guitar, Ping Pong, and a Dream: Baltimore's Community Schools Are a Focal Point for a Better Life," *Sun*, April 18, 1971, 6.

30. "Mrs. Ferguson Named Service Coordinator," *Afro*, October 29, 1968, 7; and Williams, *Politics of Public Housing*, 179.

31. Fred Rasmussen, "Slain Civil Rights Activist Mourned by Civic Leaders: Marguerite Campbell Died at Her Home," *Sun*, November 10, 1995, B1; and Raul Evans, "Mrs. Campbell Slated for 'Prime Plum Post,'" *Afro*, November 20, 1971, 21.

32. See, for example, Thomas D'Alesandro to Marguerite Campbell, March 20, 1968; Marguerite J. Campbell to William D. Schaefer, July 3, 1968; Marguerite J. Campbell to Louis Zawatzky, November 19, 1968; Marguerite Campbell to Herbert Katzenberger, October 3, 1969; and "The Enquirer Salutes . . ." *Maryland Enquirer*, December 1969, 1, all in folder "23. Marguerite Campbell Community Relations Specialist," box 450, 26, 9, BCA. See also Marguerite Campbell to Joseph Smith, March 31, 1970, folder "329 Black and White (3)," box 492, 26, 9, BCA.

33. Morton S. Baratz, "The Community Action Program in Baltimore City, 1965–1967," in Bachrach and Baratz, *Power and Poverty*, 194–195.

34. Lee Lassiter, "Welfare: Reform or Revolt—'Income, Dignity, Democracy,'" *News-American*, May 1, 1969, folder "Social Welfare," MR, VF, EPFL.

35. "Mothers on Welfare Tell of Their Troubles," *Afro*, September 6, 1966, 1, 23.

36. "Welfare Mothers Sleep-In at DPW," *Afro*, May 13, 1969, 13; and "Welfare Sit-In Protests Delays," *Sun*, May 13, 1969, C13.

37. B. T. Bentley, "Parren Mitchell: 'We Can Do More,'" *Evening Sun*, February 5, 1986, 15; Bradford Jacobs, "Mitchells of the Middle," *Evening Sun*, September 28, 1965, A20; Stephen J. Lynton, "Mitchell Announces Resignation," *Sun*, June 26, 1968, C7, C24; CAA, "Summary Program Report"; and Chambers, "Poverty Marchers Protesting Cuts."

38. Thomas J. D'Alesandro III to James F. Garrett, January 15, 1970, and Maurice A. Harmon to Thomas D'Alesandro III, February 3, 1970, folder "270 Department of Public Welfare (2)," box 486, 26, 9, BCA; and Stephen J. Lynton, "Mandel Urged to Increase Welfare Grants," *Sun*, March 11, 1969, C6.

39. Stephen J. Lynton, "Cost of War Cutting City Poverty Aid," *Sun*, May 3, 1967, C28.

40. Daniel Drosdoff, "Jobs Proposal, Legal Aid Voted," *Sun*, May 18, 1966, C30; and Stephen J. Lynton, "Housing Aid Urged on City," *Sun*, August 15, 1967, C14.

41. Helen Henry, "Welfare Boss Leads a Crowded Life," *Sun*, September 3, 1967, C1.

42. Henry, "Welfare Boss."

43. "2 Speak Out on Welfare," *Sun*, January 21, 1969, C13.

44. "Social Aides Ask 25% Raise," *Sun*, December 19, 1968, A17.

45. Lassiter, "Welfare: Reform or Revolt."

46. "Fredrick P. McGehan, "City Agency on Nutrition Is Requested," *Sun*, October, 15, 1968, C7; and "City's Public Health Plans Called Confusing, Inefficient," *Sun*, December 13, 1968, C24, C12.

47. McGehan, "City Agency," C7.

48. "W.S. Grants for Expectant Mothers," *Afro*, May 9, 1964, 15.

49. Bill Sykes to William Donald Schaefer, July 23, 1974, folder "Mayor's Office of Human Resources," box 410, 26, 9, BCA.

50. "Work-Incentive Cut Is Criticized," *Sun*, June 26, 1968, C24.

51. Harris Chaiklin, Richard Sterne, and Paul J. Ephross, "Community Organization and Services to Improve Family Living II" (Baltimore: University of Maryland School of Social Work Research Center, June 1969), frontispiece.

52. Baltimore City Department of Social Services, "An Evaluation of the Effect of Decentralization on the Delivery of Income Maintenance and Social Services," (Baltimore: Department of Social Services, November 1974), 17; and George J. Washnis, *Municipal Decentralization and Neighborhood Resources: Case Studies of Twelve Cities* (New York: Praeger, 1972).

53. Stetz, "War Stories."

54. Daniel Drosdoff, "Local Legal Aid Office Opens," *Sun*, February 1, 1967, C24; and "Bar Unit Told Poor Receive Justice Without Legal Aid," *Sun*, February 11, 1966, C6.

55. Drosdoff, "Local Legal Aid," C24.

56. Stephen J. Lynton, "Legal Aid Bureau to Offer Help to Indigent Groups," *Sun*, November 21, 1968, C10.

57. Helen Henry, "The Life and Times of a Welfare Worker," *Sun*, February 7, 1965, FY1.

58. Quoted in Martha J. Bailey and Sheldon Danziger, "Legacies of the War on Poverty," in *Legacies of the War on Poverty*, ed. Martha J. Bailey and Sheldon Danziger (New York: Russell Sage Foundation, 2013).

59. "Welfare Agency Lacks Medicare Staff," *Sun*, June 11, 1966, B20.

60. Whitney B. Smyth, "Druid Health Center Well Received," *Sun*, n.d., folder "Baltimore-Health Department-Druid Hill District," MR, VF, EPFL.

61. "City's Public Health Plans Called Confusing, Inefficient," *Sun*, December 13, 1968, C24, C12.

62. "The Meal the Mayor Wouldn't Eat," July 15, 1966, folder "Poverty/Rights Action Center: The Birth of a Movement," box 19, 27, 10, National Council of Negro Women Papers, Bethune House, Washington, DC.

63. "The Meal," NCNW Papers; Stetz, "War Stories"; and Williams, *Politics of Public Housing*.

64. Health and Welfare Council of the Baltimore Area, *Social Welfare Planning in Baltimore City*; CAA, "Summary Program Report."

65. James R. Conant, "Slum 'Hangover' Hampers Life in Housing Areas," *Evening Sun*, May 26, 1962, A1, A6; "Council Speeds Bill for Riot Overtime Pay," *Sun*, May 21, 1968, C8; CAA, "Summary Program Report," 5–6; and Williams, *Politics of Public Housing*, 163.

66. "Poor Deplore Slum Services," *Sun*, December 15, 1967, C14.

67. Community Action Agency, "Community Action Agency," folder "355 Community Action Agency (2)," box 497, 26, 9, BCA.

68. On residents' concerns about sanitation and housing, see Marguerite J. Campbell to William D. Schaefer, July 3, 1968, folder "23. Marguerite Campbell Community Relations Specialist," box 450, 26, 9, BCA; "Comment: Public Relations (Social Welfare Style) Can Have Devastating By-Products," *CRC Newsletter*, August–September 1969, 4, folder "362 Community Relations Commission (2)," box 498, 26, 9, BCA; and Sanitation Committee to Jacob Bonnett, n.d., folder "107 CAC Community Action Anti-Poverty Program (6)," box 377, 25, 9, BCA.

69. Annelise Orleck, *Storming Caesars Palace: How Black Mothers Fought Their Own War on Poverty* (Boston: Beacon, 2005).

Chapter 4

1. Quoted in Michael Honey, *Going Down Jericho Road* (New York: W. W. Norton, 2008), 298.

2. "City Workers Plan to Take Strike Vote," *Sun*, September 3, 1968, C18.

3. "City Workers Plan."

4. Windham, *Knocking on Labor's Door*; and Eileen Boris and Jennifer Klein, *Caring for America: Home Healthcare Workers in the Shadow of the Welfare State* (New York: Oxford University Press, 2015).

5. Calvin L. Fleet to Howard W. Jackson, September 2, 1938, folder "D-1-1137 (2)," box 234, 20, 9, BCA.

6. Joseph E. Slater, *Public Workers: Government Employee Unions, the Law, and the State, 1900–1962* (Ithaca, NY: IRL, 2004).

7. "Wasted Experience," *Sun*, February 10, 1960, 16.

8. Bob Hastings to Tom Morgan, August 11, 1959, folder "12 Organizing by State, Maryland, August 1957–October 1961," box 85, AFSCME President Zander Collection, Archives of Labor and Urban Affairs, Walter P. Reuther Library, Wayne State University Detroit (hereafter Reuther); Henry L. Trewhitt, "Union on Move into State Jobs," *Sun*, January 17, 1961, 36; William MacNeil, "A Union's Role in the Federal Government," *Oasis* 20, no. 6, (June 1960): 12; and John Walsh, *Labor Struggles in the Post Office: From Selective Lobbying to Collective Bargaining* (Armonk, NY: M. E. Sharpe, 1992).

9. "City Employees—Know Your CMEA," *Hall Light*, June 1961, 1; and "Kowzan Resents 'Outside' Union," *Sun*, January 22, 1960, 40.

10. "Wars Have Always Benefited Colored, Templeton Tells Municipal Employees," *Afro*, April 25, 1942, 10; and Elizabeth Reitze to Theodore McKeldin, November 17, 1964, folder "291 Pension Study Committee," box 409, 25, 9, BCA.

11. "Revision of CMEA By-Laws," *Hall Light* (September 1954): 1–2; and "Hearing of Importance to Membership," *Hall Light*, April 1960, 1.

12. "Firemen's Union Seen as Biased," *Sun*, May 31, 1960, 30; "Firemen Admitted to Union Protest Back-Dues Penalty," *Afro*, July 30, 1960, 1, 3; and "Urban Unit Backs Union Bid to Negro Firefighters," *Morning Sun*, August 2, 1960, 19.

13. "'We Won't Pay It': Firemen Reject $25 Penalty," *Afro*, August 6, 1960, 1–2; "D.C. Parley Hears Charges of Bias in City Fire Union," *Sun*, February 19, 1961, 20; and Frank Somerville, "Firefighters in Agreement," *Sun*, May 9, 1961, 38.

14. Raymond Clarke, interview with Jane Berger, Baltimore, April 18, 2007; "Maryland AFSCME Salute to Raymond H. Clarke," May 25, 1976, folder "12 Maryland Council No. 67 1976," box 129, AFSCME Collection President Wurf (hereafter Wurf); and Adam K. Jenkins, "Arena Players Score Hit in Satire/Drama," *Afro*, May 9, 1962, 15.

15. "P. J. Ciampa: AFSMCE Loses a Leader," *Public Employee* (October 1981): 7; Ernest Crofoot, interview with Jane Berger, Baltimore, July 8, 2006.

16. Richard Frank, "City Union Asks $4 Million in Hike, Benefits," *Evening Sun*, June 22, 1960, 62; "Union Asks City Employee Plan," *Sun*, December 17, 1962, 26; John Calvert (President Local 44) to Theodore McKeldin, May 9, 1963, and June 18, 1963, folder "434 Unions," box 439, 25, 9, BCA; AFSCME, AFL-CIO Local 44, "Proposal Concerning Employee Relations in Baltimore, Md.," September 4, 1964, folder "AFSCME," MR, VF, EPFL; P. J. Ciampa to Theodore R. McKeldin, January 14, 1965, folder "293 Personnel Policy and Salary Advisory Committee (3)," box 409, 25, 9, BCA; "City, County Employees Eye Strikes," *News-American*, May 23, 1966; "City Workers Want Pay Talks," *Sun*, July 1, 1966, C15; and Letter to Theodore McKeldin from Raymond Clarke and Ernest Crofoot, September 30, 1966, folder "Unions," box 376, 25, 9, BCA.

17. Crofoot, interview with Berger.

18. Personnel Policy and Salary Advisory Board, "News Release," September 7, 1964, folder "293 Personnel Policy and Salary Advisory Committee," box 409, 25, 9, BCA.

19. Joseph C. Goulden, *Jerry Wurf: Labor's Last Angry Man* (New York: Atheneum, 1982); William Serrin, "A Leader for the Little Guy," *New York Times*, September 12, 1982, section 7, 14; Joseph Hower, "Jerry Wurf, the Rise of AFSMCE, and the Fate of Labor Liberalism, 1947–1981" (PhD dissertation, Georgetown University, 2013); and "William Lucy," NAACP website, http://www.naacp.org/preview/pages/board-member-william-lucy.

20. See, for example, "More Planning Needed to Restore Our Cities," *Public Employee* (January 1968): 10; Tom Castor, "SCME Probes Welfare Plans," *Public Employee* (November 1969): 9;

and Hower, "Jerry Wurf." See also Joseph McCartin, "Bringing the State's Workers In: Time to Rectify an Imbalanced U.S. Labor History," *Labor History* 47, no. 1 (February 2006): 73–94.

21. David C. Goeller, "School Wage Boost Urged," *Sun*, July 12, 1965, S20.

22. Gerald Clark, "Teachers Militant," *Sun*, June 30, 1964, 14; and Marjorie Murphy, *Blackboard Unions: The AFT and the NEA, 1900–1980* (Ithaca, NY: Cornell University Press, 1992).

23. Lowell E. Sunderland, "Teachers Offer School Program," *Sun*, July 29, 1965, 46, 30.

24. Gene Oishi, "C.O.R.E., Teachers Union Opening Freedom School," *Sun*, July 15, 1966, C12; Oishi, "Union to Aid in Boycott by Teachers," *Sun*, January 14, 1967, B18; Rolland Dewing, "The American Federation of Teachers and Desegregation," *Journal of Negro Education* 42, no. 1 (Winter 1973), 79–92; and Jon Hale, *Freedom Schools: Student Activists in the Mississippi Civil Rights Movement* (New York: Columbia University Press, 2018), 87–88.

25. Public School Teachers Association, "Sanctions in Action," [1966], folder "Education-Baltimore 1955–1969," MR, VF, EPFL; and George Rodgers, "What's Behind School Row?" *Evening Sun*, January 16, 1967, B28.

26. Baltimore Department of Education, "Press Release Accompanying Its Response," November 19, 1967, folder "Education-Baltimore 1955–1969," MR, VF, EPFL.

27. Department of Education, "Press Release."

28. "A Community of Interests," *Oasis* 25, no. 6 (June 1965): 8.

29. "Here and There," *Oasis* 21, no. 3 (March 1961): 27; "Two Years Later," *Oasis* 24, no. 6 (June 1964): 11–13; "Promotion Plan Agreement Signed," *Government Standard* (July 31, 1964): 1; and "Postal Unions Get Formal Recognition," *Afro*, April 16, 1963, 5.

30. Kenneth Rabben, "Teachers' Union Demands Election to Choose Local 340 or NEA," *News-American*, December 2, 1966, folder "Jan.–Mar. 1967," box 139, series IV, Commission on Government Efficiency and Economy (hereafter CGEE), University of Baltimore Special Collections and Archives (hereafter UB); Gene Oishi, "Union Irked by Decision on Arrest," *Sun*, May 11, 1967, 1; Kay Mills, "'Joke of the Year,' Unionist Says of School Agreement," *Sun*, December 7, 1967, C7; and "Crosby Outlines BTU Goals," *News-American*, August 25, 1968, folder "1968," box 139, series IV, CGEE, UB.

31. "State Unionists Push Labor Law," *Sun*, January 30, 1968, C6; Bentley Orrick, "Della Pushes for a Public Strike Right," *Sun*, February 28, 1968, C22; and Betty Miller, "Defeat in Maryland, Prelude to Victory," *Public Employee* (February 1968): 11.

32. Harold Shaw, interview with Jane Berger, Baltimore, August 9, 2006.

33. Kathy Kraus, "His Job: Grappling with City Labor Problems," *News-American*, July 11, 1968, folder "1968," box 139, IV, CGEE, UB.

34. Laurie B. Green, "Race, Gender and Labor in 1960s Memphis: 'I AM A MAN' and the Meaning of Freedom," *Journal of Urban History* 30, no. 3 (2005): 465–489; and Laurie B. Green, *Plantation Mentality* (Chapel Hill: University of North Carolina Press, 2014). See also Honey, *Jericho Road*.

35. Honey, *Jericho Road*.

36. Quoted in John Nichols, "MLK: 'Our Struggle Is for Genuine Equality, Which Means Economic Equality,'" *Nation*, January 29, 2014, https://www.thenation.com/article/mlk-our-struggle-genuine-equality-which-means-economic-equality/.

37. Green, *Plantation Mentality*; and Honey, *Jericho Road*.

38. Peter B. Levy, "The Dream Deferred: The Assassination of Martin Luther King, Jr., and the Holy Week Uprisings of 1968," in *Baltimore '68*, ed. Jessica I. Elfenbein, Thomas L. Hollowak, and Elizabeth M. Nix (Philadelphia: Temple University Press, 2011), 3–25; and Mayor

Thomas D'Alesandro III, Fraser Smith, interviewer, May 2007, Baltimore 68: Riots and Rebirth Collection, University of Baltimore, http://archives.ubalt.edu/bsr/oral-histories/transcripts/dalesandro.pdf.

39. Quoted in Jonna McKone and Sheilah Kast, "Coretta Scott King's Visit to Baltimore for Economic Justice," *Maryland Morning*, WYPR, aired January 19, 2005, http://www.wypr.org/post/coretta-scott-kings-visit-baltimore-economic-justice.

40. "Strike Averted," *Sun*, December 10, 1969, 20A; and Greg Michael, "'Union Power, Soul Power': Unionizing Johns Hopkins University Hospital, 1959–1974," *Labor History* 5, no. 2 (1996): 28–66.

41. Kraus, "His Job."

42. Robert A. Erlandson, "Street, Sewer Workers Join Trash Strike," *Sun*, September 6, 1968, A1.

43. "Not to Be Tolerated," *Sun*, September 4, 1968, A10.

44. Erlandson, "Street, Sewer Workers."

45. Stephen J. Lynton, "Rights Heads Back Strike," *Sun*, September 7, 1968, A9.

46. "Strike Settlement," *Sun*, September 10, 1968, A12; "Mayor Will Sign Labor Bill Today," *Sun*, September 30, 1968, C20, C10; and "Baltimore Local 44 Sweeps Four Elections for 10,000," *Public Employee* (December 1968): 10.

47. "City's Union Voting Is Led by Local 44," *Sun*, November 27, 1968, C24; "Local 44 Wins Public Works," *Evening Sun*, November 28, 1968, D3; John B. O'Donnell Jr., "Local 44 Picked as Agent in School Workers' Election," *Sun*, December 11, 1969, C28.

48. Windham, *Knocking on Labor's Door*; Dorothy Sue Cobble, *The Other Women's Movement: Workplace Justice and Social Rights in Modern America* (Princeton, NJ: Princeton University Press, 2005); and Boris and Klein, *Caring for America*.

49. Cowie, *Stayin' Alive*.

50. Sugrue, *Origins of the Urban Crisis*.

51. Velsa M. Weaver, "Frontlash: Race and the Development of Punitive Crime Policy," *Studies in American Political Development* 21, no. 2 (Fall 2007): 230–265; and Hinton, *From the War on Poverty*, 19.

52. Hinton, *From the War on Poverty*, 11–26; Michael Lewis, "Easy Answers to Curb Crime Rates Not Available, Officials Report," *Evening Sun*, February 13, 1968, C24, C3; and Oswald Johnston, "FBI Report Show Record Rise in Crime," *Sun*, March 15, 1968, A6.

53. Lewis, "Easy Answers"; and Alan Lupo, "Boston Model Cities Tests Self-Government," *Sun*, December 29, 1968, K3.

54. Quoted in Weaver, "Frontlash," 254.

55. Hinton, *From the War on Poverty*, 63–133.

56. Durr, *Behind the Backlash*; and Antero Pietila, *Not in My Neighborhood: How Bigotry Shaped a Great American City* (Chicago: Ivan R. Dee, 2010).

57. Harry B. How Jr. to Theodore McKeldin, July 27, 1967, folder "111 Concentrated Employment Program (2)," box 378, 25, 9, BCA.

58. Kathy Kraus, "City Payroll up 1,000 Yearly: Adding New Employees as 3,000 Move Out," *News-American*, December 4, 1967, folder "Officials and Employees-Baltimore-1960-," MR, VF, EPFL. See also Commission on Governmental Efficiency and Economy, "Municipal Payroll Growth," June 1965, folder "Officials and Employees-Baltimore-1960-," MR, VF, EPFL.

59. "George Mahoney, 87, Maryland Candidate," *New York Times*, March 21, 1989, B8.

60. Quoted in Levy, "Dream Deferred," 16.

61. Quoted in Alex Csicsek, "Spiro T. Agnew and the Burning of Baltimore," in Elfenbein, Hollowak, and Nix, eds., *Baltimore '68*, 73.

62. "Leaders Hit Agnew's Nerve," *Afro*, April 13, 1968, 1.

63. Quoted in Csicsek, "Spiro T. Agnew," 76.

64. Quoted in Csicsek, "Spiro T. Agnew," 76.

65. "Agnew Insults Leaders," *Afro*, April 13, 1986, 1.

66. "All About, Ted Baby," *Afro*, April 13, 1968, 4.

67. "Agnew Says Strikers Err," *Sun*, September 8, 1968, 1.

68. "An Ill-Considered Strike," *News-American*, September 6, 1968, folder "1968," box 139, IV, CGEE, UB.

69. Stephen J. Lynton, "Resignation Announced by Mitchell," *Sun*, June 26, 1968, C24, C7.

70. Robert A. Erlandson, "Who Was the Real Target of the Council's Vote—the Mayor or Carter?" *Sun*, October 6, 1968, K1.

71. Erlandson, "Who Was the Real Target?"

72. Robert A. Erlandson, "Carter Appointment as Antipoverty Chief Rejected by Council," *Sun*, October 1, 1968, C28, C11; and "Council Kills Carter Appointment to CAA Post," *Afro*, October 1, 1968, 1.

73. Thomas D'Alesandro to Mrs. Mildred Dickerson, October 22, 1968, and "Statement by the Staff of the Community Action Agency on the Resignation of the Twelve (12) Members," n.d., folder "598 Community Action Agency Resignations," box 530, 26, 9, BCA.

74. Erlandson, "Carter Appointment."

75. "Mayor Opens New Efforts for Carter," *Sun*, October 2, 1968, C24.

76. "Mayor Opens New Efforts."

77. "Carter Describes Council as Controlled by 'Racists,'" *Sun*, October 11, 1968, C8.

78. "Mayor Opens New Efforts."

79. "Preface," in Elfenbein, Hollowak, and Nix, eds., *Baltimore '68*, xvii; and Durr, *Behind the Backlash*.

Chapter 5

1. Fred Barbash, "Welfare Workers Tackle a System That Failed Them," *Sun*, August 10, 1971, C16.

2. Barbash, "Welfare Workers."

3. Quoted in Sharon Perlman Krefetz, *Welfare Policy Making and City Politics* (New York: Praeger, 1976), 119.

4. Barbash, "Welfare Workers."

5. "Social Workers Union to Investigate Assaults," *Sun*, September 9, 1972, B6; and "Many Children from City Expected at Welfare Protest," *Sun*, March 22, 1972, A9.

6. Fred Barbash, "Analysis: Welfare Mess Lies in Faulty Paper-Pushings, Miscast Workers," *Sun*, November 12, 1971, C9.

7. "City Official Lashes Job Training Freeze," *Evening Sun*, January 6, 1973, 18.

8. Urban Services Agency, "Baltimore Model Cities Final Evaluation Report 1968–1974," no folder, box 485, SP, 9, BCA; "A Mayor Looks at Model Cities," n.d., folder "Model Cities Agency," box 151, SP, 9, BCA; and Stetz, "War Stories."

9. "Model City Plan Ready for Action," *Afro*, December 3, 1968, 26; Albert Williams to Mayor Schaefer et al., October 27, 1972, folder "Model Cities Agency," box 151, SP, 9, BCA; Charles R. Kochakian, "Model Cities Invests in Inner-City Children," *Sun*, November 4, 1970,

A11; Urban Services Agency, "Baltimore Model Cities Report"; and Jimmy Carter, "A Nomination of William G. Sykes to Be Peace Corps Deputy Director," September 19, 1979, American Presidency Project, University of California, Santa Barbara, https://www.presidency.ucsb.edu/documents/peace-corps-nomination-william-g-sykes-be-deputy-director.

10. Bill Sykes to William Donald Schaefer, July 23, 1974, folder "Mayor's Office of Human Resources," box 410, SP, 9, BCA.

11. Isaac Rehert, "Free Care Isn't Just for Poor," *Sun*, May 11, 1976, B1.

12. Jerome W. Mondesire, "State Welfare Officials Call New Workfare Laws 'Unworkable,'" *Sun*, December 28, 1972, A11.

13. Fred Barbash, "Social Work Made More Social," *Sun*, March 15, 1971, C14.

14. Barbash, "Social Work."

15. Lisa Levenstein, *Movement Without Marches: African American Women and the Politics of Poverty in Postwar Philadelphia* (Chapel Hill: University of North Carolina Press, 2010).

16. Kim Phillips-Fein, *Invisible Hands: The Businessmen's Crusade Against the New Deal* (New York: Norton, 2010); Lisa McGirr, *Suburban Warriors: The Origins of the New American Right* (Princeton, NJ: Princeton University Press, 2001); Jonathan Schoenwald, *A Time for Choosing: The Rise of Modern American Conservatism* (New York: Oxford University Press, 2001).

17. Quoted in Durr, *Behind the Backlash*, 181. See also Shelton, *Teacher Strike!*

18. See, for example, Robert Self, *American Babylon: Race and the Struggle for Postwar Oakland* (Princeton, NJ: Princeton University Press, 2003); Dan Carter, *The Politics of Rage: George Wallace, the Origins of the New Conservatism, and the Transformation of American Politics*, 2nd ed. (Baton Rouge: Louisiana State University Press, 2000); Thomas Edsall and Mary D. Edsall, *Chain Reaction: The Impact of Race, Rights, and Taxes on American Politics* (New York: Norton, 1992); and Rick Perlstein, *Nixonland: The Rise of a President and the Fracturing of America* (New York: Scribner, 2009).

19. Quoted in Walker Newell, "The Legacy of Nixon, Reagan and Horton: How the Tough on Crime Movement Enabled a New Regime of Race-Influenced Employment Discrimination," *Berkeley Journal of African American Law and Policy* 15, no. 1 (January 2013): 15.

20. [Richard Nixon], "Richard Nixon Acceptance Speech," aired August 8, 1968, C-SPAN, https://www.c-span.org/video/?4022-2/richard-nixon-1968-acceptance-speech.

21. CBS News, *Face the Nation*, aired October 27, 1968, https://www.youtube.com/watch?v=5CHELZAZW18.

22. Nixon, "Acceptance Speech."

23. López, *Dog Whistle Politics*. See also Carter, *Politics of Rage*; Perlstein, *Nixonland*; and Alexander, *New Jim Crow*, 40–48.

24. Sugrue, *Origins of the Urban Crisis*.

25. C. Fraser Smith, *William Donald Schaefer: A Political Biography* (Baltimore: Johns Hopkins University Press, 1999); Welcome, *Verda Welcome*; Kevin O'Keeffe, *Baltimore Politics 1971-1986: The Schaefer Years and the Struggle for Succession* (Washington, DC: Georgetown University Press, 1986); G. James Fleming, *Baltimore's Failure to Elect a Black Mayor in 1971* (Washington, DC: Joint Center for Political Studies, 1972).

26. Smith, *William Donald Schaefer*; Welcome, *Verda Welcome*; and Fleming, *Baltimore's Failure*.

27. Fleming, *Baltimore's Failure*.

28. Fleming, *Baltimore's Failure*.

29. Smith, *William Donald Schaefer*.

30. Marion Orr, "Baltimore: The Limits of Mayoral Control," in *Mayors in the Middle: Politics, Race and Mayoral Control of Urban Schools*, ed. Jeffrey R. Henig and Wilbur C. Rich (Princeton, NJ: Princeton University Press, 2004), 27–58; and Smith, *William Donald Schaefer*.

31. Tom Chalkley, "The City That Builds," *City Paper*, November 12, 2003; and Editorial, "Sun Endorsements for Schaefer, Clarke, Douglass," *Sun*, August 28, 1983, K6.

32. "Mayor Looks at Model Cities," BCA.

33. Between 1950 and 1977, the median income of the city's residents fell from 98 percent to 68 percent of the median suburban income. Callcott, *Negro in Maryland Politics*, 84; United States Commission on Civil Rights, United States Commission on Civil Rights, "Staff Report: Demographic, Economic, Social and Political Characteristics of Baltimore City and Baltimore County," August 1970, B9, folder "348. Civil Rights," box 495, SP, 9, BCA; and "Statement of Hon. William Donald Schaefer, Mayor of Baltimore, MD," in *Revenue Sharing: Hearings Before the Committee on Finance, United States Senate* (Washington, DC: U.S. Government Printing Office, 1972), 297–300.

34. Smith, *William Donald Schaefer*.

35. John Ruggie, "International Regimes, Transactions and Change: Embedded Liberalism in the Postwar Order," *International Organization* 36, no. 2 (Spring 1982): 379–415.

36. Kevin Boyle, "The Price of Peace: Vietnam, the Pound, and the Crisis of American Empire," *Diplomatic History* 27, no. 1 (January 2003): 37–72; Michael Mastanduno, "System Maker and Privilege Taker: U.S. Power and the International Political Economy," *World Politics* 61, no. 1 (January 2009): 121–154; Eric Helleiner, *States and the Reemergence of Global Finance: From Bretton Woods to the 1990s* (Ithaca, NY: Cornell University Press, 1994); and Joanne Gowa, *Closing the Gold Window* (Ithaca, NY: Cornell University Press, 1983).

37. Joseph C. Mills, "The International Monetary Crisis and Its Implications for Malawi," *Society of Malawi Journal* 25, no. 1 (January 1972): 26.

38. David Calleo, *The Imperious Economy* (Cambridge, MA: Harvard University Press, 1982); and Peter Gowan, *The Global Gamble: Washington's Faustian Bid for World Dominance* (London: Verso, 1999).

39. David Harvey, *A Brief History of Neoliberalism* (New York: Oxford University Press, 2005); Ronald Cox and Daniel Skidmore-Hess, *U.S. Politics and the Global Economy: Corporate Power, Conservative Shift* (Boulder, CO: Lynne Rienner, 1999); and Robert W. Burchell et al., *The New Reality of Municipal Finance: The Rise and Fall of the Intergovernmental City* (New Brunswick, NJ: Center for Urban Policy Research, Rutgers University, 1984), 236–239.

40. Burchell, *New Reality*, 236–239; John Woodruff, "Schaefer Reviews Plan to Lay Off City Employees," *Sun*, December 16, 1974, C14; Levine, "Downtown Redevelopment," 108; and Charles Levine, Irene Rubin, and George Wolohojian, *The Politics of Retrenchment: How Local Governments Manage Fiscal Stress* (Beverly Hills, CA: Sage, 1981), 134.

41. Julian Brash, "Invoking Fiscal Crisis," *Social Text* 21 (2003): 59–83.

42. Brash, "Invoking Fiscal Crisis"; Joshua B. Freeman, *Working Class New York* (New York: New Press, 2000); and Kim Phillips-Fein, *Fear City: New York's Fiscal Crisis and the Rise of Austerity Politics* (New York: Metropolitan, 2017).

43. Janet Hoffman to the President and Members of the Baltimore City Council, December 9, 1975, folder "New York City Crisis," box 283, SP, BCA; and Editorial, "One Crisis Baltimore Can Sit Out," *Sun*, October 16, 1975, A18.

44. "Baltimore: New Breed of City," *Forbes*, September 16, 1976, advertisement, p. 8.

45. Mollenkopf, *Contested City*; Katharyne Mitchell and Katherine Beckett, "Securing the Global City: Crime, Consulting, Risk, and Ratings in the Production of Urban Space," *Indiana Journal of Global Legal Studies* 15, no. 1 (Winter 2008): 75–99; Timothy J. Sinclair, "Between State and Market: Hegemony and Institutions of Collective Action Under Conditions of Capital Mobility," *Policy Science* 27 (1994): 447–446; and Daniel Rubinfelds, "Credit Ratings and the Market for General Obligation Municipal Bonds," *National Tax Journal* 26, no. 1 (March 1973): 17–27.

46. Peter S. Fisher, "Corporate Tax Incentives: The American Version of Industrial Policy," *Journal of Economic Issues* 19, no. 1 (March 1985): 1–19.

47. Fisher, "Corporate Tax Incentives"; and Robert O. Self, "Californian's Industrial Garden: Oakland and the East Bay in the Age of Deindustrialization," in *Beyond the Ruins: The Meanings of Deindustrialization*, ed. Jefferson Cowie and Joseph Heathcott (Ithaca, NY: Cornell University Press, 2003), 159–180.

Chapter 6

1. Weldon Wallace, "The Trouble with Welfare Is That There's Perpetual Crisis," *Sun*, July 29, 1974, B1.

2. "Maude Harvey, First Black Woman to Head Social Services, Dies," *Sun*, July 6, 1981, A8.

3. Wallace, "Trouble with Welfare."

4. See, for example, Maude Harvey to Richard A. Batterton, September 9, 1976, folder "Human Resources Childcare," box 251, SP, 9, BCA; Maude Harvey to Elizabeth Hight, January 30, 1975, folder "Social Services 1973–1975," box 160, SP, 9, BCA; and Quenton Lawson to Maude S. Harvey, March 8, 1976, folder "Social Services 1976," box 437, SP, 9, BCA.

5. Jerome W. Mondesire, "City Welfare Critics' Statistics Faulty," *Sun*, April 5, 1974, D4.

6. "Transcript of President's State of the Union Message to Joint Session of Congress," *New York Times*, January 23, 1971, 12; and Timothy Conlan, *From New Federalism to Devolution: Twenty-Five Years of Intergovernmental Reform* (Washington, DC: Brookings Institution, 1998).

7. "Transcript," 12. Also on New Federalism, see Mark Blyth, *Great Transformations: Economic Ideas and Institutional Change in the Twentieth Century* (Cambridge: Cambridge University Press, 2002).

8. "Transcript," 12.

9. *Revenue Sharing: Hearings Before the Committee on Finance, United States Senate* (Washington, DC: U.S. Government Printing Office, 1972). See also Conlan, *From New Federalism*; Judd and Swanstrom, *City Politics*; Patrick Larkey, *Evaluating Public Programs: The Impact of General Revenue Sharing on Municipal Government* (Princeton, NJ: Princeton University Press, 1979); Bruce Wallin, *From Revenue Sharing to Deficit Sharing: General Revenue Sharing and Cities* (Washington, DC: Georgetown University Press, 1998); and Deil Wright, "Policy Shifts in the Politics and Administration of Intergovernmental Relations, 1930s–1990s," *Annals of the American Academy of Political and Social Science* 509, no. 1 (May 1990): 60–72.

10. "Wilkins Speaks: Nixon's Devastating Plan," *Afro*, November 19, 1968, 4. See also Whitney Young, "To Be Equal: War on Poverty Fights for Life," *Afro*, March 4, 1969, 4; Young, "'Black Capitalism' No Poverty Cure," *Afro*, April 29, 1969, 30.

11. *Hearings Before the Committee on Ways and Means House of Representatives* (Washington: DC: U.S. Government Printing Office, June 1971), 218.

12. Judd and Swanstrom, *City Politics*.

13. "Mitchell Scores Nixon's Plan," *Sun*, February 15, 1971, C16.

14. "Statement of Jerry Wurf," in *Revenue Sharing: Hearings Before the Committee on Finance*, 189–209.

15. Advisory Commission on Intergovernmental Relations, *Special Revenue Sharing: An Analysis of the Administration's Grant Consolidation Proposals* (Washington, DC: United States Advisory Commission on Intergovernmental Relations, 1971); Conlan, *From New Federalism*; and Judd and Swanstrom, *City Politics*.

16. Weaver, "Frontlash"; and Katznelson, *When Affirmative Action Was White*.

17. Donald Haider, "Intergovernmental Redirection," *Annals of the American Academy of Political and Social Science* 466, no. 1 (March 1983): 165–178.

18. Judd and Swanstrom, *City Politics*, 271–286; Deil Wright, "Revenue Sharing and Structural Features of American Federalism, 1975," *Annals of the American Academy of Political and Social Science* 419 (May 1975): 100–119; Wright, "Policy Shifts," 60–72; and Wallin, *From Revenue Sharing*.

19. Department of the Treasury, *Revenue Sharing and Civil Rights* (Washington, DC: Treasury Department, [1975]) ii.

20. Deil Wright et al., *Assessing the Impacts of General Revenue Sharing in the Fifty States: A Survey of State Administrators* (Chapel Hill: University of North Carolina, 1975). GRS did give agency administrators more flexibility in organizing their programming, which many viewed positively. Wright, "General Revenue Sharing and Federalism."

21. Levine, Rubin, and Wolohojian, *Politics of Retrenchment*, 122.

22. "Pressman Says Ellis's Charge 'Fabricated,'" *Sun*, June 26, 1970, C2.

23. Stetz, "War Stories."

24. Center for Governmental Studies, "Neighborhood Decentralization," November 1973, 4–6, folder "Urban Services CAA 1972–1973," box 131, SP, 9, BCA.

25. Center for Governmental Studies, "Neighborhood Decentralization"; and Stetz, "War Stories."

26. Albert Williams to Mayor Schaefer et al., October 27, 1972, folder "Model Cities Agency," box 151, SP, 9, BCA; Urban Services Agency, "Baltimore Model Cities Final Evaluation Report 1968–1974," no folder, box 485, SP, 9, BCA; and Stetz, "War Stories."

27. William G. Sykes to Model Cities Project Directors, January 5, 1972, folder "Model Cities Agency," box 151, SP, 9, BCA.

28. William G. Sykes to All Staff Members, January 31, 1973, folder "Model Cities Agency," box 151, SP, 9, BCA.

29. F. Parachini Jr. to William Donald Schaefer, March 12, 1974, and Lenwood M. Ivey to William Donald Schaefer, March 20, 1974, folder "Model Cities/Community Action Agency 1974 +," box 151, SP, 9, BCA.

30. Mark K. Joseph to William Donald Schaefer, March 9, 1973, folder "Model Cities/CAA Merger 1972–1973," box 188, SP, 9, BCA.

31. William Donald Schaefer to Richard J. Daley, April 17, 1972; R. C. Embry Jr. to William Donald Schaefer, April 4, 1973; and Joseph to Schaefer, all folder "Model Cities Agency," box 151, SP, 9, BCA.

32. Evelyn T. Burrell, oral history, interviewed by Susan Conwell, June 25, 1976, McKeldin-Jackson Project, MHS.

33. Baltimore City Health Department (hereafter BCHD), "Baltimore Health News," January–February 1974, 118, available at the Baltimore Department of Legislative Reference.

34. BCHD, "Baltimore Health News," 118.

35. BCHD, "Baltimore Health News," 106.
36. BCHD, "Baltimore Health News," 106.
37. BCHD, "Baltimore Health News," 118; and Center for Governmental Studies, "Neighborhood Decentralization."
38. Howell Baum, *Brown in Baltimore: School Desegregation and the Limits of Liberalism* (Ithaca, NY: Cornell University Press, 2010), 147; Orr, "Baltimore: Limits of Mayoral Control," 29; Richard Benn Cramer, "Patterson's Status Unsure Following Vote," *Sun*, August 10, 1974, A1, A4; and John O'Donnell, "Patterson Fight: Who Controls the School Money?" *Evening Sun*, August 20, 1974, A10.
39. Smith, *William Donald Schaefer*, 136.
40. Kenneth Wong, *City Choices: Education and Housing* (Albany: State University of New York Press, 1990), 115.
41. "Welfare Proposal Evokes Criticism," *Sun*, March 24, 1973, B6.
42. Ben Davis, "What's a Social Worker to Do Now That the Money's Gone?" *Sun*, March 18, 1973, K3.
43. Barbara Blum, "City Serves 68% of Maryland's Welfare Cases," *News-American*, September 2, 1970, folder "Social Welfare-Baltimore-Finance," MR, VF, EPFL.
44. Jerome W. Mondesire, "State Welfare Officials Call New Workfare Laws 'Unworkable,'" *Sun*, December 28, 1972, A11.
45. Maurice A. Harmon to Janet L. Hoffmann, October 19, 1972, folder "Mayor's Office Liaison with General Assembly 1972–1973 Correspondence," box 145, SP, 9, BCA.
46. Maryland Conference of Social Workers, "The Maryland Conference of Social Workers Opposes the Takeover . . . ," and "The Relationship Between the Baltimore City Department of Social Services and the Maryland State Department of Employment and Social Services," March 22, 1973, folder "Social Services Takeover—Baltimore City Department of Social Services," box 160, SP, 9, BCA.
47. Maurice A. Harmon to William Donald Schaefer, January 31, 1973, folder "Social Services 12/71–12/73," box 160, SP, 9, BCA.
48. Quoted in Hinton, *From the War on Poverty*, 138.
49. Hinton, *From the War on Poverty*, 134–138.
50. Charles Whiteford, "Pomerleau Says Public Must Help," *Sun*, May 29, 1972, C7.
51. Patrick Gilbert, "1975 Is Seen as Pivotal Year in City Use of Heroin," *Sun*, May 9, 1975, C1.
52. Hinton, *From the War on Poverty*, 159–160; "City Gets $1.8 Million in U.S. Anti-Crime Aid," *Sun*, October 27, 1972, A11; David Ettling and Roger Twigg, "Pomerleau's Proud Progress," *Sun*, July 28, 1974, K1; and "Schaefer Defends Use of Federal Funds Law," *Sun*, March 12, 1976, C4.
53. Paul Jablow, "Layoff Worries Union Leaders," *Sun*, April 17, 1972, C18; Jeff Valentine, "Give Up Pay Hikes or Face Layoffs, City's Labor Chief Warns Unions," *Evening Sun*, May 4, 1977, A1; Douglas Watson and Curtis Riddle, "Schaefer Foresees Layoffs," *Sun*, March 2, 1978, D1; and Memo to Jerry Wurf from Donald Wasserman, February 15, 1979, folder "22 Maryland General Correspondence," box 98, Wurf, Reuther.
54. Mike Bowler, "85–90% of Teachers Join Walkout," *Sun*, February 5, 1974, A1–A2.
55. Bowler, "85–90%." See also Mike Bowler, "City Makes Plans to Keep Schools Open; Teachers Sign Up for Monday Picketing," *Sun*, February 2, 1974, A1.
56. Mike Bowler, "Teachers Call Strike, Talks Continue," *Sun*, February 4, 1974, A1.
57. Bowler, "Teachers Call Strike." The new stadium was not built.
58. Bowler, "Teachers Call Strike."

59. Bowler, "85–90%."
60. "PSTA Declares School Strike Is Over Despite Teachers' Rejection of Accord," *Sun*, March 5, 1974, A1; and Editors, "Divided Front of City Teachers," *Sun*, March 5, 1974, A14.
61. "Mayor Warns Strikers," *Sun*, July 2, 1974, A1, A8.
62. Hospital workers had staged a one-day walkout the previous year. Mary Knudson, "Hospital Union Votes to Strike This Morning," *Sun*, December 2, 1974, C1.
63. Jim Savarese to Jerry Wurf, July 8, 1974, folder "20 MD local 1195, 1974," box 137, Wurf, Reuther.
64. Jim Savarese to John Hein, February 14, 1974, folder "14 Maryland 1974," box 137, Wurf, Reuther.
65. Savarese to Wurf, Reuther.
66. Ben A. Franklin, "Baltimore Ends Its 15-Day Strike," *New York Times*, July 16, 1974, 1; and "A Second Injunction Is Issued as Baltimore Strike Continues," *New York Times*, July 10, 1974, 15. See also Don Wasserman to Jerry Wurf, July 10, 1974, folder "20 Maryland Local 1195, 1974," box 137, Wurf, Reuther; and Richard Ben Cramer, "City Union Defies Mayor, Fines Threat," *Sun*, July 8, 1974, A1. On the police officers' workplace protest, see Bill Hamilton to Tom Fitzpatrick, July 25, 1974, folder "20 Maryland Local 1195, 1974," box 137, Wurf, Reuther.
67. Richard Ben Cramer, "Court Action Delayed as Trash Grows," *Sun*, July 6, 1974, A1, A8.
68. Tracie Rozhon, "Fresh Stench of Piled Up Garbage Stirs West Baltimore Smelly Saga," *Sun*, July 10, 1974, C1–C2.
69. "'No Protection for Little Guy,'" *Sun*, July 13, 1974, A1, A8.
70. "The Week That Was," *Afro*, July 20, 1974, A4.
71. "The Week That Was"; and Memo to Ralph Flynn from Al Hamilton, "Preliminary Results on Baltimore Public Opinion Survey," August 1, 1974, folder "20 Local 1195," box 137, Wurf, Reuther.
72. Memo to Flynn from Hamilton, Wurf, Reuther.
73. Franklin, "Baltimore Ends 15-Day Strike"; Editorial, "Justice," *Evening Sun*, November 21, 1974, A20; William Donald Schaefer to Charles Benton, Francis Kuchta, Douglas Tawney, and Robert Hillman, September 25, 1974; and Robert Enten to William Donald Schaefer, April 9, 1975, all in folder "City Employees [Termination]," box 337, SP, 9, BCA.
74. Ben A. Franklin, "Striking Baltimore Police Told Work or Lose Jobs," *New York Times*, July 15, 1974, 1, 12.
75. Ben A. Franklin, "Baltimore Police Return After Ratifying New Pact," *New York Times*, July 17, 1974, 43; "Baltimore Police Rebuffed on Union," *New York Times*, July 18, 1974, 24; "Police in Baltimore Penalized on Strike," *New York Times*, July 19, 1974, 5; Smith, *William Donald Schaefer*, 129; "Statement of Jerry Wurf," *News from AFSCME*, July 31, 1974, 1, folder "21 Baltimore Strike," box 137, Wurf Collection; and "Workers Vow to Continue Baltimore's Sanitation Strike," *New York Times* July 8, 1974, 14. Local AFSCME leaders were also threatened with arrest if they did not denounce the strike. Lou Senkbeil to Jerry Wurf, July 12, 1974, folder "20 Maryland Local 1195, 1974," box 137, Wurf, Reuther.
76. Fred Barbash and Charles A. Krause, "Jail Employes [sic] Join Strikers in Baltimore," *St. Petersburg Times*, July 9, 1974, 4A.
77. Jim Flanery, "Kamka to Probe Charges in Jail Riot," *Sun*, July 15, 1974, A8.
78. Associated Press, "Police Storm Baltimore Jail, Freeing Hostages Taken During Strike by Guards," *New York Times*, July 13, 1974, 1, 35.
79. James Dilts, "Ad Dubs Baltimore 'Charm City,'" *Sun*, July 11, 1974, C1.

80. Dilts, "Ad Dubs."

81. Editorial, "Baltimore's Charms, Strikes Aside," *Sun*, July 20, 1974, A18.

82. Statement by Marvin Mandel, Governor for the State of Maryland, August 1, 1974, folder "20 Maryland," box 137, Wurf, Reuther.

83. Toledano, *Let Our Cities Burn*.

84. Toledano, *Let Our Cities Burn*. On the waning popularity of public-sector unions during the 1970s, see McCartin, "Fire the Hell out of Them." On Wurf's denial of having made the statement, see Goulden, *Labor's Last Angry Man*.

Chapter 7

1. Editorial, "The Cold Figures," *Afro*, January 1, 1977, 4.

2. "Cold Figures."

3. Stein, *Pivotal Decade*.

4. Maryland Manual On-Line, "Kalman (Buzzy) Hettleman," Department of Human Resources, maryland.gov, http://msa.maryland.gov/msa/mdmanual/18dhr/former/html/msa 15667.html.

5. Editorial, "Buddy Buddy Job Deals," *Afro*, November 6, 1976, 4.

6. Editorial, "Metro Sees the Light," *Afro*, January 29, 1977, 4.

7. Tracie Rozhon, "Minority Jobs Unit Ordered," *Sun*, December 31, 1976, B1; and Arthur W. Murphy, "Hilda Ford: Job Baroness," *Afro*, November 12, 1977, 20–21.

8. Verda F. Welcome, "Welcome Hits Pressman," *Afro*, January 29, 1977, 4.

9. Jeff Valentine, "Blacks Still Have Lower-Pay City Jobs, Despite Gains," *Evening Sun*, February 27, 1976, C1; and Baltimore Community Relations Commission, "Survey of Employment in City Government—1977" (Baltimore, 1977), available at the Baltimore Department of Legislative Reference.

10. Murphy, "Hilda Ford."

11. "Statement by Hilda E. Ford," [August 5, 1983], folder "Women's Issues 1983– Reports/Investigations," box 977, SP, 9, BCA; Hilda E. Ford to William Donald Schaefer, March 5, 1979, folder "Civil Service Commission," box 344, SP, 9, BCA; Hilda E. Ford to All Department and Agency Heads, April 12, 1979, folder "Civil Service Commission," box 344, 16, 9, BCA; and Sandy Banisky, "City Approves New Job Classification for Civil Service; 2,400 to Get Raises," *Sun*, February 12, 1981, C1.

12. "Women Seeking More Top State Jobs," *News-American*, September 1, 1978, MR, VF, EPFL.

13. "AFSCME Interim Committee on Sex Discrimination Report to International Executive Board," October 1972, folder "1 Discrimination," box 5, AFSCME Program Development (hereafter ADP), Reuther; Minutes, Interim Committee on Sex Discrimination," November 9–10, 1973, folder "4 Discrimination," box 5, APD, Reuther; "Resolution, Affirmative Action," "Resolution Sex Discrimination," and "Resolution Child Care," June 1974, folder "2 National Women's Political Caucus, 1974–1975," box 9, APD, Reuther; "Model Contract Language Prepared by AFSCME Research Department—Maternity and Childcare Leave," July 12–13, 1975, folder "12 Maternity . . . 1975," box 8, APD, Reuther; and Wendy Kahn, "Statement on OFCC Proposed Sex Discrimination Guidelines, U.S. Department of Labor," September 9, 1974, folder 9, ADP, Reuther.

14. "AFSCME Interim Committee," APD, Reuther; Ernest Crofoot, Raymond Clarke, Cecelia Fabula, Tom Keheller, Harold Shaw, and Nancy Speckman, interviews with Jane Berger,

August 18, 2007, Baltimore County; Veneda Smith, "Helping Those Who Have Lost Their Jobs," *Public Employee* (June 1983): 6; and Ernest B. Crofoot to Community Health Nurse, January 2, 1980; "City Nurses Switch Unions," *Sun*, January 17, 1980, D2; and "March Is Membership Month," *News from AFSCME* (all courtesy of Nancy Speckman).

15. U.S. Department of Commerce, *1970 Census of Population, Volume 1, Characteristics of the Population, Part 22 Maryland* (Washington, DC: U.S. Government Printing Office, 1973), 212, 228, 347; and U.S. Department of Commerce, *1990 Census of Population, Social and Economic Characteristics, Maryland* (Washington, DC: U.S. Government Printing Office, 1993), 223, 272.

16. Editorial, "The State of Black America," *New York Times*, January 20, 1977, 36.

17. Moses J. Newson, "100 AFRO Precincts Report the Results," *Afro*, November 6, 1976, 1; Elizabeth M. Oliver, "Thousands Turn Out for Carter in Historic General Election Vote," *Afro*, November 6, 1976, 1; and "You Can Ride Free of Charge to the Polls, Call If You Need a Ride," *Afro*, November 2, 1976, 1.

18. Oliver, "Thousands Turn Out."

19. "A New Beginning: Carter Becomes 39th President," *Afro*, January 22, 1977, 1.

20. Jimmy Carter, "'Our Nation's Past and Future': Address Accepting the Presidential Nomination at the Democratic National Convention in New York City," July 15, 1976, prepared by Gerhard Peters and John T. Woolley, American Presidency Project, University of California, Santa Barbara, http://www.presidency.ucsb.edu/ws/?pid=25953.

21. Susan Hartmann, "Feminism, Public Policy and the Carter Administration," in *The Carter Presidency: Policy Choices in the Post-New Deal Era*, ed. Gary Fink and Hugh Davis Graham (Lawrence: University of Kansas Press, 1998): 224–243.

22. "H.U.D. Plans to Aid Poorest Cities, Revising Community Aid Program," *New York Times*, February 19, 1977, 28. See also Conlan, *From New Federalism*; Benjamin Kleinberg, *Urban America in Transformation* (Thousand Oaks, CA: Sage, 1995); Thomas Sugrue, "Carter's Urban Policy Crisis," in Fink and Graham, eds., *Carter Presidency*, 137–157.

23. Gary Mucciaroni, *The Political Failure of Employment Policy, 1945–1982* (Pittsburgh: University of Pittsburgh Press, 1990), 11.

24. Donald Kimelman, "City Lays Off on the One Hand, Hires on Other," *Sunday Sun*, June 5, 1977, folder "Civil Service Employees," Department of Legislative Reference, City Hall, Baltimore; and "Testimony of Marion W. Pines, Director Mayor's Office of Manpower Resources, Tuesday, November 17, 1981, the House Ways and Means Committee," November 17, 1981, folder 10, box 252, SP, 9, BCA.

25. Kimelman, "City Lays Off"; and "Testimony of Marion W. Pines."

26. Cowie, *Stayin' Alive*; and Stein, *Pivotal Decade*.

27. Cowie, *Stayin' Alive*.

28. Bruce Schulman, "Slouching Toward the Supply Side: Jimmy Carter and the New American Political Economy," in Fink and Graham, eds., *Carter Presidency*, 52; W. Carl Biven, *Jimmy Carter's Economy: Policy in an Age of Limits* (Chapel Hill: University of North Carolina Press, 2002); Calleo, *Imperious Economy*, 139–153; Anthony Campagna, *Economic Policy in the Carter Administration* (Westport, CT: Praeger, 1995).

29. Timothy Barnekov et al., *Privatism and Urban Policy in Britain and the United States* (New York: Oxford University Press, 1989); Conlan, *From New Federalism*; Kleinberg, *Urban America*; Mucciaroni, *Political Failure*; Sugrue, "Carter's Urban Policy Crisis."

30. Jimmy Carter, "Remarks and Fundraising Dinner for Harry Hughes," October 10, 1978, prepared by Gerhard Peters and John T. Woolley, American Presidency Project, University of California, Santa Barbara, http://www.presidency.ucsb.edu/ws/?pid=30008.

31. Roger Wilkins, "Vernon Jordan and the Issues Vital to Blacks," *New York Times*, November 22, 1977, 25.

32. Nicholas von Hoffman, "Can Volcker Stand Up to Inflation, the Fed?" *New York Times*, December 2, 1979, section SM, 15.

33. Iwan Morgan, "Monetary Metamorphosis: The Volcker Fed and Inflation," *Journal of Policy History* 24, no. 4 (2012): 545–571; Stein, *Pivotal Decade*; Judd and Swanstrom, *City Politics*, 320; Kleinberg, *Urban America*; and Mucciaroni, *Political Failure*.

34. Morgan, "Monetary Metamorphosis"; and Stein, *Pivotal Decade*.

35. William Lucy, "Report of the International Secretary Treasurer," *Public Employee* (January 1980): 11.

36. Ellen James, "The Unemployment Rate for Baltimore City Blacks Among Highest in Nation," *Evening Sun*, November 2, 1979, C1.

37. Editorial, "The State of Black America," *New York Times*, January 20, 1977, 36.

38. Robert Reinhold, "Urban Officials Are Uneasy About Carter Aid Plan," *New York Times*, December 6, 1977, 18.

39. Roger Wilkins, "The Changing Character of Black Problems," *New York Times*, September 2, 1977, 35.

40. Vernon E. Jordan Jr., "Bulldozers Headed for Cities Again," *Afro*, November 2, 1976, 4.

41. David E. Rosenbaum, "28 Groups Protest Welfare Fund Curb," *New York Times*, July 6, 1977, 15; Philip Shabecoff, "Meany Supports Blacks' Charges of Neglect by the Administration," *New York Times*, August 31, 1977, 1; and Thomas A. Johnson, "Urban League Links Blacks' Job Plight to Recessions," *New York Times*, July 25, 1979, A10.

42. "Statement by William B. Welsh, Executive Director for Governmental Affairs, American Federation of State, County and Municipal Employees," in *Urban Policy in America Hearings Before the Subcommittee on Intergovernmental Relations of the Committee on Governmental Affairs of the U.S. Senate* (Washington, DC: U.S. Government Printing Office, 1978), 443. On AFSCME's efforts on behalf of countercyclical aid, see "Statement of Steven Pruitt, Assistant Director of Legislation, American Federation of State, County and Municipal Employees, AFL-CIO" and "Statement of the Public Employees Department, AFL-CIO," in *Targeted Fiscal Assistance to State and Local Governments, Hearings Before the Subcommittee on Revenue Sharing, Intergovernmental Revenue Impact, and Economic Problems of the Committee on Finance* (Washington, DC: U.S. Government Printing Office, 1979), 178–183, 247–248.

43. Thomas Edsall, "Young Turk Mitchell, Old Guard Get Along Now," *Sun*, November 27, 1978, C1.

44. Michael Hill, "Embry, A Man for All Causes," *Sun*, February 22, 2004, C1; Robert Douglas and Mike Powell, "Mayor Schaefer's Shadow Government," *Baltimore Magazine* (April 1980): 71; R. C. Embry Jr. to William Donald Schaefer, April 4, 1973, folder "Model Cities/CAA Merger 1972–1973," box 188, SP, 9, BCA; and Williams, *Politics of Public Housing*.

45. Jimmy Carter, "National Urban Policy Message to the Congress," March 27, 1978, prepared by Gerhard Peters and John T. Woolley, American Presidency Project, University of California, Santa Barbara, http://www.presidency.ucsb.edu/ws/?pid=30567.

46. Robert Reinhold, "President Proposes a Broad New Policy for Urban Recovery," *New York Times*, March 28, 1978, 1; and Jacques Kelly, "Officials Call Policy Major Step Forward,"

News-American, March 28, 1978, folder "Urban Policy, President Carter's," box 464, SP, 9, BCA; Gregory Squires, ed., *Unequal Partnerships: The Political Economy of Urban Redevelopment in Postwar America* (New Brunswick, NJ: Rutgers University Press, 1989); and Sugrue, "Carter's Urban Policy Crisis."

47. Thomas Johnson, "Urban League Leader Calls 1979 a 'Year of Crisis' for U.S. Blacks," *New York Times*, January 18, 1979, A1.

48. Sugrue, "Carter's Urban Policy Crisis."

49. Edsall, "Young Turk Mitchell."

50. Nathaniel Sheppard Jr., "Jordan Charges Congress Is Callous Toward Minorities," *New York Times*, August 7, 1978, D10.

51. "Cold Figures."

Chapter 8

1. Smith, *William Donald Schaefer*.

2. Quoted in Smith, *William Donald Schaefer*, 143. See also Katharine Lyall, "A Bicycle Built for Two: Public-Private Partnerships in Baltimore," *National Civic Review* 72 (1983): 531–571.

3. David Harvey, "From Managerialism to Entrepreneurialism: The Transformation in Urban Governance in Late Capitalism," in *The City Cultures Reader*, ed. Malcom Miles, Tim Hall, and Iain Borden (New York: Routledge, 2000), 51.

4. Kenneth Wong and Paul Peterson, "Urban Response to Federal Program Flexibility: Politics of Community Development Block Grant," *Urban Affairs Quarterly* 21, no. 3 (March 1986): 293–311.

5. Smith, *William Donald Schaefer*, 212.

6. Reinhold, "Urban Officials Are Uneasy"; Smith, *William Donald Schaefer*, 121; and Chalkley, "City That Builds."

7. [Joint Economic Committee of Congress], "What Baltimore Loses," *Sun*, August 18, 1981, A11; U.S. Department of Commerce, *City Government, Tourism and Economic Development, Vol. 2* (Washington, DC: U.S. Department of Commerce, 1979), 32; and U.S. Department of Housing and Community Development, Office of Evaluation Community Planning and Development, *Urban Development Action Grant Program: First Annual Report* and *Urban Development Action Grant Program: Second Annual Report* (Washington, DC: U.S. Department of Housing and Community Development, 1979, 1980).

8. Smith, *William Donald Schaefer*; and Robert Douglas and Mike Powell, "Mayor Schaefer's Shadow Government," *Baltimore Magazine* (April 1980): 69–75.

9. Smith, *William Donald Schaefer*, 203.

10. Joan Jacobson, "City Has Lost $25 Million in Bad Development Loans," *Sun*, August 2, 1992, A1.

11. Madeline Murphy, "Rumpelstiltskin, What's Next," *Afro*, May 3, 1980, 4.

12. Editorial, "Tower of Benton," *Sun*, April 17, 1980, A16.

13. L. H. Kohlman, letter to the editor, *Sun*, November 12, 1980, A20.

14. Quoted in Smith, *William Donald Schaefer*, 199–200.

15. Peter Jay, "The Mellowing of Wally," *Sun*, February 26, 1978, K4.

16. Smith, *William Donald Schaefer*, 78; Jeff Valentine, "Orlinsky Stirs as Council's Cauldron Bubbles and Boils," *Sun*, October 24, 1977, C1; and Mike Bowler, "Our Impotent City Council," *Evening Sun*, May 1, 1980, A16.

17. Kweisi Mfume, with Ron Stodghill II, *No Free Ride: From the Mean Streets to the Mainstream* (New York: Ballantine, 1996), 195.
18. Mfume, *No Free Ride*, 189.
19. Mfume, *No Free Ride*, 195.
20. Mfume, *No Free Ride*, 215–222; and History Art and Archives: The United States House of Representatives, "Kweisi Mfume," history.house.gov, http://history.house.gov/People/Detail/18186.
21. Bowler, "Our Impotent City Council," A16.
22. Smith, *William Donald Schaefer*, 78; and Valentine, "Orlinsky."
23. C. Fraser Smith, "Some Council Members Shocked," *Sun*, April 21, 1980, A1
24. "Schaefer Defends Use of the Trustee System," *Sun*, April 20, 1980, A1.
25. John Micklos, letter to the editor, *Chronicle*, May 14, 1980, folder "Shadow Government," box 340, SP, 9, BCA.
26. James A. Ulmer III, letter to the editor, *Sun*, April 30, 1980, A18.
27. Quoted in Levine, "Downtown Redevelopment," 107.
28. U.S Conference of Mayors, "The Baltimore City Loan and Guarantee Program: A Trustee System, How Your City Can Make Use of Baltimore's Approach to Creative Financing for Economic Development," April 1984, 1, available at Department of Legislative Reference, Baltimore.
29. Mfume, *No Free Ride*, 250.
30. Wong and Peterson, "Urban Response," 306.
31. Thomas Edsall, "Parren Mitchell Criticizes Mayor on Workers' Layoffs," *Sun*, June 28, 1977, C3; and Douglas and Powell, "Mayor Schaefer's Shadow Government."
32. "Poor People's Advocate Taking Fight to the Streets," *News-American*, December 17, 1978, folder "Social Welfare," MR, VF, EPFL; and Robert Embry to William Donald Schaefer, August 30, 1979, folder "Department of Housing and Community Development, 1979 [I]," box 90, SP, 9, BCA.
33. "Baltimore City Employees Fight Layoff Threat," *Public Employee* (July 1977): 7.
34. "Grapevine," *Hall Light*, April 1978, 1.
35. "Grapevine." See also "Grapevine," *Hall Light*, February 1979, 2.
36. Levine, "Downtown Redevelopment," 111–112, 116; "Saturday Forum: Henry Koellein, Jr., An Interview," *Daily Record*, February 2, 1985, 3.
37. Michael DeCourcy Hinds, "Baltimore's Story of City Homesteading," *New York Times*, January 16, 1986.
38. Levine, "Downtown Redevelopment," 112; and Ralph E. Moore, letter to editor, "Housing: The City Fails the Poor," *Sun*, November 4, 1978, A13.
39. "Neighborhood Projects Have Chance for Survival," *Afro*, October 22, 1977; and "Communities Organized to Improve Life, Inc. (COIL)" flyer, folder "Housing-Baltimore, 1970–1979," MR, VF, EPFL.
40. Thomas Kavanagh, "City Housing Policies Questioned at Sit-In," newspaper article, n.d., folder "Housing-Baltimore, 1970–1979," MR, VF, EPFL.
41. Jane A. Smith and David Rosenthal, "In Black America: A Special Report—Emergence of Black Middle Class Lags in Baltimore," *Sun*, April 8, 1988, A1, A8.
42. Editorial, "No on N, Yes on C," *Afro*, November 6, 1976, 4.
43. Smith, *William Donald Schaefer*.
44. Portia E. Badham, "Black Legislators Send Mayor a Message," *Afro*, January 26, 1980, 1–2; and "Mayor Nixes Black Caucus Demands," *Afro*, February 2, 1980, 1.

45. Levine, "Downtown Redevelopment," 119–120; Frank DeFilippo, "There's No Love Lost over Labor," *News-American*, July 29, 1983, folder "AFL-CIO," box 812, SP, 9, BCA; Bernard Berkowitz, "Rejoinder to Downtown Redevelopment as an Urban Growth Strategy: A Critical Appraisal of the Baltimore Renaissance," *Journal of Urban Affairs* 11, no. 1 (1987): 130; Judd and Swanstrom, *City Politics*, 348–349; Chalkley, "City That Builds"; and Marc Levine, "'A Third-World City in the First World': Social Exclusion, Racial Inequality, and Sustainable Development in Baltimore, Maryland," in *The Social Sustainability of Cities: Diversity and the Management of Change* (Toronto: University of Toronto Press, 2000), 134.

46. Marc V. Levine, "Response to Berkowitz Economic Development in Baltimore: Some Additional Perspectives," *Journal of Urban Affairs* 9, no. 2 (1987): 136.

47. U.S. Commission on Civil Rights, *Greater Baltimore Commitment: A Study of Urban Minority Economic Development* (Washington, DC: U.S. Government Printing Office, 1983), iii.

48. Murphy, "Rumpelstiltskin." See also Robert Stoker, "Baltimore: The Self-Evaluating City?" in *The Politics of Urban Development*, ed. Clarence Stone and Heywood Sanders (Lawrence: University Press of Kansas, 1987), 244–266; Richard Hula, "The Two Baltimores," in *Leadership and Urban Regeneration: Cities in North America and Europe*, ed. Dennis Judd and Michael Parkinson (Newbury Park, CA: Sage, 1990); and Jon Teaford, *The Tough Road to Renaissance: Urban Revitalization in America, 1940–1985* (Baltimore: Johns Hopkins University Press, 1990), 264.

49. Editorial, "Bad Time to Be Hungry," *Sun*, December 17, 1977, A14; "Rights Drive Changes in Ten Years Since King," *Sun*, April 4, 1978, C1; and Levine, "Downtown Redevelopment."

50. "Controversy over Welfare Flares Again in State," *Sun*, March 11, 1979, A1, A3.

51. Lenwood Ivey to William Donald Schaefer, December 18, 1980, folder "Urban Services Agency," box 455, SP, 9, BCA.

52. Sharon Dickman, "Welfare Budgets Shrink Along with the Hopes of the Poor," *Sun*, May 22, 1977, K3; Tom Linthicum and M. William Salganik, "Health Agency Cuts Its Budget by $4.2 Million," *Sun*, December 3, 1980, E1; Sandy Banisky, "City Has to Cut Services to Aged, Poor, Lay Off 22," *Sun*, December 6, 1980, B1; Wanda Dobson, "Spilling Blood to Avoid Red Ink," *Sun*, December 28, 1980, K2; "City Letting Our Garbage Pile Up," *Afro*, April 1, 1978, 1–2; and Clarence W. Hunter, "City Playgrounds, Pools May Shut Down," *Afro*, April 1, 1978, 1–2.

53. Helen Winternitz, "Families Tell of Hard Times," *Sun*, March 11, 1979, A1, A3.

54. Hinton, *From the War on Poverty*, 1–26.

55. Police Foundation, "Evaluation of the Urban Initiatives Anti-Crime Program: Baltimore, MD Case Study" (John F. Kennedy School of Government, for the U.S. Department of Housing and Urban Development, Office of Policy Development and Research, 1984), 43.

56. Hinton, *From the War on Poverty*, 276–306; Police Foundation, "Evaluation"; and Ron Howell, "City Beefs Up Security at Public Housing," *Evening Sun*, July 3, 1978, C20.

57. "Sun Endorsements for Schaefer, Clarke, Douglass," *Sun*, August 28, 1983, K6.

58. Kalman R. Hettleman, letter to the editor, *News-American*, March 18, 1978, folder "Social Welfare," MR, VF, EPFL.

59. Quentin R. Lawson, "Suggested Urban Policy Statement," and Robert W. McGee to Bernard Berkowitz, September 7, 1977, folder "Urban Policy," box 266, SP, BCA.

60. Sandy Banisky, "Work Load Soaring, Funds Blocked, Harried Food Stamp Offices Face Crisis" *Sun*, March 23, 1980, B8.

61. Editorial, "Park Heights Focus," *Afro*, January 26, 1980, 4.

62. Tracie Rozhon, "Ouster of City Welfare Rights Organization Opposed," *Sun*, August 1, 1979, C16.

63. Banisky, "Work Load Soaring"; Rosa Smith Washington to William Donald Schaefer, November 27, 1979, folder "Social Services [I]," box 949, SP, 9 BCA"; and William Stump, "The Cost of Welfare Is More Than Money," *News-American*, May 8, 1977, folder "Social Welfare, 1970," MR, VF, EPFL.

64. "Proposition 13," *Sun*, August 26, 1978, B1.

65. Dickman, "Welfare Budgets Shrink."

66. "U.S. Checks Welfare Rolls Against Public Payrolls," *Sun*, June 24, 1977, A1.

67. "U.S. Checks Welfare Rolls."

68. Theodore W. Hendricks, "Welfare Error Rate Denounced," *Sun*, May 6, 1978, B1.

69. Hendricks, "Welfare Error Rate."

70. "Statement by James Farmer," in *Local Distress, State Surpluses, Proposition 13: Prelude to Fiscal Crisis or New Opportunities? Hearings Before the Subcommittee on the City of the Committee on Banking, Finance and Urban Affairs, House of Representatives with the Joint Economic Committee* (Washington, DC: U.S. Government Printing Office, July 25–26, 1978), 597.

71. Jimmy Carter, "Address," October 24, 1978, Anti-Inflation Program, American Experience, Official Site, PBS, https://www.pbs.org/wgbh/americanexperience/features/carter-anti-inflation/.

72. Joseph McCartin, "'Fire the Hell out of Them: Sanitation Workers' Struggles and the Normalization of the Striker Replacement Strategy in the 1970s," *Labor: Studies in the Working-Class History of the Americas* 2, no. 3 (2005): 67–92.

73. Jerry Wurf, "President's Column," *Public Employee* (November 1977): 2.

74. "AFSCME and CSEA Unite; AFSMCE Now Largest in AFL-CIO," *Public Employee* (May 1978): 1.

75. "Wurf Tells Congressional Unit: Welfare Plan Flawed," *Public Employee* (October 1977): 4; "Wurf Says Private Sector Jobs Vital to Urban Recovery," *Public Employee* (April 1978): 3; and Jerry Wurf, "Which Way on Welfare and Jobs?" *Sun*, September 24, 1977, A15.

76. Sugrue, *Origins of the Urban Crisis*.

77. Windham, *Knocking on Labor's Door*; Stein, *Pivotal Decade*; Dorothy Sue Cobble, *The Other Women's Movement: Workplace Justice and Social Rights in Modern America* (Princeton, NJ: Princeton University Press, 2005); and Klein and Boris, *Caring for America*.

78. Goulden, *Labor's Last Angry Man*; and Francis Ryan, *AFSCME's Philadelphia Story* (Philadelphia: Temple University Press, 2010).

79. "Proposition 13: Threat to All Public Employees, Threat to All Public Services," *Public Employee* (July 1978): 1.

80. John Hanrahan, *Government for Sale: Contracting-Out the New Patronage* (Washington, DC: AFSCME, 1977), 9.

81. Hanrahan, *Government for Sale*; "Contracting-Out: The New Patronage," *Public Employee* (October 1977): 6–7; and Jerry Wurf, "President's Column," *Public Employee* (November 1977): 2.

82. Levine, "Downtown Redevelopment," 119–120.

83. Levine, "Downtown Redevelopment," 114.

84. Antero Pietila, "Outlook for City's Blacks is Unclear" *Sun*, January 6, 1980, K3; and Joseph Arnold, "Baltimore: Southern Culture and a Northern Economy," in *Snowbelt Cities: Metropolitan Politics in the Northeast and Midwest Since World War II*, ed. Richard Bernard (Bloomington: University of Illinois Press, 1990), 25–30.

85. Felicia Willett to William Donald Schaefer, March 20, 1979, folder "Department of Housing and Community Development 1979 [I]," box 90, 28, 9, BCA. (Typos in letter corrected.)

86. William Donald Schaefer to Felicia Willett, April 30, 1979, folder "Department of Housing and Community Development 1979 [I]," box 90, SP, 9, BCA.

87. Leon L. Lerner, "Dark Shadows in Harborplace's Bright Circle," *Evening Sun*, July 15, 1981, A11.

Chapter 9

1. Polly Kummel, "The Reactions in Maryland Are Predictable," *News-American*, November 11, 1980, folder "(A–Z) Reagan, Ronald (President Elect)," box 423, SP, 9, BCA.

2. James Abraham, "Reagan's Victory: Are We Doomed," *Afro*, November 8, 1980, 1.

3. U.S. Bureau of the Census, *1980 Census of Population and Housing, Census Tracts, Baltimore, Maryland, Standard Metropolitan Area* (Washington, DC: U.S Government Printing Office, 1983), P5, P83.

4. John Farrell, "Reagan Country: What Will His Election Mean for U.S. and Baltimore?" *News-American*, November 5, 1980, folder "(A–Z) Reagan, Ronald (President Elect)," box 423, SP, 9, BCA.

5. Kummel, "Reactions."

6. Farrell, "Reagan Country."

7. David Leips, "1980 Presidential General Election Results—Maryland," Atlas of U.S. Presidential Elections, http://uselectionatlas.org/RESULTS/datagraph.php?year=1980&fips=24&f=0&off=0&elect=0.

8. "Urban Services Fact Sheet," [pre–October 1981], 2, folder "Budget Cuts," box 29, SP, 9, BCA.

9. Samuel Banks, "Reagan in Baltimore: Oblivious to Desperation?" *Evening Sun*, July 28, 1982, folder "Blacks," clippings file, Department of Legislative Reference, Baltimore.

10. Ronald Reagan, "Inaugural Address," January 20, 1981, American Presidency Project, University of California, Santa Barbara, http://www.presidency.ucsb.edu/ws/?pid=43130.

11. Conlan, *From New Federalism*; Michael Luger, "Federal Tax Incentives as Industrial and Urban Policy," in *Sunbelt/Snowbelt: Urban Development and Regional Restructuring*, ed. Larry Sawers and William Tabb (New York: Oxford University Press, 1984), 201–234; George Peterson and Carol Lewis, *Reagan and the Cities* (Washington, DC: Urban Institute, 1986); Charles Murray, *Losing Ground: American Social Policy, 1950–1980* (New York: Basic, 1984); and Lawrence Mead, *Beyond Entitlement: The Social Obligations of Citizenship* (New York: Free Press, 1986).

12. "'Welfare Queen' Becomes an Issue in Reagan Campaign," *New York Times*, February 15, 1976, 51.

13. See, for example, Susan Douglas and Meredith W. Michaels, *The Mommy Myth: The Idealization of Motherhood and How It Has Undermined Women* (New York: Free Press, 2004), 173–202; Ange-Marie Hancock, *The Politics of Disgust: The Public Identity of the Welfare Queen* (New York: New York University Press, 2004); Wahneema Lubiano, "Black Ladies, Welfare Queens, and State Minstrels: Ideological War by Narrative Means," in *Race-ing Justice, En-gendering Power: Essays on Anita Hill, Clarence Thomas, and the Construction of Social Identity*, ed. Toni Morrison (New York: Pantheon, 1992), 323–363.

14. Quoted in Walker Newell, "The Legacy of Nixon, Reagan and Horton: How the Tough on Crime Movement Enabled a New Regime of Race-Influenced Employment Discrimination," *Berkeley Journal of African American Law and Policy* 15, no. 1 (January 2013): 17.

15. Newell, "Legacy," 17.

16. Dan T. Carter, *From George Wallace to Newt Gingrich: Race in the Conservative Counterrevolution, 1963–1994* (Baton Rouge: Louisiana State University Press, 1999); López, *Dog Whistle Politics*; and Alexander, *New Jim Crow*, 48–50.

17. Dudley Digges, "The First Major Urban Program of the Reagan Administration?" *Evening Sun*, July 18, 1981, A8.

18. U.S. Department of Housing and Urban Development (hereafter HUD), *The President's National Urban Policy Report, 1982* (Washington, DC: U.S. Government Printing Office, 1982), 23.

19. HUD, *Urban Policy*, 14; and Kleinberg, *Urban America*.

20. Judd and Swanstrom, *City Politics*, 295.

21. "Urban Action Grants: The Cruelest Cut of All," *News-American*, February 5, 1981, folder "Economic Conditions," MR, VF, EPFL; and "City Seen Losing $350 Million in Federal Cutbacks," *Evening Sun*, August 11, 1981, B3.

22. Harvey, *Brief History of Neoliberalism*.

23. Stein, *Pivotal Decade*.

24. Dale Russakoff, "As 3,000 CETA Workers Seek Jobs, Baltimore Braces for More Cutbacks," *Washington Post*, April 30, 1981, C4.

25. "Baltimore City: Key Issues," December 1984, 2–3, folder "Johns Hopkins University Seminar 3/12, 3–5 pm," box 709, SP, 9, BCA; and Helen Winternitz, "Families Tell of Hard Times," *Sun*, March 11, 1979, A1.

26. Burchell, *New Reality*, 10–11.

27. William Donald Schaefer, "Hearing on New Federalism," March 8, 1983, 22, folder "(A–Z) New Federalism," box 821, SP, 9, BCA.

28. Ernest Furgurson, "Baltimore 'Grantsmanship' Cited as Kind Reagan Wants Ended," *Sun*, November 24, 1981, D 4.

29. Schaefer, "Hearing on New Federalism," 31–32. On the city's struggles to attract business, see Mollenkopf, *Contested City*, 242.

30. Schaefer, "Hearing on New Federalism," 29–30.

31. "[Schaefer Testimony Before the U.S. House of Representatives Committee on Energy and Commerce]," April 6, 1981, 2, folder "Reagan Budget Cuts, WDS #141," box 841, SP, 9, BCA.

32. William Donald Schaefer, "Congressional Testimony, U.S. House of Representatives," April 6, 1981, 4, folder "Budget Cuts," box 29, SP, 9, BCA.

33. Schaefer, "Congressional Testimony," 4–5.

34. Letter to Honorable William D. Schaefer from John B. Ferron, March 24, 1981, folder "Letters of Support for Mayor Testifying Before Congress Comm WDS 141," box 731, SP, 9, BCA.

35. See correspondence in "Letters of Support for Mayor Testifying Before Congress Comm WDS 141," box 731, SP, 9, BCA.

36. Vernon Jordan Jr., "The New Regionalism," in *To Be Equal*, January 21, 1981, Folder "(A–Z) Reagan, Ronald (President Elect)," box 423, SP, 9, BCA.

37. Fred Barnes, "Reagan's Cuts Will Hurt Baltimore, Study Says," *Sun*, August 9, 1981, folder "Economic Conditions—1980s," MR, VF, EPFL.

38. Jordan, "New Regionalism."

39. Maudine Cooper, "Legislative Update," *Black Women's Agenda News and Views (A Digest)*, December 1981, n.p., folder "Women's Issues 1983—Background Info," box 977, SP, 9, BCA. See also Vernon Jordan Jr., "Fat Pentagon Can't Land Chopper but Social Programs Under Attack," *Afro*, February 28, 1981, 5.

40. Cooper, "Legislative Update."

41. See, for example, "UL Raps Reagan's State's Rights Concept" *Afro*, March 24, 1981, 7.

42. Vernon Jordan Jr., "Reagan Should Resist Benign Neglect," *Afro*, February 7, 1981, 5.

43. Jerry Wurf, "President's Column," *Public Employee* (March 1981): 2; and "AFSCME Forces Mobilize," *Public Employee* (April 1981): 3.

44. Nancy J. Schwerzler, "D.C. Rally Sends Reagan a Message; 200,000 Gather to Decry Budget Cuts," *Sun*, September 20, 1981, A1.

45. Jerry Wurf, "President's Column," *Public Employee* (April 1981): 2.

46. "Chop Slash Trim: Reagan Drops the Axe," *Public Employee* (March 1981): 3.

47. William Lucy, "Report of the International Secretary Treasurer," *Public Employee* (April 1981): 11.

48. Lucy, "Report." See also "AFSMCE Women's Advisory Committee Plans Action Agenda," *Public Employee* (April 1982): 1.

49. Lucy, "Report."

50. "Who Speaks for the Family?" *Public Employee* (June 1983): 5.

51. "AFSCME Proposes Economic Stimulus Program as Alternative to 'New Federalism,'" *Public Employee* (April 1982): 1, 7–9. For additional discussion by an AFSCME official of Reaganomics, see, for example, William Lucy, "Report International Secretary Treasurer," *Public Employee* (January 1980): 11; "What We're Up Against . . . Corporate American Makes a 'Capitol' Investment," *Public Employee* (October 1980): 4; and "Wurf Urges Full Funding for Social Programs," *Public Employee* (February 1981): 10.

52. Coalition on Women and the Budget, "Inequality of Sacrifice: The Impact of the Reagan Budget on Women" (Washington, DC: Coalition on Women and the Budget, 1984), title page.

53. Coalition, "Inequality of Sacrifice," 49–50.

54. Coalition, "Inequality of Sacrifice"; Chappell, *War on Welfare*; and Linda Gordon, "The Women's Liberation Movement," in *Feminism Unfinished: A Short, Surprising History of American Women's Movements*, ed. Dorothy Sue Cobble, Linda Gordon, and Astrid Henry (New York: Liveright, 2015), 69–146.

55. "Urban Services Fact Sheet," [pre-October 1981], 2, folder "Budget Cuts," box 29, SP, 9, BCA.

56. Laura T. Hammel, "Social Services Will 'Hurt, Hurt Badly,'" *News-American*, December 14, 1981, folder "Social Welfare, 1970–,"MR, VF, EPFL.

57. Wanda Dobson, "Plans Given to Cope with Cuts in Budget," *Evening Sun*, May 5, 1981, D2.

58. Tom Linthicum, "State Officials Still Sorting Out Details of 'New Federalism,'" *Sun*, September 20, 1981, B1–B2.

59. Linthicum, "State Officials."

60. Ernest B. Crofoot, "From the Director's Desk," *Maryland Public Employee* (June 1981): 2; and Crofoot, "From the Director's Desk," *Maryland Public Employee* (February 1983): 2.

61. Will England, "City Budget for '84 Sets Cuts in Jobs," *Sun*, April 14, 1983, A1.

62. Veneda Smith, "Helping Those Who Have Lost Their Jobs," *Public Employee* (June 1983): 6.

63. See for example, "Facing the Crisis: Social Service Planning in an Atmosphere of Uncertainty," 1981, folder "Budget Cuts," box 29, SP, 9, BCA; Hammel, "Social Services"; Department of Human Resources, "News," [1981], folder "Social Welfare, 1980–,"MR, VF, EPFL; and Letter to Walter R. Dean Jr. from Bronwyn Mayden, January 15, 1981, and Maryland Region, National Conference of Christians and Jews, Invitation to "'Budget Cuts': What Will They Be and How Will Baltimore City Be Affected," folder "Budget Cuts," box 29, SP, 9, BCA.

64. Lorraine Branham, "Local Solidarity Group Gears Washington Protests Against Budget Cuts," *Sun*, September 14, 1981, D1.

65. Frank P. L. Somerville, "Church Groups Back Rally," *Sun*, September 12, 1981, A12; James M. Abraham, "Working People Set for March on DC," *Afro*, September 15, 1981, 1–2; Lorraine Branham, "Solidarity Day Committee Expects 450–500 Busloads for DC Rally," *Sun*, September 18, 1981, D3; and Schwerzler, "DC Rally Sends Reagan a Message."

66. Abraham, "Working People Set for March."

67. "Solidarity Day in Maryland," *Public Employee* (May 1981): 13; and Ernest B. Crofoot, "From the Director's Desk," *Maryland Public Employee* (November 1981): 2.

68. National Conference of Christians and Jews, "Invitation" and "Facing the Crisis," folder "Budget Cuts," box 29, SP, 9, BCA; Social Service and Income Maintenance State Board, "Minutes," December 18, 1981, to June 21, 1984, "Department of Human Resources, Social Service and Income Maintenance Records, Maryland State Archives; and Department of Human Resources, "News," [1981], folder "Social Welfare, 1980–,"MR, VF, EPFL.

69. Department of Human Resources, "News."

70. National Conference of Christians and Jews, "Facing the Crisis"; and Hammel, "Social Services."

71. Eileen Canizan, "Children Fare Best as Human Resources Rebudgets for Cuts," *Sun*, September 24, 1981, D8.

72. Chappell, *War on Welfare*, 202, 211; and Michael Katz, *The Price of Citizenship* (Philadelphia: University of Pennsylvania Press, 2008).

73. Marshall Kaplan and Sue O'Brien, *The Governors and the New Federalism* (Boulder, CO: Westview, 1991), 4–5; Judd and Swanstrom, *City Politics*, 297, 320; Robert Thomas, "National-Local Relations and the City's Dilemma," *Annals of the American Academy of Political and Social Science* 509, no. 1 (May 1990): 115; Wright, "Policy Shifts,"; Richard Berke, "Federal Deficits Imperil an Important City Fund Source—UDAGs: UDAGs Put into Peril by U.S. Deficits," *Evening Sun*, October 8, 1985, folder "UDAGs Action Grants," box 819, SP, 9, BCA; Marc Bendick Jr. and David Rasmussen, "Enterprise Zones and Inner-City Economic Revitalization," in *Reagan and the Cities*, ed. George Peterson and Carol Lewis (Washington, DC: Urban Institute, 1986), 97–129; and George Peterson et al., eds., *The Reagan Block Grants: What Have We Learned?* (Washington, DC: Urban Institute Press, 1986), 21.

74. Alexander, *New Jim Crow*, 50.

75. Alexander, *New Jim Crow*, 51–53; and David Cole, *No Equal Justice* (New York: New Press, 1999), 141–143.

Chapter 10

1. R. B. Jones, "Urban Service Reassigns Family Service Workers," *Afro*, March 29, 1986, A1.
2. Jones, "Urban Service Reassigns."
3. The figures do not include those African American workers who were self-employed.
4. Editorial, "Two Directions at Once," *Afro*, February 21, 1981, 4.

5. Donald Kimelman, "Increased Tax Relief Weighed," *Sun*, December 12, 1978, C1; Memo to William Donald Schaefer from Bernard Berkowitz, June 26, 1978, folder "Proposition 13," box 418, SP, 9, BCA; and John W. Frece, "Hughes Opposes Limits on State Spending," *Afro*, November 7, 1981, 3.

6. Smith, *William Donald Schaefer*, 161.

7. Tom Kenworthy, "Montgomery County Sheds Its Weakling Image in State Politics," *Sunday Sun*, April 8, 1984, folder [no name], box 739, SP, 9, BCA.

8. Tom Kenworthy, "City's Lobbying Keeps Officials Busy Year Round," *Evening Sun*, September 19, 1983, D1.

9. Jack Krost, "Annapolis: Delegation from City Faces Tests," *News-American*, November 20, 1983, folder [no name], box 739, SP, 9, BCA.

10. Fraser, *William Donald Schaefer*.

11. Judd and Swanstrom, *City Politics*, 321; and Richard Berke, "City's Economy Cited as Vital to State, but State Aid Declines," *Evening Sun*, October 18, 1983, D4.

12. Todd Steiss, *Baltimore Region Employment Trends* (Baltimore: The Division, 1991), iv, 7, 22.

13. Memo to Mayor William D. Schaefer from Shirley Williams, August 5, 1981; "Summary Chart of Minorities"; and "Full-Time" [chart on city workforce racial and sex composition], [1981], all folder "Minorities 143," box 740, SP, 9, BCA.

14. Richard Nathan, Fred Doolittle, and Associates, *Reagan and the States* (Princeton, NJ: Princeton University Press, 1987), 86–88.

15. "CETA: Reagan Budget Mania Axes 300,000 Public Service Jobs," *Public Employee* (October 1981): 9.

16. Laura Hammel, "President Pledged Less Government," *News-American*, December 13, 1981, folder "Economic Conditions—1980s," MR, VF, EPFL; and Sandy Banisky, "Manpower Office Plans 40 Layoffs," *Evening Sun*, May 12, 1984, A5.

17. Lenwood Ivey to Evelina Ryce, January 24, 1983, folder "Urban Services Agency," box 455, SP, 9, BCA.

18. Athima Chansanchai, "Sallie Williams, 64, Nurse, Union Leader," *Sun*, August 23, 2002, 5B.

19. Jones, "Urban Service Reassign"; Joyce Price, "Urban Services Lays Off 21; Union Files Grievance," *News-American*, March 16, 1986, folder "UDAG's Action Grants," box 819, SP, 9, BCA; and R. B. Jones, "Urban Service Workers in Shock over Job Layoffs," *Afro*, March 15, 1986, 1–2.

20. Jones, "Urban Service Workers," 1.

21. Quoted in Stetz, "War Stories."

22. Editorial, "No Immunity to Budget Cuts," *Sun*, June 5, 1984, A6.

23. "Johns Hopkins Applied Research: A University Tries to Take on the Social Problems That Surround It," *Economist*, September 3, 2016, http://www.economist.com/news/united-states/21706340-university-tries-take-social-problems-surround-it-applied-research.

24. Jane A. Smith and David Rosenthal, "In Black America: A Special Report—Emergence of Black Middle Class Lags in Baltimore," *Sun*, April 8, 1988, A1, A8.

25. Smith and Rosenthal, "Black America."

26. Smith and Rosenthal, "Black America."

27. Gerald C. Horne, "'Privatization' Encourages Unfair Dual System," *Afro*, January 3, 1981, 5.

28. Martin Evans, "Murphy Appeals to Women Voters," *Afro*, August, 6, 1983, 1; and "NAACP Suit Charges City, State with Discrimination," *News-American*, August 31, 1983, folder "NAACP," box 814, SP, 9, BCA.

29. "Statement by Hilda E. Ford," [August 5, 1983], and "Baltimore City" [handwritten data on city employment], [1983–84], folder "Women's Issues 1983—Reports/Investigations," box 977, SP, 9, BCA; "War of Words Goes On, with Murphy Focusing on Minority Hiring," *Sun*, August 11, 1983, B8; and "State Offers Better Pensions Than the Richest Corporations," *Evening Sun*, November 18, 1975, A1.

30. James M. Abraham, "Public Workers Are Scared of Being Reaganized: DSS Staffers Fear Mass Lay-Offs," *Afro*, June 27, 1981, 1.

31. Hammel, "Social Services."

32. Michael Himowitz, "Hughes Vows Easing of Black Staff Layoffs," *Evening Sun*, June 24, 1981, B3.

33. Abraham, "Public Workers," 1–2.

34. Abraham, "Public Workers," 1–2; John Douglass, "Report to the Baltimore Metropolitan Committee: Black Employment in Maryland State Government," March 14, 1975, and John Douglass, Jacob Lima, and Yolande Marlow, "Black Employment in Maryland State Government: An Eighteen Month Follow-Up Study," January 1977, 1–2, Maryland Commission for Women, Department of Legislative Reference, City Hall, Baltimore; "Women Employed in Maryland State Government in 1979," DHR Pub. 5003, August 1980, 10–16, folder "Women's Commission," box 838, SP, 9, BCA; and "NAACP Suit," BCA.

35. Sue Williams, "Public Workers Are Scared of Being Reaganized: Hughes Promises He Won't Forget Affirmative Action," *Afro*, June 27, 1981, 1.

36. Himowitz, "Hughes Vows."

37. "States & Communities in Crisis from Reagan $42 Billion Cuts," *Public Employee* (March 1984): 8–9; U.S. Bureau of the Census, *State and Metropolitan Area Data Book 1979* (Washington, DC: U.S. Government Printing Office, 1979), 55; U.S. Bureau of the Census, *State and Metropolitan Area Data Book 1986* (Washington, DC: U.S. Government Printing Office, 1986), 570–571; and U.S. Bureau of the Census, *State and Metropolitan Area Data Book 1991* (Washington, DC: U.S. Government Printing Office, 1991), 298. Maryland employees in education include those who worked at the state's institutions of higher education.

38. C. Fraser Smith, "U.S. Work Force Cuts Hit Women, Minorities Hard," *Sun*, December 31, 1981, C1, C3.

39. Smith, "U.S. Work Force," C1.

40. Letter to Richard Gephardt from Lonis C. Ballard, March 13, 1981, folder "2 Blacks in Government (BIG) 3-10/81," box 171, National Urban League Papers, Part III, Manuscript Division, Library of Congress.

41. Smith, "U.S. Work Force," C1.

42. Robert Pear, "21% Cutback in Social Security Staff Planned," *New York Times*, April 4, 1985, A18.

43. "AFGE Local 1923 Testifies on Staffing Reduction Plan," *Local 1923 Report*, May 1985, 4, folder "Unions," History Department Files, Social Security Administration Headquarters, Woodlawn, Maryland.

44. Joseph McCartin, *Collision Course: Ronald Reagan, the Air Traffic Controllers, and the Strike That Changed America* (New York: Oxford University Press, 2011).

45. Ken Hughes, "Running on Empty, Funds, Membership Dip to Critical Low," *Federal Times*, January 22, 1990, 1. Reagan favored a performance-based rating over the unions'

seniority system. United Press International, "Burger Lifts Court Bar on Personnel Policies," *New York Times*, July 6, 1985, section 1, 8; Robert Pear, "Federal Aides Outline Plan to Cut Retirement Program" *New York Times*, November 21, 1984, A16; Associated Press, "Accord Reached on Pensions for New Federal Employees," *New York Times*, May 17, 1986, section 1, p. 8.

46. "An Affirmative Action Commitment," *Oasis* (September 1984): 11. See also "SSA Statistics," *Oasis* (January 1983): 28; "Current Status, Future Plans Examined, Downsizing in SSA," *Oasis* (February 1989): 12–14; and "Shop Talk," *Local 1923 Report*, May 1985, 1, History Department Files, Social Security Administration Headquarters, Woodlawn, Maryland.

47. Jane A. Smith and David Rosenthal, "Emergence of Black Middle Class Lags in Baltimore," *Sun*, April 8, 1988, A1; and Bart Landry, *The New Black Middle Class* (Berkeley: University of California Press, 1988).

48. U.S. Commission on Civil Rights, *Greater Baltimore Commitment: A Study of Urban Minority Economic Development* (Washington, DC: U.S. Government Printing Office, 1983), 1–2, 8.

49. Commission on Civil Rights, *Greater Baltimore*, 8.

50. Commission on Civil Rights, *Greater Baltimore*, 26.

51. "15,000 Job Seekers Apply for 20 Slots," *Afro*, April 4, 1981, 25.

52. Ann LoLordo, "While Addicts Wait for Help, Crime Goes On," *Sun*, September 20, 1983, A5; and Andrea Pawlyna, "PCP's Popularity, Crack in Rural Areas Sets Maryland Apart from Remainder of Northeast," *Sun*, June 27, 1988, 1B, 2B.

53. Ann LoLordo, "City Narcotics Squad Seeks 'Containment,'" *Sun*, September 18, 1983, A1, A14–15; and Pawlyna, "PCP's Popularity," 2B.

54. LoLordo, "While Addicts Wait."

55. LoLordo, "While Addicts Wait."

56. Randi Henderson, "Help May Depend on Addict's Means," *Sun*, June 28, 1988, 4C.

57. Henderson, "Help."

58. Ann LoLordo, "Police Hope Grim Facts Turn Use from Drugs," *Sun*, September 18, 1983, A1, A5.

59. LoLordo, "Police Hope."

60. LoLordo, "City Narcotics Squad," A15.

61. Pawlyna, "PCP's Popularity," 2B.

62. Vincent Shiraldi and Jason Ziedenberg, *Race and Incarceration in Maryland* (Washington, DC: Justice Policy Institute, 2003), 6–7, http://www.justicepolicy.org/research/2029.

63. "Baltimore Joins Top 10 in Poverty Percentage," *Baltimore Sun*, n.d., folder "(A–Z) New Federalism," box 821, SP, 9, BCA.

64. Hammel, "Social Services."

65. Hammel, "Social Services."

66. Hammel, "Social Services."

67. Some funding was restored by Congress in 1983, and states also sometimes compensated for the cuts. "AFSCME Resolution: Title XX," Resolution No. 216, AFSCME 26th International Convention, June 18–22, 1984, San Francisco, http://www.afscme.org/about/resolute/1984/r26-116.htm; Laura Hammel, "The 'Safety Net' Gets Smaller," *News-American*, December 13, 1981, folder "Economic Conditions—1980s," MR, VF, EPFL; [Joint Economic Committee of Congress], "What Baltimore Loses," *Sun*, August 18, 1981, A11; "Gird for More Cuts, Schaefer Tells City Agencies," *Sun*, November 10, 1981, D1; Judd and Swanstrom, *City Politics*, 296, 315; and Nathan and Doolittle, *Reagan and the States*.

68. Laura Hammel, "City's Federal 'Pipeline': What Will Reagan Cut?" *News-American*, November 16, 1980, folder "Economic Conditions—1980s," MR, VF, EPFL; and Portia E. Badham, "Returning School Students Face Higher Lunch Costs," *Afro*, September 5, 1981, 1.

69. "Mayor's Study Shows Cities Slashing Services in Wake of Reagan Budget Cuts," *Public Employee* (February 1982): 5; and Hammel, "Social Services."

70. Quoted in Williams, *Politics of Public Housing*, 238.

71. Beth Ruben et al., "Unhousing the Reagan Poor: The Reagan Legacy," *Journal of Sociology and Social Welfare* 19, no. 1 (March 1992): Article 8.

72. Hammel, "'Safety Net' Gets Smaller"; "City Residents March to State Capitol," *Afro*, March 28, 1981, 3; "Report Tells Concerns of the Black Elderly," *Afro*, April 11, 1981, 3; and "Elderly Blacks Will Suffer Most from Reagan's Budget Cuts," *Afro*, January 22, 1985, 20.

73. Sue Williams, "Kids Make Personal Appeal to President, Governor," *Afro*, April 4, 1981, 1–2.

74. Ron Davis, "Museum Chief Argues Against Cutting Budget," *Sun*, May 4, 1984, D2; and James Abraham, "City to Close Some Recreation Centers; Budget Blamed," *Afro*, May 9, 1981, 1.

75. "21 Will Be Laid Off in Recreation Agency," *Sun*, January 14, 1984, B12; and Abraham, "City to Close Centers."

76. Shelia Rhyne, letter to the editor, *Afro*, July 4, 1981, 4.

77. Patricia Tatum, "Welfare Righters Suing State for 'Neglect' of Needy," *Afro*, October 17, 1981, 1–2; and Tatum, "Welfare Righters Win in Court," *Afro*, October 24, 1981, 1.

78. Williams, *Politics of Public Housing*, 239.

Conclusion

1. Associated Press, "Baltimore Mayor Supports Legalization of Illicit Drugs," *New York Times*, September 30, 1988, http://www.nytimes.com/1988/09/30/us/baltimore-mayor-supports-legalization-of-illicit-drugs.html?emc=eta1.

2. Paul Valentine, "Baltimore Fights Drug War Step by Small Step," *Los Angeles Times*, June 24, 1990, http://articles.latimes.com/1990-06-24/news/mn-632_1_drug-addiction.

3. James Bock, "BUILD Seeks 'Living Wage' for Downtown Employees," *Sun*, November 21, 1993, 2B.

4. Oren Levin-Waldman, *The Political Economy of the Living Wage* (New York: M. E. Sharpe, 2005).

5. James Bock, "Labor Leaders Preach, and Preachers Urge Union Solidarity," *Sun*, May 23, 1994, 1B.

6. Quoted in Levin-Waldman, *Political Economy*, 145.

7. "BUILD's Undefined Demands," *Sun*, October 29, 1993, 18A; Marc Levine, "A Nation of Hamburger Flippers," *Sun*, July 31, 1994, E1, E4; Christopher Niedt et al., "The Effects of the Living Wage in Baltimore," Working Paper No. 119 (Washington, DC: Economic Policy Institute, 1999), 3; Stephanie Luce, *Fighting for a Living Wage* (Ithaca, NY: Cornell University Press, 2004).

8. Andrew Green, "Living Wage Becomes MD Law," *Sun*, May 9, 2009, 1A.

9. Annette Bernhardt and Laura Dresser, "Why Privatizing Government Services Would Hurt Women Workers" (Washington, DC: Institute for Women's Policy Research, 2002), 4–5.

10. U.S. Department of Commerce, *Census of Population: 1960, Volume 1, Characteristics of the Population, Part 22 Maryland* (Washington, DC: U.S. Government Printing Office, 1963), 126; U.S. Department of Commerce, *1970 Census of Population, Volume 1, Characteristics of the Population, Part 22 Maryland* (Washington, DC: U.S. Government Printing Office, 1973),

212, 228, 347; U.S. Department of Commerce, *1990 Census of Population, Social and Economic Characteristics, Maryland* (Washington, DC: U.S. Government Printing Office, 1993), 223, 272; U.S. Census, "PCT87. Sex by Industry by Class or Worker for the Employed Civilian Population 16 Years and Over [65]," Data Set: Census 2000 Summary File 4, generated by Jane Berger, using American FactFinder, http://factfinder.census.gov (November 21, 2006).

11. Brookings Institution, "Baltimore in Focus: A Profile from Census 2000," November 1, 2003, https://www.brookings.edu/research/baltimore-in-focus-a-profile-from-census-2000/.

12. "On Business People," *Evening Sun*, May 9, 1990, G2; and Laura Vozzella, "Voters OK Changes to City Council," *Sun*, November 6, 2002, 7B.

13. Glenard S. Middleton Sr., "'Comp Time' Law Will Create Sweatshops," *Sun*, June 9, 1997, 12A; Doug Donovan, "Council Finds Its Own Voice on Hotels," *Sun*, August 15, 2005, 1A, 4A.

14. "Municipal Workers Express Dissatisfaction with Deal," *Sun*, June 20, 2003, 4B.

15. Baltimore Teachers Union, "2017 Legislative Priorities," February 8, 2017, https://www.baltimoreteachers.org/2017-legislative-priorities-for-the-baltimore-teachers-union/.

16. Joe Mozingo and Timothy Phelps, "Black Power in Baltimore," *Los Angeles Times*, April 29, 2015, https://www.latimes.com/nation/la-na-black-power-20150429-story.html.

17. Levine, "Downtown Redevelopment."

18. Alexander, *New Jim Crow*.

19. López, *Dog Whistle Politics*, 105–107.

20. Marc Mauer, "Bill Clinton, 'Black Lives Matter' and the Myths of the 1994 Crime Bill," Marshall Project, April 11, 2016, https://www.themarshallproject.org/2016/04/11/bill-clinton-black-lives-and-the-myths-of-the-1994-crime-bill.

21. James DeFilippis, ed., *Urban Policy in the Time of Obama* (Minneapolis: University of Minnesota Press, 2016).

22. Lynsea Garrison, producer, "Transcript of 'Charm City,' Part 2," *New York Times*, podcast, aired June 5, 2018, https://www.nytimes.com/2018/06/05/podcasts/charm-city-part-two-transcript.html.

23. Garrison, "Transcript."

24. U.S. Department of Justice Civil Rights Division, "Investigation of the Baltimore City Police Department," August 10, 2016, 41, https://www.justice.gov/crt/file/883296/download; and Bill Keller, "David Simon on Baltimore's Anguish," Marshall Project, April 29, 2015, https://www.themarshallproject.org/2015/04/29/david-simon-on-baltimore-s-anguish.

25. Luke Broadwater, "Still Under Fire, Former Baltimore Mayor Sheila Dixon Eyes a Comeback," *Sun*, March 17, 2016, 1, 11.

26. Department of Justice, "Investigation," 42.

27. Garrison, "Transcript."

28. Christine Zhang, "Maryland's Prison Population Drops to 1980s Levels," *Sun*, April 24, 2019, https://www.baltimoresun.com/news/crime/bs-md-prison-population-vera-20190423-story.html.

29. Jaeah Lee and Edwin Rios, "7 Charts Explaining Baltimore's Economic and Racial Struggles," *Mother Jones*, May 6, 2015, https://www.motherjones.com/politics/2015/05/baltimore-race-economy-charts/.

30. Gwendolyn Mink, "Violating Women: Rights Abuses in the Welfare Police State," *Annals of the American Academy of Political and Social Science* 577, no. 1 (September 1, 2001): 79–93.

31. Glen Kessler, "Barack Obama: The 'Food Stamp President'?" *Washington Post*, December 8, 2011, https://www.washingtonpost.com/blogs/fact-checker/post/barack-obama-the-food-stamp-president/2011/12/07/gIQAzTdQdO_blog.html.

32. Kathryn J. Edin and H. Luke Shaefer, *$2.00 a Day: Living on Almost Nothing in America* (New York: Houghton Mifflin Harcourt, 2015); and Chappell, *War on Welfare*.

33. Eric Siegel, "Baltimore, Washington Trail Suburbs in Cutting Welfare Caseload Since '96," *Sun*, June 7, 2001, 22B.

34. Kathy Lally, "Md's Progress 'Dramatic' in Reducing Welfare Rolls," *Sun*, January 14, 1997, 6A.

35. Pamela Ovwigho et al., *Life on Welfare: The Active TANF Caseload in Maryland* (Baltimore: University of Maryland School of Social Work, 2004).

36. Jennifer Vey, "Building from Strength: Creating Opportunity in Greater Baltimore's Next Economy" (Washington, DC: Brookings Institution Metropolitan Policy Program, 2012), 19.

37. Associated Black Charities, "Analysis of Patterns of Employment by Race in Baltimore City and the Baltimore Metropolitan Area," prepared by Jing Li and Richard Clinch (Baltimore: Associated Black Charities, 2018), 5.

38. Baltimore Black Worker Center, "The State of Black Workers in Baltimore," https://bmoreblackworkercenter.org/our-report.

39. Stacey Hirsch, "Finding Work away from Assembly Line," *Sun*, September 18, 2005, C1.

40. Stein, *Pivotal Decade*.

41. Sarah Gantz, "Raymond James Bringing Back Alex. Brown Name," *Sun*, September 6, 2016, https://www.baltimoresun.com/business/bs-bz-alex-brown-20160906-story.html.

42. Robert Little, "New Longshoremen's Local Could Lead to Labor Conflict," *Sun*, June 11, 1999, 8A; Colin Campbell, "Port of Baltimore Breaks Records for Containers, General Cargo," *Sun*, September 29, 2017, 4D; Colin Campbell, "Port Workers to Vote Today on 6-Year Contracts," *Sun*, October 4, 2018, 4; and Marc Levinson, *The Box: How the Shipping Container Made the World Smaller and the World Economy Bigger* (Princeton, NJ: Princeton University Press, 2016).

43. Baltimore Black Worker Center, "State of Black Workers in Baltimore."

44. Associated Black Charities, "Analysis," 3; and Maryland Commission on Interracial Problems and Relations, *An American City in Transition: The Baltimore Community Self-Survey of Inter-Group Relations* ([Baltimore], 1955), 30, 32.

45. "Baltimore's Food Deserts," *Sun*, June 15, 2015, https://www.baltimoresun.com/opinion/editorial/bs-ed-food-desert-20150615-story.html; and Christina Jedra, "One in Four Baltimore Residents Live in Food Desert," *Sun*, June 10, 2015, https://www.baltimoresun.com/maryland/baltimore-city/bs-md-ci-food-desert-20150610-story.html.

46. Mayor Cuts the Ribbon to Baltimore's First New Rec Center in 10 Years," WJZ-13 CBS Baltimore, aired July 28, 2014, https://baltimore.cbslocal.com/2014/07/28/mayor-cuts-the-ribbon-on-baltimore-citys-1st-new-rec-center-in-10-years/.

47. Andrea McDaniels, "Social Workers Join List of Services at Libraries," *Sun*, September 27, 2017, 1, 15.

48. Republican National Committee, *Contract with America* (New York: Three Rivers, 1994); Stephen Barr, "Downsizing: Whose Jobs Will Be Cut?" *Washington Post*, April 3, 1995, https://www.washingtonpost.com/archive/politics/1995/04/03/downsizing-whose-jobs-will-be-cut/33913cbe-9d95-4e27-832f-4502c99f0b4a/; and Bill Clinton, "Clinton's Economic Plan: The

Speech," *New York Times*, February 18, 1993, https://www.nytimes.com/1993/02/18/us/clinton-s-economic-plan-speech-text-president-s-address-joint-session-congress.html.

49. George Will, "Back to 1900," *Sun*, January 1, 1995, 3F.

50. Reihan Salam, "Where the Jobs Aren't," *National Review*, March 31, 2011, https://www.nationalreview.com/magazine/2011/04/18/where-jobs-arent/.

51. Eric Siegel, "Urban Services Set to Vanish as Agency," *Sun*, May 23, 1993, 4B.

52. Siegel, "Urban Services."

53. Ralph Vartabedian, "The New Mission: Are Defense Mergers Good for the Industry?" *Los Angeles Times*, April 6, 1997, 2, http://articles.latimes.com/1997-04-06/business/fi-46013_1_lockheed-martin/2.

54. Steven Greenhouse, "A Watershed Moment for Public-Sector Unions," *New York Times*, February 18, 2011, https://www.nytimes.com/2011/02/19/us/19union.html.

55. Alexander Hertel-Hernandez, "How ALEC Helped Undermine Public Unions," *Washington Post*, December 17, 2014, https://www.washingtonpost.com/news/monkey-cage/wp/2014/12/17/how-alec-helped-undermine-public-unions/; and Nancy MacLean, *Democracy in Chains: The Deep History of the Radical Right's Stealth Plan for America* (New York: Viking, 2017).

56. Roberta Lynch, "Unions are About Freedom and Fairness," *On the Move* 179 (October 2017): 2, https://m.afscme31.org/on-the-move/pdf/OTM-October-2017-WEB.pdf.

57. AFSCME District Council 20, "AFSMCE: 75+ Years of History," https://www.afscme.org/about/history/75-years-of-afscme.

58. Rachel Cohen, "The Radical Teachers' Movement Comes to Baltimore," *Nation*, June 7, 2019, https://www.thenation.com/article/baltimore-teachers-union/.

59. Daniel DiSalvo, "The Trouble with Public Sector Unions," *National Review*, Fall 2010, https://www.nationalaffairs.com/publications/detail/the-trouble-with-public-sector-unions.

60. Terry Moe, *Special Interest: Teachers Unions and America's Public Schools* (Washington, DC: Brookings Institution Press, 2011); and Leo Casey, "Teachers Unions and Public Education," *Perspectives on Politics* 10, no. 1 (March 2012): 126–129.

61. AFSCME, "AFSCME: 75+."

62. Yvonne Wanger, "Saving Sandtown-Winchester: Decade-Long, Multimillion-Dollar Investment Questioned," *Sun*, May 10, 2015, http://www.baltimoresun.com/news/maryland/baltimore-city/west-baltimore/bs-md-ci-sandtown-winchester-blight-20150510-story.html.

63. Timothy Wheeler, "Bill to Help City Development Ok'ed," *Sun*, March 30, 2000, 2B.

64. Mark Reutter, "Analysis: Before City Hall Loved TIFs It Shunned Them as Bad Policy," *BaltimoreBrew*, March 23, 2016, https://www.baltimorebrew.com/2016/03/23/analysis-before-city-hall-loved-tifs-it-shunned-them-as-bad-policy/.

65. Roy Meyers, "The Port Covington TIF: Did Baltimore 'Protect This House'?" in *Tax Increment Financing and Economic Development: Uses, Structures and Impact*, 2nd edition, ed. Craig L. Johnson and Ken Kriz (Albany: State University of New York Press, 2019), 83–100; and Maximilian Tondro, "The Baltimore Development Corporation: A Case Study of Economic Development Corporations, Shadow Government, and the Fight for Public Transparency and Accountability," *Legal History Publications* 23 (2010), https://digitalcommons.law.umaryland.edu/mlh_pubs/23.

66. Edward Ericson Jr., "Checking Up on the Developers Who Get City Tax Breaks," *Sun*, June 19, 2013 (originally published in *City Paper*), https://www.baltimoresun.com/citypaper/bcp-cms-1-1507227-migrated-story-cp-20130619-mobs2-20130619-story.html.

67. Brookings, "Baltimore in Focus."
68. Meyers, "Port Covington TIF," 83.
69. Meyers, "Port Covington TIF," 93.
70. Mark Reutter, "Slow the Roll of the Port Covington TIF Subsidy, Protesters Say," *BaltimoreBrew*, May 20, 2016, https://www.baltimorebrew.com/2016/05/20/slow-the-roll-of-the-port-covington-tif-subsidy-protesters-say/; and Meyers, "Port Covington TIF," 83.
71. Reutter, "Slow the Roll."
72. Quoted in Meyers, "Port Covington TIF," 87.
73. Quoted in Editorial, "Approve Port Covington," *Sun*, September 12, 2016, 12.
74. Meyers, "Port Covington TIF," 89–97; and Fern Shen, "Port Covington Deal: Signed, Sealed and Delivered," *BaltimoreBrew*, September 28, 2016, https://www.baltimorebrew.com/2016/09/28/port-covington-tif-signed-sealed-and-delivered/.

INDEX

AFL-CIO, 80, 120, 180, 196
African American municipal workers: antipoverty activism and, 56–57, 99–103; benefits and, 48, 214, 220; community organizing and, 63, 65–67; delivery of services and, 70; female, 45, 50, 56–57, 117, 127, 214; influence of, 6–7, 34–35, 43–46, 54, 58–60, 97–98, 108, 140, 199, 206–7, 238–39; job losses, 209–15, 238; leadership and, 35, 45–46, 127, 130, 142–45, 231–33; loss of influence, 117–22, 124, 127–32, 142; middle class and, 51, 54, 206; promotions and, 49; self-advocacy and, 3–5; sexism and, 64; women's caretaking and, 74–75; workforce expansion, 47, 52–53, 167, 214
African Americans: criminalization of, 5–6, 10, 92, 94–95, 104, 162, 178, 185, 187–88, 205, 230–31, 233–34, 245; exclusion from economic development, 165–66, 171–73, 220; exclusion from policy-making, 118, 121–23; health inequalities and, 31, 72–73; income gap and, 27–28, 145; middle class, 4, 51, 215, 220; poverty and, 13, 226, 229, 238, 249n3; redevelopment concessions and, 171–72; residential segregation and, 14, 17, 30–32, 65, 67; substandard housing and services, 30–31, 74, 128, 173; voting power and, 25–26, 32, 35–36, 63. *See also* Black men; Black political power; Black women; Black workers
AFSCME. *See* American Federation of State, County and Municipal Employees (AFSCME)
Agnew, Spiro: attacks on activists, 94–96, 104–5; condemnation of protests, 88, 92, 94; dog-whistle politics and, 5, 99, 106; resignation of, 182; "silent majority" and, 78, 105
Aid to Families with Dependent Children (AFDC): advocacy for, 65–66, 102; inadequacies of, 72–73, 116, 175; minimum income proposal, 68; nutrition concerns, 73; outreach for, 69, 71; Reaganomics and, 202; replacement with TANF, 235
Alexander, Michelle, 233, 235
Allen, Phyllis, 184
American Federation of Government Employees (AFGE), 85, 146, 218–19
American Federation of State, County and Municipal Employees (AFSCME): Black activists and, 232; on CETA, 123; collective bargaining rights and, 85; critique of Schaefer, 169–70; expansion of, 139; gender equity and, 146–47; New Federalism and, 121; organizing drives, 80–81, 88–89; progressive politics and, 82–83; public critique of, 179–80; public-sector strikes and, 86–89, 95, 133–37; racial discrimination challenges, 81–82; response to Reaganomics, 195–96; urban policies and, 155–56; welfare protections and, 4, 9, 181–82; welfare rights protests and, 82, 98–99
American Federation of Teachers (AFT), 83–85
American Legislative Exchange Council (ALEC), 240–41
Anderson, Leroy, 134
antipoverty services: Black women and, 10–11, 71–75, 162; Black women employees and, 51, 56–57; city council undermining of, 95–96; community organizing and, 55–56, 60–62, 65–66; conflict with city officials, 62–63, 70; critique of welfare system, 68–70, 235–36; decentralization

antipoverty services (*continued*)
of, 70; entitlements and, 10–11, 37, 69–70; federal funding for, 7, 39–44, 58–59, 75, 100, 195; job creation advocacy and, 67; layoffs in, 205, 211–15; loss of funding for, 118, 121, 123, 126–28, 132, 173–77, 224–25; nutrition programs, 69, 73; older African Americans and, 73; planning participation and, 40–42; public scrutiny of, 59, 162, 177–79. *See also* human-services agencies; War on Poverty

Aronin, Geraldine, 66

Association of Classified Municipal Employees, 79

Association of Community Organizations for Reform Now (ACORN), 232

Bachrach, Peter, 60
Baker, Frank, 165
Baker, Goldie, 62
Ball, Robert, 218
Ballard, Lonis, 218
Baltimore: anticrime funds, 131–32; anti-Reaganomics in, 185–86; austerity policies of, 6, 8, 111–13, 115, 140–41; Black leadership in, 231–33; business influence in, 39–40; commercial redevelopment and, 8–9, 156–57, 161–63, 165, 169, 171–72; concessions for African Americans, 171–72; crime rates in, 92–93; deindustrialization in, 14, 28–29, 91, 110, 173, 190, 237; economic inequality in, 2, 12, 14, 169, 173–78, 182–83, 191, 223–24, 265n33; FEPC and, 22, 25–26, 32; homesteading initiatives, 170–71; industrial development in, 14–15; Jim Crow system in, 12–14, 19, 21, 23, 30–32; job creation and, 236; living-wage law in, 229; manufacturing jobs and, 9–10, 13–14; media depictions of strikes in, 137–39; outer city residents and, 109, 174, 182, 191; postindustrial, 205, 236–38; postwar boom times, 12–14, 21–22, 27–28; public-private partnerships and, 8, 162, 164–66; state funding for, 208–9; tax revenue and, 109, 173, 191, 210; TIFs and, 242–44; uprising after King assassination, 88, 91–92, 94, 105; waterfront gentrification and, 8, 160–63, 168, 170, 182–83, 237; white supremacy in, 3, 14

Baltimoreans United in Leadership Development (BUILD), 228, 232, 244
Baltimore Black Worker Center, 237
Baltimore Chamber of Commerce, 86
Baltimore City Council: African Americans on, 7, 26, 42, 48–49, 108, 207, 233; commercial redevelopment and, 39; conflict with CAA, 43, 62, 70, 101, 125; conservative influence on, 59–60, 62, 70–71, 95–96; EEOC and, 48; exclusion from economic planning, 166, 168; FEPC and, 25–26, 32–33; hiring-preference ordinance, 50; housing segregation laws and, 17; protests against, 44
Baltimore Development Corporation (BDC), 165, 243
Baltimore Emergency Relief Commission, 20
Baltimore Firefighters Association, 80
Baltimore Jewish Council, 21, 25
Baltimore Neighborhood Commons, Inc., 67
Baltimore Police Department (BPD): African American neighborhoods and, 131–32, 176, 234; artificial increases of crime rates, 92; Black leadership in, 233; brutality and, 1, 50, 64, 136; community-relations centers and, 70; expansion of, 131–32, 206; minority hiring in, 50, 136; Narcotics Task Force, 222; strikes and, 135–38; targeting of Black men, 234–35; War on Drugs and, 206; zero tolerance policies, 234–35. *See also* law enforcement
Baltimore Teachers Union (BTU), 4, 83–86, 90, 133–34, 232, 241
Baltimore Urban League (BUL), 20–21, 23–26, 44
Baltimore Working Women, 145
Banks, Samuel, 186
Barnes, Michael D., 218
Bascom, Marion, 49
Bauman, Robert E., 130
Bell, Valerie, 229
Benton, Charles, 143, 165
Berezin, Joan, 65
Biemiller, Andrew, 120
Black Lives Matter, 1
Black men: criminal justice system and, 10, 188, 206, 223, 233–35; deindustrialization and, 28–29, 32, 37, 190; employment

discrimination and, 38; industrial sector and, 13–16, 26–28, 32; leadership positions and, 51; low-wage jobs and, 23, 237–38; public-sector employment and, 4, 35, 51–54, 145, 147, 206, 210, 231; unemployment and, 4, 10, 14, 34, 38
Black Panthers, 57, 73
Black political power: Baltimore City Council and, 7, 26, 42, 48–49, 108, 207; Jim Crow system and, 13; municipal government and, 34, 40, 42–43, 144; Reagan and, 185, 207–9; Schaefer and, 108, 171–72; school system control, 129
Black women: antipoverty services and, 10–11, 56–57, 71–75, 162; CAA and, 62; caretaking and, 29–32, 71–72, 74–75, 175; community organizing and, 55–56, 62, 64–67; discrimination and, 51; domestic work and, 12–13, 16, 27; economic insecurity and, 14, 29–32, 38–39; federal jobs and, 23, 27, 51; income gap and, 216; low-wage jobs and, 51, 237–38; municipal leadership and, 45–46, 127, 130; NAACP and, 18–19; public-sector employment and, 4, 10, 35, 50–54, 56–57, 66–67, 205–6, 231–32; state jobs and, 52, 216; welfare system and, 32, 162, 175; work stoppages and, 90
Black workers: civil rights activism and, 24–25; exclusion from social safety net, 29–30; fair employment measures, 25–26; federal agencies and, 23–24, 27; industrial jobs and, 20, 24, 26–29, 32; low-wage jobs and, 14–16, 24, 27–28, 140; professional jobs and, 25; public-sector employment and, 3–5, 10, 33–35, 42, 47–54; wartime demands for, 16. *See also* African American municipal workers; employment discrimination
Blount, Clarence, 57, 66, 212
Blount, Gordine, 65
Bowler, Mike, 167
Brackett, Pearl Cole, 3, 64–65
Brailey, F. Troy, 20, 24, 94
Brailey, Troy, 80
Brewer, Nellie, 56
Brown, Harts, 53
Brown, Roger, 68–69, 89
Buck, Charles R., Jr., 200
BUL. *See* Baltimore Urban League (BUL)

Bunton, George, 201
Burns, Clarence, 167
Burrell, Aloha, 74
Burrell, Evelyn, 127
Bush, George W., 235
Butler, Anna, 12–13

CAA. *See* Community Action Agency (CAA)
CAC. *See* Community Action Commission (CAC)
Campbell, Marguerite, 65, 67
Caplan, Reuben, 63
Carter, Jimmy: African American support for, 147–48; anticrime investment and, 161, 175–76; anti-inflation efforts and, 151–53; CETA and, 149; economic policies and, 141–42, 148, 150–53, 158–59, 162, 183; employment policies and, 148–49; federal downsizing and, 179; UDAGS and, 159, 162, 164; urban policies and, 148–49, 154–58
Carter, Walter, 63, 66–67, 95–96, 101, 125
CETA. *See* Comprehensive Employment and Training Act of 1973 (CETA)
Chappell, Marissa, 39
Chavis, James, 143
Cheeks, Bob, 226
Cheney, Dick, 111
Ciampa, P. J., 81, 87
Citizen's Housing and Planning Association, 21
Citywide Coalition Against Displacement, 171
Citywide Young People's Forum, 18–19
Civic Interest Group (CIG), 36, 89
civil rights activists: backlash against, 78, 91–92; Black criminality rhetoric, 78, 94–95, 162, 185, 223; BUL and, 20–21; collective bargaining rights and, 77; direct-action campaigns, 19, 36, 53; employment discrimination and, 13, 21–25, 35; labor rights and, 16, 22–25, 32, 47; municipal government and, 3–4, 35, 42; NAACP and, 17–21; public-sector and, 35, 232; religious leaders and, 16, 21; response to Reaganomics, 194; voting rights and, 25, 36–37
Civil Rights Act of 1964, 37
Civil Service Commission (CSC), 49–50

Clark, Charlotte, 62
Clarke, Mary Pat, 168
Clarke, Raymond, 4, 77, 80, 86, 134–35, 147, 200
Classified Municipal Employees Association (CMEA), 79–80, 89, 169–70
Clean Block campaigns, 31, 74
Clinton, Bill, 233, 235, 239
Coalition of American Public Employees, 179
Coalition of Black Trade Unionists, 82
Coates, Helen, 136
Coates, Warrington E., 135
Cole, Juanita, 27
Collins, George W., 36
Communities Organized to Improve Life, Inc., 171
Community Action Agency (CAA): Black women staffers, 62, 75; community organizing and, 60–63, 66; conflict with city council, 62, 70, 125; job creation advocacy and, 67; Legal Aid advocacy, 70–71; loss of funding for, 126; recreational programming, 74; War on Poverty grants and, 43, 61
Community Action Commission (CAC), 43–45, 61, 95–96, 101, 145
Community Action Program, 42
Community Development Block Grants (CDBGs), 122, 149, 158
community organizing: antipoverty services and, 60–62, 65–66; Black women and, 62, 64–67; CAA and, 62–63, 66; Model Cities program and, 45, 63, 96; neighborhood improvements and, 62–63
Community Relations Commission (CRC), 48–49, 81
Comprehensive Employment and Training Act of 1973 (CETA), 122–23, 149, 211, 226
Concerned Citizens' Committee, 89–90
Congressional Black Caucus, 61, 151, 217
Congress of Racial Equality (CORE), 21, 49, 63, 84, 89, 179
Cooper, Maudine, 195
Cowie, Jefferson, 4, 91
CRC. *See* Community Relations Commission (CRC)
Crofoot, Ernest, 81–83, 86, 134, 146
Crosby, Dennis, 4, 77, 84, 86
Cummings, Elijah, 1

D'Alesandro, Thomas, III: civil service system review, 49–50; collective bargaining rights and, 86, 89–90; community relations and, 65; decentralization and, 70; nomination of Carter to CAA, 95–96; protest response, 88
D'Alesandro, Thomas, Jr., 26
Davis, Benjamin, 129
Democrats: conservative economic policies and, 153, 158–59, 230; criticism of government workers, 99; division in, 7–8, 10; labor movement and, 7, 240; Nixon's targeting of, 94, 104; urban policies and, 154; voter dissatisfaction with, 104; War on Poverty and, 34
Department of Education, 128–29
Department of Health, 69, 73, 101, 128
Department of Housing and Urban Development, 37, 154, 224
Department of Public Welfare (DPW): activist leadership and, 102; client advocates in, 70, 98–99, 101; critique of welfare inadequacies, 68–69; insensitivity in, 65–66; on women's invisible labor, 71, 94
Department of Social Services (DSS), 102, 116–17, 129–30, 177–78
de Toledano, Ralph, 139
Dickman, Sharon, 177
Dirksen, Everett, 93
DiSalvo, Daniel, 241
Dixon, Walter, 26, 48
dog-whistle politics: critique of antipoverty services and, 178, 236; Nixon and, 106, 119; Reagan and, 5, 184–85, 187–88; Republicans and, 5–6, 205, 236
Douglas, Leander, 63
Douglass, John, 216
Douglass, Robert L., 49
DPW. *See* Department of Public Welfare (DPW)
drug use: addiction treatment and, 222; crack cocaine epidemic, 203–4, 222, 234; crime rates and, 222; drug arrests in Baltimore, 131, 178, 206; law enforcement and, 132, 203, 221–23; medicalization and, 228, 234; opiate abuse, 222; prevention programs, 203, 222–23; racially biased policies, 204, 206, 223
DSS. *See* Department of Social Services (DSS)

Economic Development Agency, 157
Economic Opportunity Act (EOA), 37, 40, 42
economic policies: antipoverty strategies and, 37–40; austerity policies and, 111–13, 176–77; Bretton Woods system and, 110–11; deindustrialization and, 110; financialization of, 6, 142, 153, 190, 230–31, 237; free-market antistatism and, 187, 194, 207; full-employment and, 149–50; general revenue sharing (GRS) and, 119–20, 267n20; laissez-faire capitalism and, 104; neoliberalism and, 6, 8–11, 100, 111, 151, 153; special revenue sharing and, 121–22; stagflation and, 150, 159, 179; structural adjustment programs, 190; trickle-down, 158, 231; Washington Consensus, 189; wealth production and, 190
Edwards, Elva, 63, 126–27
Edwards, Herbert O., 40
EEOC. *See* Equal Employment Opportunities Commission (EEOC)
Eisenhower, Dwight, 39, 42
elected officials: austerity policies and, 6, 100, 112–14; Black electorate influence and, 3, 6–7; block grants and, 7, 117; concerns for investment, 158–59; dislike of community participation, 120; dislike of DPW client advocacy, 98–100; dog-whistle politics and, 5–6; federal funding restrictions on, 58–59; increased authority of, 118–21, 124, 142, 161, 206; low-income participation and, 34, 42; policy contexts of, 8, 230; pressured for antipoverty services, 56, 75; pressured for equal employment, 25, 31–32; privatization of public services, 213–14; underrepresentation of African Americans, 142–44
Embry, Robert C., Jr., 127, 156–57, 163
employment discrimination: African Americans and, 12–13, 15–16, 38, 216–17; Baltimore City Hall and, 33–34; Black income gap and, 27–28; civil rights activism and, 13, 21–25, 35; CRC and, 48–49; EEOC and, 26, 48; federal ban on, 22–23, 32; FEPC and, 22, 25–26; labor exploitation and, 15–16; low-wage jobs and, 15–16, 24, 236–38; municipal government and, 18, 33–34, 48, 142–45, 214; prevention of unionization and, 15–16; seniority and, 216–17
Equal Employment Opportunities Commission (EEOC), 26, 48, 80

Fair Employment Practices Commission (FEPC), 22, 25–26, 32
Farmer, James, 179
federal government: African American employees and, 23–24, 34, 52–53, 59, 67, 85, 217–18; anticrime legislation and, 93, 131; antipoverty services, 3, 10, 37, 41–43, 55–56, 58, 69, 75, 100–101; Black women employees and, 23, 27, 51; block grants and, 7, 121–23, 149; categorical grants and, 121–23; contracting out, 181–82; distribution of intergovernmental revenue, 208–9; downsizing and, 179–80, 187, 217–20, 231, 239; employment discrimination ban, 22–23, 32; expansion of, 53, 103; gendered caretaking relief and, 71–74; health care and, 69, 72; job creation and, 9, 37–38, 47, 53; law enforcement funding, 173; nutrition programs, 73; unionization and, 79, 85, 241; urban redevelopment and, 39–40, 173. *See also* Great Society reforms; New Federalism; War on Poverty
feminist organizations, 9, 186, 196–98
FEPC. *See* Fair Employment Practices Commission (FEPC)
Ferguson, F. Eulalian, 65
Ferron, John B., 193
Fisher, Peter S., 114
Food Stamps, 10, 37, 69, 73, 202, 224–25
Ford, Gerald, 93, 113, 122
Ford, Hilda, 144–45, 214
Foster, Joan, 62
Friedman, Milton, 111
Froelicher, Frances, 166

Garland-Bey, Maxine, 211
gender: African American urban history and, 4, 13; caretaking and, 72–75, 225–27; Great Society reforms and, 71–72; municipal employment and, 35; racial rhetoric and, 10; Reaganomics and, 196–97, 206–7; unions and, 146–47; welfare protections and, 29–30, 196–97. *See also* Black women; women

general revenue sharing (GRS), 119–21, 124, 267n20
Gingrich, Newt, 239
Gray, Freddie, 1–2, 235
Greater Baltimore Committee (GBC), 39–40, 157, 162–63
Great Society reforms, 34–37, 39, 47, 58, 71–73, 75
Green, Pat, 211
Greenspan, Alan, 150
Gresser, Anne, 134

Harmon, Maurice, 102–3, 130
Harris, Patricia Roberts, 148, 154
Harvey, David, 163
Harvey, Maude S., 116–17, 129–30, 143, 245
Haysbert, Raymond V., 143, 213
Health and Welfare Council of the Baltimore Area, Inc. (HWC), 40, 43
health care: community-based service, 101–2; desegregation in, 72; inequalities in, 31, 72–73; insurance and, 72–73; loss of funding for, 128, 226; privatization of, 213–14; unionization and, 77, 88
Helms, Jesse, 5, 139
Henry, Annie, 88
Hettleman, Kalman, 143, 176, 178, 200
Hinton, Elizabeth, 93, 131, 175
Hinton, Robert E., Jr., 41
Hoffman, Janet, 208
Horne, Gerald C., 214
Hospital and Nursing Homes Employee Union, 88
housing: decreased spending on public, 226; discrimination in, 17, 63; federal funding for, 73; law enforcement and, 131–32, 176; open, 50, 94, 167; resident decision-making, 45, 62–63, 157; subsidizing luxury/middle class, 171; substandard, 14, 30–31, 74, 128, 171, 173, 226–27
Housing and Community Development Act of 1974, 122
Houston, Charles, 19, 29
How, Harry, Jr., 93
human-services agencies: activism and, 56–57, 75, 98, 100–101, 103, 118, 125; African American employees and, 51–52, 57, 94, 144, 207; influence on policy-making, 59, 69, 97; layoffs in, 10, 215, 221; loss of funding for, 173, 175, 212; loss of influence, 118, 127, 130–31, 139, 142–43, 161, 177, 206, 221; low-wage jobs and, 51–52; New Federalism and, 118, 124, 128; public hostility towards, 173, 177; resistance to Reaganomics, 186, 199–200. *See also* antipoverty services; welfare system

industrial sector, 13–16, 26–29, 32, 37–38. *See also* manufacturing
Interdenominational Ministerial Alliance, 40–41, 49, 89, 171, 232
International Brotherhood of Teamsters, 80
Irby, Nathan C., Jr., 133
Ivey, Lenwood, 125–27, 212

Jackson, Jesse, 148
Jackson, Kieffer A., 18
Jackson, Lillie May, 18, 23, 26, 53, 94, 107
Jacobson, Joan, 165
Janus v. AFSCME Council 31, 241
Jim Crow system, 12–14, 17, 19, 21, 30–32
Job Corps, 39
Johnson, Lyndon: anticrime legislation and, 92–93; Civil Rights Act of 1964, 37; community participation and, 42, 44; economic policies and, 111; Great Society reforms, 34, 36–37, 47, 58; growth liberalism and, 38; health insurance and, 72; Kerner Report, 92; national poverty level, 83; Voting Rights Act of 1965, 37; War on Poverty and, 67, 73
Johnson, Veronica, 212
Jones, Edmond, 69
Jones, Ronald, 205
Jones, Tawanda, 1, 11
Jones, Thomas Oliver, 87
Jordan, Vernon, Jr., 151, 155, 158, 194
Joseph, Mark K., 127

Keller, Kimberlee, 229
Kennedy, John F., 19, 34–36, 85
Kerner Report, 92
Key, Addie, 223
King, Coretta Scott, 88
King, Martin Luther, Jr., 76, 78, 87–88, 92, 94
Koellein, Henry, Jr., 170
Kohlman, L. H., 166

labor, 13–14, 16, 22, 28–29, 180. *See also* organized labor; public-sector unions

Lane, Dorothy E., 133
Langford, Beatrice, 70
law enforcement: African American neighborhoods and, 131–32, 176; anticrime investment, 132, 175–76, 203–4; expansion of, 6, 217, 223; mass incarceration and, 10, 131, 223, 233–35; as responders to urban poverty, 118, 131, 221; targeting of Black men, 188, 206, 223, 233–35; war on crime, 93, 118, 122, 131–32; War on Drugs and, 203–4, 206, 221–23. *See also* Baltimore Police Department (BPD)
Lawson, James, 87
Lawson, Quentin, 176
Lazarus, Esther, 68, 102
Lerner, Leon, 183
Levine, Marc, 172
liberalism, 5–6, 8–11, 38–39, 110, 230
Linaweaver, F. Pierce, 51, 89
Lively, Walter, 43, 89–90
Loeb, Henry, 87
Lucy, William, 82–83, 153, 180, 196

Madden, Martina, 62
Mahoney, George, 94
Mandel, Marvin, 136, 138–39
manufacturing: decline in, 28, 34, 47; effects of mechanization on, 13–14, 28–29, 32, 37; job losses, 4, 9, 14, 28, 38; relocation of, 37–38; unionization and, 10. *See also* industrial sector
Marshall, Thurgood, 18–19
Maryland Classified Employees Association (MCEA), 79
Maryland Commission on Interracial Problems and Relations, 52
Maryland School Teachers Association, 84
Massinga, Ruth, 200
Matthews, Bernice, 238
McCartin, Joseph, 179
McCarty, Margaret, 46, 51, 65
McCauley, John A., 224
McKeldin, Theodore, 25, 41, 44, 49, 59, 65, 73, 93
Medicaid, 10, 37, 47, 72, 226
Medicare, 10, 37, 47, 72
Meyers, William J., 95
Mfume, Kweisi, 166–67, 169, 184
Middleton, Glenard S., Sr., 232, 241
Miklos, John, 168

Mikulski, Barbara, 68–69
Mitchell, Clarence, 19, 22–23, 60
Mitchell, Clarence, III, 107–8
Mitchell, Juanita Jackson: on African American planning participation, 41; civil rights activism and, 18–19, 21, 23, 36, 94, 107; desegregation and, 31
Mitchell, Parren: anti-inflation efforts and, 151–52; CAA and, 3, 61–62, 67, 95–96, 101, 107, 244; Congressional work, 148, 154, 158; critique of Schaefer, 169, 171; fight for racial and economic justice, 60–61; Legal Aid advocacy, 70–71; on New Federalism, 121; protests and, 55, 58, 66
Model Cities program, 37, 45, 63, 96, 101, 122, 125–26
Moe, Terry, 242
Moir, Earlyne, 81
Moore, Ralph, 171
Moore, Robert, 43
Morgan State University, 17, 41, 43, 60, 64, 167
Moseley, Laura, 200
Mother Rescuers from Poverty, 62, 65–66, 73
Moynihan, Daniel Patrick, 38
municipal government: civil rights activism and, 3–4; community participation and, 44–45; democratic decision-making in, 42, 67, 75; downsizing and, 239–40; employment discrimination and, 18, 33–34, 48, 142–45, 214; federal funding for, 58–59; gender bias in, 145–46; job cuts in, 209–15, 227; job training and, 81–82; low-wage jobs and, 81, 83, 88; minority hiring in, 48–52; 1960s growth in, 47; privatization of, 213–14, 229, 239–40; public services and, 8, 74–75, 173–75, 224–25; race relations in, 80–81; resistance to Reaganomics, 198–203; shift of authority in, 117–22, 124, 206, 208, 215; union activism and, 3–4, 6, 76–91, 97; white control of, 46, 118, 143–45. *See also* African American municipal workers; public-sector employment
Murphy, Carl, 17, 21
Murphy, John, 16
Murphy, Madeline, 61, 166
Murphy, William, 1

Murray, Carolyn, 99
Musgrove, George, 216

National Association for the Advancement of Colored People (NAACP): antipoverty funds and, 41; Baltimore activism and, 17–20; female leadership in, 18–19; labor rights and, 19–20, 22–25, 214; sanitation worker strike and, 89; on SSA employment, 53; voter-registration drives, 36
National Education Association (NEA), 83–84
National Organization for Women, 197
National Right to Work, 241
National Urban League (NUL), 151, 155, 158, 194–95
Negro American Labor Council (NALC), 20, 80
Neighborhood Action Coalition, 223
Neighborhood Housing Action Committee, 63
neoliberalism: Bush and, 235; Carter and, 153; economic policies and, 6, 8–9, 151, 230; impact of, 10–11, 231; inflation control and, 150; Nixon and, 100, 110–11, 142; Reagan and, 185, 189, 199, 206–7; white conservatives and, 235; work and marriage in, 235, 238
Newbold, Robert T., Jr., 40
New Federalism: authority of elected officials and, 117–21, 124, 142; civil rights activist opposition to, 120–21; exclusion of African Americans planners, 118, 121–23; general revenue sharing (GRS) and, 119–21, 124; mayoral authority and, 124–25, 128–29, 131; Reaganomics and, 192–95, 199, 206–7; shift in municipal power relations, 117–18, 121–22, 124, 206–9, 215; undermining of community participation, 120, 124, 127–28; union challenges to, 118, 120–21
Newman, Joseph, 222
New Right, 162, 179
Nixon, Richard: block grants and, 7, 121–22; dog-whistle politics and, 5, 104–6, 119, 178; economic policies and, 99–100, 110–11; grant-in-aid programs, 123; law-and-order approach, 96, 118, 131; New Federalism and, 117–19, 142; rescinding of War on Poverty, 103; "silent majority" and, 104–5

Obama, Barack, 234, 236
Office of Economic Opportunity (OEO), 61
O'Malley, Martin, 233–34
Omnibus Crime Control and Safe Streets Act of 1968, 122
organized labor: activism and, 76–80; African Americans and, 3–5, 80; antipoverty planning and, 42; conservative rhetoric and, 5; employee/professional associations and, 79–80; employer prevention of, 15–16; federal unions and, 79, 85; job creation advocacy and, 9; mayoral battles and, 132; New Deal protections for, 22; private-sector, 9; public schools and, 83–85; race relations in, 80–81; response to Reaganomics, 194; welfare state defense by, 9. See also public-sector unions
Orleck, Annelise, 75
Orlinsky, Walter, 166

Parker, Davetta, 234
Passano, William, 26
Patterson, Ronald, 129
Personal Responsibility and Work Opportunity Act, 235
Pines, Marion, 101, 149
Pitts, Tilghman G., Jr., 71
Plank, Kevin, 243
Pomerleau, Donald, 137
Port Covington TIF, 244
Pressman, Hyman, 144
public policy: Black leaders and, 40, 78, 130, 143, 221; community participation and, 59–60; conservative rhetoric and, 240, 242; corporate power and, 180, 199, 206; elected officials and, 120; neoliberal reforms, 6, 8, 10; New Federalism and, 117–21; organized labor and, 9, 180, 196; public-sector workers and, 5–6; racist rhetoric and, 5–6, 9–10; women and, 46. See also urban policies
public schools: African American control of, 129; community participation and, 45; community schools and, 64, 74; desegregation in, 18, 31; free lunch programs, 69, 73; sanctions for improvement of, 84–85;

strikes and, 133–34; unionization and, 83–86
Public School Teachers Association (PSTA), 83–84, 86, 133–34
public-sector employment: benefits of, 48, 214–15; Black activists and, 231–33; Black men in leadership, 51–52; Black women in, 4, 10, 35, 50–54, 56–57, 66–67, 141, 231; conservative rhetoric and, 5–6; critique of, 93–94, 178–79; downsizing and, 209–15, 238–40; gender equity and, 147; job losses, 10, 220–21; privatization of, 179, 181, 213, 229; Reaganomics and, 206; residency requirements for, 140–41; strikes and, 86–90, 118; women in, 52, 141; workforce expansion, 34. *See also* African American municipal workers; municipal government
public-sector unions: African American employees and, 4–5, 78, 80–82, 85; backlash against, 91, 133, 135–38; Black activists and, 3–5, 232–33; collective bargaining rights and, 85–86, 89–90, 133, 180, 233; conservative rhetoric and, 5, 138, 240–41; critique of Schaefer, 169–70; economic justice and, 229, 233, 241–42; education and, 84; gender equity and, 146–47; mobilization of, 3–4, 88, 91; municipal influence of, 83, 85, 90, 136–37; policy-making and, 118, 132; public services advocacy and, 4, 186, 240; race relations in, 80; resistance to downsizing, 180; resistance to Reaganomics, 195–97, 200–201; strikes and, 76–77, 86–87, 89, 132–36; unionizing drives and, 76–91; vilification of, 7, 179–81; working conditions and, 214–15. *See also* organized labor
Public Services International, 82

Randolph, A. Philip, 20
Rawlings, Pete, 216
Rawlings-Blake, Stephanie, 238
Reagan, Ronald: anti-federal aid, 185; anti-unionism of, 5, 139, 219; dog-whistle politics and, 5, 184–85, 187–88; election of, 184; federal downsizing and, 187; global free trade and, 189–90, 194; military spending and, 187; municipal opposition to, 185–86; neoliberalism and, 206–7; New Federalism and, 192–95, 199, 206–9; targeting of urban funding, 188–89; tax cuts and, 187, 202; welfare system rhetoric, 188
Reaganomics: anticrime investment and, 203–4; Baltimore opposition to, 185–86; Black urban criminality discourse, 231; direct-action campaigns, 199, 201–2; gendered implications of, 196–98, 206–7; liberal response to, 194–98; municipal resistance, 198–203; privatization of public services, 213–14; public-sector downsizing and, 206, 209–21; public-sector union resistance, 195–97, 200–201; states' rights and, 7, 119, 184, 195, 206–7; urban policies and, 186, 190–93, 204; welfare cuts and, 186–88, 193, 195–206, 223–27
Republicans: Black urban criminality discourse, 5, 9–10, 92, 94–95, 104, 230; block grants and, 236; delegitimization of liberalism and, 5, 8–10; dog-whistle politics and, 5–6, 205, 236; downsizing and, 230; law-and-order approach, 233; "silent majority" and, 78, 104–5; targeting of unions, 240–41
Revo-Cohen, Lynn, 218
Rhyne, Shelia, 227
Roosevelt, Franklin, 19, 39
Rouse, James, 39, 160
Roy, Melvin G., 41
Ruggie, John, 110
Rumsfeld, Donald, 111, 113
Russell, George L., 51, 107
Ryce, Evelina, 211

Sachs, Leon, 21, 25, 49
sanitation worker strike, 76, 86–90, 95, 133–38
Schaefer, William Donald: affirmative action plan, 144; African American support for, 107–8; antipoverty services and, 126; austerity policies and, 8, 111–13, 115, 124, 132, 162, 176–77; block grants and, 117; business tax-relief and, 8, 113–15; city boosterism and, 108–9; commercial redevelopment and, 8–9, 110, 161–64, 182–85, 193; concessions for strikers, 136–37; control of public schools, 128–29; covert

Schaefer, William Donald (*continued*)
decision-making by, 164–72; creation of USA, 126–27; critique of, 169–71, 176; employment practices, 143–44; federal aid advocacy, 186, 188–94, 209; New Federalism and, 124–25, 128–29, 131; 1971 mayoral election, 107–8; quasi-public corporations and, 8, 164–65, 172; retribution by, 167, 169, 176; TIFs and, 243; tourism promotion, 8, 138, 161–62, 164, 170, 229
Schmoke, Kurt, 228–29, 233–35, 239, 242
Self, Robert, 39
Self-Help Housing, 62–63, 74
Service Employees International Union, 88
Shaw, Harold, 86
Shriver, Sargent, 41
Shultz, George, 111
Singletary, Elrae, 175, 225
Slater, Joseph, 79
Sledge, Barbara, 219
Smeal, Eleanor, 197
Smith, C. Fraser, 129, 165
Smith, Charlie, 222
Snipes, Daisy, 65
Social Security Administration (SSA), 23, 53, 85, 146, 217–20
Sollars, Mary, 96
state government: African American employees and, 52, 216–17; expansion of, 52; federal funding and, 192–93, 195; general revenue sharing (GRS) and, 119–21, 124; layoffs in, 215–18; public services cuts, 174, 196, 200–201, 224–25; representation in, 236; transfer of DSS employees to, 117, 129–30
Stein, Judith, 142, 190
Stevenson, Mary, 102
Stockman, David, 189
Storey, Zelma, 65
Student Non-Violent Coordinating Committee (SNCC), 41
Students for a Democratic Society (SDS), 41, 43
Sykes, William, 101, 126

TANF. *See* Temporary Aid to Needy Families (TANF)
Tavernise, Sabrina, 234
tax increment financing (TIF), 242–44
Tayback, Matthew, 69, 73

Teaford, Jon C., 60
Templeton, Furman, 21
Temporary Aid to Needy Families (TANF), 235–36
Thompson, Linda, 201
Thornton, Theodore, Jr., 215
Title XX, 122–23, 224
tourism industry, 8, 138, 161–62, 164, 170–71, 228–29
Truman, Harry, 23, 32
Turner, Mary, 175, 225

U-JOIN. *See* Union for Jobs or Income Now (U-JOIN)
Ulmer, James A., III, 168
unemployment, 4, 10, 14, 38, 148–49, 153–54
Union for Jobs or Income Now (U-JOIN), 43–44, 67, 89
Urban Development Action Grants (UDAGs), 157, 159, 161, 163–64, 192
Urban Initiatives Anti-Crime Program, 175
urban policies: African American displacement and, 39; African American participation in, 42; AFSCME and, 155–56; austerity policies and, 112–15; Black women and, 45–46; business influence on, 39–40, 42; Carter and, 148–49, 154–58; commercial redevelopment and, 156–57; community participation and, 44–46; Department of Housing and Urban Development, 37, 154; federal funding for, 7, 39–40; Great Society initiatives and, 37; neoliberalism and, 100; NUL and, 155; public-private partnerships, 142; Reaganomics and, 186, 190–93; women's employment and, 39
Urban Services Agency (USA), 126–27, 174, 205, 211–12, 240
U.S. Commission on Civil Rights, 53, 172, 220
U.S. Post Office, 23, 85, 221

Violent Crime Control and Law Enforcement Act of 1994, 234
Volcker, Paul, 152–53
voting rights, 9, 25–26, 35–37

Walker, Scott, 241
Wallace, Pete, 27
Ward, Elizabeth, 61

War on Drugs, 203–4, 206, 221–22
War on Poverty: activist critique of, 67; community participation and, 44; defense of, 100; elderly and, 73–74; entitlements and, 37; exclusion of working women, 39; federal funding for, 55, 59–61; health care and, 72–73; local oversight of, 43–44; municipal employment and, 3, 6; public-sector growth and, 34; recreational programming, 74; undermining of, 96, 122–23, 127–28, 175
Washington, Leola, 102
Washington Consensus, 189
Waxter, T. J. S., 16
Welcome, Verda F., 26, 144
Welfare Rights Organization, 82, 98, 169, 226–27
welfare system: Black criminality rhetoric, 11, 162, 178, 212, 223, 230–31, 235, 245; Black workers in, 5, 29–30, 32; budget cuts and, 186–88, 193, 195–206, 215, 223–27; conservative rhetoric and, 6–7, 129–30, 236; defense of, 9, 186; health insurance and, 72–73; inadequacies of, 68–72, 116–17, 174; postwar measures, 22; public scrutiny of, 177–78, 208; wealth redistribution and, 37, 57, 75, 106, 153, 176, 187–88, 245; welfare rights protests and, 65–66. *See also* antipoverty services
Wendler, Joan, 138
White, McCall, 24
White, Walter, 19
white flight, 6, 25, 28, 93, 109, 115, 173
whites: Black disenfranchisement and, 25–26; civil rights backlash, 92; dog-whistle politics and, 5, 105–6; as elected officials, 7–9, 25; employment discrimination and, 15–16, 20; homesteading initiatives, 170–71; hostility to municipal employees, 93–94; identity politics and, 120; municipal leadership and, 46, 118, 143–45; wage differentials and, 15, 27; welfare protections and, 13
white supremacy, 3, 14, 31, 37, 78, 188, 206
Wilkins, Roy, 120
Will, George, 239
Willett, Felicia, 182–83
Williams, Rhonda, 51
Williams, Sallie, 212
Williams, Sue, 217
Williamson, Richard, 192
Windham, Lane, 3, 77, 180
Wise, Shirley, 45
Wohl, Rachel, 201
women: antipoverty services and, 71; caretaking and, 224, 226–27; CETA and, 149; federal jobs and, 71; impact of Reaganomics on, 196–98, 206–7; income gap and, 145, 216; Job Corps and, 39; municipal leadership and, 145; poverty and, 197–98, 236, 238; public policy and, 46; public-sector employment and, 52, 141, 145–46; public-sector unions and, 146–47; public services cuts and, 175, 224–27; unpaid labor and, 57, 198; welfare protections and, 14, 22, 29–30. *See also* Black women
Wong, Kenneth, 129
Wright, Blacka, 229
Wright, Madeline, 244
Wurf, Jerry, 82, 87, 121, 137, 139, 180–81, 196

Young, Whitney, Jr., 155

ACKNOWLEDGMENTS

It is a pleasure to have the opportunity to thank the many people who helped to make this book a reality. My deepest gratitude goes to Kevin Boyle for his generous guidance and support. He serves as a model that historians can achieve great success while also practicing kindness and exercising humility. Similarly, Susan Hartmann has been a tremendous source of ever-thoughtful advice and wisdom and a person whose integrity inspires me. And Ken Goings's sage counsel and quick wit kept me grounded and focused. In addition, the professors I had at the University of Massachusetts–Amherst and the Ohio State University profoundly shaped the ways I have learned to study and interpret history. Particular thanks go to Bruce Laurie, Carl Nightingale, Steve Nissenbaum, Kathy Peiss, Brigitte Søland, and Judy Wu.

I am grateful to the many scholars who have guided me and provided influential feedback on my work. Jennifer Klein offered critical advice early on through her thoughtful editing of an article that was included in a special edition on privatization of the *International Journal of Labor and Working-Class History*. I am grateful as well to the reviewers of that article whose insights also inform this book. Eileen Boris has led by example and is the epitome of a scholar-activist. Generous praise from Lisbeth Cohen helped me remain determined to finish the project even as the demands of family life and sandwich generation-ing made that outcome uncertain. The book has benefited as well from the thoughtful commentaries and insights of Nancy MacLean, Joe McCartin, Alice O'Connor, and Will Jones, among others.

* * *

As much as scholars have influenced me, I owe a tremendous debt to the Baltimoreans who were willing to share their memories with me. Three generations of one family in particular helped me to see the chronology I describe in this book. Thanks to Apral and Gina and your grandmother, mother, and aunts. I also benefited from conversations with multiple leaders and workers affiliated with the American Federation of State, County, and Municipal Employees. In particular, I feel deeply fortunate to have had the opportunity to speak with Raymond Clarke and Ernest Crofoot. I can only hope that I did their stories justice; I know how important they are.

I would also like to thank the members of my women's writing group at the ILR School at Cornell University. You gave me much-needed guidance that I continue to value. In addition, faculty and staff at Moravian College, particularly Sandra Aguilar, Chris Hunt, and Robert LaRue, have helped me fine-tune my thinking. And I also remain very appreciative of the research assistance from former students Miles Barros, Keri Lindenmuth, Zach Rivenbark, and Leah Tiber.

I am deeply indebted to the anonymous reviewers of this book. They encouraged me to return it to its roots and also helped me to better situate and frame it. I thank them for the seriousness with which they took their task. Bob Lockhart's trenchant insights and many important suggestions have also helped to transform this book. And his patience has been a saving grace.

Multiple archivists and librarians have given me the gift of their superpowers. I spent long days—in my coat—in the underfunded, underheated, but proudly staffed Baltimore City Archives. In addition, I received invaluable support at both the Walter P. Reuther Library and the Archives of Labor and Urban Affairs at Wayne State University and in the Special Collections of the University of Baltimore. Amazing librarians at the Enoch Pratt Free Library in Baltimore assisted me in countless ways. And there was nothing more humbling while I was doing research for this book than sharing space in the library's Periodical Room with city residents who were waiting for their turn to peruse the employment ads in a hard copy of *The Sunday Sun*. Those job seekers hardened my determination to tell this story.

Fellowship support from the Ohio State University, the University of Massachusetts–Amherst, and the Woodrow Wilson Foundation provided me with the luxury of time to work on this project. That time would have been unproductive had it not included precious hours spent with graduate school friends. Among them are Audra Jennings, Alison Efford, Melissa Guy, and especially Jacki Della Rosa Caron.

This book certainly would not have been possible without the tremendous education I received as a student in the Baltimore City Public School system. Even as critics—both conservative and progressive alike—belittled the quality of urban public education, I was fortunate to have teachers who taught me with passion and encouraged me to stand proud and speak my mind. In many ways, they were the inspiration for this book. My most profound gratitude goes to Mrs. Louise Simms of Western High School, who taught me to take my ideas seriously and to study what intrigued me as long as I did so with humility and an open mind.

I also want to extend thanks to the Gallagher family for many years of support. A special shout-out goes to my nieces and nephews: Olivia and Jonathan Manchand; Daniel, Thomas, and Isabella Gallagher; Finley and Quincy Muldoon, Owen and Charlotte Solis; and Nikolai Berger. I hope you like seeing your name in a book, and I also hope you write your own book someday!

To my oldest and dearest friends, the Western gang, I am so grateful for decades of uproarious laughter and countless hours of counsel, serious discussion, and critical engagement. Shannon Avery, Lisa Arnquist, Eve Oishi, and Pam Haag, I can't acknowledge you enough. And to Rob Hewes, thank you for sharing my passion for Baltimore and for being willing to talk to me about it—endlessly. You will find your insights here.

This book is dedicated to my parents, Donald and Margaret Berger. Born during the Depression in Jim Crow Baltimore, they later resisted the lure of white flight and the suburbs and gave me the gift of an urban childhood. The lessons they taught me about race and politics infuse this book, and their values make me proud. And to my sister Susan Berger, you are my rock.

Finally, to my nuclear family, thank you for your patience during the many hours Mommy spent working on her book. Leigh and Cass, you are the lights of my life. And Julie, I will be eternally grateful for the many conversations, multiple readings and rereadings, editorial and tech support, and so much more. I could never have done this without you.

Lightning Source UK Ltd.
Milton Keynes UK
UKHW011253080921
390216UK00006B/324/J